Communications
in Computer and Information

Andrzej Dziech   Andrzej Czyżewski (Eds.)

Multimedia Communications, Services and Security

6th International Conference, MCSS 2013
Krakow, Poland, June 6-7, 2013
Proceedings

 Springer

Volume Editors

Andrzej Dziech
AGH University of Science and Technology
Department of Telecommunications
Krakow, Poland
E-mail: adzie@tlen.pl

Andrzej Czyżewski
Gdansk University of Technology
Multimedia Systems Department
Gdansk, Poland
E-mail: indect@sound.eti.pg.gda.pl

ISSN 1865-0929   e-ISSN 1865-0937
ISBN 978-3-642-38558-2   e-ISBN 978-3-642-38559-9
DOI 10.1007/978-3-642-38559-9
Springer Heidelberg Dordrecht London New York

Library of Congress Control Number: 2013938651

CR Subject Classification (1998): I.2.10, I.4, I.5, I.2, K.6.5, K.4, K.5, H.3, H.4, C.2, E.3

Typesetting: Camera-ready by author, data conversion by Scientific Publishing Services, Chennai, India

Printed on acid-free paper

Springer is part of Springer Science+Business Media (www.springer.com)

Preface

The Multimedia Communications, Services and Security (MCSS) conferences in recent years have become one of the notable scientific forums for exchanging ideas and monitoring the development of multimedia technology in applications related to the broadly defined public safety problems. From among many interesting topics of papers that were submitted for this year's 6th MCSS conference, some deserve special attention because of the importance of the matters raised in the research and applications topics.

The rapid growth of modern methods of video surveillance, also those that protect the privacy of individuals in public places, is reflected in increasing number of on-going projects in this area, bringing new opportunities in the field of improving the balance between the security and privacy rights of citizens. In the last few years many publications regarding automatic video content analysis have been presented. However, the systems researched are usually focused on a single type of object, e.g., human or vehicle activity. No equally efficient approach to the problem of video analytics in the fully dynamic environments had been proposed before new sophisticated hardware and software solutions were introduced to this domain, as is reflected by achievements presented in some papers included in this year's conference edition. This remark applies also to the processing of audio signals carried out in order to identify dangerous situations, including an analysis of the emotional state of the speaker.

Owing to the developments in signal processing, a rapid prototyping of real-time hardware/software solutions has entered the domain of video processing algorithms development. We also witness considerable progress in objectivized, user experience-related assessments of video quality and in new watermarking algorithms applications. Automatic reasoning mechanisms were developed, being more efficient than before which provide the semi-automatic identification of security threats and dangers based on ontology related to traffic. The rapid growth of methods and algorithms applied to the prevention of cyberspace terrorism and new ways of data protection is also reflected in the presented paper subjects. The above examples are only a fragmentary view of the rich program of the 6th MCSS conference paper presentations, which, as in previous years, were accompanied by an interesting exhibition of technological achievements and thematic workshop sessions.

June 2013

Andrzej Dziech
Andrzej Czyżewski

Organization

The International Conference on Multimedia Communications, Services and Security (MCSS 2013) was organized by AGH University of Science and Technology.

Executive Committee

General Chair

Andrzej Dziech — AGH University of Science and Technology, Poland

Committee Chairs

Andrzej Dziech — AGH University of Science and Technology, Poland

Andrzej Czyżewski — Gdansk University of Technology, Poland

Technical Program Committee

Atta Badii	University of Reading, UK
Remigiusz Baran	Kielce University of Technology, Poland
Alexander Bekiarski	Technical University - Sofia, Bulgaria
Fernando Boavida	University of Coimbra, Portugal
Eduardo Cerqueira	Federal University of Para, Brazil
Ryszard Choras	University of Technology and Life Sciences, Poland
Michele Colajanni	University of Modena and Reggio Emilia, Italy
Marilia Curado	University of Coimbra, Portugal
Andrzej Czyzewski	Gdansk University of Technology, Poland
Adam Dąbrowski	Poznan University of Technology, Poland
Anne Demoisy	Skynet Belgacom, Belgium
Marek Domański	Poznan University of Technology, Poland
Andrzej Duda	Grenoble Institute of Technology, France
Andrzej Dziech	AGH University of Science and Technology, Poland
Andrzej Głowacz	AGH University of Science and Technology, Poland
Michał Grega	AGH University of Science and Technology, Poland
Nils Johanning	InnoTec Data, Poland
Jozef Juhár	Technical University of Kosice, Slovakia

Organizing Committee

Jacek Dańda	AGH University of Science and Technology, Poland
Jan Derkacz	AGH University of Science and Technology, Poland
Sabina Drzewicka	AGH University of Science and Technology, Poland
Andrzej Głowacz	AGH University of Science and Technology, Poland
Michał Grega	AGH University of Science and Technology, Poland
Piotr Guzik	AGH University of Science and Technology, Poland
Paweł Korus	AGH University of Science and Technology, Poland
Mikołaj Leszczuk	AGH University of Science and Technology, Poland
Andrzej Matiolański	AGH University of Science and Technology, Poland
Michał Pawłowski	AGH University of Science and Technology, Poland
Małgorzata Janiszewska	AGH University of Science and Technology, Poland
Krzysztof Rusek	AGH University of Science and Technology, Poland

Sponsoring Institutions

- Institute of Electrical and Electronics Engineers (IEEE)
- AGH University of Science and Technology, Department of Telecommunications

Table of Contents

Rule-Based Knowledge Management
in Social Threat Monitor*

Mateusz Baran and Antoni Ligęza

AGH University of Science and Technology
al. Mickiewicza 30, 30-059 Krakow, Poland
{matb,ligeza}@agh.edu.pl

Abstract. Social Threat Monitor (STM) is a Web system incorporating a relational database and GIS component for enregistration of user provided data on threats. In contrast to typical Crime Mapping Systems — where only authorized services, such as Police, are allowed and responsible for selective threat reporting — in case of STM all registered citizens can input threat data of interest. Registered data can be spatially visualized allowing easy browsing of reports. Wide, distributed and unlimited access makes this kind of service a new quality on the way to threat monitoring and safety improvement. However, due to a huge volumes of complex, multi-aspect data, automated knowledge management appears indispensable. In this paper a Rule-Based System for report processing and knowledge management is proposed. A new taxonomy of rules for complex knowledge management tasks is put forward. The rules are used to assess report admissibility, access restriction, perform basic processing and threat inference. Special ECA-type rules provide immediate reaction to dangerous situations and run statistical analysis of gathered data. The rules are written in Prolog.

Keywords: Knowledge Management, Rule-Based Systems, GIS, INDECT.

1 Introduction

Improving citizen safety with use of modern technologies has become an issue of primary importance in contemporary world. It is a matter of concern of local authorities, governments and even international organizations. Most of the activities are focused on monitoring — both human operator and automatic — of dedicated areas. Apart from classical solutions, technologically advanced research are going on. The INDECT Project is a perfect example of interdisciplinary FP7 Project aimed at citizen safety improvement in urban environments by variety of modern information processing technologies and tools.

* The research presented in this paper is carried out within the EU FP7 INDECT Project: "Intelligent information system supporting observation, searching and detection for security of citizens in urban environment" (http://indect-project.eu)

A. Dziech and A. Czyżewski (Eds.): MCSS 2013, CCIS 368, pp. 1–12, 2013.
© Springer-Verlag Berlin Heidelberg 2013

Social Threat Monitor (STM) is one of the tools being developed within the WP4 package of tasks in the INDECT Project. It is a kind of social Web system incorporating a relational database and GIS[1] component for enregistration of user provided data on threats. However, in contrast to typical Crime Mapping Systems — where only authorized services, such as Police, are allowed and responsible for selective threat reporting — in case of STM all registered citizens can input threat data of interest. The system is widely accessible for public for data inspection, and simultaneously new data on threats can be a matter of massive, parallel input.

Registered data can be spatially visualized allowing easy browsing, search focused on types, area, time, severity, etc., and generation of reports. Wide, distributed and unlimited access makes this kind of service a new quality on the way to threat monitoring and safety improvement. However, due to a huge volumes of complex, multi-aspect data *automated knowledge management* appears indispensable.

In this paper a conceptual design of Rule-Based System for input data processing, report generation and knowledge management suitable for STM is proposed. A new taxonomy of rules for complex knowledge management tasks are put forward. The rules are used to assess report admissibility, access restriction, perform basic processing and threat inference. Special ECA-type[2] rules provide immediate reaction to dangerous situations and run statistical analysis of gathered data. The rules are written in PROLOG.

Note that conceptual design of rule-based systems and knowledge-based systems [21,11] still remains a great challenge. Rule-based systems are a perhaps best know, special case of tools for efficient knowledge management. Some development of new methodologies for design of such systems can be observed [22,16], including the formalized XTT2 method [23] as well as visualization of rule-based models [19] or even modeling rules in a collaborative environment [1]. This paper follows some principles of such modern rule-based systems development.

2   Social Threat Monitor

Social Threat Monitor (STM) is a system for distributed knowledge acquisition, gathering and organizing knowledge on threats of various nature. The system leverages the social networks concepts and GIS component to support communities in improving safety of citizens in urban environments. STM is a web system for citizen provided information, automatic knowledge extraction and management. In fact, STM is a good example of a conceptually simple *people-to-people* social service based on advanced knowledge management technology. A general idea of the system is presented in Fig. 1.

---

[1] Geographic information system — a system for capturing, storing and managing of geographical data [24].
[2] Event Condition Action or ECA-rules; such rules are triggered by an Event, and if the Condition is satisfied, the Action is executed.

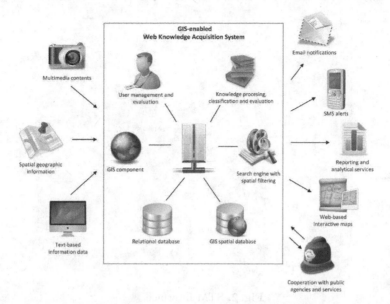

Fig. 1. General idea of STM (source: `http://vigil.ia.agh.edu.pl/dokuwiki/doku.php?id=pub:stm:man:overview`)

STM enables citizens to *share the information* about threats they encounter. Reported threats can be immediately viewed by other users; in fact the system works on-line, 24x7 hours. The users of STM can observe and evaluate the data presented in the system. They can vote on the individual threats (to express their concern), comment and discuss. Reported threats are monitored by police officers (and other distinguished services) who can make their own announcements and use the system for internal investigations.

The main method of STM usage is through WWW interface. It exposes full functionality to each major group of users: citizens (unregistered), citizens (registered users), police (services) officers and administrators. Additionally an API for querying the system for threats and reporting is provided.

Support for gathering and processing of context data from mobile devices (smartphones, tablets) is outside of the scope of the project. However users can put additional data in their reports, such as photos. This data is not processed by the STM.

Figure 2 shows the user interface of STM. Threats are displayed as icons over a map, their position corresponds to location of the threat. Icons display the category of threat or, when there are two or more threats close to each other, a round icon with their count is shown (this feature is scale-dependent).

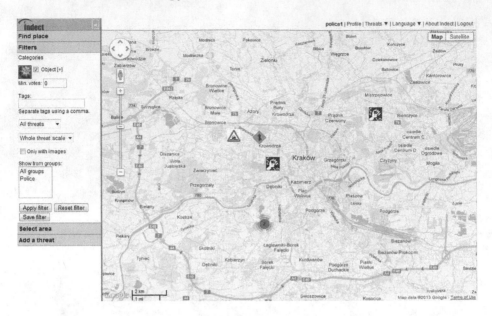

Fig. 2. STM interface

Left panel provides basic functionality for users. These are (in top to bottom order):

- finding a location,
- filtering of threats to be displayed on map,
- selecting an area,
- adding new threats.

The first functionality makes navigation on a map easier. The user can find area he finds interesting faster.

Filtering makes finding interesting reports easier. For example, if a user is looking for reports about natural disasters, holes in streets should not be visible on the map. It is also possible to display threats only in certain area selected by user.

The last functionality is adding new threats. Only registered users can add new threats. The user can specify a number of parameters like severity or category.

Users can also vote on threats while they are browsing them. Votes express how many people find it important. Based on votes on user's entries, his/her credibility is determined, what gives three-dimensional importance classification: how important user thinks the threat is, how credible he is and how many people find the issue noteworthy.

Reported threads are categorized with a predefined taxonomy (Fig. 3). The tree-like structure corresponds to the natural way of thinking about them, for example a tornado is a natural disaster or arms dealing is a crime. Its advantage

Fig. 3. Threat taxonomy

over flat categorization is easier expression of conditions regarding more then one non-divisible threat type.

The database stores all information supplied by reporting user. There are also a few attributes filled in a different way. The core set of attributes associated with a threat is as follows:

- title of threat,
- description (text),
- user reporting the threat,
- category of entry (w.r.t. the predefined taxonomy),
- number of votes,
- image connected with report,
- time of creation,
- time when threat ends,
- place on map the report is attached to,
- scale of threat.

The most complete technical documentation on the Social Threat Monitor is covered by two recent INDECT Reports D4.14 [13] (technical details) and D9.30 [14] (a user-oriented manual).

3   Rule-Based Systems

Rule-Based System are perhaps the most widely used and best known tool for knowledge specification [8]. They can often take quite complex forms and be composed in a complex, network-like structure [11]. However, in majority of systems there is no clear distinction among different types of rules. A simple taxonomy of rules was proposed perhaps for the first time in [9]. Below, an outline of a taxonomy of rule types for knowledge management in STM is put forward. Note that diversified types of rules define in fact their *roles* in the system.

For the sake of knowledge management within STM we have distinguished the following types and subtypes of rules:

Constraint Definition Rules — these are rules defining constraints imposed on data and knowledge within the system of interest; they can be subdivide into:

- *input constraint rules* — defining constraints on admissible input data,
- *state constraint rules* — detecting inconsistency in the knowledge base,
- *conflict resolution rules* — rules specifying how the system should behave in case of conflict,

Deduction Rules — rules producing new chunks of knowledge,

Procedural Rules — rules assuring execution of some predefined procedures or actions; we have:

- *numerical processing rules* — numerical procedures or function values have to be calculated,
- *symbolic processing rules* — special symbolic procedures (e.g. text processing) is necessary,
- *input-output rules* — data is to be input or output,
- *other operational rules* — other operations are to be executed,

Aggregation Rules — rules for data/knowledge aggregation (or fusion),

Control Rules — rules performing typical inference control operations.

Note that, rules can modify the state of the knowledge base through *assert* and *retract* operations [11]; hence, not only if-then-else or a case-like constructs can be imitated, but various types of loops can be defined as well.

It is also important to notice, that there are several mechanisms for invoking rules:

- *positive preconditions* — facts that must be valid to fire a rule,
- *negative preconditions* — facts that must be known to be false to fire a rule,
- *excluding conditions* — conditions, which — if satisfied — eliminate a rule from operation,
- *events* — external event triggering a rule,
- *time* — rules can be activated by examining internal clock.

Note also, that practically, any combination of the above may be in use. Finally, rules may point out to other rules in a direct way (the so-called *next rule* and *else rule* mechanism [11]).

4 Example Rules for STM

There are several areas where Rule-Based Systems may prove to be useful in
STM. The general purpose is atomization of typical maintenance and reporting tasks with well-defined conditions and actions. Some examples are reported
below:

Constraint Definition Rules for preservation and inconsistency detection.
Some example proposed rules include:

- Checking if reported threat is admissible for given position, e.g. if a pothole
  is reported on a road.

```
possibleAnywhere(threat(robbery)).
admissibleLocationType(threat(crossing), road).
admissibleLocationType(threat(pothole), road).
forbiddenLocationType(threat(earthquake), ocean).

admissible(Threat, Location) :- possibleAnywhere(Threat).
admissible(Threat, Location) :-
    admissibleLocationType(Threat, LocType),
    isOfType(Location, LocType),
    forbiddenLocationType(Threat, ForbLocType),
    not(isOfType(Location, ForbLocType)).
```

- Checking if two contradictory threats are not reported close to each other,
  e.g. fire and flooding.

```
contradictoryImpl(Threat1, Threat2) :-
    close(Threat1, Threat2),
    Threat1 = threat(fire), Threat2 = threat(flooding).
contradictory(Threat1, Threat2) :-
    contradictoryImpl(Threat1, Threat2).
contradictory(Threat1, Threat2) :-
    contradictoryImpl(Threat2, Threat1).
```

- Checking if a report is not duplicated, e.g. two reports of fire in the same
  house.

```
hasDuplicate(Threat, Duplicate) :-
    threatRadius(Threat,Radius),
    location(Threat, Loc),
    report(Threat2),
    location(Threat2, Loc2),
    isInside(Loc, Radius, Loc2),
    Duplicate = Threat2.
```

- Checking if user is not sending reports too quickly. Too frequent reporting suggest it is done by some automated procedure, which is undesired.

```
tooFrequentReporting(Threat, PrevThreat, MinTimeBetweenReports) :-
    time(PrevThreat, PrevTime),
    time(Threat, CurTime),
    MinTime is PrevTime + MinTimeBetweenReports,
    CurTime > MinTime.
```

In such cases threat should not be checked in and user should be notified about problem with their report.

Procedural Rules — basic data processing, filtering and refinement for the purpose of internal representation.

Some proposed rules include:

- If threat is reported in an area under monitoring, it is send for review by policeman currently watching this area.

```
sendForReview(Threat) :-
    location(Threat, Loc),
    monitored(Loc).
```

- If threat is voted on, increase credibility of user that reported it.

```
increaseCredibility(Threat) :-
    reporter(Threat, User),
    credibility(User, PrevCred),
    retractall(credibility(User, _)),
    CurCred is PrevCred + 1,
    assert(credibility(User, CurCred)).
```

Aggregation Rules — record (evidence) accumulation.

Some proposed rules include:

- Marking areas with higher than average number or severity of threats.

```
areaType(Subarea, Area, Level) :-
    Threshold is averageNumberOfThreats(Area) + const,
    averageNumberOfThreats(Subarea) > Threshold,
    Level = level(high).
areaType(Subarea, Area, Level) :-
    Threshold is averageNumberOfThreats(Area) - const,
    averageNumberOfThreats(Subarea) > Threshold,
    Level = Level(average).
areaType(Subarea, Area, Level) :- Level = level(low).
```

- Marking areas with increased number or severity of threats compared to previous period. For example increased number of fire reports can indicate that they were caused by an arsonist.

```
threatNumberIncrease(Area, ThreatType) :-
    type(ThType),
    threatNumber(Area, ThType, NumberNow, currentTimePerion),
    threatNumber(Area, ThType, NumberThen, previousTimePeriod),
    Threshold is NumberThen + margin,
    NumberNow > Threshold,
    ThreatType = ThType.
```

Rules of this type are primarily used for generating timely reports for authorities and the police.

Procedural Rules — triggered by events, i.e. ECA-type rules.
Some proposed rules include:

– If a fire is reported during drought, alarm firefighters (certain threats are more dangerous under specific conditions).

```
emergency(threat(fire), Conditions) :- drought(Conditions).
```

– If a report has a picture, user's credibility is above a certain threshold, category suggests immediate action (robbery, fire, drought) and the threat has high scale it should be immediately reviewed.

```
review(Threat, CredThreshold, ScaleThreshold) :-
    hasPicture(Threat),
    reporter(Threat, User),
    credibility(User, Cred),
    Cred > CredThreshold,
    urgent(Threat),
    scale(Threat, Scale),
    Scale > ScaleThreshold.
```

Aggregation Rules — activated by clock, i.e. monitoring-type statistical rules fired after predefined period of time.
Proposed rules include:

– Time-based running of statistical analysis of threat data.

Deduction Rules — both forward chaining and backward chaining is possible.
Some proposed rules include:

– Threat abduction and deduction rules, e.g. a car accident or fallen tree can be the cause of traffic jam on the same road.

```
directEffect(threat(pothole), threat(trafficJam)) :-
    sameRoad(threat(pothole), threat(trafficJam)).
directEffect(threat(fallenTree), threat(trafficJam)) :-
    sameRoad(threat(fallenTree), threat(trafficJam)).
directEffect(threat(trafficJam), threat(carAccident)) :-
```

```
      sameRoad(threat(trafficJam), threat(carAccident)).
  directEffect(threat(thunder), threat(fire)) :-
      nearbyLocation(threat(thunder), threat(fire)).
  canCause(Cause, Effect) :-
      directEffect(Cause, Effect).
  canCause(Cause, Effect) :-
      directEffect(Cause, MiddleEffect),
      canCause(MiddleEffect, Effect).
```

– Rules for selection of threats to present to the user. If there are too many
  low scale threats of similar type in an area, some of them can be hidden or
  clustered to expose less common threats.

5   Related Work

Crime Mapping service http://www.crimemapping.com/, available for the USA,
allows authorities to inform citizens about threats in their area. Though the information presented is similar, STM allows multi-directional exchange of reports. The functional specification of STM, usability and interoperability is
much more reach. The same applies to Metropolitan Police Crime Mapping
http://maps.met.police.uk/ displays aggregated crime information for Bor-
oughs, Wards and Sub-wards in London. Historical trends are shown too. Crime-
Stat [7] is a crime mapping program designed to compute spatial statistics of
incidents. Its output can be displayed in a geographic information system (GIS)
program.

There are many possible improvements and areas for future work. Among
the most important are automatic reporting of threats. When multiple users are
running from one place they are probably running away from a threat. Another
objective would be the use of rule-based description for specification of security
policies for given contexts, e.g. [20]. The system could learn user usage habits
exposing features he uses most often. It could be automatically informed about
new threats in selected area via e-mail or SMS. A practical development of rule
bases in a distributed, web-based environment could be performed in the future
using a wiki system [18].

6   Concluding Remarks

The paper presents knowledge management issues in the Social Threat Monitor — a system for acquisition, storage, and presentation of threats, developed
within the INDECT Project. For efficient, automatic knowledge management
the conceptual design of rules-based technology is put forward. A new taxonomy of rules was introduced. Example rules, presented with PROLOG notation
illustrate the knowledge processing activities.

One of the important issues concerning rule-based systems is the verification
of the rule-base. This was not considered here, but the Authors are aware of this

issue [10,5,11]. In fact for the XTT2 rule representation a practical verification tool was developed [17]. Another issue consists in efficient design of the rule-base; here technologies based on BPMN can be useful [6]. Finally, an interesting issue for further research is automated plan generation under time constraints and in multi-agent system, which can be considered as reaction for threats by security services [3].

References

1. Adrian, W.T., Bobek, S., Nalepa, G.J., Kaczor, K., Kluza, K.: How to reason by HeaRT in a semantic knowledge-based wiki. In: Proceedings of the 23rd IEEE International Conference on Tools with Artificial Intelligence, ICTAI 2011, Boca Raton, Florida, USA, pp. 438–441 (November 2011), http://ieeexplore.ieee.org/xpls/abs_all.jsp?arnumber=6103361&tag=1
2. Adrian, W.T., Ciężkowski, P., Kaczor, K., Ligęza, A., Nalepa, G.J.: Web-based knowledge acquisition and management system supporting collaboration for improving safety in urban environment. In: Dziech, A., Czyżewski, A. (eds.) MCSS 2012. CCIS, vol. 287, pp. 1–12. Springer, Heidelberg (2012), http://link.springer.com/book/10.1007/978-3-642-30721-8/page/1
3. Baki, B., Bouzid, M., Ligęza, A., Mouaddib, A.I.: A centralized planning technique with temporal constraints and uncertainty for multi-agent systems. Journal of Experimental and Theoretical Artificial Intelligence 18(3), 331–364 (2006)
4. Caballé, S., Daradoumis, T., Xhafa, F., Conesa, J.: Enhancing knowledge management in online collaborative learning. International Journal of Software Engineering and Knowledge Engineering 20(4), 485–497 (2010)
5. Coenen, F., et al.: Validation and verification of knowledge-based systems: report on eurovav99. The Knowledge Engineering Review 15(2), 187–196 (2000)
6. Kluza, K., Maślanka, T., Nalepa, G.J., Ligęza, A.: Proposal of representing BPMN diagrams with XTT2-based business rules. In: Brazier, F.M., Nieuwenhuis, K., Pavlin, G., Warnier, M., Badica, C. (eds.) Intelligent Distributed Computing V. SCI, vol. 382, pp. 243–248. Springer, Heidelberg (2011), http://www.springerlink.com/content/d44n334p05772263/
7. Levine, N.: Crime mapping and the crimestat program. Geographical Analysis 38(1), 41–56 (2006), http://dx.doi.org/10.1111/j.0016-7363.2005.00673.x
8. Liebowitz, J. (ed.): The Handbook of Applied Expert Systems. CRC Press, Boca Raton (1998)
9. Ligęza, A.: Expert systems approach to decision support. European Journal of Operational Research 37(1), 100–110 (1988)
10. Ligęza, A.: Intelligent data and knowledge analysis and verification; towards a taxonomy of specific problems. In: Vermesan, A., Coenen, F. (eds.) Validation and Verification of Knowledge Based Systems: Theory, Tools and Practice, pp. 313–325. Kluwer Academic Publishers (1999)
11. Ligęza, A.: Logical Foundations for Rule-Based Systems. Springer, Heidelberg (2006)
12. Ligęza, A., Adrian, W.T., Ernst, S., Nalepa, G.J., Szpyrka, M., Czapko, M., Grzesiak, P., Krzych, M.: Prototypes of a web system for citizen provided information, automatic knowledge extraction, knowledge management and GIS integration. In: Dziech, A., Czyżewski, A. (eds.) MCSS 2011. CCIS, vol. 149, pp. 268–276. Springer, Heidelberg (2011)

13. Ligęza, A., Adrian, W.T., Kaczor, K., Nalepa, G.J., Ciężkowski, P., Żywioł, M., Grzesiak, P.: Web system for citizen provided information, automatic knowledge extraction, knowledge management and GIS integration. INDECT D4.14 technical report
14. Ligęza, A., Adrian, W.T., Kaczor, K., Nalepa, G.J., Ciężkowski, P., Żywioł, M., Grzesiak, P.: Web system for citizen provided information, automatic knowledge extraction, knowledge management and GIS integration. INDECT D9.30 technical report
15. Ligęza, A., Ernst, S., Nowaczyk, S., Nalepa, G.J., Szpyrka, M., Furmańska, W.T., Czapko, M., Grzesiak, P., Kałuża, M., Krzych, M.: Towards enregistration of threats in urban environments: practical consideration for a GIS-enabled web knowledge acquisition system. In: Dańda, J., Derkacz, J., Głowacz, A. (eds.) MCSS 2010: IEEE International Conference on Multimedia Communications, Services and Security, Kraków, Poland, May 6-7, pp. 152–158 (2010)
16. Ligęza, A., Nalepa, G.J.: A study of methodological issues in design and development of rule-based systems: proposal of a new approach. Wiley Interdisciplinary Reviews: Data Mining and Knowledge Discovery 1(2), 117–137 (2011)
17. Nalepa, G.J., Bobek, S., Ligęza, A., Kaczor, K.: HalVA - rule analysis framework for XTT2 rules. In: Bassiliades, N., Governatori, G., Paschke, A. (eds.) RuleML 2011 - Europe. LNCS, vol. 6826, pp. 337–344. Springer, Heidelberg (2011), http://www.springerlink.com/content/c276374nh9682jm6/
18. Nalepa, G.J.: PlWiki – A generic semantic wiki architecture. In: Nguyen, N.T., Kowalczyk, R., Chen, S.-M. (eds.) ICCCI 2009. LNCS, vol. 5796, pp. 345–356. Springer, Heidelberg (2009)
19. Nalepa, G.J., Kluza, K.: UML representation for rule-based application models with XTT2-based business rules. International Journal of Software Engineering and Knowledge Engineering (IJSEKE) 22(4), 485–524 (2012), http://www.worldscientific.com/doi/abs/10.1142/S021819401250012X
20. Nalepa, G.J., Ligęza, A.: Designing reliable Web security systems using rule-based systems approach. In: Menasalvas, E., Segovia, J., Szczepaniak, P.S. (eds.) AWIC 2003. LNCS (LNAI), vol. 2663, pp. 124–133. Springer, Heidelberg (2003)
21. Nalepa, G.J., Ligęza, A.: Conceptual modelling and automated implementation of rule-based systems. In: Software Engineering: Evolution and Emerging Technologies, Frontiers in Artificial Intelligence and Applications, vol. 130, pp. 330–340. IOS Press, Amsterdam (2005)
22. Nalepa, G.J., Ligęza, A.: HeKatE methodology, hybrid engineering of intelligent systems. International Journal of Applied Mathematics and Computer Science 20(1), 35–53 (2010)
23. Nalepa, G.J., Ligęza, A., Kaczor, K.: Formalization and modeling of rules using the XTT2 method. International Journal on Artificial Intelligence Tools 20(6), 1107–1125 (2011)
24. Open Geospatial Consortium: OpenGIS geography markup language (GML) implementation specification, version 2.1.2, http://www.opengeospatial.org/standards/gml

Multiagent System for Pattern Searching in Billing Data*

Łukasz Bęben and Bartłomiej Śnieżyński

AGH University of Science and Technology
Faculty of Computer Science, Electronics and Telecommunications
Department of Computer Science
30 Mickiewicza Av., 30-059 Krakow, Poland
bartlomiej.sniezynski@agh.edu.pl

Abstract. In this paper we present an agent-based pattern searching system using a distributed Apriori algorithm to analyse billing data. In the paper, we briefly present the problem of pattern mining. Next, we discuss related research focusing on distributed versions of Apriori algorithm and agent-based data mining software. Paper continues with an explanation of architecture and algorithms used in the system. We propose an original distribution mechanism allowing to split data into smaller chunks and also orthogonally distribute candidate patterns support calculation (in the same computation task). Experimental results on both generated and real-world data show that for different conditions other distribution policies give better speedup. The system is implemented using Erlang and can be used in heterogeneous hardware environment. This, together with multi-agent architecture gives flexibility in the system configuration and extension.

Keywords: data mining, multi-agent systems, criminal analysis.

1 Introduction

Public security is an area of governments' interests which is getting more and more important these days. With appropriate tools, such as data analysis with data mining, some threats could be avoided [1]. Data mining can also be used during investigation by criminal analysts for suspected entities discovering.

There are several data mining tools developed in the criminal analysis domain. The most popular is *Pattern Tracer* developed by *i2 Ltd.* [2]. Another tool is Mammoth (see [3]). Unlike traditional statistical methods, the result of such analysis has a form of information about a structure of the data instead of a numeric value. The structure can be represented by relationships, patterns, rules or dependencies. For example, we can discover a pattern showing that often person A calls person B, and next person B calls person C.

---

* The research leading to the results described in the paper has received funding from the European Community's Seventh Framework Program (FP7/2007-2013) under grant agreement n° 218086.

A. Dziech and A. Czyżewski (Eds.): MCSS 2013, CCIS 368, pp. 13–24, 2013.

Table 1. Table of 6 transactions and 4 elements

Transactions	A_1	A_2	A_3	A_4
t_1	0	1	1	0
t_2	1	1	1	0
t_3	0	0	1	1
t_4	1	1	0	0
t_5	0	0	0	1
t_6	0	1	1	0

Unfortunately, because of the algorithmic complexity of the problem, both tools mentioned above are unable to process large data sets. Therefore we decided to prepare parallel version of data mining algorithm Apriori which uses weighted load-balancing [4] upgraded with orthogonal data-split to process portions of data in parallel. We decided to apply an agent-based architecture to distribute computations. As a result, we obtained a flexible architecture allowing to extend the system very easily.

In the following section we describe the idea of pattern searching. This section may be skipped by a reader familiar with data mining techniques. After such theoretical introduction, we present related research. Next, we show our system architecture and algorithms used by the agents. Finally, we present experimental results on both generated and real-world data.

2   Patterns

In this section we give a brief overview of pattern searching problem in billing domain. We consider input data in a form of event sequences, which represent phone calls between exactly two entities (phone or *IMEI* numbers). However, similar processing can be performed for other types of data.

Before the analysis process begins, input data (sequence of calls) has to be transformed into transactions using a sliding window of the given span. As a consequence we get a set of transactions, as illustrated in Table 1.

Columns $A_1, A_2, \ldots, A_n$ represent *elements* (pairs of *objects* representing callers). Set $A = \{A_1, A_2, \ldots, A_n\}$ is the set of elements. There are observations in subsequent rows also known as *transactions*. 1 in row t_i in the column A_j means that call A_j is present in the i-th transaction corresponding to the i-th time window.

The result of the basic pattern searching analysis is the set of frequent patterns:

$$W = \{W_1, W_2, \ldots, W_p\}. \tag{1}$$

Each pattern $W_l \subseteq A$ is a set consisting of elements:

$$W_l = \{A_{l_1}, A_{l_2}, \ldots, A_{l_k}\}, \tag{2}$$

where $A_{l_i} \in A$. Discovering the pattern W_l in the data means that elements (calls) $A_{l_1}, A_{l_2}, \ldots, A_{l_k}$ often occur together which may represent some suspected activity.

With each discovered pattern W_i its support denoted as $sup(W_i)$ representing the number of its occurrences in the data is associated. In order to search patterns, a user has to provide a minimum support sup_{min} and only patterns for which support is not less than the sup_{min} are discovered. They are called frequent patterns.

For the data presented in Table 1 and $sup_{min} = 3$ the following frequent patterns will be discovered: $\{A_2\}, \{A_3\}, \{A_2, A_3\}$.

This example is useful to present an important Apriori property of frequent sets: if the pattern W_l is a frequent pattern, its subpattern $W_l' \subset W_l$ is also frequent. This property is used by the most popular Apriori algorithm. It is an iterative algorithm, which in successive iterations finds larger patterns. Based on the frequent patterns of size x it generates the candidate patterns of size $x + 1$. Then it calculates their support and patterns, which are found too few times are removed.

3   Related Research

Apriori algorithm is one of the most popular data mining techniques. However, its original version suffers from efficiency problems. Therefore, several parallel versions of this algorithm were developed. Most popular ones are presented below.

In [5] the Apriori algorithm was implemented using an approach proposed by Bodon [6]. In this approach the Trie structure is used for candidate patterns support counting, which tends to be faster than when using a hash map structure. The database is split into disjoint parts and each part is sent to a worker thread. Each worker performs candidate patterns support counting on its database portion and sends the results to a master thread, which aggregates the data from workers. The master thread is responsible for candidate patterns pruning and new candidate patterns generation. The article points out the problem of an optimal database distribution in order to balance workload among the workers. This concerns especially the final iterations of the algorithm, when there are only few candidate patterns to check and still the whole database has to be processed.

In [7] the implementation of Apriori-based frequent itemset mining algorithm on MapReduce is presented. In the article, it is pointed out that every distributed implementation of the algorithm faces problems of proper load balancing and computation nodes failures. The MapReduce deals with all of these and tends to be a natural solution. Even though, the problem of counting support for a small number of candidate itemsets in the final iterations still occurs. The idea of counting i-itemsets, (i+1)-itemsets ... (i+n)-itemsets(candidate itemsets from the following iterations) in one iteration is proposed. However, generating too many candidates may overload workers and is addressed by estimating workers capabilities and limiting the candidates to the estimated worker capacity. The Trie structure is used for candidate itemsets support counting.

Yu [4] describes a weighted load-balancing parallel Apriori algorithm for pattern mining. Here, the goal is also to limit database scans by storing metadata and distributing work properly. Metadata is a structure which for every item assigns Transaction IDentification (TID) in which this item appears. Working threads are used to calculate support for given candidate itemsets. Work distribution takes into account not only the number of candidate itemsets but also the number of transactions in which these itemsets' subitemsets appear. Experimental results on a cluster with 16 processors show that proposed technique is faster more than 10 times than parallel Apriori algorithm using a Trie structure.

In our research we decided to use an agent-based technology to implement distributed version of Apriori algorithm. Good survey of the multi-agent based distributed data mining can be found in [8].

Agents may be located in different sites which allows to mine data in their original locations. As a consequence, the data may be left in the original place. It may be especially important when network traffic has to be limited or if data can not be transmitted because of the security reasons [9,10].

Agents can be also used to provide better scalability. Work [11] presents a multi-agent system for large scale data mining. The system is composed of data mining agents, facilitator for coordinating the agents, and user interface. Agents are used to perform data query on their data and results are aggregated.

4   System Architecture

System architecture is presented in Fig. 1. The system consists of two types of agents:

Exploring Agent responsible for data exploration;
Counting Agent responsible for candidate patterns support counting.

The system is working in the following way. Exploring agent chooses a *Task* from the available set of tasks. The task is defined as a pair consisting of: input data, and minimal support. In order to perform the data exploration, Exploring Agent autonomously creates a number of Counting Agents and uses distributed version of Apriori algorithm described in the next section. The number of created agents may depend on the characteristics of the task.

The system is implemented using Erlang, taking advantage of its simple language-level distribution features and message passing concurrent programming. As a result, the system is relatively simple and can be used in heterogeneous hardware environments. This, together with a multi-agent architecture gives a flexibility in the system configuration. It also allows to extend the system capabilities – the same architecture allowed to implement parallel versions of machine learning algorithms C4.5, and Naïve Bayes.

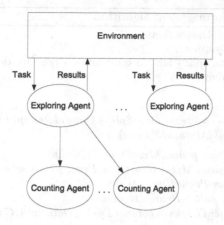

Fig. 1. System architecture

5 Algorithms

At the beginning of processing a given task, the Exploring Agent creates appropriate number of CountingAgents and calculates the metadata of the database as in [4] (see Algorithm 1). The metadata is a structure which for every item (or set of items) assigns Transaction IDentification (TID) which it appears in. The support of a candidate pattern can be obtained by counting the intersection of metadata created for items present in the candidate pattern.

The Exploring Agent spawns Counting Agents which perform candidate patterns support counting. Counting Agents are spawned at the beginning of the algorithm and awaiting the computation task. In the i-th iteration the metadata for candidate patterns of size $i - 1$ is sent to Counting Agents. Counting Agents are responsible for generating candidate patterns and the support counting using Metadata (see Algorithm 3). The Counting Agent takes a pair of candidate patterns form the previous iteration and checks whether they can form a new candidate pattern(they differ only by one item) and if so, calculates the support for the new candidate pattern – a metadata for the created candidate pattern is the intersection of the pair's candidate pattern metadata and the support is just the length of the obtained metadata. The support counting algorithm is presented as Algorithm 4. Results from each Counting Agent are then aggregated in the Exploring Agent. The Exploring Agent performs candidate patterns pruning (removing candidate patterns with support lower than min_{sup}) and updates the metadata (metadata from previous step is replaced with results for current candidate patterns). When there are no candidate patterns left, frequent patterns discovered so far are returned.

The workload can be distributed amongst Counting Agents in different manners. The database can be split into disjoint parts, analyzed by each Counting Agent separately and the results can be aggregated by summing the counted

---

Algorithm 1. Exploring Agent algorithm

Input: Data - list of Transactions,
MinSup - minimum support,
DataSplit, CandidatesSplit - how to split data for computations
Result: Frequent Itemsets

1 **begin**
2      $Result := []$
3      $CountingAgents :=$ create $DataSplit * CandidatesSplit$ CountingAgents
4      $Metadata := buildMetadata(Data)$

5      $PrunedItemsets := prune(MetaData, MinSup)$
6      $MetaData := updateMeta(MetaData, PrunedItemsets)$
7   **while** *not empty PrunedItemsets* **do**
8          $Result := Result + PrunedItemsets$
9          $CountingAgentTasks = balanceTasks(DataSplit, CandidatesSplit)$

10   send $CountingAgentsTasks$ to $CountingAgents$
11   receive $CountingAgentsCounts$ from $CountingAgents$
12   join $CountingAgentsCounts$

13         $PrunedItemsets = prune(CountingAgentsCounts, MinSup)$
14         $Metadata = updateMeta(Metadata, PrunedItemsets)$
15   **end**
16   stop workers $CountingAgents$
17   **return** $Result$
18 **end**

---

support from each part. Splitting the database is referred to as Data Split – the database is split into *DataSplit* disjoint parts and *DataSplit* Counting Agents are created.

Another way is to split candidate patterns so as to balance the workload amongst the Counting Agents as proposed in [4] – the results are acquired by just joining candidate patterns from Counting Agents (see Algorithm 2). Balancing candidate pattern relies on estimating the work needed to count a support for new candidate patterns using pruned candidate patterns from the previous iteration and can be estimated as a maximum number of operations needed for counting intersection of metadata for two candidate patterns that produce the new candidate pattern: for A, B – candidate patterns from previous iteration, $A \cup B$ – potential new candidate pattern, $intersect\_estimate(A \cup B) = length(A_{metadata}) * length(B_{metadata})$, where $length(X_{metadata})$ is a number of transactions in which X occurs. Metadata for candidate patterns is distributed amongst Counting Agents so as to balance the estimates. Candidate patterns balancing is referred to as Candidates Split – candidate patterns are split into *CandidatesSplit* disjoint parts and *Candidatespattern* Counting Agents are created. The balancing is performed using *balanceTasks* procedure (Algorithm 1, line 9).

Presented policies can also be used together and the candidate patterns distribution can be calculated for each database part separately in order to achieve the best load balancing – candidate patterns can be balanced for each database part separately. When both *DataSplit* and *CandidatesSplit* values are greater than 1, *DataSplit* ∗ *CandidatesSplit* Counting Agents are spawned and the candidate patterns are balanced for each database part separately.

In the current implementation *DataSplit* and *CandidatesSplit* are parameters provided by the user.

Algorithm 2. Exploring Agent : join support counts from Counting Agents

Input: CountingAgentsCounts - supports returned from Counting Agents
Result: Support counts from the whole database

```
1  begin
2      Result := map()
        // counts for CandidateSet are tagged with DataId
3      foreach DataId, CandidateSet, Count in CountingAgentsCounts do
4          if CandidateSet in Result then
               // join data from different database parts
5              Result[CandidateSet]+ = Count
6          end
7          else
8              Result[CandidateSet] := Count
9          end
10     end
11     return Result
12  end
```

Algorithm 3. Counting Agent algorithm

```
1  begin
2      while not stop do
3          receive DataId, SetsToCheck, MetaData
4          Counts := countSupport(SetsToCheck, MetaData)
5          send back DataId, Counts
6      end
7  end
```

---

6   Experimental Results

Experiments were performed to test the system's performance. Both real billing data and synthetic datasets were used in the experiments. The synthetic data was generated using IBM data generator.

Algorithm 4. Counting Agent : support counting

Input: SetsToCheck, MetaData
Result: Support counts for CandidateSets

1 **begin**
2     $Supports := map()$
3   **foreach** (Set_A, Set_B) *in SetsToCheck* **do**
4   **if** $Set_A \cup Set_B$ *forms CandidateSet* **then**
5             $supports[CandidateSet] :=$
            $length(MetaData(Set_A) \cap MetaData(Set_B))$
6   **end**
7   **end**
8   **return** *Supports*
9 **end**

6.1 Setup

The experiments were performed on a single machine with Intel^{TM}Core^{TM}i5-450M Processor (3M cache, 2.40 GHz), 4GB RAM on Ubuntu 10.10. The experiments were performed for different Data Split and Candidates Split amongst Counting Agents. We have chosen the following splits:

DataSplit=1, CandidatesSplit=1 which corresponds to a classical Apriori implementation, without paralelization, and may be used as a reference;
DataSplit=4, CandidatesSplit=1 in which only data is partitioned and corresponds to simple Apriori paralelization;
DataSplit=1, CandidatesSplit=4 where we partition candidate sets and do not partition data which corresponds to technique used in [4];
DataSplit=2, CandidatesSplit=2 which is full partitioning.

Calculations were repeated 5 times to eliminate the noise and the average time is presented in figures. The experiments showed that the optimal balancing policy depends on the dataset characteristics and support, therefore different policies for datasets are presented.

6.2 Generated Data

The data was generated using the IBM Data Generator. Results for T10I4D50K-N10K and T10I4D50KN100K are presented in Fig. 2 (a), (b), respectively. The number after T stands for the average transaction length, I stands for the average pattern length, D is the number of transactions in the database and N stands for total number of items.

For the T10I4D50KN10K, when support is small, splitting the candidate patterns amongst the workers gives better speedup. Because of the small support, there are a lot of candidate patterns produced and the number of patterns is substantially bigger than the number of transactions to process. It changes as the support gets bigger, since less candidate patterns are produced and the number of transactions determines the execution time. For support values 0.005 and larger DataSplit=4 gives the best results.

For the T10I4D50KN100K splitting the database amongst the workers was a better policy for all support values. The reason is that the number of transactions is greater than the number of candidate patterns generated.

6.3   Billing Data

A real-world billing data was also used in the experiments. The results are shown for a dataset including 3 months billing data and the time window span is 10 hours. The dataset contains 12k transactions. The results are shown in Fig. 2 (c). Here also DataSplit=4 gave the best speedup, because there are not many candidate patterns generated, and the number of transactions determines the execution time. Results of other configurations are much worse.

Let us check the results of the pattern searching. The following pattern example was discovered in experiments: 610960222 → 771390331, 613413849 → 61377413849, 771390331 → 613413849. When we go back to the original data, we can see the emerging pattern (table 2): 610960222 → 771390331 → 613413849 → 61377413849. During investigation, criminal analyst should check these numbers. Even if they occur rarely in the billing data, they appear together which may suggest suspected behaviour.

Table 2. Example pattern occurring in a billing data

Time	Call
$2005 - 01 - 07, 12 : 05 : 50$	$613413849 \to 61377413849$
$2005 - 01 - 07, 19 : 23 : 17$	$613413849 \to 61377413849$
$2005 - 01 - 08, 16 : 19 : 00$	$771390331 \to 613413849$
$2005 - 01 - 08, 17 : 53 : 00$	$610960222 \to 771390331$
$2005 - 01 - 09, 13 : 25 : 01$	$613413849 \to 61377413849$
$2005 - 03 - 17, 12 : 43 : 00$	$771390331 \to 613413849$
$2005 - 03 - 17, 13 : 14 : 57$	$613413849 \to 61377413849$
$2005 - 03 - 17, 14 : 14 : 00$	$771390331 \to 613413849$
$2005 - 03 - 17, 14 : 29 : 39$	$613413849 \to 61377413849$
$2005 - 03 - 17, 16 : 41 : 00$	$610960222 \to 771390331$
$2005 - 03 - 17, 17 : 12 : 00$	$771390331 \to 613413849$
$2005 - 03 - 18, 10 : 24 : 00$	$610960222 \to 771390331$
$2005 - 03 - 18, 10 : 58 : 00$	$771390331 \to 613413849$
$2005 - 03 - 18, 11 : 06 : 00$	$610960222 \to 771390331$
$2005 - 03 - 18, 11 : 27 : 57$	$613413849 \to 61377413849$
$2005 - 03 - 18, 18 : 07 : 00$	$771390331 \to 613413849$
$2005 - 03 - 18, 20 : 06 : 00$	$610960222 \to 771390331$
$2005 - 03 - 18, 20 : 40 : 00$	$771390331 \to 613413849$

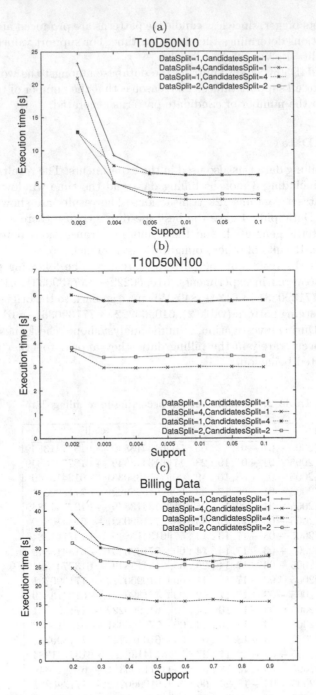

Fig. 2. Average execution time for selected balancing policies and various support values for generated data T10I4D50KN10K (a), T10I4D50KN100K (b), and real-world billing data (c)

7   Conclusions

This paper summarizes our experience in multi-agent implementation of pattern searching system designed to mine patterns in billing data. We have presented theory related to pattern searching, system design, algorithms, and experimental results on generated and real-world data. Results show that various partitioning gives the best results in various conditions. Data split gives good results if there is a lot of transactions, while candidates split is good for many candidate patterns.

Future works will be performed in several directions. Firstly, we would like to add learning capabilities to Exploring Agent (Exploring Agent will have an architecture proposed in [12]). Learning will be used to determine the distribution method. Next, we are planning other applications of the mining system, like Internet Identity Analysis [13] and Focused Web Crawling [14]. Last but not least, we would like to test the system on a cluster and simulate various conditions like CPU availability or network speed limits.

References

1. Seifert, J.W.: Data mining: An overview. CRS Report for Congress (2004)
2. i2 Ltd: i2 Pattern Tracer (2009) http://www.i2.co.uk/
3. Świerczek, A., Dębski, R., Włodek, P., Śnieżyński, B.: Integrating applications developed for heterogeneous platforms: Building an environment for criminal analysts. In: Dziech, A., Czyżewski, A. (eds.) MCSS 2011. CCIS, vol. 149, pp. 19–27. Springer, Heidelberg (2011)
4. Yu, K.M., Zhou, J.L.: A weighted load-balancing parallel apriori algorithm for association rule mining. In: IEEE International Conference on Granular Computing, GrC 2008, pp. 756–761 (August 2008)
5. Ye, Y., Chiang, C.C.: A parallel apriori algorithm for frequent itemsets mining. In: Fourth International Conference on Software Engineering Research, Management and Applications, pp. 87–93 (August 2006)
6. Bodon, F.: A fast apriori implementation. In: Proceedings of the IEEE ICDM Workshop on Frequent Itemset Mining Implementations. CEUR Workshop Proceedings, vol. 90 (2003)
7. Lin, M.Y., Lee, P.Y., Hsueh, S.C.: Apriori-based frequent itemset mining algorithms on mapreduce. In: ICUIMC 2012 Proceedings of the 6th International Conference on Ubiquitous Information Management and Communication Article No. 76 (2012)
8. Moemeng, C., Gorodetsky, V., Zuo, Z., Yang, Y., Zhang, C.: Agent-based distributed data mining: A survey. In: Cao, L. (ed.) Data Mining and Multi-agent Integration, pp. 47–58. Springer, US (2009)
9. Klusch, M., Lodi, S., Gianluca, M.: The role of agents in distributed data mining: issues and benefits. In: IEEE/WIC International Conference on Intelligent Agent Technology, IAT 2003, pp. 211–217 (October 2003)
10. Li, X., Ni, J.: Deploying mobile agents in distributed data mining. In: Washio, T., Zhou, Z.-H., Huang, J.Z., Hu, X., Li, J., Xie, C., He, J., Zou, D., Li, K.-C., Freire, M.M. (eds.) PAKDD 2007. LNCS (LNAI), vol. 4819, pp. 322–331. Springer, Heidelberg (2007)

11. Kargupta, H., Hamzaoglu, I., Stafford, B.: Scalable, distributed data mining using an agent based architecture. In: Proceedings the Third International Conference on the Knowledge Discovery and Data Mining, pp. 211–214. AAAI Press, Menlo Park (1997)
12. Śnieżyński, B.: An architecture for learning agents. In: Bubak, M., van Albada, G.D., Dongarra, J., Sloot, P.M.A. (eds.) ICCS 2008, Part III. LNCS, vol. 5103, pp. 722–730. Springer, Heidelberg (2008)
13. Wilaszek, K., Wójcik, T., Opaliński, A., Turek, W.: Internet identity analysis and similarities detection. In: Dziech, A., Czyżewski, A. (eds.) MCSS 2012. CCIS, vol. 287, pp. 369–379. Springer, Heidelberg (2012)
14. Turek, W., Opalinski, A., Kisiel-Dorohinicki, M.: Extensible web crawler – towards multimedia material analysis. In: Dziech, A., Czyżewski, A. (eds.) MCSS 2011. CCIS, vol. 149, pp. 183–190. Springer, Heidelberg (2011)

Mobile Context-Based Framework for Monitoring Threats in Urban Environment[*]

Szymon Bobek, Grzegorz J. Nalepa, and Weronika T. Adrian

AGH University of Science and Technology
al. Mickiewicza 30, 30-059 Krakow, Poland
{szymon.bobek,gjn,wta}@agh.edu.pl

Abstract. With a rapid evolution of mobile devices, the idea of context awareness has gained a remarkable popularity in recent years. Modern smartphones and tablets are equipped with a variety of sensors including accelerometers, gyroscopes, pressure gauges, light and GPS sensors. Additionally, the devices become computationally powerful which allows real-time processing of data gathered by their sensors. Universal access to the Internet via WiFi hot-spots and GSM network makes mobile devices perfect platforms for ubiquitous computing. Although there exist numerous frameworks for context-aware systems, they are usually dedicated to static, centralized, client-server architectures. There is still space for research in a field of context modeling and reasoning for mobile devices. In this paper, we propose a lightweight context-aware framework for mobile devices that uses data gathered by mobile device sensors and perform on-line reasoning about possible threats, based on the information provided by the Social Threat Monitor system developed in the INDECT project.

Keywords: context-awareness, mobile computing, GIS, knowledge management, INDECT.

1 Introduction

Distributed reporting and notification systems for citizen security have become common and widely expected and adopted in recent years. Within the scope of the INDECT[1] project such solutions are being developed and evaluated. Principal objectives of the project include engaging citizens into active participation in the authorities efforts to provide instant notification for a number of security threats in a given neighborhood or a wider location. The threats can be considered in different categories, such as crime, natural disasters, accidents or traffic related events.

A system called *Social Threat Monitor* (STM) that meets the above mentioned needs was developed. The STM is a GIS-based solution that assists citizens in

---

[*] The research presented in this paper is carried out within the EU FP7 INDECT Project: "Intelligent information system supporting observation, searching and detection for security of citizens in urban environment" (http://indect-project.eu).
[1] See http://indect-project.eu

reporting security threats together with their severity and location. The threats are classified using a general top-level ontology, with domain ontologies supporting the detailed specification of threats. The information about the threats is stored in a knowledge base of the system which allows lightweight reasoning with the gathered facts. All the threats can be located on a web-accessible map that can be analyzed by a group of users, e.g., police officials, regular citizens, etc.

The current version of the system is a web-based solution, composed of a server-side GIS-based service providing access to the knowledge base and a web client. Therefore, a standard-compliant web browser is expected to be used as the main user interface. Another method for interfacing with the system on the application level is provided by a dedicated API that allows posing queries and making updates of the knowledge base.

An apparent limitation of the current system is related to the use of mobile devices on the client side. In the first generation of the system, an implicit assumption was made, that the user has a standard web browser available. Moreover, this browser should be used with a standard (for regular desktop and laptop computers) point-and-click user interface. However, currently the most common use case scenario includes the use of a mobile handheld device, such as a smartphone or a tablet, with a number of multimodal interfaces and sensors. Therefore, a need for a new front-end for the system became apparent. The principal objective of this paper is to propose and discuss a design of a prototype of such a system. It uses the context-aware application paradigm that improves usability from the user perspective, and simplifies the use of multi sensor data available on the mobile devices.

The rest of the paper is organized as follows. In Section 2, issues of context modeling and reasoning in mobile devices are discussed. This leads to presenting the motivation of the development of a new STM front-end in Section 3. The architecture of the system is presented in Section 4. A practical use case scenario is briefly introduced in Section 6. Finally, summary and directions for future work are given in Section 7.

2   Context in Mobile Computing

Research in the area of pervasive computing and ambient intelligence aims to make use of context information to allow devices or applications behave in a context-aware way. Dey [10] defines context as *any information that can be used to characterize the situation of an entity*, where *an entity is a person, place, or object that is considered relevant to the interaction between a user and an application, including the user and application themselves.*

The *information* in Dey's definition may be:

- location of the user (spatial context),
- presence or absence of other devices and users (social context),
- time (temporal context),
- user *behavior* or *activity* (activity recognition, behavior modeling), and
- other environmental data gathered by microphones, light sensors, etc.

Raw information captured by the device sensors is usually useless without further preprocessing and interpretation. Thus, the main challenges in context-aware systems are context modeling and context-based reasoning. There have been done a lot of research regarding context modeling. Various methods of knowledge representation were used, e.g., rules and logic [8,19,25], ontologies [7,30], object-oriented languages (CML, ORM) [12], context lattices [32] or processes [14].

In the area of context-based reasoning, the following approaches were developed: machine learning and probabilistic inference [5,31], decision trees [18], rule-based and logic-based reasoning [25,19,8]. Although there are a lot of frameworks and middlewares developed for context-aware systems, they are usually limited to a specific domain and designed without taking into consideration mobile platforms. Examples include CoBrA [6] and SOUPA [7] for building smart meeting rooms, GAIA [26] for active spaces, Context Toolkit [8], etc.

There is still space for research in a field of lightweight context modeling and context reasoning targeted at mobile devices. Some attempts were made to develop such frameworks, like SOCAM [11], or Context Torrent [13]. However, these frameworks do not provide full support for all of the challenges that we believe are crucial for mobile computing, with respect to the context modeling and context-based reasoning:

1. **energy efficiency** – most of the sensors, when turned on all the time, decrease the mobile device battery level very fast. This reflects on usability of the system and ecological aspects regarding energy saving.
2. **privacy** – most of the users do not want to send information about their location, activities, and other private data to external servers. Hence, the context reasoning should be performed by the mobile device.
3. **resource limitations** – although mobile phones and tablets are becoming computationally powerful, the context aware system has to consume as low CPU and memory resources as possible in order to be transparent to the user and other applications.

All of these require from the modeling language and inference engine to be simple and lightweight. Aforementioned challenges were usually approached by the programmers at the very last phase of the development of context-aware application, or were not approached at all. We believe that solutions to these challenges should be provided by the framework architecture. This will oblige the programmer to build context-aware application in an efficient way, making the development easier and less error prone.

3 Motivation

The primary objective of research that lead to the development of STM was to build a semantically enriched environment for collaborative knowledge management. Using it, local communities should be able to share information about road traffic dangers and threats, i.e. closed roads, holes in the pavements and streets, dangerous districts or events that impede a normal traffic. STM was aimed to be a community portal that allows citizens to participate and cooperate in order to improve the security in the urban environment. Within the task several system prototypes have been developed [2,3,29]. The subsequent versions of the STM system have used intelligent processing to provide possibly most useful knowledge to the users. Categorization of threats and possibility of inferring new facts based on the ones entered by users was introduced.

The latest development of the system [16] included a redesign that emphasizes the social aspects of the system. It defined the application as a platform to exchange information about dangers and their location among citizens and with public services. The objective of the application is to help civilians and public services to improve safety in urban areas and detect dangers faster. Users are able to browse threats in selected area and submit information about a threat by adding comments and photos. Moreover, public services are able to inform people about dangers and to monitor threats and decide if an intervention is needed. The main limitation remained the user interface (UI) which should be intuitive and easy to use, potentially adaptable to various hardware platforms including desktop and mobiles. In fact, so far the system was not designed to use mobile devices on the client side. Nevertheless, currently the most common use case scenario includes the use of a mobile handheld device, such as a smartphone or tablet. Such a device has a number of multimodal interfaces and sensors, e.g. gesture based interface, GPS, etc. Therefore, a need for a new front-end for STM became apparent.

The idea comes down to propose a design of a prototype of such a front-end. It is based on the the context-aware application paradigm that improves usability from the user perspective. Moreover, it simplifies the user of multi sensor data available on the mobile devices. The principal idea is presented in Figure 1.

Being in a given situation, and location (i.e., context) the user can be automatically notified by their mobile device about the threats relevant to him and the situation. Relevance to the person may be related to their role defined in the STM system, as well as the context, e.g. a person who walks should not be bothered by warnings relevant only to drivers in the same location. The use of data fusion from the sensors and multimodal interfaces of the mobile device allows to limit the amount of data the user would have to provide to the system. In fact, we propose a major paradigm shift on the front-end side. Whereas the original interface of STM was mostly query-based, here we propose a push-based UI where the user is automatically notified only about the information relevant to him. The system automatically uses the context data from the mobile device, as well as the data acquired from the STM server to perform reasoning for the user. In the following section, the architecture of the system is discussed.

4   Context-Based STM Front-End Architecture

The proposed system is based on a service-oriented architecture (see Figure 2). It consists of three main elements:

1. sensors service – responsible for gathering data from sensors and performing initial preprocessing of them,

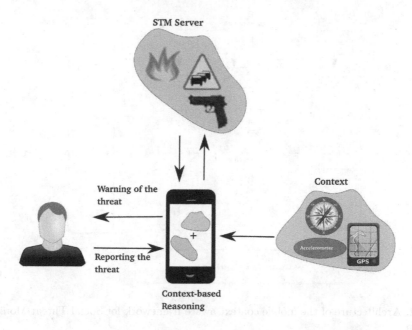

Fig. 1. Context-based front-end for Social Threat Monitor

2. inference service – responsible for context based reasoning and knowledge management. It provides TCP/IP API for context-aware applications,
3. working memory middleware – acting as an intelligent proxy between sensors service and the inference service.

Sensors Service
The Sensor Service gathers data directly form mobile device sensors. Due to the different possible sensor types (GPS, Accelerometer, Bluetooth), different methods for interpreting these data are required. Hence, each sensor has its own interpreter module that is responsible for initial preprocessing of the raw data. Data preprocessing is triggered by the Working Memory Middleware.

Inference Service
The inference service is responsible for performing reasoning, based on the model (knowledge base) and the working memory elements (facts). The service is capable of managing many models transparently switching between them. The reasoning task is performed by HeaRT [4,1]. It is a lightweight rule-based inference engine that uses XTT2 [24] notation for knowledge representation. It is written in Prolog and can be installed on mobile device together with tuProlog[2] interpreter, providing autonomous inference service. Moreover, the HeaRT inference engine, in contrary to other rule-based inference engines, provides custom

---

[2] See http://alice.unibo.it/xwiki/bin/view/Main/

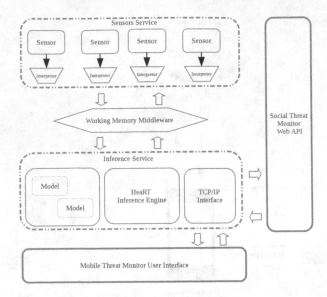

Fig. 2. Architecture of the mobile context aware framework for Social Threat Monitor system

verification module that can be used for automatic optimization of knowledge base (see Section 7 for details).

The inference service provides a TCP/IP interface for context-aware applications that may query HeaRT for important information. An exemplary query may concern listing all possible threats. This will require the inference engine to determine a context of the user (decide if the user is a driver, a cyclist, a pedestrian, decide where the user is, or where he or she will be in a nearest future). Based on this facts and on the data pulled from Social Threat Monitor system, the inference service will return the list of all the threats relevant for the user.

Working Memory Middleware
The Working Memory Middleware is responsible for exchanging information between sensors service and inference service. The working memory is shared between all models stored within the inference service, acting as a *knowledge cache*. Therefore, it minimizes the number of required requests to the sensors service, improving power efficiency of the entire system.

5   Context-Based Knowledge Management

The context aware framework presented in this paper uses XTT2 notation for knowledge representation. XTT2 [24] is a visual knowledge representation method for rule-based systems [17,23] where rules are stored in tables connected with each other creating a graph (see Figure 3).

The XTT2 has a textual representation called HMR. An example of a rule written in HMR language is presented below. The rule is referenced in Figure 3, in table *Today*.

```
xrule Today/1: [day in [sat,sun]] ==>[today set weekend].
```

The HMR representation is used by the HeaRT inference engine, which provides several inference modes, including:

Data-Driven which can be used to find all possible information that can be inferred from given data.

Goal-Driven which can be used to find only a specific information that can be inferred from a specific subset of XTT2 tables.

These inference modes allow the efficient reasoning in structured knowledge bases, like XTT2. Only the tables that lead to desired solution are fired, and no rules are fired without purpose, making the inference process less resource-consuming. Detailed description of the inference algorithms for XTT2 rule bases, can be found in [20]. For the purpuse of context processing a process-based description could also be used, see [15].

The HeaRT inference engine provide a callback mechanism that allows to query external sources for information. The external source could be: database, user, or in our case working memory middleware and Social Threat Monitor system. Callbacks are associated with attributes, defined as e.g.:

```
xattr [ name: day,
class: simple,
type: day,
comm: in,
callback: [ask_working_memory,[day]]
    ].
```

The *comm* element in the attribute definition determines behavior of a callback. There are three different types of such behavior:

comm: in – the callback is obliged to pull the value of the attribute from external source,

comm: out – the callback is obliged to push the value of the attribute to external source,

comm: inter – the callback should not assert nor retract any information from external source.

More about callback mechanism can be found in [22].

6   Use Case Scenario

An exemplary XTT2 model (see Figure 3) presented in this section allows to alert users about threats in a context-aware way. The system takes into consideration spatial (localization of the user) and temporal (time of a day) contexts, as well

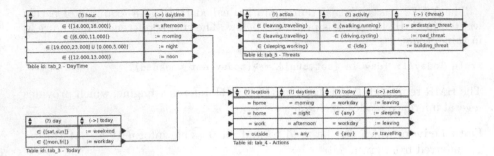

Fig. 3. Example of the model for a mobile threat monitor

as user activities. This allow the intelligent threats filtering. For instance, the model will prevent from warning a user who is driving a car about threats that are applicable to pedestrians only. This is achieved by selecting only these rules that are valid in current context.

Information about threats is fetched from Social Threat Monitor system via callbacks using the WEB API (see [2] for details). Information about user localization, time of a day, and user activities is pulled from a working memory middleware via callback mechanism. The working memory middleware obtains this information from sensors interpreters (for example: location from GPS sensor interpreter, activity like walking or running from accelerometer sensor interpreter, etc.).

Taking into consideration an example from Figure 3, and assuming that it is Monday, 8 o'clock am, and the user is driving a car, the system will process following rules: (1) rule 1 from *DayTime* table, (2) rule 2 from *Today* table, (3) rule 4 from *Actions* table, (4) and rule 2 from *Threats* table.

This inference chain will trigger several callbacks, including one that is assigned to `road_threats` in the *Threats* table. The callback will fetch all road threats from Social Threat Monitor system that are located near the user and assign it to `road_threats` attribute.

The application that implements Mobile Threat Monitor interface will be able to pull all information about threats from inference service via TCP/IP API and display it to the user.

7   Summary and Future Work

In this paper, we presented a mobile context-aware framework that uses data gathered by mobile device sensors and perform on-line reasoning about possible threats, based on the information provided by the Social Threat Monitor system. We argue that our solution addresses main challenges in mobile context-aware computing, that includes (1) *energy efficiency*, (2) *privacy*, and (3) *resource limitations*. The framework is designed in a service oriented architecture that includes:

1. *inference service*, that uses HeaRT inference engine to provide on-line efficient reasoning, preserving the (2) and (3);

2. *working memory middleware*, that works as knowledge cache minimizing the number of required requests to the sensors service, improving power efficiency of the entire system, preserving (1) and (2);
3. *sensor service*, that is responsible for gathering and initial preprocessing of the raw sensor data.

Future work includes more improvements towards power efficiency, and automatic optimization of knowledge bases, as well as intelligibility and usability of the system. The framework presented in this paper may be extended for additional functionalities, including:

Automatic threat reporting – The application could report anomalies in user behavior to the Social Threat Monitor system. When similar anomaly will be reported by many users, an alert will be raised. For instance, if a number of users start running from a building, there is probably a fire.

Learning user usage habits – The working memory middleware could learn user usage habits, to optimize sensors sampling. For instance, if there is no point in sampling accelerometer sensor at night with a high frequency, where there is high probability that the user will not move.

Intelligibility – Rule based system have a high capabilities of self-explaining their decisions. According to Dey [9], this is crucial factor of the system usability. The framework could provide mechanisms that will allow explaining its decision and asking user for corrections.

Automatic model optimization – HeaRT inference engine provides a verification plug-in that allows detecting anomalies such as: rules subsumption, redundancy and contradiction. Hence, a mechanism that will perform automatic optimization of an existing XTT2 model could be implemented [21].

There is also a possibility of a formal verification of systems developed with the presented approach. For example, a Petri net model for a context-aware application can be design. Some possibilities of including rule-based systems into Petri net models have been studied in [28] and [27]. It is possible to adopt these solutions to our needs.

References

1. Adrian, W.T., Bobek, S., Nalepa, G.J., Kaczor, K., Kluza, K.: How to reason by HeaRT in a semantic knowledge-based wiki. In: Proceedings of the 23rd IEEE International Conference on Tools with Artificial Intelligence, ICTAI 2011. pp. 438–441. Boca Raton, Florida, USA (November 2011)
2. Adrian, W.T., Ciężkowski, P., Kaczor, K., Ligęza, A., Nalepa, G.J.: Web-based knowledge acquisition and management system supporting collaboration for improving safety in urban environment. In: Dziech, A., Czyżewski, A. (eds.) MCSS 2012. CCIS, vol. 287, pp. 1–12. Springer, Heidelberg (2012),
http://link.springer.com/book/10.1007/978-3-642-30721-8/page/1

3. Adrian, W.T., Waliszko, J., Ligęza, A., Nalepa, G.J., Kaczor, K.: Description logic reasoning in an ontology-based system for citizen safety in urban environment. In: Mercier-Laurent, E., et al. (eds.) AI4KM 2012: 1st International Workshop on Artificial Intelligence for Knowledge Management at the Biennial European Conference on Artificial Intelligence (ECAI 2012), Montpellier, France, August 28, pp. 63–67 (2012)
4. Bobek, S.: Heart rule inference engine in intelligent systems. PAR Pomiary Automatyka Robotyka 15(12), 226–228 (2011) ISSN 1427-9126
5. Bui, H.H., Venkatesh, S., West, G.A.W.: Tracking and surveillance in wide-area spatial environments using the abstract hidden markov model. IJPRAI 15(1), 177–195 (2001), http://dblp.uni-trier.de/db/journals/ijprai/ijprai15.html#BuiVW01
6. Chen, H., Finin, T.W., Joshi, A.: Semantic web in the context broker architecture. In: PerCom, pp. 277–286. IEEE Computer Society (2004)
7. Chen, H., Perich, F., Finin, T.W., Joshi, A.: Soupa: Standard ontology for ubiquitous and pervasive applications. In: 1st Annual International Conference on Mobile and Ubiquitous Systems (MobiQuitous 2004), Networking and Services, Cambridge, MA, USA, August 22-25, pp. 258–267. IEEE Computer Society (2004)
8. Dey, A.K.: Understanding and using context. Personal Ubiquitous Comput. 5(1), 4–7 (2001)
9. Dey, A.K.: Modeling and intelligibility in ambient environments. J. Ambient Intell. Smart Environ. 1(1), 57–62 (2009)
10. Dey, A.K.: Providing architectural support for building context-aware applications. Ph.D. thesis, Atlanta, GA, USA (2000), aAI9994400
11. Gu, T., Pung, H.K., Zhang, D.Q., Wang, X.H.: A middleware for building context-aware mobile services. In: Proceedings of IEEE Vehicular Technology Conference (VTC) (2004)
12. Henricksen, K., Indulska, J., Rakotonirainy, A.: Modeling context information in pervasive computing systems. In: Mattern, F., Naghshineh, M. (eds.) PERVASIVE 2002. LNCS, vol. 2414, pp. 167–180. Springer, Heidelberg (2002), http://dl.acm.org/citation.cfm?id=646867.706693
13. Hu, D.H., Dong, F., li Wang, C.: A semantic context management framework on mobile device âĹŮ
14. Jaroucheh, Z., Liu, X., Smith, S.: Recognize contextual situation in pervasive environments using process mining techniques. J. Ambient Intelligence and Humanized Computing 2(1), 53–69 (2011)
15. Kluza, K., Maślanka, T., Nalepa, G.J., Ligęza, A.: Proposal of representing BPMN diagrams with XTT2-based business rules. In: Brazier, F.M.T., Nieuwenhuis, K., Pavlin, G., Warnier, M., Badica, C. (eds.) Intelligent Distributed Computing V. SCI, vol. 382, pp. 243–248. Springer, Heidelberg (2011), http://www.springerlink.com/content/d44n334p05772263/
16. Ligęza, A., Adrian, W.T., Ciężkowski, P.: Towards collaborative knowledge engineering for improving local safety in urban environment. In: Canadas, J., Nalepa, G.J., Baumeister, J. (eds.) 8th Workshop on Knowledge Engineering and Software Engineering (KESE 2012) at the at the biennial European Conference on Artificial Intelligence (ECAI 2012), Montpellier, France, August 28, pp. 58–61 (2012), http://ceur-ws.org/Vol-949/
17. Ligęza, A., Nalepa, G.J.: A study of methodological issues in design and development of rule-based systems: proposal of a new approach. Wiley Interdisciplinary Reviews: Data Mining and Knowledge Discovery 1(2), 117–137 (2011)

18. Logan, B., Healey, J., Philipose, M., Tapia, E.M., Intille, S.S.: A long-term evaluation of sensing modalities for activity recognition. In: Krumm, J., Abowd, G.D., Seneviratne, A., Strang, T. (eds.) UbiComp 2007. LNCS, vol. 4717, pp. 483–500. Springer, Heidelberg (2007), http://dl.acm.org/citation.cfm?id=1771592.1771620
19. Loke, S.W.: Representing and reasoning with situations for context-aware pervasive computing: a logic programming perspective. Knowl. Eng. Rev. 19(3), 213–233 (2004), http://dx.doi.org/10.1017/S0269888905000263
20. Nalepa, G.J., Bobek, S., Ligęza, A., Kaczor, K.: Algorithms for rule inference in modularized rule bases. In: Bassiliades, N., Governatori, G., Paschke, A. (eds.) RuleML 2011 - Europe. LNCS, vol. 6826, pp. 305–312. Springer, Heidelberg (2011)
21. Nalepa, G.J., Bobek, S., Ligęza, A., Kaczor, K.: HalVA - rule analysis framework for XTT2 rules. In: Bassiliades, N., Governatori, G., Paschke, A. (eds.) RuleML 2011 - Europe. LNCS, vol. 6826, pp. 337–344. Springer, Heidelberg (2011), http://www.springerlink.com/content/c276374nh9682jm6/
22. Nalepa, G.J.: Architecture of the HeaRT hybrid rule engine. In: Rutkowski, L., Scherer, R., Tadeusiewicz, R., Zadeh, L.A., Zurada, J.M. (eds.) ICAISC 2010, Part II. LNCS, vol. 6114, pp. 598–605. Springer, Heidelberg (2010)
23. Nalepa, G.J., Kluza, K.: UML representation for rule-based application models with XTT2-based business rules. International Journal of Software Engineering and Knowledge Engineering (IJSEKE) 22(4), 485–524 (2012), http://www.worldscientific.com/doi/abs/10.1142/S021819401250012X
24. Nalepa, G.J., Ligęza, A., Kaczor, K.: Formalization and modeling of rules using the XTT2 method. International Journal on Artificial Intelligence Tools 20(6), 1107–1125 (2011)
25. Ranganathan, A., Campbell, R.H.: An infrastructure for context-awareness based on first order logic. Personal Ubiquitous Comput. 7(6), 353–364 (2003), http://dx.doi.org/10.1007/s00779-003-0251-x
26. Ranganathan, A., McGrath, R.E., Campbell, R.H., Mickunas, M.D.: Use of ontologies in a pervasive computing environment. Knowl. Eng. Rev. 18(3), 209–220 (2003)
27. Szpyrka, M.: Design and analysis of rule-based systems with adder designer. In: Cotta, C., Reich, S., Schaefer, R., Ligęza, A. (eds.) Knowledge-Driven Computing: knowledge engineering and intelligent computations. SCI, vol. 102, pp. 255–271. Springer, Heidelberg (2008)
28. Szpyrka, M., Szmuc, T.: Decision tables in petri net models. In: Kryszkiewicz, M., Peters, J.F., Rybiński, H., Skowron, A. (eds.) RSEISP 2007. LNCS (LNAI), vol. 4585, pp. 648–657. Springer, Heidelberg (2007)
29. Waliszko, J., Adrian, W.T., Ligęza, A.: Traffic danger ontology for citizen safety web system. In: Dziech, A., Czyżewski, A. (eds.) MCSS 2011. CCIS, vol. 149, pp. 165–173. Springer, Heidelberg (2011)
30. Wang, X., Zhang, D., Gu, T., Pung, H.K.: Ontology based context modeling and reasoning using owl. In: PerCom Workshops, pp. 18–22 (2004)
31. Ye, J., Coyle, L., Dobson, S.A., Nixon, P.: Representing and manipulating situation hierarchies using situation lattices. Revue d Intelligence Artificielle 22(5), 647–667 (2008)
32. Ye, J., Dobson, S.: Exploring semantics in activity recognition using context lattices. J. Ambient Intell. Smart Environ. 2(4), 389–407 (2010)

Anchor-Free Localization Algorithm with Low-Complexity Method for Node Distance Estimation Enhancement Using ToA

Vladimír Cipov, Ľubomír Doboš, and Ján Papaj

Department of Electronics and Multimedia Communications,
Faculty of Electrical Engineering and Informatics, Technical University of Košice,
Letná 9, 042 00 Košice, Slovak Republic
{vladimir.cipov,lubomir.dobos,jan.papaj}@tuke.sk

Abstract. We introduce the anchor-free localization algorithm using Time of Arrival node distance estimation technique. ToA using Ultra Wide-Band communication technology is preferred, because it is one of the most promising approaches of the mobile positioning and has a great potential for accurate ranging especially in the harsh indoor environment. Due to very wide bandwidth of the UWB systems, these systems are capable resolving individual multipath components in the received Channel Impulse Response and determining their time of their arrival very precisely. We propose a low-complexity method for mitigation of the Undetected Direct Path effect which causes considerable errors in the node distance estimation. The method combines the mean of the time delay differences of the reflected paths detected in the measured channel power delay profile, overall channel impulse response length and Mean Excess Delay calculated relative to the first detected path. The positioning algorithm has been simulated in LoS, NLoS(OLoS) and NLoS(UDP) communication conditions.

Keywords: Anchor-free localization, NLoS, UDP mitigation, Time of Arrival.

1 Introduction

In the field of mobile communication, the wireless nodes location problem has gained increasing interest. Location estimation is a complex problem. It has been investigated extensively in the literature, where authors solved various problems. Within a few years, positioning techniques have achieved different stages of evolution - from the basic location methods based on cellular communication to the methods based on the ad-hoc node communication often without any points that create the network infrastructure. In such cases we are talking about the Anchor-free localization.

Currently, the research teams have aim to solve just this type of positioning, where different algorithms have been developed in order to provide anchor-free localization such as SALAM [6], SPA [2] or Improved-MDS [1].

The anchor-free localization method has been simulated in this paper which is based on the main steps typical for the two last mentioned algorithms. In the first step the

A. Dziech and A. Czyżewski (Eds.): MCSS 2013, CCIS 368, pp. 36–47, 2013.

Improved MDS (Multidimensional Scaling) principle has been used in order to create the partial node Local Coordinate Systems (LCSs). As the second step, in which the partial LCSs are joined together to one Global Coordinate System (GCS), the geometric methods of shifting, rotation and mirroring of the LCSs have been utilized. The simulated algorithm is classified as the Range-based[1] in which the Time of Arrival (ToA) ranging technique has been used in order to estimate the node distances. This type of node distance determination techniques belongs to the one of the most precise, but it is also very vulnerable to the node communication conditions. The successful indoor applications of the ToA ranging techniques require the identification process of the type of communication environment which is very challenging task.

The remainder of this paper is organized as follows: In Section 2, we describe the basic approaches of ToA estimation problem using relevant related works. Section 3 deals with the explanation of the Anchor-free positioning algorithm. The proposed low-complexity NLoS-UDP mitigation method is explained in section 4. For understandable explanation, we utilize the concrete example of the received Channel Impulse Response (CIR). The improvements in node distance estimation of this method are also reported and discussed in this section. Finally the simulation results of the algorithm in different types of the communication environment are described. Section 5 concludes this paper.

2   The Time of Arrival Estimation Problem

Time of Arrival is the ranging technique where the node distance d can be estimated simply as the product of the measured signal propagation delay ToA and the speed of light c $(c=3 \cdot 10^8 m.s^{-1})$ [3]:

$$d = c \cdot ToA \qquad (1)$$

The ToA estimation accuracy depends on different primary and secondary conditions. However, the conditions mostly influencing the node distance estimation accuracy are precision of transmitter-receiver time synchronization, used system bandwidth, multipath signal propagation and Non Line of Sight communication. The ranging error caused by multipath propagation is inversely proportional to the system bandwidth [5]. It is generally true that when the bandwidth of the system increases, the time-domain resolution and thus the accuracy of ToA estimation and node distance determination increase.

Alsindi classifies three types of communication environment [10]:

Line-of-Sight with Dominant-Direct-Path (LoS-DDP). In this case the direct path is the strongest and the first detected path in the channel profile and it can be detected by the receiver. There are no considerable obstacles between the transmitter and the receiver. However, the indoor radio propagation channel is characterized as site-specific, exhibiting severe multipath propagation and low probability of LoS signal propagation between the transmitter and receiver [5].

---

[1] In the Range-based localization techniques the unknown node positions are determined according to the measured received signal parameters using one of the known ranging techniques that are converted to the node distances.

Non Line-of-Sight with Non Dominant-Direct-Path (NLoS-NDDP), named also as Obstructed LoS (OLoS). Typical LoS communication between a transmitter and a receiver does not exist. In NDDP channel profile, the direct path is not the strongest path of the CIR, however, it is still detectable because it is received above the detection threshold of the receiver.

Non Line-of-Sight with Undetected-Direct-Path (NLoS-UDP). In UDP channels, the direct path goes below the detection threshold of the receiver while other paths are still detectable. The receiver assumes the first detected peak as a direct path which causes considerable distance estimation errors and consequently increasing of the node distance determination error. In the case when UDP is identified, the next step is to find ways, how to resolve the assumed direct path arrival time from the received channel power delay profile in order to minimize the ranging error. This error is defined as the difference between the estimated time of arrival of the received signal and its true time of arrival [5].

Therefore, the classification of the communication channel to DDP and UDP seems to be sufficient [5]. In the Fig. 1 the basic steps for channel identification are depicted. At first the LoS/NLoS channel identification should be performed. In order to identify the channel conditions the statistical Kurtosis Parameter (KP) can be used [11]. It is defined as the ratio of the fourth order moment of the data to the square of the second order moment. For the received CIR the value of KP is calculated. According to the set detection threshold, which represents the limit between the LoS and NLoS environment, the channel identification can be performed. If KP takes the values above the defined threshold it goes of LoS condition and vice versa, if it takes the values less than the defined threshold it goes of NLoS condition. However, identification using only NLoS occurrence rather than UDP identification is not enough. Two UDP identification approaches that use the binary hypothesis testing of the defined channel parameters and an application of neural network architecture (NNA) design have been proposed [5]. The team of prof. Pahlavan from Worcester Polytechnic Institute elaborately deals with the Time of Arrival estimation problem [5], [7], [8], [9], [10].

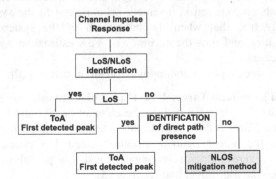

Fig. 1. Diagram of ToA determination process according to identified communication environment

3   Brief Overview of the Anchor-Free Localization Algorithm

The localization algorithm runs for each node separately and uses only one-hop communication, which prevents the network congestion. It consists of two main stages:

I.   **Formation of the Local Coordinate Systems (LCSs)**, where the Improved MDS-MAP technique is utilized in order to determine the relative node positions in LCS [1]. Two steps precede the MDS procedure.

   • **Node distance estimations** based on the ranging techniques such as Received Signal Strength (RSS) or Time of Arrival (ToA). In our simulations the second approach has been used (see section 4.1).

   • **Formation of the matrices (Distance Matrix - DM) containing the neighboring node distances** derived in the previous step from the measured data.

II. **Formation of the Global Coordinate System (GCS).** This process is also called the Network Coordinate System building [2] in where the partial Local Coordinate Systems are connected and unified in the same direction.

3.1   Formation of the Local Coordinate Systems

The aim of this process is formation of partial LCSs belonging to each node in the network. One LCS consists of the actual node relative position (this node is located at the centre of its LCS where its coordinates are set to [0,0]) and relative positions of its one-hop adjacent nodes.

Since the described positioning algorithm belongs to the Range-based localization techniques, the *node distance estimation procedure* is based on the localization parameters measurements. As it was mentioned some of the distance estimation techniques can be used in order to determine the node distances.

After this step each node is able to fill up the first row and column of its *distance matrix*[2], where the cells represent the pair of the particular nodes, because it knows its distances to the one-hop adjacent nodes. Then the missing node distances are filled up in the DM. This process is based on the node communication procedure of such nodes, which belong into the LCS of the given node, Fig. 2.

The node "ID1" sends a message containing its identification to the one-hop adjacent nodes in the network. The adjacent nodes add to the message the information about the distance to the node "ID1" and send this message forward to their one-hop

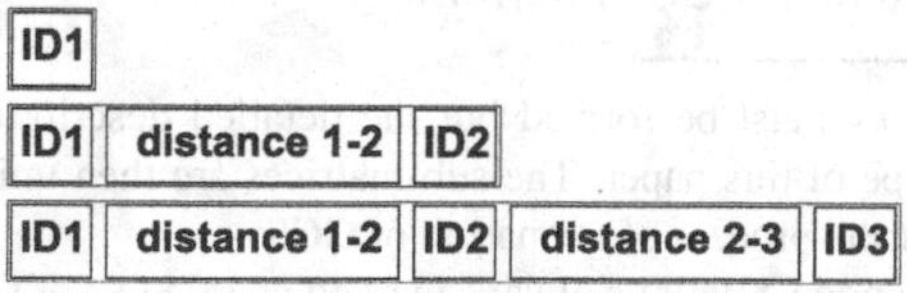

Fig. 2. Example of node communication procedure for finding the distance of nodes 2 and 3 served by node 1

---

[2] The rows and columns in the distance matrix are indexed according to the node ID.

adjacent neighbors. These neighbors repeat this process. They add the information to the message about their distance to the node, from which they receive the message and send it forward to their adjacent nodes. The nodes which receive such message check: if "ID1" is identical with its node ID, it stores the information about the distance between the nodes "ID2" and "ID3" into its distance matrix. For other nodes, when "ID1" is not identical with their node ID this message is ignored and not sent forward again.

The DM contains the node pair distances, is symmetrical and has zeros in the main diagonal. The formed distance matrix is used as the input to the MDS method in order to form the LCS of each node. It is possible that some cells of the node DM can not be determined, because the given node pair is not in communication rage. This situation can be solved by omitting of the rows and columns which contain the largest number of zeros until the DM contains zeros only on main diagonal[3].

3.2   Formation of the Global Coordinate System

Now, the network node LCSs are formed, but have different directions. The partial LCSs must be joined together, because they are *shifted*, *rotated* and *mirrored* according to each other. Using such operations, the partial LCSs can be joined into the one Global Coordinate System. The procedure of the GCS formation is explained using two LCSs of the nodes "A" and "B"[4]. For the sake of clarity, the nodes of the second LCS are marked by an apostrophe, Fig. 3.

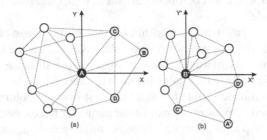

Fig. 3. LCSs of the nodes "A" and "B" used for problem explanation

The LCS(B) is joined with the LCS(A). Presence of the node "B" located in the LCS(A) (and vice versa, the node "A" located in the LCS(B)) is crucial. Similarly, it is advantageous, if the third common node is located in LCS(A) and LCS(B) simultaneously which is needed in process of mirroring[5].

---

[3] The distance sub-matrices must be formed but the detailed description of the sub-matrices formation is out of scope of this paper. The sub-matrices are then unified together using the procedure described for the process of formation of GCS.

[4] The LCS or GCS of the node X will be always marked as LCS(X) or GCS(X).

[5] The unification and mirroring of two LCSs can be carried out also without the third common node. However this procedure is lengthy, it utilizes the comparison of information about the measured node distances and detected mutual node distances using both mirrored and non-mirrored LCS separately, but its detailed description is out of scope of this paper.

At first the centre of the LCS(B) must be shifted to the node "A", Fig. 4. The procedure of shifting is carried out by subtraction of the coordinates of the node "A" from the coordinates of each node.

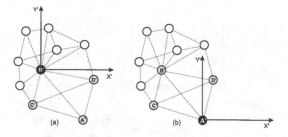

Fig. 4. LCS(B) shifted to the node "A" ((a) before and (b) after shifting respectively)

Next, both LCSs must be oriented in the same direction, in other words, LCS(A) must be rotated by an angle α and LCS(B) must be rotated by an angle β. They can be expressed for positive and negative y_B, y_B' respectively as, Fig. 5:

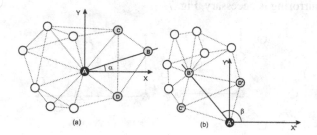

Fig. 5. Calculation of angles for rotation process

$$\alpha = \arccos\frac{x_B}{D_{AB}}; \quad \beta = \arccos\frac{x_B'}{D_{AB}'} \quad (2)$$

$$\alpha = -\arccos\frac{x_B}{D_{AB}}; \quad \beta = -\arccos\frac{x_B'}{D_{AB}'}$$

$[x_B, y_B]$ represent the coordinates of the node "B" and D_{AB} represents the distance between the nodes "A" and "B". Similarly for $[x_B', y_B']$ and D_{AB}'.

Then both LCSs will rotate in the direction negative to the size of α and β. For this process it is necessary to calculate the angle δ, which represents the angle BAX_i (X_i represents i^{th} node). For positive and negative y_i respectively:

$$\delta_i = \arccos\frac{x_i}{D_{Ai}}; \quad \delta_i = -\arccos\frac{x_i}{D_{Ai}} \quad (3)$$

The point coordinates will be recalculated for positive and negative result of $\delta - \alpha$ as:

$$x_i = D_{Ai}\cos(\delta_i - \alpha); \quad y_i = D_{Ai}\sin(\delta_i - \alpha)$$
$$x_i = -D_{Ai}\cos(\delta_i - \alpha); \quad y_i = D_{Ai}\sin(\delta_i - \alpha) \tag{4}$$

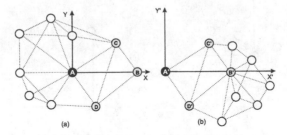

(a)   (b)

Fig. 6. LCSs oriented in the same direction

The same procedure can be applied also for the rotation of the LCS(B). After rotation, a point "C", which is common for both LCSs, must be found. According to its location, it will be decided about the need of mirroring. If "C" has not the same sign of the y-axis, mirroring is necessary, Fig. 7.

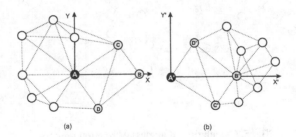

(a)   (b)

Fig. 7. Test for the need of mirroring (mirroring is needed)

Mirroring is carried out by simple change of the sign of the y-axis for each node in LCS. Now both LCSs can be joined together, Fig. 8.

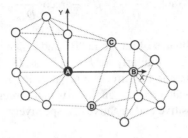

Fig. 8. LCS(B) joined to the LCS(A)

4   Simulations and Results

In our simulations we have used the existing model of the wireless channel impulse response generation for IEEE 802.15.4a ultra wideband technology [4]. It provides the generation of the channel impulse response for different types of communication environment such as residential, office, open outdoor and industrial. We have used the CIR for "LoS and NLoS OFFICE" environment.

Our simulations are based on a prior knowledge of the communication conditions without any channel identification procedure. In the most cases the ToA of the received signal is assumed as the ToA of the first detected path. The problem occurs, when the direct path is missing in the received signal channel impulse response. This fact causes considerable distance estimation errors, witch leads to the incorrect localization. For NLoS mitigation problem, especially in case of NLoS communication with UDP, the low-complexity NLoS mitigation technique for ToA estimation has been proposed and it is described in the following part.

4.1   Description of the Proposed Low-Complexity UDP Mitigation Method

The description of the method is explained using the concrete example of the transmitter-receiver pair 10m distant.

Assume the CIR received at the receiver site as is depicted in Fig. 9. *Detection threshold* represents the sensitivity of the receiver and it is set to 50mV[6]. All paths (multipath components) received and identified above this detection threshold can be used for ToA estimation. It can be seen that in the received CIR the direct path is missing and it is necessary to estimate its assumed time of arrival $ToA_{assumed\text{-}LoS}$.

At first the parameter, named *"Correction parameter"* – C_{LoS}, must be calculated.

$$C_{LoS} = \left(\frac{TD_{mean}}{d(CIR)} \right) \cdot \tau_m \tag{5}$$

It will be subsequently subtracted from the time of arrival of the first detected path $ToA_{Lp(1)}$ representing the first multipath component. TD_{mean} represents the mean of the time differences between the pairs of the paths received above the detection threshold. $L_{p(max)}$ denotes the serial number of the last received path and number of received paths simultaneously, $L_{p(i)}$ the serial number of the i-*th* received path. $d(CIR)$ represents the total length of the CIR that is expressed as the difference between the ToA of the last received multipath component $ToA_{Lp(max)}$ and the ToA of the first multipath component $ToA_{Lp(1)}$. τ_m is the Mean Excess Delay calculated relative to the first detected path.

$$TD_{mean} = \frac{\sum_{i=2}^{L_{p(max)}} (ToA_i - ToA_{i-1})}{L_{p(max)} - 1} \tag{6}$$

$$d(CIR) = ToA_{Lp(max)} - ToA_{Lp(1)} \tag{7}$$

---

[6] The infinite dynamic range of the receiver has been assumed.

In the next expression P_i represents the power of the ith received path and ToA_i its time of arrival.

$$\tau_m = \frac{\sum\limits_{i=1}^{L_{p(max)}} ToA_i |P_i|^2}{\sum\limits_{i=1}^{L_{p(max)}} |P_i|^2} \tag{8}$$

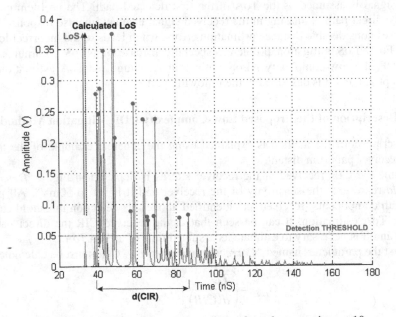

Fig. 9. Received CIR at the receiver distant from the transmitter at 10m

After the calculation of the *Correction parameter* the assumed time of arrival of the direct path can be expressed as:

$$ToA_{assumed-LoS} = ToA_{Lp(1)} - C_{LoS} \tag{9}$$

In Table 1 the parameters of the received multipath components corresponding with the depicted CIR in Fig. 9 are introduced. The calculated parameters for *Correction parameter* calculation have the following values:

- $TD_{mean} = 3{,}8334$ ns; $d(CIR) = 47{,}6667$ ns; $\tau_m = 50{,}1908$ ns;
- $C_{LoS} = 4{,}0363$ ns;

The introduced procedure for ToA determination enhancement causes the improvement of the ToA estimation and subsequently also the improvement of node the distance estimation:

- $ToA_{Lp(1)} = 38{,}3333$ ns; → *Node distance ($ToA_{Lp(1)}$)* = $11{,}4900$ m ;
- $ToA_{assumed-LoS} = 34{,}2970$ ns. → *Node distance ($ToA_{assumed-LoS}$)* = $10{,}2891$ m;

Table 1. Power, Time of Arrival and Time differences of the received multipath components

i	P_i[V]	ToA_i[ns]	$ToA_i - ToA_{i-1}$[ns]
1	0.0823	38,3333	---
2	0.2774	39,6666	1,3333
3	0.2445	41,0000	1,3333
4	0.2858	41,6666	0,6667
5	0.3468	43,3333	1,6667
6	0.3739	48,0000	4,6667
7	0.3455	48,6666	0,6667
8	0.0893	57,0000	8,3334
9	0.2611	58,6666	10,0000
10	0.2359	63,6666	5,0000
11	0.0776	65,3333	1,6667
12	0.0740	66,0000	0,6667
13	0.0805	69,0000	3,0000
14	0.2355	69,6666	6,0000
15	0.1062	75,3333	5,6667
16	0.0749	81,6666	6,3333
17	0.0796	86,0000	4,3334

4.2 Obtained Results of the Proposed Method in Process of Distance Estimation and after Its Implementation to the Positioning Algorithm

The proposed method has been tested on 1000-times randomly generated CIRs for transmitter-receiver pairs distant randomly at the distance from 0m to 15m. Only the harsh NLoS-UDP condition has been assumed. Generally, the distance estimation error has been reduced by 35,78%. The estimated ToA of the direct path has been improved in 74,5% of cases. In the Table 2, the comparison of the distance estimation error using ToA of the first detected path and the assumed calculated ToA of the missing direct path can be found respectively.

Table 2. Distance estimation error for nodes randomly distant at 0-15m

ToA estimation method	Distance estimation error [m]
$ToA_{Lp(1)}$	1,4356
$ToA_{assumed-LoS}$	0,9220

The proposed ToA estimation method has been tested also in Anchor-free positioning algorithm described in the section 3. The impact of the proposed NLoS-UDP mitigation method on the potential enhancement of the localization error using this algorithm has been studied. For completeness, also the LoS and NLoS (Obstructed Line-of-Sight) node communication conditions have been simulated. The obtained results are introduced in Table 3.

Our simulations were carried out in MATLAB programming environment and for statistical relevance were repeated one hundred times. The network consisting of the 50 mobile nodes deployed on the area of 50x50m with all receivers' radio range of 15m has been used. Note that the precise time synchronization between nodes has been assumed.

The proposed UDP mitigation method has achieved the reduction of the relative localization error after the first stage of the algorithm, LCSs formation, of 18,11% and total relative distance estimation error of 35,61%. However we have expected the better result of the total localization error improvement. Despite the fact that the significant improvement of the node distance estimation has been reached, it is not sufficient for plausible reduction of the total localization error of the presented algorithm. Only small improvement of the localization accuracy has been enrolled.

Table 3. Obtained results of the localization process after implementation of the proposed UDP mitigation method to the Anchor-free positioning algorithm[7]

Type of office environment	Total Localization error (GCS) [%]	Localization error after 1st stage (LCS) [%]	Node distance estimation error [m]	Number of successfully localized nodes
NLoS-UDP	19,89	3,89	0,953	47,23
	20,41	4,75	1,480	47,64
NLoS (OLoS)	3,51	0,21	0,014	47,85
LoS-DDP	0,44	0,03	0,002	47,45

5   Conclusion

The first simulations of the proposed low complexity method for node distance estimation enhancement using Time of Arrival are presented in this paper. The article is focused on the ToA estimation problem in harsh UDP environment where direct path is unavailable and on potential improvement of its ToA determination. The simulation results of the node distance estimation technique seem to be promising, but it is worth mentioning, that the simulations have been carried out in ideal communication conditions, especially with the precise time synchronization of mobile terminals which is very difficult to achieve in practice. Additionally, in the case of direct path presence (LoS/OLoS case), the model assumes the precise arrival time of the first detected path. These assumptions have affected the achieved simulation results that consequentially seem to be better than in reality. As a future work, it would be useful to compare

---

[7] If the localization error is expressed in %, we assume that error of 100% represent the value of the network size 50m. The results achieved after the implementation of the proposed method of the UDP mitigation are marked grey.

the simulations with the measurements of the channel impulse response that suffer from the impact of the real communication environment.

Acknowledgments. This work has been performed partially in the framework of the EU ICT Project INDECT (FP7 - 218086) and by the Ministry of Education of Slovak Republic under research VEGA 1/0386/12 and under research project ITMS-26220220155 supported by the Research & Development Operational Programme funded by the ERDF.

References

1. Shang, Y., Ruml, W.: Improved MDS-based localization. In: Twenty-Third Annual Joint Conference of the IEEE Computer and Communications Societies, INFOCOM 2004, Hong Kong, March 7-11, vol. 4, pp. 2640–2651 (2004)
2. Čapkun, S., Hamdi, M., Hubaux, J.P.: GPS-free positioning in mobile ad hoc networks. Cluster Computing 5(2), 157–167 (2002)
3. Decarli, N., Dardari, D., Geizici, S., D'amico, A.A.: LOS/NLOS Detection for UWB Signals: A Comparative Study Using Experimental Data. In: IEEE International Symposium on Wireless Pervasive Computing (ISWPC), Modena, Italy, May 5-7 (2010)
4. Molisch, A.F., et al.: IEEE 802.15.4a Channel Model – Final Report. Tech. Rep., Document IEEE 802.1504-0062-02-004a (2005)
5. Heidari, M., Alsindi, N.A., Pahlavan, K.: UDP identification and error mitigation in toa-based indoor localization systems using neural network architecture. IEEE Transactions on Wireless Communications 8(7), 3597–3607 (2009)
6. Youssef, A.A.: SALAM: A Scalable anchor-free localization algorithm for wireless sensor networks. In: Dissertation, p. 192. Faculty of the Graduate School of the University of Maryland, College Park (2006)
7. Alsindi, N., Duan, C., Jinyun Zhang Tsuboi, T.: NLOS channel identification and mitigation in Ultra Wideband ToA-based Wireless Sensor Networks. In: 6th Workshop on Positioning, Navigation and Communication, WPNC 2009, March 19, pp. 59–66 (2009)
8. Alavi, B.: Distance Measurement Error Modeling for Time-of-Arrival based indoor geolocation. In: Dissertation, p. 171. Faculty of Worcester Polytechnic Institute, Department of Electrical and Computer Engineering, Worcester (April 2006)
9. Alsindi, N.: Indoor Cooperative Localization for Ultra Wideband Wireless Sensor Networks. In: Dissertation, p. 149. Faculty of Worcester Polytechnic Institute, Department of Electrical and Computer Engineering, Worcester (April 2008)
10. Alsindi, N.: Performance of TOA Estimation Algorithms in Different Indoor Multipath Conditions. In: Diploma work, p. 111. Faculty of Worcester Polytechnic Institute, Department of Electrical and Computer Engineering, Worcester (April 2004)
11. Güvenc, I., Chong, C.-C., Watanabe, F.: NLOS Identification and Mitigation for UWB Localization Systems. In: Wireless Communications and Networking Conference, WCNC 2007, March 11-15, pp. 1571–1576 (2007)

Visual Detection of People Movement Rules Violation in Crowded Indoor Scenes

Piotr Dalka and Piotr Bratoszewski

Multimedia Systems Department
Gdansk University of Technology
Gdansk, Poland
{piotr.dalka,bratoszewski}@sound.eti.pg.gda.pl

Abstract. The paper presents a camera-independent framework for detecting violations of two typical people movement rules that are in force in many public transit terminals: moving in the wrong direction or across designated lanes. Low-level image processing is based on object detection with Gaussian Mixture Models and employs Kalman filters with conflict resolving extensions for the object tracking. In order to allow an effective event recognition in a crowded environment, the algorithm for event detection is supplemented with the optical-flow based analysis in order to obtain pixel-level velocity characteristics. The proposed solution is evaluated with multi-camera, real-life recordings from an airport terminal. Results are discussed and compared with a traditional approach that does not include optical flow based direction of movement analysis.

Keywords: movement event detection, Gaussian Mixture Model, Kalman filters, optical flow.

1 Introduction

Increasing number of video monitoring cameras entails a need for tools for automatic analysis of video streams applied to detecting events of interest and to presenting them to a system operator for validation and interpretation. Hence, real-time analysis of all video streams can be applied, instead of data storing only or optional post-analysis approach.

The task of automatic event detection in video streams acquired from surveillance cameras may be related to outdoor or indoor scenes. Outdoor analysis is devoted mainly to road traffic in order to find various rules violations such as wrong-way driving, U-turning, excessive speed, etc. [1][2][3]. Solutions aimed at indoor video processing usually recognize larger variety of tasks. They range from simple intrusion detection in restricted areas [4] to advanced human action recognition, such as bending [5], pointing, answering a phone or embracing [6][7].

The main challenge in the visual human activity analysis is related to the people density in a camera field of view; in crowded scenes, frequent occlusions between moving persons significantly hinder event detection. One solution to the problem is related to a favorable camera setup: in the paper [8] a method for simultaneously

A. Dziech and A. Czyżewski (Eds.): MCSS 2013, CCIS 368, pp. 48–58, 2013.

tracking all people in a dense crowd is presented where occlusions are overcome by placing cameras at a high elevation and tracking the heads of the people only. However, such a solution cannot by applied in general and often an automatic event detection system has to be deployed using existing installations with cameras mounted to a low ceiling.

The majority of event detection systems utilizing fixed surveillance cameras follows the same general processing scheme: firstly, pixels belonging to moving objects are detected in video streams, then they are tracked in consequent frames and, finally, the gathered data is used to detect events of interest. The survey of human tracking methods in complex scenes may be found in [9]. In general, they are based on spatio-temporal blobs matching or they use 3D human shape and pose models of various coarseness.

The solution proposed in the paper employs blob-based object tracking utilizing Kalman filters with extensions providing conflict resolving in more complex situations [10]. However, this approach fails in case of event detection in crowded scenes. Therefore, it is supplemented with an optical flow analysis in order to limit ratio of false positive alarms. A rule-based approach is used to detect persons violating moving rules that are often in force in large public transport terminals. Actions detected are: wrong direction of movement on a one-way lane and moving across lanes restricted with ropes or belts.

The paper is organized as follow. In the section 2, a general description of the video processing framework is provided. Details regarding moving object detection and event recognition algorithms are presented in sections 3 and 4. Section 5 describes experiments carried out using a real-life installation in an airport terminal and their results. The paper is concluded in section 6.

2   General Video Processing Framework

The video processing framework used for detection of movement rules violation comprises of several video processing modules (Fig. 1). They are executed in a multi-threaded manner which makes the real-time processing of video streams possible. First, moving objects are detected in video frames acquired from a surveillance camera. It is performed with an adaptive background scene model based on Gaussian mixtures [11]. Five distributions are used to model each image pixel in order to allow multiple colors describing a background pixel appearance. The background model is initialized using additional, "warm-up" fragments at the beginning of each analyzed recording. Their length is chosen according to the GMM learning coefficient value and is equal approx. 2 minutes. After this period the model is properly initialized and the event detection procedures are started.

The background subtraction algorithm is supplemented with shadow detection and removal module in order to obtain actual silhouettes of objects [12]. Then, object tracking with Kalman filters is performed in order to provide spatio-temporal continuity of blob tracking. The implemented method utilizes appearance-based blob matching in order to handle conflict situations (passing by, partial occlusions, merging, splitting etc.) as described in [10]. However, this approach is not sufficient in case of crowded scenes as, due to conflict resolving routines involved, it does not provide reliable information regarding objects' instantaneous speeds and directions of movements. Therefore, it is supplemented with the optical-flow based analysis in order to estimate pixel-level speed velocity characteristics. Next, a combined blob behavior analysis is performed in order to detect events in areas annotated manually in video frames. The results of event detection are sent to a system operator as event alarms and are stored in the database for future references.

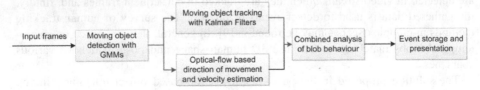

Fig. 1. General scheme of the visual event detection algorithm

3 Object Detection with the Direction of Movement

In order to detect violations of movement rules in the crowded scenes, a new solution has been developed that combines moving object detection based on the GMMs [11] with the results of an optical flow in order to find pixel-level direction of movement of all objects. The GMMs algorithm provides pixel-level accurate information related to locations of moving objects, including the ones that stopped for a short amount of time. However, it does not provide any information related to the direction of movement. On the other hand, the optical flow algorithm delivers data regarding object velocity vectors, however it is not able to provide exact object locations and boundaries. Therefore, a combination of the GMMs and optical flow methods is employed in order to obtain both the pixel-level velocities and exact object silhouettes.

Image analysis is performed for each input video frame I (Fig. 2a). In the frame, moving objects are detected with the GMMs. As a result, a binary mask G containing pixels belonging to moving objects is obtained (Fig. 2b). Simultaneously, a dense optical flow is calculated in the same area with the algorithm proposed by Farneback [13]. The optical flow found in the current frame is set as an initial estimate of the optical flow in the following frame. An important parameter of the algorithm is the windows size W_O that has to be set according to the typical object size and speed in order to provide sufficient overlap of moving object images in neighboring video frames. If the window value is too small, the resulting optical flow map for a moving object is very fragmented and heterogeneous; high window values result in the averaged map that lacks required resolution and prevents separation of neighboring objects moving in different directions.

As the result of optical flow calculation, a 2D flow field O is obtained for the frame t that is defined with the following relation:

$$I_{t-1}(x, y) \cong I_t(x + O(x, y, 0), y + O(x, y, 1)) \tag{1}$$

where $O(x,y,n)$ denotes n-th element of the flow field $\mathbf{O}$ at (x,y) coordinates. Therefore, the flow field $\mathbf{O}$ contains velocity vectors (v_x, v_y) for each pixel of the image I_t (Fig. 2c). Next, a new binary mask $\mathbf{M}$ is created that combines results of object detection with GMMs and with the optical flow:

$$M(x, y) = \begin{cases} 1, & \text{if } G(x, y) > 0 \text{ and } \sqrt{v_x^2 + v_y^2} > V_{\min} \\ 0, & \text{otherwise} \end{cases} \tag{2}$$

The mask $\mathbf{M}$ denotes location of all pixels that move with the required speed (at least $V_{\min}$, Fig. 2d). Speed thresholding allows to filter out all objects that are temporarily stationary and therefore cannot trigger movement related events.

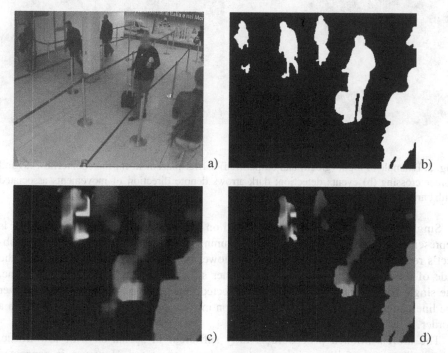

Fig. 2. Object detection supplemented with the direction of movement: a) input video frame $\mathbf{I}$, b) results of object detection with GMMs $\mathbf{G}$, c) result of object detection with optical flow $\mathbf{O}$, d) combined mask $\mathbf{M}$; colors in c) and d) denote different directions of movement while luminance is directly proportional to the velocity vector magnitude

4 Movement Rules Violation Event Detection

There are two types of real events that are detected in the framework: crossing a border (e.g. moving across lanes restricted with straps) and counterflow (i.e. wrong direction of movement). Despite the different meaning, both event types are detected with the same algorithm and its configuration determines the meaning of the event.

The main configuration parameter for the algorithm is the placement of two barriers in the image: the input one and the output one (Fig. 3). The barriers denote the order in which they have to be crossed in order to trigger a particular event in the defined location. Barriers should be oriented perpendicular to the direction of object movement that would indicate the event. Using two barriers instead of only one significantly reduces number of false positives results that could be triggered by objects moving close to a barrier.

a)   b)

Fig. 3. Example of input (green) and output (red) barrier placement for the counterflow (a) and border crossing (b) events detection; dark arrows denote direction of movements associated with barriers

Single barrier crossing is detected based on object tracking results; each object is represented by a rectangle (Fig.6, right column). Whenever a defined hot spot of object's rectangle (usually the middle of the lower border of the rectangle) changes the side of the barrier and remains on the other side for the required amount of time, the single barrier crossing sub-event is detected. Side changing is detected whenever the line connecting object's hot spot position in two adjacent frames intersects with a border.

The aforementioned procedure is fully sufficient in scenarios with low traffic, where silhouettes of all moving objects are clearly separated. However, in congested scenes where occlusions are common, this approach would generate many false positives due to object tracking conflict resolving procedure that often causes chaotic movements of rectangles denoting objects locations and sizes. Therefore, accidental barrier crossings may be triggered by nearby objects.

In order to improve accuracy of events detection, the object direction of movement is validated whenever barrier crossing event is detected, using the optical flow $\mathbf{O}$ and a binary mask $\mathbf{M}$. Let $R = \{x, y, w, h\}$ denote an object's location (top-left corner) and size in the moment the barrier crossing is detected. The number of pixels of an object analyzed N_A in order to validate the direction of movement is given with the equation:

$$N_A = \sum_{i=x}^{x+w-1} \sum_{j=y}^{y+h-1} \begin{cases} 1, & \text{if } M_{ij} > 0 \\ 0, & \text{if } M_{ij} = 0 \end{cases} \tag{3}$$

where M_{ij} denotes the element of the matrix $\mathbf{M}$ at coordinates (i,j).

With each barrier b the required direction of movement α_b is associated. The number of pixels of an object N_V fulfilling direction of movement criterion is given as follows:

$$N_V = \sum_{i=x}^{x+w-1} \sum_{j=y}^{y+h-1} \begin{cases} 1, & \text{if } M_{ij} > 0 \text{ and } |\alpha_b - \alpha_{ij}| < \Delta\alpha \\ 0, & \text{otherwise} \end{cases} \tag{4}$$

where $\Delta\alpha > 0$ denotes the maximum allowed deviation of the pixel direction of movement from the expected direction α_b defined for a barrier, and α_{ij} denotes the direction of movement of a pixel (i,j) calculated from the optical flow matrix $\mathbf{O}$:

$$\alpha_{ij} = \text{atan } 2(O(i,j,1), O(i,j,0)) \tag{5}$$

where $O(i,j,0)$ and $O(i,j,1)$ correspond with the optical flow vector field horizontal and vertical components, respectively, for the pixel (i,j).

The ratio of object pixels with valid direction of movement r is given with the equation:

$$r = \frac{N_V}{N_A} \tag{6}$$

The object direction of movement during barrier crossing is considered valid if the ratio r exceeds the defined threshold T_r. This condition assures that when a crossing event is detected for a given object, the tracker associated with it does contain the defined ratio of pixels moving in the required direction.

Validation of the object direction of movement is performed both for the input and output barrier and it must be satisfied in order to detect the event.

5 Experiments and Results

For the purpose of experiments regarding detection of movement rules violation real-life recordings from two surveillance cameras have been used. The cameras are installed in Linate Airport located in the close vicinity of Milano, Italy (Fig. 4). They provide streams with PAL resolution at 15 frames per second. The first camera (Filter1) observes the lanes established with ropes that are designed to form a queue of passengers awaiting for a security control. Sometimes it happens that a person does not wish to follow the strap-defined corridors but chooses the faster way under the ropes and across the lanes instead. In order to detect such events, the detector has been configured with the barriers pictured in Fig. 3a. Another event that also might occur in the same area is related to the wrong direction of movements within the lane. The respective detector configuration is shown in Fig. 3b.

The second camera (Filter2) is located in the area in front of the security control. In the left side of the frame, rope lanes are visible. The event set for detection in this camera field of view is related to entering the lanes under the ropes. As two possible directions of movement (from the bottom or from the right side) are possible in this scene, two detectors are deployed for this video stream (Fig. 5).

Fig. 4. Sample video frames from recordings from camera Filter1 (top) and Filter2 (bottom)

Fig. 5. Example of input (green) and output (red) barrier placement for the two variants of the border crossing event; dark arrows denote direction of movements associated with barriers

Nine hours of recordings from each camera, spanning over three days, have been automatically analyzed in order to detect all events of interest. The values of the algorithm parameters have been determined during initial experiments and are provided in Table 1. The window size W_O for optical flow calculation has been set by viewing optical flow map superimposed on the input frames and finding the optimal value that provides both intra-object homogeneity and inter-object separation. The value for the threshold T_r has been found as the one that provides the best results in terms of limiting the ratio of false positive detections while maintaining the ratio of true positives as high as possible.

Table 1. Algorithm parameters values used during experiments

Parameter	Value for Filter1 camera	Value for Filter2 camera
W_O [pixels]	15	15
V_{min} [pixels/frame]	0.75	0.25
$\Delta\alpha$ [°]	30	30
T_r	0.15	0.2

Results of analysis have been validated with ground-truth data that has been gathered manually by viewing the recordings. Sample events are presented in Fig. 6.

Due to impossibility to predict when events of interest might occur, it was decided to stage some events in order to gather a valuable video material for experiments. Thus 31 events have been performed by actors. Remaining events (28) are the real ones captured in recordings.

The detailed results of event detection are shown in Table 2. True positives TP denote number of correctly detected events. False negatives FN represent events that were missed and false positives FP mark false detections. Performance measures used are defined as follows:

$$accuracy = \frac{TP}{TP + FP + FN} \tag{7}$$

$$precision = \frac{TP}{TP + FP} \tag{8}$$

$$recall = \frac{TP}{TP + FN} \tag{9}$$

The proposed algorithm is able to detect over 80% of real events. This result, although low at the first sight, is satisfactory taking into account highly variable flow rate of people. The majority of missed events is caused by unfavorable placements of cameras that make silhouettes of persons performing forbidden events susceptible to occlusion by other persons closer to the camera. All situations presented in Fig. 6 have been detected successfully.

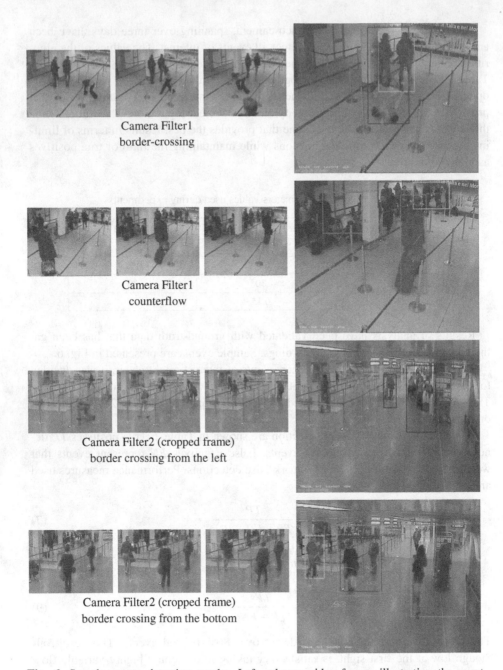

Fig. 6. Sample events detection results. Left column: video frames illustrating the event, right column: visualization of the algorithm, where orange lines denote barriers, multi-colored rectangles – object trackers and multi-colored semi-transparent layers – velocities of objects exceeding minimum speed threshold (different directions of movement are represented with different hues while velocity vector magnitude is directly proportional to the layer luminance)

Table 2. Summary results of detection of people movement rules violation events

Measure	Camera		Together
	Filter1	Filter2	
Number of events	45	14	59
Events detected (*TP*)	37	12	49
Events missed (*FN*)	8	2	10
False detections (*FP*)	20	12	32
Accuracy	0.57	0.46	0.54
Precision	0.65	0.50	0.60
Recall	0.82	0.86	0.83

It may be noticed that event detection performance measures for both cameras are similar. Taking into account different fields of views of the cameras (distinct viewing angles and scene compositions) it may be stated that the solution presented is universal and may be applied to a variety of surveillance installations.

Table 3 presents the advantage of using the method proposed that includes analysis of the pixel-level direction of movement of object in the process of event detection. Comparing with the traditional approach using Kalman filter based object tracking only, the number of false positives has been reduced by 70 (78% of FPs) for the Filter1 camera and by 20 (63% of FPs) for the Filter2 camera. These results significantly increase the accuracy and precision measures.

Table 3. The advantage of employing object detection with direction of movement analysis in the process of event detection

Measure	Without direction of movement analysis (standard approach)			With direction of movement analysis (proposed method)		
	Filter1	Filter2	Together	Filter1	Filter2	Together
False detections (*FP*)	90	32	122	20	12	32
Accuracy	0.27	0.26	0.27	0.57	0.46	0.54
Precision	0.29	0.27	0.29	0.65	0.50	0.60

6   Conclusions

The paper presents a framework for visual detection of events in crowded indoor scenes. Especially violations of people movement rules in public transport terminals are recognized. The system is able to detect over 80% of real events and is robust to camera viewing angles or scene composition. Including optical-flow derived velocity data in the process of event detection allows for a significant reduction of false positive alarms.

Further work will be focused on increasing the accuracy of event detection. It may be accomplished by switching from the blob-based tracking to visual clues tracking in order to make event recognition possible in case of severe occlusions. This approach might reduce the number of false positives as well.

Acknowledgements. Research funded by European Commission within the project ADDPRIV (Automatic Data relevancy Discrimination for a PRIVacy-sensitive video surveillance). The project No. 261653 is a part of the European Seventh Framework Program (FP7).

References

1. Dong, N., Jia, Z., Shao, J., Xiong, Z., et al.: Traffic abnormality detection through directional motion behavior map. In: 7th IEEE International Conference on Advanced Video and Signal Based Surveillance, pp. 80–84 (2010)
2. Veeraraghavan, H., Schrater, P., Papanikolopoulos, N.: Switching Kalman filter-based approach for tracking and event detection at traffic intersections. In: Proc. IEEE Mediterrean Conference on Control and Automation Intelligent Control, pp. 1167–1172 (2005)
3. Tusch, R., Pletzer, F., Mudunuri, M., Kraetschmer, A., et al.: LOOK2 - a video-based system for real-time notification of relevant traffic events. In: IEEE International Conference on Multimedia and Expo Workshops, p. 670 (2012)
4. Spirito, M., Regazzoni, C.S., Marcenaro, L.: Automatic detection of dangerous events for underground surveillance. In: Proc. IEEE Conf. Adv. Video Signal Based Surveillance, pp. 195–200 (2005)
5. Ellwart, D., Czyzewski, A.: Camera angle invariant shape recognition in surveillance systems. In: Proc of the 3rd International Symposium on Intelligent and Interactive Multimedia: Systems and Services, Baltimore, USA, vol. 6, pp. 33–40 (2010)
6. Takahashi, M., Naemura, M., Fujii, M., Satoh, S.: Human action recognition in crowded surveillance video sequences by using features taken from key-point trajectories. In: Computer Vision and Pattern Recognition (CVPR) Workshops, pp. 9–16 (2011)
7. Laptev, I., Marszalek, M., Schmid, C., Rozenfeld, B.: Learning realistic human actions from movies. In: IEEE Conference on Computer Vision and Pattern Recognition (2008)
8. Eshel, R., Moses, Y.: Homography based multiple camera detection and tracking of people in a dense crowd. In: IEEE Conference on Computer Vision and Pattern Recognition (2008)
9. Zhao, T., Nevatia, R.: Tracking multiple humans in complex situations. IEEE Transactions on Pattern Analysis and Machine Intelligence 26(9), 1208–1221 (2004)
10. Czyzewski, A., Szwoch, G., Dalka, P., et al.: Multi-stage video analysis framework. In: Lin, W. (ed.) Video Surveillance, pp. 147–172. InTech, Rijeka (2011)
11. Stauffer, C., Grimson, W.E.: Adaptive background mixture models for real-time tracking. In: Proc. of IEEE Conf. on Computer Vision and Pattern Recognition, pp. 246–252 (1999)
12. Czyzewski, A., Dalka, P.: Moving object detection and tracking for the purpose of multimodal surveillance system in urban areas. In: Tsihrintzis, G.A., Virvou, M., Howlett, R.J., Jain, L.C. (eds.) New Direct. in Intel. Interac. Multimedia. SCI, vol. 142, pp. 75–84. Springer, Berlin (2008)
13. Farnebäck, G.: Two-frame motion estimation based on polynomial expansion. In: Bigun, J., Gustavsson, T. (eds.) SCIA 2003. LNCS, vol. 2749, pp. 363–370. Springer, Heidelberg (2003)

Survey of Recent Developments in Quality Assessment for Target Recognition Video

Mikołaj Leszczuk[1] and Joel Dumke[2]

[1] AGH University of Science and Technology, Krakow, Poland
leszczuk@agh.edu.pl
http://www.agh.edu.pl/
[2] Institute for Telecommunication Sciences, Boulder CO, USA
jdumke@its.bldrdoc.gov
http://www.its.bldrdoc.gov/

Abstract. Users of video to perform tasks require sufficient video quality to recognize the information needed for their application. Therefore, the fundamental measure of video quality in these applications is the success rate of these recognition tasks, which is referred to as visual intelligibility or acuity. One of the major causes of reduction of visual intelligibility is loss of data through various forms of compression. Additionally, the characteristics of the scene being captured have a direct effect on visual intelligibility and on the performance of a compression operation-specifically, the size of the target of interest, the lighting conditions, and the temporal complexity of the scene. This paper presents a survey of recent developments in quality assessment for target recognition video, which is including performed series of tests to study the effects and interactions of compression and scene characteristics. An additional goal was to test existing and develop new objective measurements.

Keywords: compression, MOS (Mean Opinion Score), quality assessment, target recognition video.

1 Introduction

The transmission and analysis of video is often used for a variety of applications outside the entertainment sector. Generally this class of (task-based) video is used to perform a specific recognition task. Examples of these applications include security, public safety, remote command and control, telemedicine, and sign language. The Quality of Experience (QoE) concept for video content used for entertainment differs materially from the QoE of video used for recognition tasks because in the latter case, the subjective satisfaction of the user depends upon achieving the given task, e.g., event detection or object recognition. Additionally, the quality of video used by a human observer is largely separate from the objective video quality useful in computer vision [20]. Therefore, in these applications it is crucial to measure and ultimately optimize task-based video quality. This is discussed in more detail in [18].

Enormous work, mainly driven by the Video Quality Experts Group (VQEG) [26], has been carried out for the past several years in the area of consumer video quality.

A. Dziech and A. Czyżewski (Eds.): MCSS 2013, CCIS 368, pp. 59–70, 2013.

The VQEG is a group of experts from various backgrounds and affiliations, including participants from several internationally recognized organizations, working in the field of video quality assessment. The group was formed in October of 1997 at a meeting of video quality experts. The majority of participants are active in the International Telecommunication Union (ITU) and VQEG combines the expertise and resources found in several ITU Study Groups to work towards a common goal [26]. Unfortunately, many of the VQEG and ITU methods and recommendations (like ITU's Absolute Category Rating – ACR – described in ITU-T P.800 [10]) are not appropriate for the type of testing and research that task-based video, including CCTV requirements.

This paper is organized as follows. Section 2 describes related state-of-the-art work and motivation. In section 3, a survey of recent developments in quality assessment for target recognition tasks is presented. Section 4 concludes the paper and details the future work.

2   Related State-of-the-Art Work and Motivation

Subjective recognition metrics, described below, have been proposed over the past decade. They usually combine aspects of Quality of Recognition (QoR) and QoE. Some of these metrics have been not focused on public safety practitioners as subjects, but rather on naive participants. The metrics are not context specific, and they do not apply video surveillance-oriented standardized discrimination levels.

One notable metric is Ghinea's Quality of Perception (QoP) [4], [5]. Unfortunately, the QoP metric does not wholly fit video surveillance needs. It targets mainly video deterioration caused by frame rate measured in Frames Per Second (FPS), whereas FPS does not necessarily affect the quality of Closed-Circuit Television (CCTV) and the required bandwidth [14]. The metric has been proven for rather low, legacy resolutions, and tested on rather small groups of subjects (10 instead of standardized 24 valid, correlating subjects). Furthermore, a video recognition quality metric specific to a video surveillance context requires tests in a fully controlled environment [9] with standardized discrimination levels (avoiding vague questions) and with reduced impact of subliminal cues [12].

Another metric worth mentioning is QoP's offshoot, Strohmeier's Open Profiling of Quality (OPQ) [3]. This metric puts more stress on video quality than on recognition/discrimination levels. Its application context, being focused on 3D, is also different than video surveillance which requires 2D. Like the previous metric, this one also does not apply standardized discrimination levels, allowing subjects to use their own vocabulary. The approach is qualitative rather than quantitative, whereas public safety practitioners prefer the latter for public procurement. The OPQ model is somewhat content/subject-oriented, while a more generalized metric framework is needed for video surveillance.

OPQ partly utilizes free sorting, as used in [15]. Free sorting is also applied in the method called Interpretation Based Quality (IBQ) [6], [13], adapted from [2] and [23]. Unfortunately, these approaches only allow mapping relational rather than absolute quality.

Furthermore, there exists only a very limited set of quality standards for task-based video applications. Therefore, it is still necessary to define the requirements for such systems from the camera, to broadcast, to display. The nature of these requirements will depend on the task being performed.

European Norm No. 50132 [1] was created to ensure that European CCTV systems are deployed under the same rules and requirements. The existence of a standard has opened an international market of CCTV devices and technologies. By selecting components that are consistent with the standard, a user can achieve a properly working CCTV system. This technical regulation deals with different parts of a CCTV system including acquisition, transmission, storage, and playback of surveillance video. The standard consists of such sections as lenses, cameras, local and main control units, monitors, recording and hard copy equipment, video transmission, video motion detection equipment, and ancillary equipment. This norm is hardware-oriented as it is intended to unify European law in this field; thus, it does not define the quality of video from the point of view of recognition tasks.

The VQiPS (Video Quality in Public Safety) Working Group, established in 2009 and supported by the U.S. Department of Homeland Security's Office for Interoperability and Compatibility, has been developing a user guide for public safety video applications. The aim of the guide is to provide the potential consumers of public safety video equipment with research and specifications that best fit their particular application. The process of developing the guide will have a further beneficial effect of identifying areas in which adequate research has not yet been conducted, so that such gaps may be filled. A challenge for this particular work is ensuring that it is understandable to public safety practitioners, who may have little knowledge of video technology [20].

Internationally, the number of people and organizations interested in this area continues to grow, and there is currently enough interest to motivate the creation of a task-based video project under VQEG. At one of the recent meetings of VQEG, a new project was formed for task-based video quality research. The Quality Assessment for Recognition Tasks (QART) project addresses precisely the problem of lack of quality standards for video monitoring [17]. The initiative is co-chaired by Public Safety Communications Research (PSCR) program, U.S.A., and AGH University of Science and Technology in Krakow, Poland. Other members include research teams from Belgium, France, Germany, and South Korea. The purpose of QART is exactly the same as the other VQEG projects – to advance the field of quality assessment for task-based video through collaboration in the development of test methods, performance specifications and standards for task-based video, as well as predictive models based on network and other relevant parameters [24].

3   Recent Developments

This section describes recent developments related to results of pilot trials on car and object recognition applications. Furthermore, the section presents some details of the VQiPS multimedia database of reference recordings and results as well as methods for automatic classification of entire sequences.

3.1   Results of Pilot Trial on Car Recognition Application

This research, conducted on an AGH University car parking lot, was dedicated to an emerging area of human and machine quality optimization in video monitoring systems. QoE in monitoring systems defines an ability to recognize some specific actions and detect some objects. New video quality recommendations have been developed in order to assure an acceptable level of recognition/detection accuracy. This involved adjusting video codec parameters and constant control with respect to the current video characteristics and intended recognition/detection actions. The purpose of the tests was to analyze human versus machine ability to recognize car registration numbers on video material recorder using a CCTV camera. Video sequences used in the tests were compressed using an H.264 codec.

Recognizing the growing importance of video in delivering a range of public safety services, let us consider a license plate recognition task based on video streaming in constrained networking conditions. Video technology should allow users to perform the required function successfully. This subsection demonstrates people's ability to recognize car registration numbers in video material recorded using a CCTV camera and compressed with the H.264/AVC codec. An example frame from the license plate recognition task is shown in Fig 1. The usage case is presented in literature [21].

Fig. 1. Example frame from the license plate recognition task

Video streaming services still face the problem of limited bandwidth access. While for wired connections bandwidth is generally available in the order of megabits, higher bit rates are not particularly common for wireless links. This poses problems for mobile users who cannot expect a stable high bandwidth.

Therefore a solution for streaming video services across such access connections is transcoding of video streams. The result is transcoding bit-rate (and quality) scaling to personalize the stream sent according to the current parameters of the access link. Scaling video sequence quality may be provided in compression, space and time. Scaling of compression usually involves varying the codec Quantization Parameter (QP). Scaling of space means reducing the effective image resolution, resulting in increased granularity when attempts are made to restore the original content on the screen. Scaling of time amounts to the rejection of frames, i.e. reducing the number of

FPS sent. However, frame rates are commonly kept intact, as their deterioration does not necessarily result in bit-rate savings due to inter-frame coding [14].

The abovementioned scaling methods inevitably lead to lower perceived quality of end-user services (QoE). Therefore the scaling process should be monitored for QoE levels. This makes it possible to not only control but also maximize QoE levels depending on the prevailing transmission conditions. In the event of failure to achieve a satisfactory QoE level, the operator may intentionally interrupt the service, which may help preserve network resources for other users.

To develop accurate objective measurements (models) for video quality, subjective experiments have been performed. The ITU-T P.910 Recommendation "Subjective video quality assessment methods for multimedia applications" [11] addressed the methodology for performing subjective tests in a rigorous manner.

One important conclusion is that for a bit rate as low as 180 kbit/s the detection probability is over 80% even if the visual quality of the video is very low. Moreover, the detection probability depends strongly on the SRC (over all detection probability varies from 0 (sic!) to over 90%) [19].

More results were presented in [18], [19] and [21].

3.2   Results of Pilot Trial on Object Recognition Application

Within a similar psychophysical experiment, conducted at the Institute for Telecommunication Sciences, clips that were shown were produced using the following four categories of lighting condition scenarios:

1. Outdoor, daylight,
2. Indoor, bright with flashing lights,
3. Indoor, dim with flashing lights, and
4. Indoor, dark with flashing lights.

Three different distances were used to create the clips:

1. 5.2 meters for indoor scenarios,
2. 10.9 meters for outdoor scenarios, objects close, and
3. 14.6 meters for outdoors scenarios, objects far.

37 subjects were gathered for each of the tests. Each subject was asked to fill out a test form, which included demographic and professional experience questions as well as the results of the vision tests. The form also informed subjects about the purpose of the experiment, what kind of videos would be presented, the subject's task, and what objects would be shown in the videos. Viewing conditions in the room where the test took place followed Recommendation ITU-R BT.500-12 [9] and Recommendation ITU-T P.910 (Fig. 2). Subjects could take break during the test, but this option was rarely used.

Assessment principles for the maximization of task-based video quality are a relatively new field. Section 7.3 of ITU-T P.912 ("Subjects") [12] says that, "Subjects who are experts in the application field of the target recognition video should be used.

The number of subjects should follow the recommendations of ITU-T P.910." Expert subjects (police officers, doctors, etc.) are costly and difficult to hire compared to non-expert subjects (colleagues, friends, students, pensioners). Nevertheless, to the best of the authors' knowledge, this expert subject issue has not been verified in any specific academic research. There do exist some applicable ideas incorporated from industry. For example, large television companies hire expert subjects to monitor their quality [25]. However, there is no evidence that these companies have applied any serious effort to determine how these people compare to non-expert subjects. Almost all Mean Opinion Score (MOS) quality tests focus on non-experts. There is a belief that people who have more video knowledge or experience would give different results, but that has not ever been rigorously studied. In this test, we compared groups of subjects assessing video quality for task-based video. Once a comparison has been made for task-based video, amendments to standards could be developed that will assist researchers of task-based video quality.

Fig. 2. A photo of the test environment used in psychophysical experiments

In the recognition psychophysical experiment performed by NTIA-ITS, two groups (non-paid professional and paid non-professional) achieved almost the same results, so both subject groups can be equally treated as "motivated subjects." Nevertheless, in contrast to the experiments with "motivated subjects," there is a great difference between results of "motivated subjects" and "unmotivated subjects" [16].

"Motivated subjects" had more correct answers in all kinds of scenario groups – about 82%, which is 17% more than for "unmotivated subjects."[1] As in the "unmotivated subjects" experiment, the worst results were gathered for inside, dark, moving scenarios (42.4%), and the best for inside, bright light, moving scenarios (96.5%), which were well recognized also in "unmotivated subjects" experiment ("unmotivated subjects" did also perform well for those questions) [16].

More information about the videos and scenarios is included in [27] and [28]. More detailed results have been presented in [16].

3.3   VQiPS Multimedia Database of Reference Recordings and Results

The approach taken by VQiPS was to remain application-agnostic. Instead of attempting to individually address each of the many public safety video applications, the approach has been based on their common features. Most importantly, as mentioned previously, each application consists of some type of recognition task. The ability to achieve a recognition task is influenced by many parameters, and five of them have been selected as being of particular importance. They are:

— **Target size.** Specifies whether the anticipated region of interest in the video occupies a relatively small or large percentage of the frame.
— **Level of motion.** Specifies the anticipated level of motion in the scene.
— **Lighting level.** Specifies the anticipated lighting level of the scene.
— **Discrimination level.** Specifies the level of detail required from the video.
— **Usage time frame.** Specifies whether the video will need to be analyzed in real-time or recorded for later analysis.

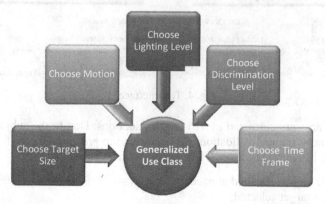

Fig. 3. Classification of video into Generalized Use Classes as proposed by VQiPS

---

[1] We are defining these subjects solely by their performance. There is no other reason they are categorized as unmotivated.

These parameters form what are referred to as Generalized Use Classes, or GUCs [28]. Fig 3 is a representation of the GUC determination process.

The aim of the research was to develop algorithms that would automatically support classification of input sequences into one of the GUCs. Usage time frame and discrimination level are scenario-related parameters and they cannot be set solely based on video analysis. As VQiPS had previously conducted some research on level of motion, the research approached the remaining parameters: target size and lighting level. A description of the GUC aspect does not define particular characteristics of the targets, which could be used as a criterion for automatic algorithms. As a result, the task was to obtain opinions of end-users, such as police officers, about essential objects included in the footage obtained from video surveillance and their size and lighting level. It was necessary to create an intuitive and easily accessible tool that would perform the research. A web-based interface was created, allowing end-users to:

— Watch the video sample,
— Select targets by drawing on the frames and describing them,
— Select the lighting level of the whole sequence and particular targets.

Fig. 4 presents the developed tool.

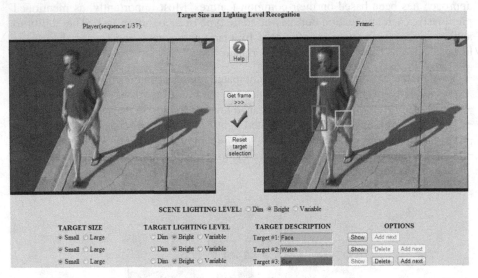

Fig. 4. The interface

The set of answers consisted of 616 target selections. Due to the subjective nature of the experiment, manual validation was performed to prepare data for further analysis and reduce its ambiguity level. The excluded entries contained [22]:

— two or more targets selected at once,
— no particular target selected,
— the same target selected more than once by one of the end-users.

After the validation process, there were 553 reasonable answers [22].

More detailed results have been presented in [22].

3.4   Methods for Automatic Classification of Entire Sequences into Generalized Use Classes

After determining the thresholds for the static classifiers of GUC lighting level and target size, the work focused on automatic methods for classifying sequences. Because the study was not devoted to research into target detection and tracking, data generated by the appropriate methods implemented using third party software (Node Station) [24] were used. Analysis and further work on algorithms was performed in Mathworks MATLAB, based on XML files generated by the Node Station during analysis of the input sequences. They contained coordinates of every detected and tracked target within the frames. Saving the data into XML files provided flexibility of further usage. As a result, the algorithms we worked on were based on image processing of each video frame. The algorithms were segmented into two steps: preparation of data obtained from the Node Station into a set of significant Region of Interest (ROI) coordinates, and determination of the size and lighting level for each target on the basis of pre-defined metrics. To evaluate automatic classifiers, sequences used in a previous study on thresholds during web tests performed by end-users, were used as input files. These footages were divided into two equal sets: testing and training. Fig 5 presents the developed classification method.

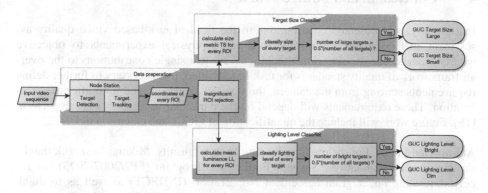

Fig. 5. Block diagram of specified GUC classification method

The first module of the method needs to detect, track and numerically describe targets within the existing input sequence. This research was not restricted to the development of these methods, therefore we applied qualitative checks to the performance of the tools available to us, which were scripts supported by the Computer Vision System Toolbox provided with MATLAB R2011b, and the Node Station detection and tracking system. The performance of the first was poor, and it would require further development in order to achieve a similar efficiency to the second. As a result, the Node Station software [24] was used in this research.

The object detection module implemented in the Node Station is based on a Gaussian Mixture Models of a background and the codebook method [24]. In this research we used the first detector mode, which means that objects were detected on the basis of picture elements that differ from the background [7], [8]. The aim of the Node Station authors was to use the system to detect moving objects within a static area.

For the sequence in which the background was moving (for example footage taken in a car during a pursuit), the system detects multiple objects, supposedly in a random manner. Therefore, it was necessary to impose similar assumption to the input footage of our system. The set of sequences that did not meet these conditions was rejected. In order to use this set, it would be necessary to process files with other detection and tracking systems that would recognize objects in the footage captured with a moving camera and detect static objects.

The results of the experiment revealed that the problem of binary classification of target size is general and difficult to determine by experts. Consequently, the developed automatic method of target size classification allows us to determine the GUC parameter with compliance levels of 70% with end-users' opinion, which is a satisfactory result indicating the indecision of users. Lighting levels of the entire sequence can be classified with an efficiency reaching 93%. A user guide for public safety defines very common features of video sequences. As a result, the classification into GUCs of any footage by a computer algorithm cannot be taken as a certain result, therefore it should be verified manually [22].

More detailed results have been presented in [22].

4   Conclusion and Future Work

In summary, we presented contributions to the field of task-based video quality assessment methodologies from subjective psychophysical experiments to objective quality models. The developed methodologies are just single contributions to the overall framework of quality standards for task-based video. It is necessary to further define requirements starting from the camera, through the broadcast, and until after the presentation. These requirements will depend on the particular tasks users wish to perform [18]. Future work will include the quantification of GUCs and extension of P.912.

Acknowledgment. For the research leading to these results, Mikołaj Leszczuk thanks the European Community's Seventh Framework Program (FP7/2007-2013) for received funding under grant agreement No. 218086 (INDECT) as well as to thank AGH University of Science and Technology for received funding under Department of Telecommunications statutory work. Joel Dumke thanks the U.S. Department of Homeland Security Office for Interoperability and Compatibility for received funding for the research under the Public Safety Communications Research program.

References

[1] CENELEC EN 50132, Alarm systems. CCTV surveillance systems for use in security applications, European Committee for Electro-technical Standardization European Norm (2011)

[2] Picard, D., Dacremont, C., Valentin, D., Giboreau, A.: Perceptual dimensions of tactile textures. Acta Psychologica 114(2), 165–184 (2003),
http://www.sciencedirect.com/science/
article/pii/S0001691803000751

[3] Strohmeier, D., Jumisko-Pyykko, S., Kunze, K.: Open profiling of quality: a mixed method approach to understanding multimodal quality perception. Adv. Multimedia 2010, 3:1–3:17 (January 2010), http://dx.doi.org/10.1155/2010/658980

[4] Ghinea, G., Thomas, J.P.: QoS impact on user perception and understanding of multimedia video clips. In: Proceedings of the Sixth ACM International Conference on Multimedia, ser. MULTIMEDIA 1998, pp. 49–54. ACM, New York (1998), http://doi.acm.org/10.1145/290747.290754

[5] Ghinea, G., Chen, S.Y.: Measuring quality of perception in distributed multimedia: Verbalizers vs. imagers. Computers in Human Behavior 24(4), 1317–1329 (2008)

[6] Nyman, G., Radun, J., Leisti, T., Oja, J., Ojanen, H., Olives, J.L., Vuori, T., Hakkinen, J.: What do users really perceive — probing the subjective image quality experience. In: Proceedings of the SPIE International Symposium on Electronic Imaging 2006: Imaging Quality and System Performance III, vol. 6059, pp. 1–7 (2006)

[7] Szwoch, G., Dalka, P.: Identification of regions of interest in video for a traffic monitoring system. In: Proc. 1st Intern. Conf. on Information Technology, pp. 337–340 (May 2008)

[8] Szwoch, G., Dalka, P., Czyżewski, A.: Objects classification based on their physical sizes for detection of events in camera images. In: 2008 Signal Processing Algorithms, Architectures, Arrangements, and Applications (SPA), pp. 15–20 (September 2008)

[9] ITU-R BT.500-12, Methodology for the subjective assessment of the quality of television pictures, International Telecommunication Union Recommendation, Rev. 12 (2009), http://www.itu.int/rec/R-REC-BT.500-12-200909-I

[10] ITU-T P.800, Methods for subjective determination of transmission quality, International Telecommunication Union Recommendation (1996), http://www.itu.int/rec/T-REC-P.800-199608-I

[11] ITU-T P.910, Subjective video quality assessment methods for multimedia applications, International Telecommunication Union Recommendation (1999), http://www.itu.int/rec/T-REC-P.910-200804-I

[12] ITU-T P.912, Subjective video quality assessment methods for recognition tasks, International Telecommunication Union Recommendation (2008), http://www.itu.int/rec/T-REC-P.912-200808-I

[13] Radun, J., Leisti, T., Hakkinen, J., Ojanen, H., Olives, J.L., Vuori, T., Nyman, G.: Content and quality: Interpretation-based estimation of image quality. ACM Transactions on Applied Perception 4(4), 2:1–2:15 (2008), http://doi.acm.org/10.1145/1278760.1278762

[14] Janowski, L., Romaniak, P.: QoE as a function of frame rate and resolution changes. In: Zeadally, S., Cerqueira, E., Curado, M., Leszczuk, M. (eds.) FMN 2010. LNCS, vol. 6157, pp. 34–45. Springer, Heidelberg (2010), http://dx.doi.org/10.1007/978-3-642-13789-1_4

[15] Duplaga, M., Leszczuk, M., Papir, Z., Przelaskowski, A.: Evaluation of quality retaining diagnostic credibility for surgery video recordings. In: Sebillo, M., Vitiello, G., Schaefer, G. (eds.) VISUAL 2008. LNCS, vol. 5188, pp. 227–230. Springer, Heidelberg (2008)

[16] Leszczuk, M.I., Koń, A., Dumke, J., Janowski, L.: Redefining ITU-T P.912 recommendation requirements for subjects of quality assessments in recognition tasks. In: Dziech, A., Czyżewski, A. (eds.) MCSS 2012. CCIS, vol. 287, pp. 188–199. Springer, Heidelberg (2012)

[17] Leszczuk, M., Dumke, J.: The Quality Assessment for Recognition Tasks (QART), VQEG (July 2012), http://www.its.bldrdoc.gov/vqeg/project-pages/qart/qart.aspx

[18] Leszczuk, M.: Assessing task-based video quality — A journey from subjective psycho-physical experiments to objective quality models. In: Dziech, A., Czyżewski, A. (eds.) MCSS 2011. CCIS, vol. 149, pp. 91–99. Springer, Heidelberg (2011)

[19] Leszczuk, M.: Optimizing task-based video quality; A journey from subjective psycho-physical experiments to objective quality optimization. Springer Multimedia Tools and Applications (2012), doi:10.1007/s11042-012-1161-6

[20] Leszczuk, M., Stange, I., Ford, C.: Determining image quality requirements for recognition tasks in generalized public safety video applications: Definitions, testing, standardization, and current trends. In: IEEE International Symposium on Broadband Multimedia Systems and Broadcasting (BMSB), pp. 1–5 (2011)

[21] Leszczuk, M., Janowski, L., Romaniak, P., Głowacz, A., Mirek, R.: Quality assessment for a licence plate recognition task based on a video streamed in limited networking conditions. In: Dziech, A., Czyżewski, A. (eds.) MCSS 2011. CCIS, vol. 149, pp. 10–18. Springer, Heidelberg (2011)

[22] Witkowski, M., Leszczuk, M.I.: Classification of Video Sequences into Specified Generalized Use Classes of Target Size and Lighting Level. In: The IEEE Symposium on Broadband Multimedia Systems and Broadcasting, June 27-29. Yonsei University, Seoul (2012)

[23] Faye, P., Bremaud, D., Daubin, M.D., Courcoux, P., Giboreau, A., Nicod, H.: Perceptive free sorting and verbalization tasks with naive subjects: an alternative to descriptive mappings. Food Quality and Preference 15(7-8), 781–791 (2004) Fifth Rose Marie Pangborn Sensory Science Symposium,
http://www.sciencedirect.com/science/article/pii/S0950329304000540

[24] Szczuko, P., Romaniak, P., Leszczuk, M., Mirek, R., Pleva, M., Ondas, S., Szwoch, G., Korus, P., Kollmitzer, C., Dalka, P., Kotus, J., Ciarkowski, A., Dąbrowski, A., Pawłowski, P., Marciniak, T., Weychan, R., Misiorek, F.: D1.2, report on NS and CS hardware construction. The INDECT Consortium: Intelligent Information System Supporting Observation, Searching and Detection for Security of Citizens in Urban Environment, European Seventh Framework Program FP7-218086-collaborative project, Europa, Tech. Rep, cop (2010)

[25] Spangler, T.: Golden eyes. Multichannel News (October 2009)

[26] The Video Quality Experts Group, VQEG (July 2012), http://www.vqeg.org/

[27] VQiPS, Recorded-video quality tests for object recognition tasks, U.S. Department of Homeland Security's Office for Interoperability and Compatibility (June 2011),
http://www.pscr.gov/outreach/safecom/vqips_reports/RecVidObjRecogn.pdf

[28] VQiPS, Video quality tests for object recognition applications," U.S. Department of Homeland Security's Office for Interoperability and Compatibility (June 2010),
http://www.safecomprogram.gov/library/Lists/Library/Attachments/231/Video_Quality_Tests_for_Object_Recognition_Applications.pdf

Selective Robust Image Encryption
for Social Networks

Ahmet Emir Dirik[1,2] and Nasir Memon[2,3]

[1] Electronic Engineering Dept., Faculty of Engineering and Architecture,
Uludag University, Bursa, 16059, Turkey
[2] Center for Interdisciplinary Studies in Security and Privacy,
NYU, Abu Dhabi, UAE
[3] Computer Science & Engineering Dept.,
Polytechnic Institute of NYU, USA

Abstract. Current image encryption schemes do not achieve robustness to lossy compression and downsizing without sacrificing image quality. In this paper, we introduce a selective robust image encryption scheme for online social networks that provides a trade-off between robustness and security. With the selective encryption property, users have an option to share a blurred version of the original image and only a specific group of people having the right key can access the full content. Our method is based on the fact that image resizing and compression can be modeled as a low pass process which alters and/or removes high frequency components of image pixels. We achieve robustness to compression and downsizing by adjusting and shuffling DCT coefficients. Experimental results show that the proposed method can be applied in real world applications and social networks with satisfactory image quality.

Keywords: image encryption, robustness, privacy, social networks.

1 Introduction

With the advent of image sharing tools and online social networks, privacy is becoming an increasing concern. When a user shares an image, she may reveal sensitive information related to her private life. Besides, some shared images may contain offensive, embarrassing, or inappropriate content. Consider a scenario where John, a member of a social network would like to share an image. However, due to some privacy concerns, he wants to make the full content available only to a specific group of people. One solution is to design a client-to-client security mechanism for image distribution for Facebook and similar Web 2.0 services [7], [12]. Similar to file encryption, when a sender uploads an image to an online social network, the shared image can be encrypted using a secret key. This key can be associated with the users' social network account and can be shared only with the accounts which are authorized by the sender.

A serious challenge for such a scheme is that social network providers typically re-compress the image or modify the dimension and quality of uploaded images.

A. Dziech and A. Czyżewski (Eds.): MCSS 2013, CCIS 368, pp. 71–81, 2013.
© Springer-Verlag Berlin Heidelberg 2013

In this case, classic encryption schemes [1], [4], [5] fail due to unpredictable image modifications performed by the social network provider. Therefore, the decryption of the original image becomes impossible at the receiving end.

For the above reasons, current social networks such as Facebook, Twitter, etc. may need image encryption systems which are robust to image transformations such as downsizing, cropping, and, compression. It is also desired that image decryption should yield acceptable image quality at the receiver/viewer end, even after the lossy manipulations performed by the social networking provider. Current robust image encryption schemes do not preserve acceptable image quality without sacrificing the level of protection of the encrypted content [11], [13], [15].

Design of a robust image encryption system [2], [6], [12] has to consider the trade off between security and robustness to image transformations. There have been a couple of approaches that have ben proposed for robust image encryption. One approach is to shuffle large image blocks like a jig saw puzzle [12]. This may not provide reasonable security, since attacks against the encryption scheme would be straightforward and even without such attacks, the image content may still be conceivable after encryption. Another approach is to shuffle DCT coefficients of the original image which have same spatial frequencies based on a secret key [9]. This approach requires the receiver to reshuffle DCT frequencies using the shared key and constructs the original image. Although this method is robust to JPEG compression, it has problems with image resizing and may yield low image quality after decryption [9].

In this paper, we introduce a robust image encryption scheme for online social networks taking into account the design challenges introduced above and discuss different trade-offs between robustness and security. Our method is based on the fact that image resizing and compression can be modeled as low pass processing which alters and/or removes high frequency components of image pixels. A robust image encryption scheme has to handle such deformations at high spatial frequencies after decryption. This fact limits pixel-wise shuffling along the image because it spreads out the image spectrum without considering any lossy image processing after encryption.

Hence we propose an approach similar to [9] that employs shuffling of low and mid spatial frequency components in the transform domain, by utilizing DCT coefficients. The drawback of DCT shuffling is that it causes distortions in the image and yields dark or white noisy blocks since some pixel values can exceed the maximum value (255) after shuffling. Thus, the actual pixel values cannot be restored even without lossy operations after encryption. We propose below an approach that provides alleviates this problem and provides better distortion-security tradeoff.

2   Encryption Method

In order to get better distortion after decompression, the main idea of the proposed method is to shuffle DCT coefficients having equal frequencies. DCT coefficients are shuffled independently based on a secret key. The resulting content can then be decrypted if the correct decryption key is provided.

(a) PSNR 39.06 dB   (b) PSNR 50.85 dB

Fig. 1. Effect of DCT scaling on decrypted image quality. (a) and (b) are decrypted images of Fig. 2.b and Fig. 2.c. DCT scaling and decreasing the contrast as in Fig. 2.c improves the PSNR significantly. Notice the distorted small blocks on the wall in (a).

Instead of shuffling all 64 DCT coefficients, only middle and high DCT frequencies can be shuffled during encryption. As a result, selective encryption [10] can be achieved. In this case, robustness of the encryption method to lossy processes and distortions also increases since DCT 0 frequency contains most of the content of the image and it is not affected from lossy operations significantly. However, with this encryption scheme, people may opt using selective or full encryption methods based on their security and privacy concerns.

One of the drawbacks of equal frequency shuffling is that encrypted 8 by 8 spatial blocks may have unexpected dark or light tones. This problem can be handled by limiting the power of DCT coefficients during encryption. In this paper we choose an empirically determined scaling factor to limit the power of DCT coefficients. However the power of DCT frequencies can be adjusted adaptively for less encryption-decryption distortion.

An example of such encryption distortion is visible in Fig. 1.a. It is seen in the figure that there are some noisy blocks on the wall in the image on the left. The original image of Fig. 1 and its encrypted and compressed versions are depicted in Fig. 2. In Fig. 2 two different encrypted forms are presented. The encrypted image on the left side has been created by DCT shuffling. On the other hand the encrypted image on the right side has been created by DCT scaling during shuffling. This means that all DCT coefficients are scaled down with a specific factor α before the encryption. Here, α has been selected as 2. This scaling has an effect of limiting DCT coefficient powers and narrowing the range of the image histogram as it is seen in Fig. 2.e. Dark and high tones in the histogram in Fig. 2.d does not appear in Fig. 2.e. In the decryption step, during reshuffling, all DCT coefficients are upscaled with the same factor α used in the encryption step. This step restores the actual DCT powers and corrects the range of the decrypted image histogram. As a result, better image quality in terms of PSNR is achieved. For instance, the decrypted image in Fig. 1.b has been encrypted

(a) Original image

(b) Encryption result with no (c) Encryption with DCT co-
DCT coefficient scaling. efficient scaling. Contrast nar-
rowed.

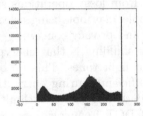 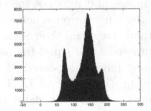

(d) Histogram of image (b)   (e) Histogram of image (c)

Fig. 2. Encrypted and JPEG compressed versions of the original image in (a) with their corresponding histograms. In (b) the original image has been encrypted with DCT shuffling. In (c) DCT coefficients has been scaled for better image quality. See Fig. 1.

with DCT scaling factor 2 and has 50.85 dB PSNR. On the other hand, the same image encrypted without DCT scaling has 39.06 dB after the decryption (Fig. 1.a).

The security of the proposed scheme is based on the strength of the key using shuffling DCT frequencies. In image encryption literature, chaos based methods [3],[8],[14] are widely used due to the desired properties of chaotic sequences such as they are unpredictable, non-periodic, and have good avalanche effect. Thus utilizing chaotic sequences would be one of the alternative choices for DCT shuffling. In this paper instead of discussing chaos based properties we will particularly focus on the robustness of the proposed encryption method.

Fig. 3. Restaurant image : [436x684] pixels

(a) Full encryption result

(b) Decryption after JPEG compression (Q80)

Fig. 4. Full encryption with JPEG compression (Q80)

An example of full encryption with 64 DCT frequencies and a decryption result after JPEG compression with quality 80 are given in Fig. 3 and 4. In Fig. 3 an
image to be encrypted is shown. In Fig. 4, both encrypted and decrypted versions
of the image in Fig 3 are provided. An example of the selective encryption method
is given in Fig. 5. In this figure both selectively encrypted image and its decrypted
form after JPEG compression with quality factor Q80 are provided. It is seen
from the figure that selective encryption preserves main content but not reveal

(a) Selective encryption result

(b) Decryption after JPEG compression (Q80)

Fig. 5. Selective encryption (63 DCT coefficients) with JPEG compression Q80

the details of the original image. All details can only be accessed if a right key is provided. Besides selective encryption are not affected from external distortions significantly as shown in Fig. 5.

Since equal DCT frequencies are shuffled during encryption instead of shuffling all DCT coefficients, the proposed scheme gains robustness not only for JPEG compression but also downsizing. To test this property, we took the image shown in Fig. 6 and encrypted using 63 DCT coefficients except DCT 0 frequency. Then, the encrypted image was compressed with JPEG quality Q75 and downsized with a factor 0.90. The encrypted image and its distorted and decrypted version are shown in Fig. 7. It is seen from the figure that even after compression and downsizing, introduced method yields a satisfactory image quality after the decryption.

3   Experimental Results

As stated in the introduction, encrypted images can be distorted with uncontrolled operations such as lossy compression, downsizing just after being shared. Even if the encrypted image would lose information, we would like to attain reasonable image quality after decryption. To evaluate the applicability of the proposed method we conducted an experimental setup involving 100 images

Fig. 6. Boy image : [436x684] pixels

(a) Selective encryption result

(b) Decryption after downsizing (0.90) and JPEG compression (Q75)

Fig. 7. Selective encryption with JPEG compression (Q75) and downsizing (0.90)

taken from the Greenspun's image database[1]. First, we tested the robustness property so all images were compressed with JPEG with quality factors ranging from Q100 to Q50. Second, we applied JPEG compression (Q75) and downsizing together to the encrypted images. Here, downsizing ratios are selected from 0.9 to 0.5. In all of the experiments, DCT scaling ratio α is fixed to 2.

The result of the first experiment is provided as box plot in Fig. 8. Here, 100 images were encrypted and compressed with different JPEG quality factors. The

---

[1] http://philip.greenspun.com

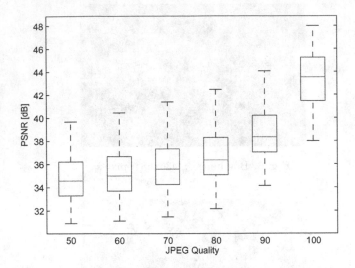

Fig. 8. Robustness to different JPEG compression levels in terms of PSNR

Table 1. Average PSNR [dB] values after JPEG compression and decryption for full and selective encryption

	Q100	Q80	Q60
Full (64 coef)	43.3786	36.7855	35.3165
Selective (63 coef)	43.6511	36.8365	35.3490
Selective (62 coef)	44.1216	36.9211	35.4014

PSNR was measured for each encrypted image after compression and decryption steps. The PSNR statistics of each individual experiment are depicted with different boxes. In each box, the central red line shows the median of the data, and the edges of the box shape are 25th and 75th percentiles. Dotted lines show the extreme data points. From the figure it is seen that reducing the JPEG quality factor for encrypted images result in degradation of the quality, as well. However, the median of PSNR for Q50 is close to 35 dB which still provides a reasonable image quality. The average PSNR values for Q100, Q80, and Q60 are also provided in Table 1. In this experiment we also evaluated the robustness of selective encryption in which DCT 0 and/or near DCT 0 frequencies were not shuffled. This makes the appearance of the encrypted image not fully random revealing the rough content of the original image. Thus, 100 images were also encrypted shuffling 63 and 62 DCT frequencies and compressed with Q100, Q80, and Q60 quality factors. For 63 coefficient case, DCT 0 frequency was not touched during encryption. For 62 coefficient case, DCT 0 and DCT 1 frequencies were not shuffled. The mean of the PSNR values of compressed and decrypted images

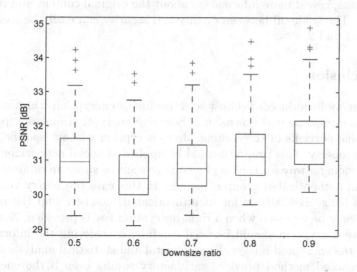

Fig. 9. Robustness to downsizing and compressing (Q75) in terms of PSNR

Table 2. Average PSNR [dB] values after JPEG compression (Q75), downsizing and decryption for full and selective encryption

	0.9	0.8	0.6
Full (64 coef)	31.6953	31.3111	30.6843
Selective (63 coef)	33.8296	33.6610	33.4120
Selective (62 coef)	34.0918	33.9536	33.7904

are provided in Table 1 for two selective encryption cases. It is intuitive that average PSNR values are better for selective cases than the full encryption case where all DCT frequencies are shuffled. This is because, for the selective case, the main content is visible and not shuffled during the encryption. Thus, in selective case, the content of the original image is not affected much from the compression and downsizing, resulting a better looking decrypted image in terms of PSNR.

In the second experiment, the robustness of the encryption method to both JPEG compression and downsizing is evaluated. First, images were encrypted. Then they were compressed with JPEG quality factor 75 and reduced their dimensions with downsizing factor ranging from 0.9 to 0.5. PSNR statistics of decrypted images for different downsizing factors are given in Fig. 9. It is seen from the figure that the median PSNR values are between 30dB and 32dB for different downsizing factors. This shows the efficacy of the proposed method under lossy compression and different downsizing operations. A more detailed analysis of full and selective encryption cases are provided in Table 2. Similar to the results in the first experiment, it is seen from the table that the average PSNR becomes better for selective encryption cases. However shuffling less coefficients, reveal more information about the original content and reduces the security. The trade-off between quality and security can easily be seen from both Tables 1 and 2.

4   Conclusion

In this paper we introduced a robust selective image encryption which survives from lossy compression and downsizing. Selective encryption makes it possible to reveal some portions of the content after encryption without sacrificing the robustness property. This property could be applied in social networking applications, providing a way for the users who may want to share an original image only with an authenticated group of people. In this case the blurry version of the original image is available for unauthenticated members and the original version will only be accessed when a right decryption key is provided. Nevertheless, selective encryption should be used carefully considering the information revealed by the encrypted images. Experimental and statistical analysis suggest that the proposed method provides satisfactory results even if the encrypted image is compressed with low JPEG quality factors and downsized afterwards. Considering both quality and security issues, introduced method could be a good option to employ in social networking applications compared to jig-saw like encryption schemes. Moreover the proposed method can be used in any encryption system or application where robustness to any external distortions and/or lossy processes are required. Compared to the similar robust encryption schemes, proposed method provides better image quality in terms of PSNR.

Acknowledgement. This work was partially supported by the Center for Interdisciplinary Studies in Security and Privacy, NYU, Abu Dhabi.

References

1. Chen, G., Mao, Y., Chui, C.: A symmetric image encryption scheme based on 3d chaotic cat maps. Chaos, Solitons & Fractals 21(3), 749–761 (2004)
2. Dirik, A.E.: Image encryption scheme for print and scan channel. In: International Conference on Applied and Computational Mathematics, ICACM (2012)
3. Gao, H., Zhang, Y., Liang, S., Li, D.: A new chaotic algorithm for image encryption. Chaos, Solitons & Fractals 29(2), 393–399 (2006)
4. Guan, Z., Huang, F., Guan, W.: Chaos-based image encryption algorithm. Physics Letters A 346(1), 153–157 (2005)
5. Guo, J., et al.: A new chaotic key-based design for image encryption and decryption. In: Proceedings of the 2000 IEEE International Symposium on Circuits and Systems, ISCAS 2000, vol. 4, pp. 49–52. IEEE (2000)
6. Haas, B., Dirik, A.E., Nawaz, Y.: Image encryption for print-and-scan channels using pixel position permutation, US Patent App. 12/317,955 (December 31, 2008)
7. Hassinen, M., Mussalo, P.: Client controlled security for web applications. In: 30th Anniversary The IEEE Conference on Local Computer Networks, pp. 810–816. IEEE (2005)

8. Li, S., Zheng, X.: Cryptanalysis of a chaotic image encryption method. In: IEEE International Symposium on Circuits and Systems, ISCAS 2002, vol. 2, pp. II-708–II-711. IEEE (2002)
9. Li, W., Yu, N.: A robust chaos-based image encryption scheme. In: IEEE International Conference on Multimedia and Expo., ICME 2009, pp. 1034–1037. IEEE (2009)
10. Liu, X., Eskicioglu, A.: Selective encryption of multimedia content in distribution networks: Challenges and new directions. In: IASTED Communications, Internet & Information Technology (CIIT), USA (2003)
11. Podesser, M., Schmidt, H., Uhl, A.: Selective bitplane encryption for secure transmission of image data in mobile environments. In: Proceedings of the 5th IEEE Nordic Signal Processing Symposium (NORSIG 2002), pp. 4–6 (2002)
12. Poller, A., Steinebach, M., Liu, H.: Robust image obfuscation for privacy protection in web 2.0 applications. In: Society of Photo-Optical Instrumentation Engineers (SPIE). Conference Series, vol. 8303, p. 1 (2012)
13. Yekkala, A., Veni Madhavan, C.: Bit plane encoding and encryption. Pattern Recognition and Machine Intelligence, 103–110 (2007)
14. Zhang, L., Liao, X., Wang, X.: An image encryption approach based on chaotic maps. Chaos, Solitons & Fractals 24(3), 759–765 (2005)
15. Zhou, Y., Panetta, K., Agaian, S.: Image encryption using discrete parametric cosine transform. In: 2009 Conference Record of the Forty-Third Asilomar Conference on Signals, Systems and Computers, pp. 395–399. IEEE (2009)

Feature Recycling Cascaded SVM Classifier Based on Feature Selection of HOGs for Pedestrian Detection

Alexandros Gavriilidis, Carsten Stahlschmidt,
Jörg Velten, and Anton Kummert

Faculty of Electrical Engineering and Media Technologies
University of Wuppertal
D-42119 Wuppertal, Germany
{gavriilidis,stahlschmidt,velten,kummert}@uni-wuppertal.de

Abstract. Since to pedestrian detection in driver assistance as well as surveillance systems is a challenging task of the recent years this paper introduces a fast cascaded classifier based on linear and non-linear support vector machines (SVMs). To yield high and accurate detection rates, histogram of oriented gradients (HOGs) will be preselected by the fisher score. These features will be a basis for the training algorithm of the cascaded classifier. A non-maximum suppression algorithm will be used and evaluated in respect to reject HOG features which have a huge overlap in a joint image area. By variation of the non-maximum suppression parameter different numbers of preselected HOG features will be used to create the cascaded classifier. The different cascaded classifiers will be evaluated and compared between each other and in relation to the HOG procedure from Dalal and Triggs combined with a support vector machine.

Keywords: Pedestrian Detection, Cascaded Classifier, Feature Selection, Support Vector Machine.

1 Introduction

Fast, accurate and robust object detection is required in many driver assistance [5] as well as surveillance systems. To overcome these requirements many different approaches are available. In [9] a pedestrian detection algorithm based on Haar and HOG features is presented. The Haar features will be used with AdaBoost to preselect region of interests (ROIs) with low computing costs and a high detection rate. Remaining ROIs have many of false positive detections and will be evaluated by a libSVM combined with HOG features [3]. Increasing the speed of object detection based on a single classifier [3] in multi scales and large images can be reached by use of cascaded classifiers. The idea of cascaded classifiers is based on rejection of image areas without the object of interest with low computational cost and a high detection rate for the object of interest. Each subsequent stage can increase the computational costs for the object detection

A. Dziech and A. Czyżewski (Eds.): MCSS 2013, CCIS 368, pp. 82–94, 2013.

because the number of ROIs in the image will be reduced by each stage of the cascade. In [10] a training for a support vector machine based on the idea of AdaBoost is presented. Inside the cascade different HOG blocks will be randomly chosen and a certain number of SVMs will be trained by what the best SVM classification result will be added to the strong classifier of the current cascade stage. Due to the whole training set is used to compute the false and true positive rates each stage will be limited by a maximum acceptable false positive rate and a minimum acceptable detection rate respectively. To increase the performance of an object detection algorithm and to reduce the training complexity, feature selection can be considered. Different methods to select features are presented in [1]. The F-Score presented in [1] as well as the SVM weights will be used to produce a sorted list of feature weights, whereupon a large value of a weight indicates a feature which is more suitable to distinguish between the positive and negative training data. A list with ranked features can be used to select just the best features for the training procedure of a SVM classifier. The F-Score is a filter based ranking procedure which means no detection algorithm like AdaBoost or a SVM are necessary for the feature ranking or selection.

The remainder of the paper is structured as follows. First, preliminary considerations will include the basic formulation of a SVM as presented in [7] and the description of the used HOG features of [3]. Section three include the feature ranking procedure and the feature selection algorithm which is based on a non-maximum suppression algorithm. Results from this section will be used for the training procedure of the cascaded SVMs which will be described in section four. Section five inlcudes the evaluation and comparision of different feature selection results as well as the detection performance of the cascaded classifier. The last section includes conclusions and results.

2   Preliminary Considerations

2.1   Support Vector Machine

In [7] the support vector machine (SVM) is described which has been developed first by Vladimir Vapnik [2]. Since the SVM training algorithm used in this paper is based on the sequential minimal optimization (SMO) algorithm of J. C. Platt the basic equations of the linear and non-linear SVM will be extracted as described in paper [7]. The current paper does not change the optimization problem described in [7], so the formulation of the optimization problem can be found in [7]. A training set is defined as

$$(y_i, \mathbf{x}_i), i = 1, \ldots, N \in \mathbb{N}, \tag{1}$$

where $y_i \in \{-1, 1\}$ is the label information for positive $(y_i = +1)$ and negative $(y_i = -1)$ training examples and $\mathbf{x}_i \in \mathbb{R}^m$ with $m \in \mathbb{N} \backslash \{0\}$ includes the calculated feature values of the current training example y_i. The SVM in its linear form tries to find a hyperplane to seperate the positive from the negative training examples which can be seen in figure 1. The linear SVM equation is defined as

$$u_L = \mathbf{w}^T \cdot \mathbf{x} - b_L, \tag{2}$$

where $\mathbf{w} \in \mathbb{R}^m$ is the normal vector to the hyperplane, $\mathbf{x} \in \mathbb{R}^m$ is the input vector and $b_L \in \mathbb{R}$ is a threshold to shift the hyperplane. In [7] it is described

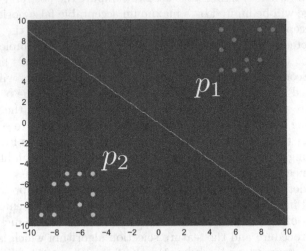

Fig. 1. The red area (right upper corner of the figure) includes the positive data points and the blue area (left lower corner) includes the negative data points. Both sets have been seperated by the SVM with the largest gap between the different sets. The points p_1 (positive example) and p_2 (negative example) have the smallest distance to the seperating line.

$u_L = 0$ is the seperating hyperplane and if $u_L > 0$ the input vector will be classified as a positive example and if $u_L < 0$ as a negative example. Here, the case $u_L >= 0$ will be defined as a positive example too. Because of not every problem is linear separable, the equation for a non-linear SVM as described in [7] is defined as

$$u_{NL} = \sum_{i=1}^{N} y_i \alpha_i K(\mathbf{x}_i, \mathbf{x}) - b_{NL}, \tag{3}$$

where $K(\mathbf{x}_i, \mathbf{x})$ is a kernel function to calculate the similarity between a training vector $\mathbf{x}_i$ and the input vector $\mathbf{x}$, $\alpha_i \geq 0 \; \forall \; i$ are Lagrange multipliers from the optimization problem, y_i is the label information of the training vector and b_{NL} is a threshold like b_L of equation (2). Due to [7] the normal vector $\mathbf{w}$ and the threshold b_L of equation (2) can be calculated by the determined Lagrange multipliers α_i. The normal vector $\mathbf{w}$ will be calculated by

$$\mathbf{w} = \sum_{i=1}^{N} y_i \alpha_i \mathbf{x}_i \tag{4}$$

and the threshold b_L will be calculated with

$$b_L = \frac{\sum_{h=1}^{M} (\mathbf{w}^T \cdot \mathbf{x}_h - y_h)}{M}, \tag{5}$$

where $\mathbf{x}_h$ with $\alpha_h > 0$ are the so called support vectors and $M \in \mathbb{N}\backslash\{0\}, M \leq N$ is the number of positive α_h. By means of this relationship it is possible to train a SVM machine and save the linear as well the non-linear SVM parameter for an object detection task.

2.2   Histogram of Oriented Gradients

The histogram of oriented gradient (HOG) feature introduced in [3] will be used for the training of the SVM cascade. To compare different feature selection results and cascade properties, the block size of a HOG feature will be 2×2 and the cell size of a HOG feature will be 16×16 pixel. Here, the feature selection result and the resulting SVM cascade are of interest for the evaluation, not the different HOG features. In figure 2 the calculated histograms of one HOG block can be seen where the whole block is normalized by L1-norm as described in [3]. Due to the use of the integral image representation presented

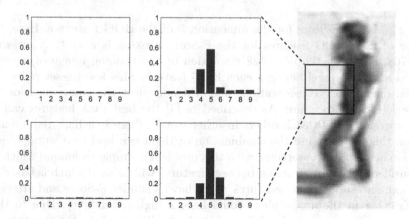

Fig. 2. On the right hand side of the image, the positive object (a pedestrian in 64×128 resolution) is shown where the rectangle represents the HOG block with 2×2 cells inside. On the left hand side, the calculated histograms of each cell with nine orientations are shown.

in [8], trilinear interpolation as described in [3] is not used here. The whole feature vector $\mathbf{x} \in \mathbb{R}^m$ includes all $m = 36$ entries of the four histograms shown in figure 2.

3   Feature Selection with Fisher Score

In this paper, the fisher score, also called F-Score, will be used to rank a set of features, which is defined and used in [6]. The difference between the F-Score in [1] and [6] is based on the weighting of the numerator and denominator with the number of used samples in the current class (e.g. positive or negative examples). Since the equation of F-Score presented in [6] is more general, it will be used for feature ranking. The equation is defined as

$$F_r = \frac{\sum_{j=1}^{c} n_j(\mu_j - \mu)^2}{\sum_{j=1}^{c} n_j\sigma_j^2} \qquad (6)$$

where c defines the different classes (e.g. positive or negative with $c = 2$), μ_j, σ_j are the mean and variance of class j, respectively, with $n_j \in \mathbb{N}\setminus\{0\}$ the number of samples, and μ, σ are the mean and the variance over all classes, respectively. A large value F_r of the r-th feature represents a much better separation of the different classes based on this single feature. To use the F-Score for the HOG features, each of the $m = 36$ dimensions is evaluated with equation (6) and the results are summarized by

$$F_r = \frac{\sum_{k=1}^{m} F_{r,k}}{m} \qquad (7)$$

where $F_{r,k}$ is the F-Score for the dimension k of the HOG feature r. Here, the number of used HOG features for the F-Score ranking is $r = 1, \ldots, n_r$ with $n_r = 768$, based on the 64×128 resolution of the training image of figure 2 and a step of two pixel between each HOG feature. This feature set reduction is based on memory considerations and will not effect the comparison of the feature selection procedure. As described in [4] the best rank features can be highly correlated with each other. In other words, there is a high redundancy between this features and the combination of them can lead to a worse object detection accuracy. To overcome with this problem a simple technique which do not consider mutual information between features will be used which is based on non-maximum suppression. Features which have a similar F-Score and are close to each other in the image plane could have a high redundancy. Due to this, the non-maximum suppression is based on the position and the F-Score value of the current feature. The algorithm 1 selects now a subset $\mathcal{F}_S$ of features from the ranked feature set $\mathcal{F}_R = \{F_1, \ldots, F_{n_r}\}$ which has been created with the F-Score presented in equation (6). Each time a maximum has been found, all features which are overlapping in the image plane up to a factor $overlap$ between [0 100) in percent, as described in algorithm 1, will be removed from the set $\mathcal{F}_R$. For the calculation of the overlap, the block width value of 32 pixel will be used because of no other block width and cell width properties will be used as described in subsection 2.2.

Algorithm 1. Non-Maximum Suppression Nearest Neighbour

Input: $\mathcal{F_R}$ is set of ranked features
$\qquad$ $\mathcal{F_N}$ is set of neglected features
$\qquad$ Value $overlap \in [0\ 100]$ in percent
Output: $\mathcal{F_S} \subset \mathcal{F_R}$ of selected features
$\qquad$ Value $n_s \in \mathbb{N}$ counts number of selected features
1: $\mathcal{F_R} \leftarrow \{F_r | r = 1, \ldots, n_r\}$
2: $\mathcal{F_N} \leftarrow \emptyset$
3: $n_s \leftarrow 0$
4: **while** $\mathcal{F_R} \neq \emptyset$ **do**
5: $\qquad$ find next possible maximum in $\mathcal{F_R} \backslash \mathcal{F_N}$
6: $\qquad$ remove selected maximum from $\mathcal{F_R}$ and append to $\mathcal{F_S}$
7: $\qquad$ remove all features from $\mathcal{F_R}$ which are overlapping more than $overlap$ in the
$\qquad$ image plane with the selected maximum
8: $\qquad$ add all removed features to $\mathcal{F_N}$
9: $\qquad$ $n_s \leftarrow n_s + 1$
10: **end while**

---

4 Training of Cascaded Linear and Non-linear SVM Classifiers

The selected features $\mathcal{F_S} = \{F_1, \ldots, F_{n_s}\}$ are ordered by F_1 with the highest F-Score value and F_{n_s} with the smallest F-Score value. The set of training examples with $c = 2$ classes will now be divided into the number of positive samples $N_p \in \mathbb{N} \backslash \{0\}$ and negative examples $N_n \in \mathbb{N} \backslash \{0\}$ where

$$\underbrace{(y_1, \mathbf{x}_1), \ldots, (y_{N_p}, \mathbf{x}_{N_p})}_{\mathcal{T_P} := \text{positive examples}}, \underbrace{(y_{N_p+1}, \mathbf{x}_{N_p+1}), \ldots, (y_N, \mathbf{x}_N)}_{\mathcal{T_N} := \text{negative examples}}, N = N_p + N_n. \quad (8)$$

For the cascaded SVM classifier it is necessary to define a linear and non-linear adjustable threshold to increase the detection rate of one SVM cascade stage. To increase the detection rate of the linear SVM classifier

$$b_L := b_L - \Delta_{b_L} \quad (9)$$

with $\Delta_{b_L} = 0.5$ will be used. Each time b_L will be decreased by Δ_{b_L}, the false positive and the true positive rate of the current SVM classifier will be increased. For the non-linear SVM classifier the output u_{NL} will be transformed to

$$u_{NL_{new}} = \frac{1}{1 + e^{-u_{NL}}} \quad (10)$$

where $u_{NL} = 0$ yields $u_{NL_{new}} = u_{NL_{border}} = 0.5$, which is the margin between positive and negative examples. The non-linear SVM classifier will now be adjusted by decreasing the decision threshold

$$u_{NL_{border}} := u_{NL_{border}} - \Delta_{u_{NL}} \quad (11)$$

Algorithm 2. Training Cascade of SVMs

Input: $\mathcal{F}_S$ set of selected features
   $\mathcal{T}_P$ positive and $\mathcal{T}_N$ negative training sets with N_p, N_n examples
   $\mathcal{V}_P$ positive and $\mathcal{V}_N$ negative validation sets
   f_{max} maximum acceptable false positive rate
   d_{min} minimum acceptable true positive rate
Output: A l-Level ($l \in \mathbb{N}\backslash\{0\}$) cascaded linear and non-linear SVM classifier
   $\mathcal{F}_C$ ordered set of features for cascaded SVM classifier

1: $f_0 \leftarrow 1, \mathcal{F}_C \leftarrow \emptyset, l \leftarrow 1, f_l \leftarrow f_{l-1} \cdot f_{max}$
2: remove first entry of $\mathcal{F}_S$ and append it to $\mathcal{F}_C, n_s \leftarrow n_s - 1$
3: **while** $\mathcal{F}_S \neq \emptyset$ and $\mathcal{T}_N \neq \emptyset$ **do**
4:   $f_{best} \leftarrow 1, d_{best} \leftarrow 0, b_{cas} \leftarrow false, b_{cas}$ establishes a new cascade stage
5:   **for** all entries $F_v \in \mathcal{F}_S, v = 1, \ldots, n_s$ **do**
6:     use all features $\mathcal{F}_C \cup F_v$ to train a SVM classifier
7:     $d_{cur} \leftarrow 0, f_{cur} \leftarrow 0$, current true and false positive rates
8:     evaluate linear SVM classifier with $\mathcal{V}_P, \mathcal{V}_N$ to calculate d_{cur}, f_{cur}
9:     **while** $d_{cur} \leq d_{min}$ and $f_{cur} < f_l$ **do**
10:       decrease threshold b_L as defined in equation (9)
11:       evaluate linear SVM classifier with $\mathcal{V}_P, \mathcal{V}_N$ to calculate d_{cur}, f_{cur}
12:     **end while**
13:     **if** $d_{cur} \geq d_{best}$ and $f_{cur} < f_{best}$ **then**
14:       $d_{best} \leftarrow d_{cur}, f_{best} \leftarrow f_{cur}$, best true and false positive rates
15:       save F_v as F_{best} best feature of current iteration
16:       **if** $d_{best} > d_{min}$ and $f_{best} < f_l$ **then**
17:         $b_{cas} \leftarrow true$
18:       **end if**
19:     **end if**
20:   **end for**
21:   **if** $b_{cas} = true$ **then**
22:     $d_{cur} \leftarrow 0, f_{cur} \leftarrow 0, u_{NL_{border}} \leftarrow 0.5$
23:     evaluate non-linear SVM with $\mathcal{F}_C \cup F_{best}$ and $\mathcal{V}_P, \mathcal{V}_N$ to calculate d_{cur}, f_{cur}
24:     **while** $d_{cur} \leq d_{min}$ and $u_{NL_{border}} > \Delta_{u_{NL}}$ **do**
25:       decrease threshold $u_{NL_{border}}$ as defined in equation (11)
26:       evaluate non-linear SVM with $\mathcal{V}_P, \mathcal{V}_N$ to calculate d_{cur}, f_{cur}
27:     **end while**
28:     save linear and non-linear thresholds and SVM parameter
29:     remove all by linear SVM correct classified examples from $\mathcal{T}_N$
30:     $l \leftarrow l + 1, f_l \leftarrow f_{l-1} \cdot f_{best}$
31:   **end if**
32:   **if** no F_{best} found **then**
33:     remove first entry from $\mathcal{F}_S$ and append to $\mathcal{F}_C, n_s \leftarrow n_s - 1$
34:   **else**
35:     remove F_{best} from $\mathcal{F}_S$ and append to $\mathcal{F}_C, n_s \leftarrow n_s - 1$
36:   **end if**
37: **end while**
38: **if** $\mathcal{T}_N \neq \emptyset$ **then**
39:   train last SVM classifier with all features of $\mathcal{F}_C$
40:   save best linear and non-linear solutions
41: **end if**

---

with $\Delta_{u_{NL}} = 0.025$ which yields an increasing of the false positive and true positive rate, where $u_{NL_{border}} > 0$ has to be fulfilled. In other words, the SVM decision to be a positive example increases due to $u_{NL_{new}} < u_{NL_{border}}$ is the SVM output for a negative validation example. The transformation of u_{NL} to $u_{NL_{new}}$ is important for runtime considerations. The evaluation of the non-linear SVM classifier would be too expensive if the threshold u_{NL} would be decreased with a constant factor until a certain true positive rate would be achieved.

5 Evaluation

The HOG feature selection result trained with the algorithm 2 will be compared with the normal HOG descriptor presented in [3] with a cell size of 16×16 pixel and a block size of 2×2 cells including 9 orientations in each cell. A SVM will be used to train a linear and non-linear classifier based on the normal HOG descriptor. Selected HOG features have the same propertiers of block, cell size and number of orientations as the HOG features of the normal HOG descriptor. The kernel of the SVM will be a radial basis function (RBF) defined as $K(\mathbf{x}_i, \mathbf{x}) = e^{-\gamma \cdot \|\mathbf{x}_i - \mathbf{x}\|^2}$, with $\gamma = 0.05$. To compare the different results of the approaches, the values γ of the kernel and $C = 1000$ of the SVM will not be adjusted.

For training and testing, the INRIA dataset is used which is divided into 1230 positive, 12180 negative examples for training and 580 positive, 4530 negative examples for validation, respectively. Some examples of the INRIA set can be seen in figure 3. Two cascaded SVM classifiers have been trained with the overlap factors 62.50 percent and 68.75 percent of the non-maximum suppression

Fig. 3. The examples on top of this figure are positive examples for training and testing. Examples at the bottom are negative examples of the INRIA dataset. All examples are scaled to 64×128.

algorithm. The factor *overlap* = 62.50 yields a feature set of 20 selected HOG features and the factor *overlap* = 68.75 a set of 28 selected HOG features. In other words, a small overlap factor decrease the number of selectable features and a large overlap factor increase the number of selectable features, respectively. To accept a new cascade stage, the minimum acceptable true positive rate is set to $d_{min} = 0.99$ and the maximum acceptable false positive rate $f_{max} = 0.7$ restrict the number of cascade stages based on the number of available features, as it can be seen in algorithm 2.

First, the linear detection result of the different approaches will be compared. In figure 4, the different ROC curves can be seen. Since the trained SVM classifier

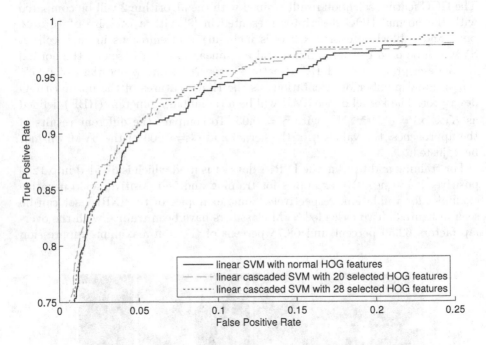

Fig. 4. The blue coloured solid line presents the ROC curve of the normal HOG procedure with a linear SVM classifier result. The cyan coloured dashed line shows the linear SVM result of the 4-Level cascaded SVM with 20 selected HOG features and the magenta coloured dotted line shows the results of the 4-Level cascaded SVM with 28 selected HOG features.

based on the feature vector of the normal HOG procedure will not be adjusted in the decision threshold, as defined in equation (9), results of the different approaches will be compared in a certain point on the ROC curves. The linear SVM of the normal HOG procedure with a decision threshold of $u_L \geq 0$ for positive and $u_L < 0$ for negative classified examples achieves a true positive rate of 0.931 and a false positive rate of 0.083, as shown in table 1. The 4-Level cascaded linear SVM classifer with 20 selected HOG features perform as best in this point. To use more and more features for the feature recycling cascade does not necessarily improve the result of the cascaded linear SVM classifier as it can be seen in table 1.

Table 1. The ROC curve values of the linear classifiers of figure 4 are compared on the true positive (TP) point 0.931

Classifier	TP	FP
normal HOG SVM classifier	0.931	0.08300
cascaded HOG SVM classifier with 20 features	0.931	0.06225
cascaded HOG SVM classifier with 28 features	0.931	0.07307

Now, the non-linear stages will be compared. To do this, the linear SVM output trained with the normal HOG descriptor feature vector will be used as a single cascade stage before the non-linear SVM output of the normal HOG descriptor. In other words, the normal HOG descriptor trained with a SVM will be used as a 1-Level cascaded classifier with a linear and non-linear cascade stage. Due to this, the decision output of the linear stages will be used to calculate the ROC curves of the non-linear classifier stages. In the case of the normal HOG procedure there is just the single linear SVM output as the input for the non-linear SVM classifier. For the cascaded HOG SVM classifiers with selected features, the ouput of l cascaded linear SVM classifiers will be used as input for the l-Level cascaded non-linear SVM classifiers. In other words, the non-linear stages have no propability to reach a true positive rate of 100 percent. The maximum true positive rate which can be reached by the non-linear SVM classifiers is the best true positive rate of the linear decision which can be seen in figure 5. To compare the results, the true positive rate of the normal HOG procedure with the linear SVM output will be used at the same point as in table 1. The non-linear cascade stages are now able to reduce the false positive rate of the linear SVM result. Table 2 includes the three points on the ROC curves where the different approaches can be compared at the same point of the linear stages. In figure 5 it can be seen that the cascaded linear non-linear SVM classifier with the normal HOG descriptor feature vector performs better than the 4-Level cascaded classifier with 20 selected HOG features. The 4-Level cascaded SVM classifier with 28 selected HOG features is nearly above all the best result.

Table 2. The ROC curve values of the non-linear classifiers of figure 5 are compared on the true positive (TP) point 0.931

Classifier	TP	FP
normal HOG SVM classifier	0.931	0.026490
cascaded HOG SVM classifier with 20 features	0.931	0.011700
cascaded HOG SVM classifier with 28 features	0.931	0.009492

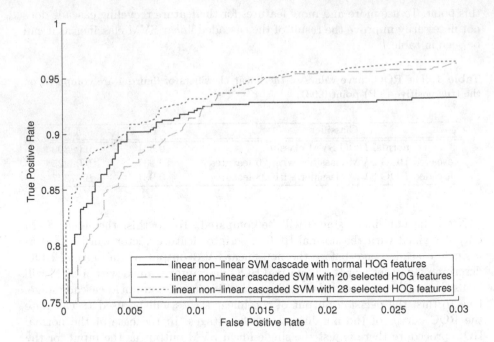

Fig. 5. The blue coloured solid line presents the ROC curve of the normal HOG procedure with a non-linear SVM result cascaded with a previous linear SVM result. The cyan coloured dashed line shows the non-linear SVM result of the 4-Level cascaded SVM with 20 selected HOG features and the magenta coloured dotted line shows the results of the 4-Level cascaded SVM with 28 selected HOG features.

Besides the classifier accuracy, the main improvement of the feature recycling cascaded classifier is based on the computation of the HOG features. To detect an object inside of an image, many subwindows have to be examined. A feature vector of the normal HOG procedure has to be calculated for each detection window (subwindow) inside of a ROI in the image. Due to the size of the normal HOG descriptor, as defined in [3], the time for computing the whole feature vector and to use the feature vector for a linear and non-linear SVM classifier needs a lot of time. A normal cascaded classifier like presented in [10], which allows the use of new features in every cascade stage, has to caclulate the current feature vector of each cascaded stage. The benefit of a cascade is the rejection of false positives with a small computational effort, but computation of features in each stage is also very time-consuming. Since the feature recycling cascade presented in this paper is based on the idea of using calculated features of previous cascade stages, in the same order as they has been calculated, computational costs are reduced in relation to a cascade presented in [10]. Computational cost of each cascade stage is reduced to the calculation of the new features of the current cascade stage and the new evaluation of the feature vector with the new SVM parameter.

The different approaches have been compared in relation to the speed of scanning an image with a sliding window. The speedup between the normal HOG descriptor and the cascaded HOG SVM classifiers is not surprising but the speedup between the feature recycling cascade and the not recycling cascade is interesting. A feature recycling cascaded classifier needs 78.44 percent of the computation time of the normal cascade. The speedup has been computed over a video sequence with 366 frames where the time of detection in each frame has been averaged over the whole video sequence. The speedup is presented as a relative value, since information about absolut values of computing times are to dependent on used hard- and software components.

6   Conclusions

A feature recycling cascaded classifier based on HOG feature selection and SVM classification has been presented in this paper. This cascaded classifier uses calculated features of one cascaded stage for the feature vector of the next cascaded stage. The feature vector will be increased by new features from stage to stage where just the new features have to be calculated for using the SVM classifier of stage l for a linear or non-linear classification. The feature recycling cascaded classifier needs 78.44 percent of computation time of the not feature recycling cascaded classifier. Time difference of the normal HOG descriptor used with an SVM is not compared to the cascade classifiers because of no direct comparability of speed. Since the number of used HOG features $(20, 28)$ for the cascaded classifiers is close to the 21 HOG features included in the normal HOG descriptor, no huge performance difference between the normal HOG descriptor and the cascaded classifier can be seen. The use of more HOG features can increase the performance. Since the focus of this paper is based on the comparison between the performance of the new feature recycling cascade and the well known HOG procedure of [3] and the comparison of speed between a feature recycling cascade and a not feature recycling cascade, the number of selected features should be close to the number of features included in the normal HOG descriptor. A drawback of the feature recycling cascaded classifier can be the not reversibility of selected features in previous cascade steps. In other words, the sequence of selected features cannot be changed in following cascade steps. Different features in cascade steps could increase the accuracy of the cascaded classifier but would also increase the computational costs of calculating these features.

Acknowledgement. The research leading to these results has received funding from the European Community's Seventh Framework Programme (FP7 / 2007 - 2013) under grant agreement no. 218086.

References

1. Chang, Y.W., Lin, C.J.: Feature Ranking Using Linear SVM. Journal of Machine Learning Research - Proceedings Track 3, 53–64 (2008)
2. Cortes, C., Vapnik, V.: Support Vector Networks. Machine Learning 20, 273–297 (1995)
3. Dalal, N., Triggs, B.: Histograms of Oriented Gradients for Human Detection. In: Proceedings of the IEEE Computer Society Conference on Computer Vision and Pattern Recognition, CVPR 2005, San Diego, California, USA, vol. 1, pp. 886–893 (June 2005)
4. Ding, C., Peng, H.: Minimum Redundancy Feature Selection from Microarray Gene Expression Data. In: Proceedings of the 2nd IEEE Computer Society Conference on Bioinformatics, CSB 2003, Stanford, CA, USA, pp. 523–528 (August 2003)
5. Haselhoff, A., Hoehmann, L., Nunn, C., Meuter, M., Kummert, A.: On Occlusion-Handling for People Detection Fusion in Multi-camera Networks. In: Dziech, A., Czyżewski, A. (eds.) MCSS 2011. CCIS, vol. 149, pp. 113–119. Springer, Heidelberg (2011)
6. He, X., Cai, D., Niyogi, P.: Laplacian Score for Feature Selection. In: Neural Information Processing Systems, vol. 18, pp. 507–514. MIT Press, Lake Tahoe (2005)
7. Platt, J.C.: Sequential Minimal Optimization: A Fast Algorithm for Training Support Vector Machines. Tech. rep., Microsoft Research (April 1998)
8. Viola, P., Jones, M.: Rapid Object Detection Using a Boosted Cascade of Simple Features. In: Proceedings of the IEEE Computer Society Conference on Computer Vision and Pattern Recognition, CVPR 2001, Kauai, HI, USA, vol. 1, pp. 511–518 (December 2001)
9. Xing, W., Zhao, Y., Cheng, R., Xu, J., Lv, S., Wang, X.: Fast Pedestrian Detection Based on Haar Pre-Detection. International Journal of Computer and Communication Engineering 1(3), 207–209 (2012)
10. Zhu, Q., Avidan, S., Yeh, M.C., Cheng, K.T.: Fast Human Detection Using a Cascade of Histograms of Oriented Gradients. In: Proceedings of the IEEE Computer Society Conference on Computer Vision and Pattern Recognition, CVPR 2006, New York, USA, vol. 2, pp. 1491–1498 (June 2006)

Two Methods for Detecting Malware

Maciej Korczyński, Gilles Berger-Sabbatel, and Andrzej Duda

Grenoble Institute of Technology, CNRS Grenoble Informatics Laboratory
UMR 5217 681, rue de la Passerelle,
BP 72 38402 Saint Martin d'Hères Cedex, France
{Maciej.Korczynski,Gilles.Berger-Sabbatel,Andrzej.Duda}@imag.fr

Abstract. In this paper, we present two ways of detecting malware. The first one takes advantage of a platform that we have developed. The platform includes tools for capturing malware, running code in a controlled environment, and analyzing its interactions with external entities. The platform enables us to detect malware based on the observation of its communication behavior. The second approach uses a method for detecting encrypted Skype traffic and classifying Skype service flows such as voice calls, skypeOut, video conferencing, chat, file upload and download in Skype traffic. The method is based on the Statistical Protocol IDentification (SPID) that analyzes statistical values of some traffic attributes. We apply the method to identify malicious traffic—we have successfully detected the propagation of Worm.Win32.Skipi.b that spreads over the Skype messenger by sending infected messages to all Skype contacts on a victim machine.

1 Introduction

In this paper, we consider the problem of detecting malware. The standard detection method consists of identifying malware by searching some patterns in the code (a signature). The signature method however suffers from several drawbacks and needs to be enhanced with other approaches. We consider two other methods that may provide an additional possibility of detecting malware. The first one is based on the observation of the communication behavior caused by suspected code. It takes advantage of our platform for botnet-related malware analysis. It is composed of tools for capturing malware, running code in a controlled environment, and analyzing its interactions with external entities.

The second method provides a means for detecting encrypted Skype traffic and classifying Skype service flows such as voice calls, skypeOut, video conferencing, chat, file upload and download in Skype traffic. The method is based on the Statistical Protocol IDentification (SPID) that analyzes statistical values of some traffic attributes. We apply the method to identify malicious traffic—we have successfully detected the propagation of Worm.Win32.Skipi.b that spreads over the Skype messenger by sending infected messages to all Skype contacts on a victim machine. We have focused on the selection of an appropriate set of attribute meters based on propagation characteristics to classify malicious flows with high accuracy.

A. Dziech and A. Czyżewski (Eds.): MCSS 2013, CCIS 368, pp. 95–106, 2013.

2   Platform for Botnet-Related Malware Analysis

We have presented the design of the platform for botnet-related malware analysis and its applications in the previous work [1,2,3]. It has the following functionalities (cf. Figure 1):

- *Malware capture*: for this purpose, we use Dionaea, which a popular low-interaction honeypot, that mainly captures malware propagated through vulnerabilities in the Microsoft SMB services.
- *Malware classification*: as soon as malware is captured, it is automatically classified according to the network connections it attempts to perform to contact its command and control service (C&C) [3]. To this end, malware is run on a virtual machine without actual connection to the Internet but with a DNS service provided by the host machine. The queried DNS addresses and attempted connections are observed and recorded with the MWNA software tool briefly described in Section 2.1. This allows detecting malware with really unknown behavior thus avoiding the analysis of already known malware.
- *Analysis of malware network activity*: it is performed under the control of an operator using MWNA. The analysis focuses on identifying the C&C and detecting malicious activities.

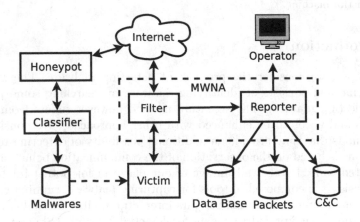

Fig. 1. Architecture of the platform

2.1   MWNA

MWNA (Malware Network Analyzer) runs on a gateway between a computer (real or virtual) infected by malware (the victim) and the Internet. It is composed of two programs communicating through TCP sockets, the *filter*, and the *reporter*:

– *The filter*: it uses the *netfilter_ queue* mechanism of Linux to intercept packets flowing through the network stack in the kernel. The process of packet matching can be specified by rules (drop, trace, higher-level analysis, etc.). Packets are analyzed up to the application level when necessary. It controls connection establishment, its termination, and DNS activity (queries and replies). A number of application-level protocols can be detected and at least partially analyzed even if they do not run on their standard ports: IRC, HTTP, SMTP. The HTTPS protocol is identified and verified up to the point it enters the encrypted mode (but certificates are not currently checked). The NTP, IPP, and the Netbios Name and Session service protocols are verified when they run on their standard ports. Unknown textual protocols can also be detected.

The *filter* includes a system of dynamically loaded plugins allowing to extend it with higher level functionalities that include monitoring and blocking of malicious activities:

- Interaction with C&C: in the current state of the program, C&C can mainly be detected as IRC-based protocols. C&C based on non standard textual or binary protocols and HTTP can also be detected with few false positives. When C&C interaction through IRC is detected, all communication between the victim and the attacker is recorded.
- ICMP and TCP scans are detected and blocked.
- Denial of Service attacks (DoS): TCP SYN flooding, UDP flooding, and HTTP flooding attacks are detected and blocked by dropping packets sent to the attacked host.
- Mail transmission attempts are detected and can optionally be blocked by resetting the connection to the mail server.
- Spam transmission can be detected based on attempts to send a mail through multiple relays or to multiple different destinations.
- The HTTP payload is analyzed to detect the transmission of Windows executables. The detection is based on the identification of executable headers and does not rely on the Content-type headers or file name extensions.

As the *filter* is interfaced with the kernel, it must be executed with the administrator privileges. Detected events are sent to the *reporter* using a very simple textual protocol.

– *The reporter*: it is in charge of displaying messages for the operator, recording events in a Sqlite database, storing communication traces in a file, and recording C&C interactions. It does not need to be executed with the administrator privileges.

The separation of MWNA into several processes has several advantages:

– As the *reporter* runs without administrator privileges, it can use high level tools such as database or graphic user interface without security risks.
– High latency operations (e.g. user interaction, disk I/O) are removed from the critical path of packet processing.

- Better performance can be achieved on multi-core architectures.
- The *reporter* can be run on a separate machine or on a production network, without security risks.
- The *reporter* could be eventually replaced with a program performing a fully automatic analysis of the malware network activity.

2.2   Detecting Malware Activities

In this section, we will present two examples of malware activities. In the first one, we will present the graphic interface of *Mwna* with the malware that at the first glance seems to attempt sending a spam. The second example is the malware actually sending spam.

2.3   Port Scanning Malware

Figure 2 presents a screen capture of the reporter while analyzing malware captured in December 2012. The title bar of the window shows the MD5 digest of the malware. The line under the menu bar shows that the C&C has been identified as IRC and presents the IP address and the port number.

The right text area under the line indicates the DNS replies. In the studied case, there is only a reply to a TXT query on lap.viridinikasihc.net and a query on the address of the host machine. The reply to the TXT query seems to be some kind of encrypted data, which should include the address of the C&C.

The left text area shows the detected malicious activities: in this case, an attempt to send a spam is detected, because a compromised machine tries to

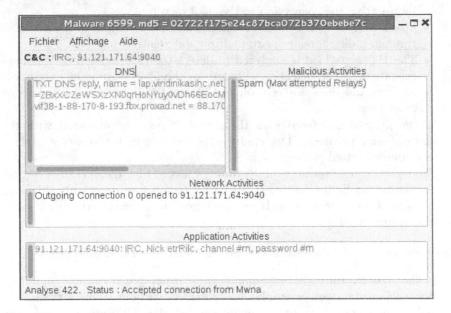

Fig. 2. Screen capture of Mwna

connect to different SMTP servers. All these attempts fail, as the access provider only allows connections to its own SMTP server.

The text area under the previous ones displays network activities: in this case, only the connection to the IRC server.

The bottom text area displays the application-level activities: in this case, the malware joins an IRC channel.

At this point, the tool indicates that spam transmission is attempted, but there are two problems:

- The addresses of the SMTP servers are not DNS resolved,
- There is not enough data exchanged to specify a spam payload and a list of recipients.

We have redirected the connections to the SMTP port to a program that emulates a SMTP server without actually transmitting messages, but we did not find any transmission once the connection is set up. Finally, if we disable the spam detection feature, we can see that these connection attempts are in fact scans on the SMTP port, probably with the goal of discovering open mail relays.

2.4 Spam Sending Malware

In this second example, the malware communicates with its C&C using a modified IRC protocol identified as an *unknown textual protocol*.

Four DNS queries try to find the mail servers of AOL, Yahoo, Google, and Hotmail, which seems typical for spam sending malware. Then, the malware downloads several files from HTTP servers. Five of them are Windows executables and two others are queries to get the official IP address and a domain name of the machine on which the malware runs.

Then, the malware attempts to connect to mail servers and spam transmission is detected.

As in the previous case, we have analyzed the malware while the SMTP traffic is redirected to a local program. We could see two other downloads that appear to be encrypted data, hence, the spam payload and the recipient list may be contained in these files or encapsulated in the downloaded executable files. 383 mails have been sent in 5 minutes using 83 connections to many mail relay addresses. In most connections, the malware only sent one mail, or no mail at all, but in 17 cases, it sent up to 164 emails. All these mails are advertisements for a russian site selling drugs.

2.5 Discussion

These two examples show that our platform allows to detect and identify malicious activities of malware. Spam transmissions seem to be the most frequent activity. In this case, we are able to gather enough data to determine the strategy of spamming tools and to intercept the spam payload.

3   Classification Method of Encrypted Skype Traffic

In this section, we present the second method for detecting malware activities. More specifically, we identify malicious flows concealed in encrypted TCP Skype traffic tunneled over the TLS/SSL protocol [4]. We have considered a worm called Worm.Win32.Skipi.b alias Skipi [5] that spreads over the Skype Instant Messaging (IM) system.

We apply a method for classifying Skype service flows [6,7] based on the Statistical Protocol IDentification (SPID) algorithm [8]. SPID is based on *traffic models* that contain a set of *attribute fingerprints* represented as probability distributions. They are created through frequency analysis of traffic properties called *attribute meters* of application layer data or flow features. An example of such an attribute meter is *byte frequency* that measures the frequency at which all of the possible 255 values occur in a packet. Other attribute meters defined in detail later include for instance byte offset, byte re-occurring, direction change, and packet size.

SPID operates in three steps. First, packets are classified into bi-directional flows. All connections are represented as 5-tuples according to the source IP address, source port, destination IP address, destination port, and transport layer protocol. However, only packets carrying data are significant, because the analysis is based on both the application layer data and flow features. Then, each flow is analyzed in terms of attribute meters to obtain a collection of attribute fingerprints associated with a particular type of traffic.

In the initial training phase, the method creates *traffic models*—attribute fingerprints representative for the traffic we want to detect. During the classification phase, the method computes attribute fingerprints on the flows to classify and compares them with traffic models by means of the Kullback-Leibler (K-L) divergence [9]:

$$D(P||Q) = K\text{-}L(P,Q) = \sum_{x \in X} P(x) log_2 \frac{P(x)}{Q(x)}. \tag{1}$$

The K-L divergence is a measure of the difference between two probability distributions $P(x)$ and $Q(x)$. $P(x)$ represents the distribution of a particular attribute of an observed flow and $Q(x)$ is the distribution corresponding to a known traffic model. Classification consists in comparing $P(x)$ with all known traffic models and selecting the protocol with the smallest average divergence $D(P||Q)$ and greater than a given threshold. We need to correctly set the divergence threshold to decrease the false positive rate for known traffic models—we only take into consideration the K-L divergence average values above the threshold.

In the first phase, it detects Skype traffic after a TCP three-way handshake based on the first five packets of the connection by considering some attribute meters reflecting application level data. Then, it changes the set of attribute meters to payload independent features to detect service flows in the Skype traffic: voice/video, skypeOut, chat, and file transfer. This phase requires a larger number of packets to analyze to be effective: our calibration sets this value to

Table 1. Attribute meters used in classification

No.	Attribute meter name	Inspected bytes per packet	Inspected packets per flow
1	byte-frequency	100	8
2	action-reaction of first bytes	3	6
3	byte value offset hash meter	32	4
4	first 4 packets byte reoccurring distance with byte	32	4
5	first 4 packets first 16 byte pairs	17	4
6	first 4 ordered direction packet size	0	4
7	first packet per direction first N byte nibbles	~8	1
8	packet size distribution	0	All
9	direction packet size distribution	0	All
10	byte pairs reoccurring count	32	All
11	first server packet first bit positions	~16	1

450 packets. Finally, the method considers more packets (the threshold is set to 760) to further distinguish between voice and video flows, and between file upload and download.

3.1   Attribute Meters for Skype

Table 1 presents the set of attribute meters that we have defined for classifying Skype traffic.

- **byte frequency:** in each packet it measures and returns the frequency of individual bytes in the payload. Encrypted data seems to have equally distributed byte frequencies, whereas the plain text may exhibit different distributions. The SSL protocol tends to provide some unencrypted information related to a session, such as SSL version, message type, compression method selected by the server, etc., in the first bytes of the encrypted packets.
- **action-reaction of first bytes:** it creates hash values based on the first 3 bytes of each packet that was sent in a different direction than the previous one. It is better to analyze packets sent alternately in different directions instead of looking at all packets, because we can easily analyze the request-response phase between a client and a server. The meter is especially useful in primary identification of a SSL Skype connection.
- **byte value offset hash:** it combines individual byte values in each packet with the offset at which the bytes are positioned. The meter considers up to 32 bytes of the 4 first packets. The SSL is one of the protocols that use several positions in particular packets (e.g. in Client Hello or Server Hello messages). As a result, the combination of bytes with their positions provides some additional information with respect to the byte frequency.
- **first 4 packets byte reoccurring distance with byte:** it creates a short hash value (usually a 4-bit representation) and combines it with the distance between the two occurrences. The measurement detects the bytes that occurred more than once within 16 previous bytes. It was specifically created to

identify banners in plain text packets like e.g. TT in HTTP GET and POST messages, but it also applies to the case of the encrypted SSL content.

- **first 4 packets first 16 byte pairs:** it combines neighboring bytes in a 16-bit value and converts to a 8 bit hash value (the size is determined by the fingerprint length). It analyzes only application layer data regardless of the flow information, i.e. packet size, directions, or inter-arrival times. The meter indicates that there are some specific, not random two-byte combinations like e.g. list compression methods supported by the client in the SSL Client Hello message sent to the server.

- **first 4 ordered direction packet size:** the meter returns the compressed version of the packet size that represents a range in which the packet lies instead of the exact value. Measurements are separately done for each of four first packets in connection and the returned value is associated with the packet direction and the order number. It is a flow based attribute created for early traffic recognition.

- **first packet per direction first N byte nibbles:** it analyzes the first packet in each direction and inspects its first few bytes depending on the fingerprint length (8 bytes for a fingerprint length of 256). It provides a measure combining the packet direction, byte offset, and a compact representation of the byte value so-called *nibble*, (it divides a byte into two 4-bit groups, performs an XOR calculation, and returns the resulting 4-bit value). The first packet in each direction and the first few bytes corresponding to these packets say a lot about the application layer protocol and might also provide some hidden information of the underlying service.

- **packet size distribution:** it computes the distribution of the packet size. It provides some hints about the encrypted flows, because the size of Skype packets is somehow deterministic depending on the type of traffic.

- **direction packet size distribution:** this attribute is very similar to the first 4 ordered direction packet size meter. The only difference is that it inspects all packets in a connection and does not mark each measurement with the order number of the packet in a connection. It is an example of a flow based attribute especially suitable for detailed Skype classification: it is able to classify flows in which packet sizes per direction are different, which enables to distinguish file upload from download.

- **byte pairs reoccurring count:** it detects bytes that reoccur in two consecutive packets. In addition, it takes into account the direction of a given packet and its predecessor.

- **first server packet first bit positions:** it looks into the first few bytes of the first packet coming from the server, inspects each bit, and returns the bit values with respect to the bit offset position. The idea is that when connecting to TCP-based services, the server sends some typical welcome messages.

3.2   Identification of Malicious Skype Flows

Finally, we want to test our detection method with malicious flows concealed in Skype traffic. We have considered a worm called Worm.Win32.Skipi.b alias

Skipi that spreads over the IM system by sending URL-embedded encrypted chat messages to all Skype contacts on a victim machine. We have selected an appropriate set of attribute meters to use in the SPID algorithm to detect malicious traffic.

Worms propagating in chat messengers have become one of security threats in recent years [10,11,12]. However, existing Internet worm detection mechanisms [13] cannot be directly applied to the detection of malicious flows spreading via instant messengers. The mechanisms cannot distinguish between the encrypted legitimate traffic and messages generated by worms: an infected user does nothing but sending correctly looking messages to other end users.

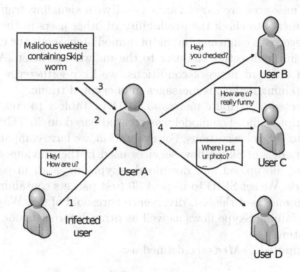

Fig. 3. Propagation of the Skipi worm

In our experiments, we obtain the ground truth information (the traffic generated by Skipi) by running the worm on a laptop having Skype installed. The Skype client had a small number of contacts so that it could easily spread the worm to them. Figure 3 illustrates the propagation process of Skipi through the Skype instant messenger. Let us assume that user A receives a chat message from one of his/her friends after the friend was infected by Skipi (Step 1). The worm message is composed of a selection of some text strings to convince the receiver to open a malicious link to a photo. An example of such a message sent by the worm is shown below:

```
On 30/03/2011, at 10:19, user wrote:
> how are u ? :)
On 30/03/2011, at 10:19, user wrote:
> I used photoshop and edited it
On 30/03/2011, at 10:19, user wrote:
```

```
> http://www.%infectedURL%.jpg
On 30/03/2011, at 10:19, user wrote:
> oops sorry please don't look there :S
On 30/03/2011, at 10:19, user wrote:
> :)
```

When user A clicks on the link to download the photo, it actually points to the URL where a copy of the Skipi worm is located (Step 2). Once the worm copy is downloaded (Step 3) and executed on the system, it starts to propagate by sending similar messages to all active entries in the contact list (Step 4). We focus on analyzing and detecting worm propagation traffic. We have observed that malicious messages are closely associated with signaling traffic: the client sends TCP segments to check the availability of other users in the contact list. As soon as, it receives a confirmation, Skipi immediately sends the chat messages containing the link redirecting the user to the malware location. After running the malware in different network conditions, we have gathered a collection of TCP flows containing malicious messages in encrypted traffic.

We have selected 6 attribute meters: 3, 7–11 in Table 1 to create the fingerprints of the Skipi traffic. The model was created based on 30 TCP connections corresponding to 1484 observations. For evaluation, we have compared the traffic model with 6 models of Skype flow services used in the previous classification, i.e. voice, video, file upload and download, skypeOut, and, in particular, the legal chat service. We set SPID to inspect 30 first packets containing payload in each connection and used the K-L divergence threshold of 0.8. We run the tests with traces containing Skype flows as well as other Internet traffic composed of various applications.

We have computed *F-Measure* defined as:

$$Precision = \frac{TP}{TP + FP}, \tag{2}$$

$$Recall = \frac{TP}{TP + FN}, \tag{3}$$

$$F\text{-}Measure = \frac{2 * Precision * Recall}{Precision + Recall}, \tag{4}$$

for all flows and for each of 6 selected attribute meters. The True Positive (TP) term refers to all malicious Skype flows that were correctly identified as Skipi, False Positives (FPs) refer to all flows that were incorrectly identified as Skipi traffic. Finally, False Negatives (FNs) represent all flows of Skipi traffic that were incorrectly identified as legitimate Skype service flows or other Internet traffic.

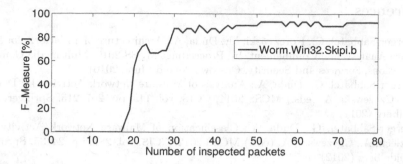

Fig. 4. Detection of the Skipi worm: the F-Measure in function of the number of inspected packets

Figure 4 presents the F-Measure in function of the number of inspected packets with payload: it rapidly rises after the 18th packet, while after inspecting 30 packets, the F-Measure is equal to 87.5% with Recall of 100%. This means themethod has detected all malicious flows with no False Negatives, which is early enough to take prevention actions such as blocking Skype traffic of the user sending malicious chat messages to all Skype contacts after the first attempt. The figure also shows that after the 45th packet, the F-Measure becomes flat due to the fact that two-way communication between the Skipi worm and the victim user contains between 40 and 140 packets depending on the message sent through the chat messenger.

4 Conclusions

In this paper, we have presented two methods of detecting malware that go beyond the traditional signature based detection. The first one is based on the observation of the communication behavior caused by suspected code. The detection uses a platform with tools for capturing malware, running code in a controlled environment, and analyzing their interactions with external entities. The second approach uses a method for detecting encrypted Skype traffic and classifying Skype service flows such as voice calls, skypeOut, video conferencing, chat, file upload and download in Skype traffic. The method is based on the Statistical Protocol IDentification (SPID) that analyzes statistical values of some traffic attributes. We have applied the method to identify malicious traffic—we have successfully detected the propagation of Worm.Win32.Skipi.b that spreads over the Skype messenger by sending infected messages to all Skype contacts on a victim machine.

Acknowledgments. This work was partially supported by the EC FP7 project INDECT under contract 218086.

References

1. Berger-Sabbatel, G., Korczyński, M., Duda, A.: Architecture of a Platform for Malware Analysis and Confinement. In: Proceedings MCSS 2010: Multimedia Communications, Services and Security, Cracow, Poland (June 2010)
2. Berger-Sabbatel, G., Duda, A.: Analysis of Malware Network Activity. In: Dziech, A., Czyżewski, A. (eds.) MCSS 2011. CCIS, vol. 149, pp. 207–215. Springer, Heidelberg (2011)
3. Berger-Sabbatel, G., Duda, A.: Classification of Malware Network Activity. In: Dziech, A., Czyżewski, A. (eds.) MCSS 2012. CCIS, vol. 287, pp. 24–35. Springer, Heidelberg (2012)
4. Dierks, T., Rescorla, E.: The Transport Layer Security (TLS) Protocol, Version 1.2. RFC 5246 (August 2008)
5. Cuong, N.C.: Skype-New Target of the Worm Spreading via IM (May 2010), http://blog.bkav.com
6. Korczyński, M.: Classifying Application Flows and Intrusion Detection in the Internet Traffic. PhD thesis, École Doctorale Mathématiques, Sciences et Technologies de l'Information, Informatique (EDMSTII), Grenoble, France (November 2012)
7. Korczyński, M., Duda, A.: Classifying Service Flows in the Encrypted Skype Traffic. In: 2012 IEEE International Conference on Communications, ICC 2012, pp. 1064–1068 (June 2012)
8. Hjelmvik, E., John, W.: Statistical Protocol Identification with SPID: Preliminary Results. In: Proceedings of 6th Swedish National Computer Networking Workshop (May 2009)
9. Kullback, S., Leibler, R.A.: On information and sufficiency. Annals of Mathematical Statistics 22, 49–86 (1951)
10. Leavitt, N.: Instant Messaging: A New Target for Hackers. Computer 38(7), 20–23 (2005)
11. Swoyer, S.: Enterprise Systems: IM Security Exploits Explode in 2007 (August 2008), http://www.esj.com
12. Kaspersky Lab Detects New IM Worms Capable of Spreading via Almost All Instant Messengers (August 2010), http://www.kaspersky.com
13. Yan, G., Xiao, Z., Eidenbenz, S.: Catching Instant Messaging Worms with Change-Point Detection Techniques. In: Proceedings of the 1st Usenix Workshop on Large-Scale Exploits and Emergent Threats, pp. 1–10. USENIX Association (2008)

Audio-Visual Surveillance System
for Application in Bank Operating Room

Józef Kotus[1], Kuba Lopatka[1], Andrzej Czyżewski[1], and Georgis Bogdanis[2]

[1] Gdańsk University of Technology, Faculty of Electronics,
Telecommunications and Informatics, Multimedia Systems Department, Gdańsk, Poland
[2] Informatic Systems Designing and Applications Agency Microsystem, Sopot, Poland
{joseph,klopatka,andcz}@multimed.org

Abstract. An audio-visual surveillance system able to detect, classify and to localize acoustic events in a bank operating room is presented. Algorithms for detection and classification of abnormal acoustic events, such as screams or gunshots are introduced. Two types of detectors are employed to detect impulsive sounds and vocal activity. A Support Vector Machine (SVM) classifier is used to discern between the different classes of acoustic events. The methods for calculating the direction of coming sound employing an acoustic vector sensor are presented. The localization is achieved by calculating the DOA (Direction of Arrival) histogram. The evaluation of the system based on experiments conducted in a real bank operating room is given. Results of sound event detection, classification and localization are given and discussed. The system proves efficient for the task of automatic surveillance of the bank operating room.

Keywords: sound detection, sound source localization, audio surveillance.

1 Introduction

An audio-visual surveillance system for application in bank operating room is presented. The system implements the acoustic event detection, classification and localization algorithms for recognizing safety threats. This work provides a continuation of the previous research in which the algorithms were developed [1, 2]. Here their practical application and evaluation in real conditions are presented. According to the concept diagram, presented in Fig. 1, the input signals originate from the multichannel acoustic vector sensor (AVS). Next, the signal processing is performed. Initially, the detection of acoustic events is carried out. Subsequently, the detected events are classified to determine if the event poses any threat or not. Finally, the acoustic direction of arrival (DOA) is determined using the multichannel signals from the AVS. The techniques for detection and classification, as well as the localization algorithm, are described in the next sections.

The algorithms operate in realistic conditions, with a significant level of disturbing noise and room reflections presence. In the following sections an attempt to assess the performance of the employed signal processing techniques in such difficult conditions is made. The results gathered from the analysis of live audio data and recorded situations including arranged threats are presented. It is shown that the performance of the system is sufficient to detect alarming situations.

A. Dziech and A. Czyżewski (Eds.): MCSS 2013, CCIS 368, pp. 107–120, 2013.

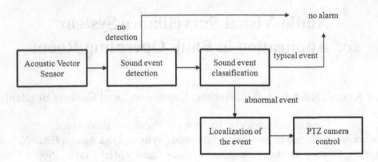

Fig. 1. Concept diagram of the audio-visual bank operating hall surveillance system

2   Acoustic Event Detection and Classification

In the state-of-the art research on acoustic event recognition the most popular approach is to employ generative (e.g. Gaussian Mixture Models or Hidden Markov Models) or discriminative (e.g. Support Vector Machines, Artificial Neural Networks) pattern recognition algorithms to discern between predefined types of sounds basing on the extraction or spectral, temporal or perceptual features [3-4]. Some works follow the so-called *detection by classification* approach, in which the classifier operates online and the decision concerning foreground acoustic event presence is made based on results of classification [4]. Another approach, denoted *detection and classification* separates the process into two operations – detection is responsible for separating the foreground event from the acoustic background; classification – for recognizing the type of detected sound [5]. In our work we follow the second approach. In consequtive subsections the algorithms for detecting and classifying acoustic events will be briefly introduced.

The bank operating hall is an indoor acoustic environment in which most sounds are generated by people and comprise:

-    background cocktail-party noise,
-    foreground voice activity,
-    stamping,
-    other sounds (e.g. chairs moving with a squeak, safes beeping, people steps, objects being put down on desks etc.).

These sounds are considered typical elements of the acoustic environment. We define the following classes of acoustic events in order to discern between them: *speech, scream, gunshot, stamp, chair, beep* and *other*. To detect and to recognize the events we use two types of detectors and one classification algorithm, which will be introduced in the following subsections.

2.1   Detection

Two types of detectors are employed. *Impulse detector* is designed to detect short impulsive sounds (e.g. stamps) [2]. *Speech detector* is intended to detect tonal sounds, and voice activity in particular [1]. The impulse detector algorithm is based on comparing the instantaneous equivalent sound level L with the threshold t. The sound level is calculated according to the formula as in Eq. (1):

$$L[dB] = 20 \cdot \log\left(\sqrt{\frac{1}{N} L_{norm} \sum_{n=1}^{N} (x[n])^2} \right) \tag{1}$$

where $x[n]$ represents the discrete time signal and $N = 512$ samples (at 48000 samples per second) equals to the length of the analysis frame. The parameter L_{norm} (normalization level) assures that the result is expressed in dB SPL (relative to 20 µPa). The speech detector is based on the parameter peak-valley difference (PVD) defined in Eq. (2) [6]:

$$PVD = \frac{\sum_{k=1}^{N/2} X(k) \cdot P(k)}{\sum_{k=1}^{N/2} P(k)} - \frac{\sum_{k=1}^{N/2} X(k) \cdot (1 - P(k))}{\sum_{k=1}^{N/2} (1 - P(k))} \tag{2}$$

The PVD parameter is calculated from the signal power spectrum $X(k)$ calculated in 4096 sample frames. The vector P contains locations of the spectral peaks. In order to calculate the parameter value, locations of the spectral peaks must be known. Herewith, we employed a simple search algorithm capable of finding the spectral peaks. The detection threshold t is obtained by adding a 10 dB margin to the average sound level in case of impulse detection or multiplying the median PVD value by 2 in case of speech detector. The threshold is smoothed using exponential averaging according to Eq. (3):

$$t = t_{old} \cdot (1 - \alpha) + t_{new} \cdot \alpha \tag{3}$$

The exponential averaging enables an adaptation of the detection algorithm. The new threshold value t_{new} utilized in Eq. 3 is introduced in order to consider the changes in the acoustic background. The constant α is related to the detector adaptation time and is obtained from the formula in Eq. (4), which in this case provides an assumed value of 10 minutes, yielding α equal to $1.8 \cdot 10^{-5}$.

$$T_{adapt}[s] = \frac{N}{SR \cdot \alpha} \tag{4}$$

where SR denotes the sampling rate – in this case 48000 S/s and N denotes the length of the detector frame – 512 samples for the impulse detector and 4096 samples for the speech detector.

2.2   Classification

A Support Vector Machine classifier (SVM) was used to classify the events. The seven classes of events (*speech, scream, gunshot, stamp, chair, beep, other*) are recognised. Therefore, a multiclass SVM with 1-vs-all approach was employed. A set of 55 features was used for the classification. Further details concerning classification and calculation of the features can be found in related publications [7-11].

3   Acoustic Events Localization

Acoustic vector sensors were first applied to acoustic source localization in the air by Raangs et al. in 2002, who used measured sound intensity vector to localize a single monopole source [12]. A more recent development is the application of acoustic vector sensors to the problem of localizing multiple sources in the far field. In 2009, Basten et al. applied the MUSIC method to localize up to two sources using a single acoustic vector sensor [13]. In the same year Wind et al. applied the same method to localize up to four sources using two acoustic vector sensors [14, 15].

The authors' experiences with the sound source localization based on the sound intensity methods performed in the time domain or in the frequency domain were presented in the previous papers [16, 17]. The developed algorithm used for acoustic events localization works in the frequency domain. Its block diagram is depicted in Fig. 2. The multichannel acoustic vector sensor produces the following signals: sound pressure p and three orthogonal particle velocity components u_x, u_y, u_z. The essential functionality of the localization algorithm is its connection with the acoustic event detection module (described in details in section 2.1). The detection module (block 4 indicated by gray shading) operates on acoustic pressure signal only. The detection procedure is performed in parallel to the localization process. Signal set by the detection module affects the operation of the units 5, 7 and 10.

In the block 2 the acoustical signals are buffered and prepared for FFT (Fast Fourier Transform) calculation. The Hanning window was applied. Subsequently, the 4096 point FFT calculation for each signal is performed, with the sampling frequency equal to 48 kS/s (frequency resolution: 11.7 Hz). Such parameters provide a sufficient spectral resolution for sound source localization. The overlap degree was equal to 50%. The FFT calculation was performed for each acoustic component (p, u_x, u_y, u_z), separately. This operation yields transformed signals: $X_p(i)$, $X_{ux}(i)$, $X_{uy}(i)$, $X_{uz}(i)$, where i (ranging from 0 to 4095) denotes the index of the spectral bin. The matrix X now contains information about the direction of arrival of every spectral component of the signal.

$$\mathbf{X} = \begin{bmatrix} X_p(i) & X_{ux}(i) & X_{uy}(i) & X_{uy}(i) \end{bmatrix} = \begin{bmatrix} \Im\{p(n)\} & \Im\{u_x(n)\} & \Im\{u_y(n)\} & \Im\{u_z(n)\} \end{bmatrix} \quad (5)$$

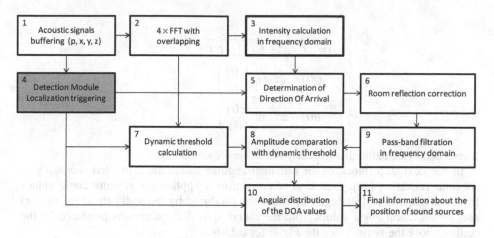

Fig. 2. The block diagram of the proposed algorithm

To extract the information about DOA from the signals in the frequency domain, the sound intensity in the frequency domain is computed (block 3 of Fig. 2). The sound intensity vector is defined and calculated according to Eq. (6).

$$\vec{I}(i) = \begin{bmatrix} I_x(i) \\ I_y(i) \\ I_z(i) \end{bmatrix} = \begin{bmatrix} X_p(i) \cdot \overline{X_{ux}(i)} \\ X_p(i) \cdot \overline{X_{uy}(i)} \\ X_p(i) \cdot \overline{X_{uz}(i)} \end{bmatrix} \tag{6}$$

where:

$I_x(i)$ – sound intensity component for x direction for i-th spectral components,
$X_p(i)$ – coefficients of complex spectrum for i-th spectral components for acoustic pressure signal,
$\overline{X_{ux}(i)}$, conjugated spectrum coefficients for particle velocity in x direction.

The calculation of sound intensity components in the frequency domain is the most important part of the localization algorithm. These data are used in the block 5. Before the calculation of the direction of arrival for particular frequencies, the signal from the detection module is included in the calculation.

The positive state on the detection module output initiates the following actions:

- the dynamic threshold calculation in the frequency domain is suspended (block 7),
- time distribution of direction of arrival (DOA) is prepared to be calculated (block 10),
- the calculation process of DOA for detected sound event begins (block 5).

In the block 5 the angular values for azimuth and elevation for i-th spectral components are computed according to Eq. (7):

$$\begin{cases} r(i) = \sqrt{I_x(i)^2 + I_y(i)^2 + I_z(i)^2} \\ \varphi(i) = \arctan\left(\dfrac{I_x(i)}{I_y(i)}\right) \\ \theta(i) = \arcsin\left(\dfrac{I_z(i)}{r(i)}\right) \end{cases} \qquad (7)$$

where $\varphi(i)$ is the azimuth angle, $\theta(i)$ and is the elevation angle.

In the next step (block 6) the obtained angular values are corrected according to specular reflection [18]. This kind of correction is applied for azimuth angle values from the range: 0 to 180 degrees (reflections produced by the wall behind the sensor) and for elevation angle values from the range: 0 to -90 (reflections produced by the ceiling above the sensor) -see the Fig. 5 for details.

The most of the acoustic energy for the speech signal is contained in the frequency range from 200 to 4000 Hz. For better separation of the considered speech signal from the other disturbing components the additional filtration in the frequency domain was applied, calculated in the block 9. At the output of this block DOA values are limited to the frequency range from 200 to 4000 Hz. After that the next step of the localization algorithm can be executed, within the block 8. In such a case the data from blocks 7 and 9 are used. For a better understanding this step the explanation of block 7 is provided below. The computation of the dynamic threshold is performed for all frequency components in the FFT spectrum independently, according to Eq. (8):

$$\left|X_{p\_th}[n]\right| = \left|X_{p\_old}[n]\right| \cdot (1 - \alpha) + \left|X_{p\_new}[n]\right| \cdot \alpha \qquad (8)$$

where: $|X_{p\_th}[n]|$ - is the magnitude of the acoustic pressure which will be used to calculate the dynamic threshold, n – component number of the FFT spectrum, indices old and new mean the earlier and the present value of $|X_p[n]|$, respectively and the constant α is related to the spectrum adaptation time and in this case equal to 0.05.

The time averaging process is carried out when the detector module returns 0 (no event detected). As it was mentioned before, the averaging process is suspended when the event detection occurs. In that case the final average values are used as the dynamic threshold.

In the block 8 the values from the block 9 are compared with the dynamic threshold obtained from the block 7 according to the condition expressed by formula (9):

$$L_{p\_event}[n] \geq L_{p\_th}[n] + 10 \qquad (9)$$

where: L_{p_event} – sound pressure level for considered acoustic event, L_{p_th} – sound pressure level of dynamic threshold, n – point number of the FFT spectrum.

If the condition expressed by Eq. (9) is true for a given FFT component, the DOA values computed in the block 9 (corrected and filtered azimuth and elevation values for particular FFT components) are used to compute the angular distribution of azimuth and elevation. This operation is performed in the block 10. It is important to emphasize that the azimuth and elevation distributions are prepared to be calculated every time when a new acoustic event is detected (because the algorithm is working in the real time, the data computed for the last event are erased and the new empty tables are prepared). Both angular distributions (both for azimuth and elevation) are computed using the sound intensity value for given angular values according to (10):

$$\begin{cases} F_A[\varphi] = \sum I_\varphi \\ F_E[\theta] = \sum I_\theta \end{cases} \tag{10}$$

where $F_A[\varphi]$ is the azimuth distribution, $F_E[\theta]$ is the elevation distribution, I_φ – the intensity value for given azimuth angle, I_θ – the intensity value for given elevation angle.

Finally, the values stored in the tables $F_A[\varphi]$ and $F_E[\theta]$ are smoothed by means of weighted moving average and Hanning window coefficients (window length was equal to 5), according to (11):

$$\begin{cases} F_{SA}[\varphi] = \sum_{n=-2}^{n=2} F_A[\varphi + n] \cdot h_n \\ F_{SE}[\theta] = \sum_{n=-2}^{n=2} F_E[\theta + n] \cdot h_n \end{cases} \tag{11}$$

where: $F_{SA}[\varphi]$ is the smoothed azimuth distribution, $F_{SE}[\theta]$ is the smoothed elevation distribution, n – index number, h_n – Hanning window coefficients (window length was equal to 5 frames).

The maximum values of the tables $F_{SA}[\varphi]$ and $F_{SE}[\theta]$ indicate the current position of the considered acoustic event.

4   Results

4.1   Detection and Classification Results

First, an experiment was conducted in order to assess the detection and the classification of typical acoustic events. A 13-hour-long signal registered in the bank operating hall was analysed (recorded from 7:00 a.m. to 8:00 p. m.). The ground truth data concerning the position of sound sources were unknown. The detailed results of sound source localization were presented in section 4.2. The results of event detection are presented in Tab. 1. In total 1026 acoustic events were detected. It is visible that stamping (547 detections) are the prevailing sounds. Other events are also frequently present (368 detections). Only 84 speech events were recognised, which can be explained by the fact that speech is often present in the background as cocktail-party noise and the detectors adapt to that background by adjusting the detection threshold according to Eqs. 3 and 4. The sound of moving chairs and money safe beeps were seldom detected (23 and 4 occurrences, respectively). No threatening sound events were detected during that period.

Table 1. Number of detected events

Type of event:	speech	other	stamp	chair	beep
number of detecteed events:	84	368	547	23	4

total: **1026**

In Fig. 3 the distribution of events per hour of operation is presented. It is visible that during the early hours – 7 to 9 a. m. – other sounds are more frequent than stamping. Stamping becomes more frequent during the operating hours, which are 9 a.m.to 6 p. m.. Information about the movement in the bank can also be derived from the event distribution. The peak hour appears to be on 1 p. m.. Speech events are evenly distributed, since they are caused by both: the clients and the staff of the bank, who are present during the whole period.

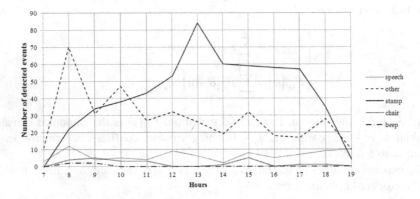

Fig. 3. Distribution of detected events per operating hour

Another important aspect is the level of the acoustic background. As it was stated in the previous sections, the threshold of acoustic event detection is adaptive, i. e. it follows the changes of sound level in the environment. The changes of the detection threshold of both detection algorithms employed are presented in Fig. 4. Again, it is visible that the peak hour is around 1 p.m. to 2 p. m.. The SPL level of the background and the median PVD reach a maximum. During the early and the late hours the threshold is lowered, which enables a detection of some more subtle sound events.

To assess the efficiency of threatening events detection, a hazardous situation was arranged. 17 people took part in an experiment organised in a real bank operating hall. The arranged situations included shouting, screams, typical conversation and robbery simulation with the use of a gun. A noise gun was used to generate gunshot sounds. A 31-minute-long signal was registered and then analysed. 74 events were detected. Sounds belonging to the following classes were emitted: *speech, scream, gunshot* and *other*. The analysis of the classification results is presented in Tab. 2. It can be observed that the threatening events are recognised with an acceptable accuracy. However, the speech sounds are often confused with other acoustic events.

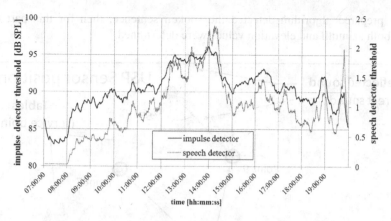

Fig. 4. Changes in detection threshold during operating hours

The analysis of the classification results is presented in Tab. 2. It can be observed that the threatening events are recognised with an acceptable accuracy. However, again speech sounds are often confused with other events. All gunshots were correctly classified, although only four shots were emitted. It is worth noting that the events in this experiment were recognised in fully realistic conditions, namely in the presence of noise (mostly cocktail-party noise).

Table 2. Results of recognition of threatening events

clasified as →	speech	scream	gunshot	other	precision	recall
Speech	24	7	0	10	1	0.58
Scream	0	21	0	4	0.75	0.84
Gunshot	0	0	4	0	1	1
Other	0	0	0	4	0.22	1
			overall correctly classified:		[53/74]	71.6%

4.2 Acoustic Events Localization Results

In the previous section the detection and classification results were presented. In this section the detection and localization functionality of the developed solution were shown. All experiments were conducted in the bank operating room The ground truth data of sound source position were available. First of all, the detection and localization tests for a single speaker were performed. The speaker was located successively in various customer service points (points 7 and 9 in Fig. 5) and the spoken sequence consisted of counting from 1 to 10. In Fig. 5 the layout of the bank operating room was shown. The position of the USP Sensor, direct sound and reflected sound paths were also depicted. The group of gray rectangles indicates the position of customers service places (tables and chairs). The size of the room: x: 20, y: 18, z: 3.5 m. 20 persons took part in the experiments.

The prepared algorithm detected the spoken sentence, then for this part of the signal both azimuth and elevation values were determined.

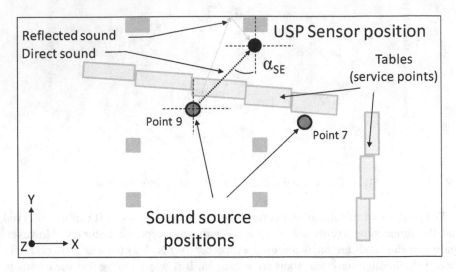

Fig. 5. Speaker positions during the sound source detection and localization experiments

The utterances were repeated three times for each particular point during this experiment. As was mentioned in section 3, only detected sound event is used for computing the azimuth and elevation values. It means that localization process is based only on the parts of the signal in which sound events were detected by the detection module (see the detection algorithm – section 2.1 and localization algorithm in section 3). In Fig. 6 the speaker detection results are depicted.

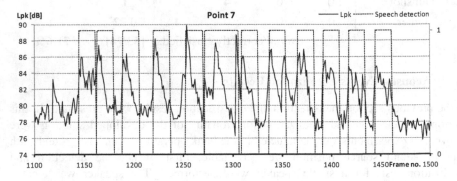

Fig. 6. Speaker detection results obtained in point 7. This signal triggered the sound source localization algorithm.

Two kinds of computation were done. First, the room reflection correction was disabled. In the second analysis the room reflections were considered. The sample results represented by the angular distributions (for azimuth and elevation) are presented in Fig. 7 (the reflection correction was disabled) and in Fig. 8 (the reflection correction was enabled). The ground truth data are also depicted. The gray dot indicates the point 7 and the black rhombus - point 9, respectively.

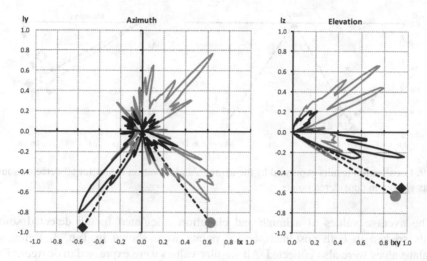

Fig. 7. Sample angular distributions for both: azimuth and elevation obtained for two speaker positions

Localization results for the same signals, however analyzed with the reflection correction were shown in Fig. 8. Imaginary sound sources were reduced, so therefore the proper position of the considered sound sources is indicated. It proves that the reflection correction is an essential part of the localization algorithm.

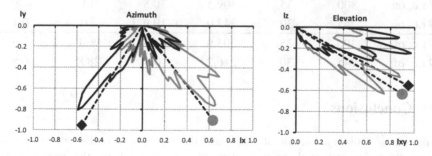

Fig. 8. Sample angular distributions both for azimuth and elevation obtained for two speaker positions

All localization results for every detected sentence are presented in Fig. 9. The average values of azimuth and elevation for considered speaker positions were calculated. They are presented in Fig. 9 .The grey empty circle corresponds to the position 7, the black empty rhombus indicates the position 9. It is important to emphasize that the obtained average angle values are very close to the reference points.

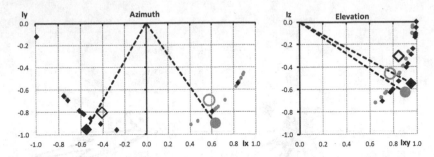

Fig. 9. Localization results expressed by the azimuth and elevation values for all detected sound events spoken in considered points

The average values of azimuth and elevation calculated for all detected sound events spoken in both customer service points were shown in Tab. 3. Reference angular values were also collected. All angular values were expressed in degrees. Tab. 3 contains also the estimated localization error (defined as a difference between the ground truth data and the calculated angles) for both settings: with and without reflection correction.

Table 3. Average results of sound source localization for particular points

Source	Ground Truth		Measurement results		Localization error	
Position	Azimuth	Elevation	Azimuth	Elevation	Azimuth	Elevation
P 7 r.c. on	300	35	309.5	30.8	9.5	4.2
P 9 r.c. on	245	30	243.0	19.9	2.0	10.1
P 7 r.c. off	300	35	203.9	-14.9	96.1	49.9
P 9 r.c. off	245	30	216.2	-0.8	28.8	30.8

5   Conclusions

On the basis of obtained results it was found that accurate acoustic event detection enables preparing essential acoustic data that were used by the sound source localization algorithm. The designed and implemented algorithm of sound source localization was practically tested in the real acoustic conditions. It was shown that the obtained average values of azimuth and elevation were close to the Ground Truth values. The error was less than 10 degrees for considered speaker positions.

It was shown that sound reflections inside operating room can seriously disturb the localization process. The proposed room acoustics influence correction procedure, which allows for obtaining better results, despite the presence of noticeable sound reflections.

The proposed methodology can significantly improve the functionality of the traditional surveillance monitoring systems. Application of acoustic vector sensor can be useful for localization of detected sound events. The described method can be applied to surveillance systems for monitoring and visualising the acoustic field of a specified area. The direction of arrival information can be used to control the Pan-Tilt-Zoom (PTZ) camera to automatically point it towards the direction of the detected sound source.

Acoustic modality offers many interesting functionalities in the automating detection and classification of hazardous situations. It is worth to emphasize that the proposed method can be a useful tool also during the offline forensic audio analysis.

Acknowledgements. Research is subsidized by the European Commission within FP7 project "INDECT" (Grant Agreement No. 218086). The presented work has been also co-financed by the European Regional Development Fund under the Innovative Economy Operational Programme, INSIGMA project no. POIG.01.01.02-00-062/09.

References

1. Łopatka, K., Kotus, J., Czyżewski, A.: Application of vector sensors to acoustic surveillance of a public interior space. Archives of Acoustics 36(4), 851–860 (2011)
2. Kotus, J., Łopatka, K., Czyżewski, A.: Detection and localization of selected acoustic events in 3d acoustic field for smart surveillance applications. Multimedia Tools and Applications (2012) (published online)
3. Cowling, M., Sitte, R.: Comparison of techniques for environmental sound recognition. Pattern Recognition Letters 24, 2895–2907 (2003)
4. Valenzise, G., Gerosa, L., Tagliasacchi, M., Antonacci, F., Sarti, A.: Scream and gunshot detection and localization for audio-surveillance systems. In: IEEE Conference on Advanced Video and Signal Based Surveillance, London, August 5–7, pp. 21–26 (2007)
5. Temko, A., Nadeu, C.: Acoustic event detection in meeting room environments. Pattern Recognition Letters 30, 1281–1288 (2009)
6. Yoo, I.-C., Yook, D.: Robust voice activity detection using the spectral peaks of vowel sounds. ETRI Journal 31(4), 451–453 (2009)
7. Zhuang, X., Zhou, X., Hasegawa-Johnson, M., Huang, T.: Real-world acoustic event detection. Pattern Recognition Letters 31, 1543–1551 (2010)
8. Rabaoui, A., et al.: Using robust features with multi-class SVMs to classify noisy sounds. In: International Symposium on Communications, Control and Signal Processing, Malta, March 12–14 (2008)
9. Łopatka, K., Zwan, P., Czyżewski, A.: Dangerous sound event recognition using support vector machine classifiers. In: Nguyen, N.T., Zgrzywa, A., Czyżewski, A. (eds.) Adv. in Multimed. and Netw. Inf. Syst. Technol. AISC, vol. 80, pp. 49–57. Springer, Heidelberg (2010)

10. Zwan, P., Czyzewski, A.: Verification of the parameterization methods in the context of automatic recognition of sounds related to danger. Journal of Digital Forensic Practice 3(1), 33–45 (2010)
11. Peeters, G.: A large set of audio features for sound description (similarity and classification) in the cuidado project. CUIDADO IST Project Report 54 (version 1.0), 1-25 (2004)
12. Raangs, R., Druyvesteyn, W.F.: Sound source localization using sound intensity measured by a three dimensional PU probe. In: AES Munich (2002)
13. Basten, T., de Bree, H.-E., Druyvesteyn, E.: Multiple incoherent sound source localization using a single vector sensor ICSV16, Krakow, Poland (2009)
14. Wind, J.W., Tijs, E., de Bree, H.-E.: Source localization using acoustic vector sensors, a MUSIC approach, NOVEM, Oxford (2009)
15. Wind, J.W.: Acoustic Source Localization, Exploring Theory and Practice. PhD Thesis, University of Twente, Enschede, The Netherlands (2009)
16. Kotus, J.: Application of passive acoustic radar to automatic localization, tracking and classification of sound sources. Information Technologies 18, 111–116 (2010)
17. Kotus, J.: Multiple sound sources localization in real time using acoustic vector sensor. In: Dziech, A., Czyżewski, A. (eds.) MCSS 2012. Communications in Computer and InfSCCISormation Science, vol. 287, pp. 168–179. Springer, Heidelberg (2012)
18. Weyna, S.: Identification of Reflection and Scattering Effects in Real Acoustic Flow Field. Archives of Acoustics 28(3), 191–203 (2003)

Depth Estimation in Image Sequences
in Single-Camera Video Surveillance Systems

Aleksander Lamża[1], Zygmunt Wróbel[1], and Andrzej Dziech[2]

[1] Department of Biomedical Computer Systems, Institute of Computer Science,
Faculty of Computer and Materials Science, University of Silesia in Katowice,
ul. Bedzinska 39, 41–200 Sosnowiec, Poland
{aleksander.lamza,zygmunt.wrobel}@us.edu.pl
[2] Department of Telecommunications of the AGH University of Science
and Technology, al. Mickiewicza 30, 30- 059 Krakow, Poland

Abstract. Depth estimation plays a key role in numerous applications, including video surveillance, target tracking, robotics or medicine. The standard method of obtaining depth information is to use stereovision systems, which require at least two cameras. In some applications this is a big hindrance because of dimensions, costs or power consumption. Therefore, there is a need to develop an efficient method of depth estimation that can be applied in single-camera vision systems. In the literature several techniques to accomplish this task can be found. However, they require either modification of the camera (in the mirror-based methods) or changing the parameters of the lens (in the focus-based methods). In this paper a new method based on image sequences from cameras with standard fixed-focal-length and fixed-focus lens is presented.

Keywords: depth estimation, optical flow, video surveillance, single-camera vision.

1 Introduction

The main objective was to propose a method that allows estimation of distance in vision systems using a single camera. Surveillance systems can be the main application of such method. It enables the use of existing surveillance infrastructure and the introduction of additional features of spatial analysis for the scenes being observed.

The primary assumption was to use video sequences from a single camera. Therefore, what will follow is a short overview of only these depth estimation methods that do not require the use of more than one camera.

One group of techniques is based on modifying the internal camera parameters. In Depth from Focus (DFF) and Depth from Defocus (DFD) methods, it is assumed that the images are taken from the same point of view, but with different focus settings. The idea of this methods is based on the concept of depth of field, which is a consequence of the inability of cameras to simultaneously focus on the planes on the scene at different depths. The depth of field of a camera

A. Dziech and A. Czyżewski (Eds.): MCSS 2013, CCIS 368, pp. 121–129, 2013.

with a given focus value corresponds to the distance between the farthest and the nearest planes on the scene, in relation to the camera, whose points appear with a satisfactory definition in acquired images, according to a given criterion. At each instant, a lens can exactly focus the points in only one plane, called the object plane [4,12].

Another group of techniques involves supplementing the camera optical system. A common approach is to attach a mirror system to the lens, which gives the original and displaced image. Thus it is possible to use methods similar to those which are used in classical stereovision [8,9].

Due to the limitations that are associated with these methods, a new method was developed which can be used in existing video systems, for example in video sureillance systems.

2   Optical Flow Estimation and Objects Detection

In the first step moving objects should be detected. For this purpose, optical flow estimation is performed, and then, on the basis of the result, motion extraction and further object detection are performed.

In a typical one-camera vision systems, two images are taken by the camera separated by a discrete time interval Δt. What may be observed at each point is the change of point's intensity value $\Delta I(x, y)$ during this time interval. Optical flow is a vector field describing this intensity change by indicating the motion of features from one image to the other.

The optical flow estimation algorithm applied in our method is based on the algorithm proposed by Brox and Bruhn [2]. The starting point for optical flow estimation is to assume that pixel intensity is not changed by the displacement:

$$I(x, y, t) = I(x + u, y + v, t + 1), \tag{1}$$

where I denotes a two-dimensional rectangular gray-scale image, and $d = (u, v, 1)$ is the displacement vector between two consecutive images: at time t and $t+1$ which is to be calculated.

In real images it is not possible to ensure constancy of pixels intensity. Therefore, small variations should be allowed, what can be achieved by using a gradient. In this way the calculated vector does not depend on the pixel values. The criterion from eq. 1 takes the following form:

$$\nabla I(x, y, t) = \nabla I(x + u, y + v, t + 1), \tag{2}$$

where $\nabla = (\delta_x, \delta_y)^T$ is the spatial gradient. For reasons of simplification, it must be assumed that the vector d is relatively small. Then the image at time $t + 1$ can be approximated by:

$$I(x, y, t + 1) \approx I(x, y, t) + \nabla I(x, y, t) \cdot d. \tag{3}$$

Thus, the estimation for vector d is then:

$$d \approx \frac{I\left(x,\, y,\, t+1\right) - I\left(x,\, y,\, t\right)}{\nabla I\left(x,\, y,\, t\right)}. \tag{4}$$

Of course, vector d can not be recovered from one gradient constraint since there is one equation with two unknowns, u and v [3]. The intensity gradient constrains the flow to a one parameter family of velocities along a line in velocity space. One common way to further constrain u is to use gradient constraints from nearby pixels (window W), assuming they share the same velocity. With many constraints there may be no velocity that simultaneously satisfies them all, so instead the velocity that minimizes the constraint errors should be found. The least-squares (LS) estimator minimizes the squared errors:

$$\sum_{(x,y)\in W} \left(I\left(x,\, y,\, t+1\right) - I\left(x,\, y,\, t\right) - \nabla I\left(x,\, y,\, t\right) \cdot d\right)^2. \tag{5}$$

The results of applying the algorithm described, including the dispacement vectors as well as motion flow visualization, are presented in Fig. 1.

Fig. 1. Optical flow estimation: (a) one frame from a sequence; (b) displacement vectors; (c) flow visualization. Image sequence from Middlebury dataset [6].

2.1 Motion Regions Extraction

Due to the nature of optical flow, the estimation is subject to noise. Therefore, it is necessary to filter out the values that introduce noise to motion information. To do this, all $\parallel d \parallel$ values are first normalized to a range $[0, 1]$, and then every value below the threshold T_α are set to zero. For the optical flow method used here the optimal value of T_α is 0.2.

Based on the calculated displacement vector matrix, motion regions can be extracted. For this purpose, the slope (s) should be determined for each vector $d = (u, v)$:

$$s = \frac{u}{v}. \tag{6}$$

After obtaining the slopes, the regions are segmented based on the direction of motion (indicated by the s value). In Fig. 2 a visualization of optical flow is presented (top) as well as the extracted regions for four directions: from left to right, from right to left, upward and downward.

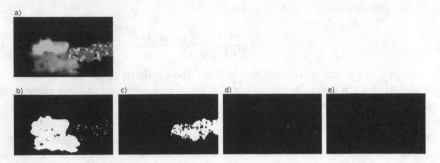

Fig. 2. Results of motion detection in four directions: (a) an input frame; (b) right to left motion; (c) left to right motion; (d) upward motion; (e) downward motion

2.2 Objects Detection

The next step is to extract moving objects from the sequence of images. For this purpose, the areas obtained in the preceding step are used. Every area is approximated by the smallest rectangle (bounding box) containing this area. This process is applied to regions extracted in four directions. Figure 3 demonstrates the results for two directions.

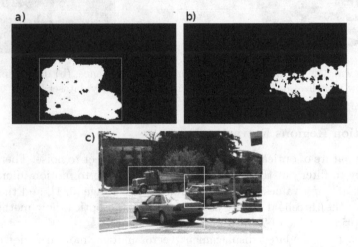

Fig. 3. Motion areas bounding boxes: (a) for right to left motion; (b) for left to right motion; (c) a frame from the video sequence with bounding boxes

Figure 3 shows that a single large area comprising a car and a truck was created. This happened because the vector d of both objects was classified as a movement to the left (due to the slight movement of the car, which from this perspective can be considered as a motion to the left). Such situations have to be eliminated before further steps of the algorithm. To achieve this, a correction coefficient can be entered.

Fig. 4. Improved motion areas bounding boxes

Coefficient c depending on the module of vector d has been proposed. Thresholds for c are determined based on the histogram of $\| d \|$ for every extracted area. The result of modifying the algorithm is shown in Fig. 4.

3   Depth Estimation

The primary objective of the method is the estimation of depth based on sequences of 2-dimensional images. The method determines the relative location of objects in 3-dimensional space and, when additional conditions are met, absolute position of objects.

3.1   Relative Object Position

In order to determine the objects' relative position in 3-dimensional space, the intersection of bounding boxes is analyzed. The method is based on the determination of the sequence in which the boxes intersect. For that purpose, the coordinates of the boxes and their intersections have to be determined. The previously selected areas of movement (masks) are overlapped on the intersecting subsets. As a result, the information on the objects' sequence is obtained. The disadvantage of the solution is the inability to determine the objects' sequence if the bounding boxes do not intersect.

3.2   Absolute Object Position

If we assume that the camera's inclination and its vertical position are known (and constant), it is possible to estimate the absolute distance of objects to the camera. In most public surveillance systems these conditions can be easily met (see fig. 5). Importantly, for the case described here, the optical axis of the camera may not be parallel to the level of the ground under surveillance.

The distance of the object to the camera (D) is calculated based on the distance between the bottom edge of the object (d_p) and the bottom edge of the image. From geometric relationships one gets:

$$D = h \cdot \frac{1 - A(d_p) \cdot \tan\theta \cdot \tan\frac{\psi}{2}}{A(d_p) \cdot \tan\frac{\psi}{2} + \tan\theta}, \tag{7}$$

where θ is the inclination of the camera, ψ is the vertical angle of view, h is the vertical position of the camera and:

$$A(d_p) = \left(1 - \frac{2d_p}{h_p}\right), \tag{8}$$

where d_p is the distance between the bottom edge of the object and the bottom edge of the image, and h_p is a height of the image. The distance D is calculated as a function of the tangent of two angles (inclination of the camera and the vertical angle of view) as well as vertical position of the camera. Both of these values must be selected individually based on the size of the monitored area. Because a situation must be avoided where the optical axis of the camera intersects the monitored area, the following relation must be held:

$$\tan\left(\theta + \frac{\psi}{2}\right) < \frac{D_{max}}{h}, \tag{9}$$

where D_{max} is the maximum viewing distance.

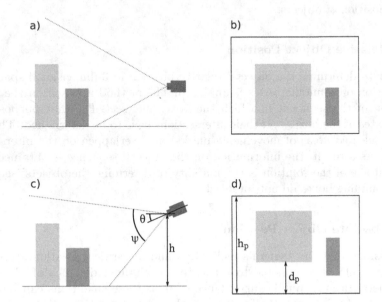

Fig. 5. Impact of inclination of the camera on the planar projection of scene: (a and b) optical axis parallel to ground, (c and d) optical axis inclined at angle θ

4 Experimental Results

In order to verify the method tests were performed with the sequences of both synthetic and real images. Sequences available in public datasets have been used: Middlebury [1,6], MIT Traffic Data Set [7,11] and QMUL Junction Dataset [5,10]. The results of the algorithm were compared with the available or prepared ground-truth data.

Below the test results for each class of images: synthetic and real are presented. For each sequence the depth estimation error, which is defined as:

$$E = 1 - \frac{\sum H_c}{H_g \cdot n}, \tag{10}$$

where H_c is the number of correct estimations per frame, H_g is the number of estimations from ground-truth, and n is the number of frames, was calculated.

In Table 1 the results for the estimation errors of the synthetic sequences (s1 to s5) are presented.

Table 1. Depth estimation error for synthetic image sequences

Images sequence	Length [frames]	Error E
s1	8	0.10
s2	8	0.08
s3	10	0.11
s4	10	0.12
s5	8	0.08

Table 2 presents the results for the estimation errors of the real sequences (r1 to r5) using the algorithm for relative object positioning.

Table 2. Depth estimation error for real image sequences (relative object position)

Images sequence	Length [frames]	Error E
r1	120	0.39
r2	80	0.28
r3	65	0.51
r4	125	0.40
r5	90	0.36

Table 3 presents the results for the estimation errors of the real sequences (the same as above) using the algorithm for absolute object positioning.

The presented data show that the absolute object positioning method produces results more than doubled in value relative to the object positioning

Table 3. Depth estimation error for real image sequences (abolute object position)

Images sequence	Length [frames]	Error E
r1	120	0.19
r2	80	0.16
r3	65	0.23
r4	125	0.13
r5	90	0.15

method. This is due to the fact that the second algorithm is based on the overlapping of objects' bounding boxes, which is not present in all frames of the image sequence.

5 Conclusion

The proposed method enables the use of single-camera vision systems (especially surveillance systems) to determine the relative positions of objects in three-dimensional space. When additional conditions are met, concerning mainly the angle of the camera, it is possible to determine the absolute distance of observed objects to the camera.

The algorithms were implemented in Matlab, without the use of additional optimizations, so their performance does not permit a practical application. It is planned that the algorithms are implemented in an efficient environment using OpenCV library, so that it would be possible to estimate the performance and the introduction of additional optimizations. The most time-consuming operation (approximately 70%) is the determination of the optic flow, so using a different method of extraction of motion from images should be taken into consideration.

After necessary improvements and optimization are made, the proposed method can be used in practical applications.

Acknowledgment. Work supported by European Regional Development Fund under INSIGMA project no. POIG.01.01.02-00-062/09.

References

1. Baker, S., Scharstein, D., Lewis, J.P., et al.: A Database and Evaluation Methodology for Optical Flow. Computer Vision, 1–8 (2007)
2. Brox, T., Bruhn, A., Papenberg, N., Weickert, J.: High accuracy optical flow estimation based on a theory for warping. In: Pajdla, T., Matas, J. (eds.) ECCV 2004. LNCS, vol. 3024, pp. 25–36. Springer, Heidelberg (2004)
3. Fleet, D.J., Weiss, Y.: Optical Flow Estimation. In: Paragios, N., Chen, Y., Faugeras, O. (eds.) Mathematical Models for Computer Vision: The Handbook, pp. 239–257. Springer (2005)

4. Gaspar, T., Oliveira, P.: New Dynamic Estimation of Depth from Focus in Active Vision Systems - Data Acquisition, LPV Observer Design, Analysis and Test. In: Proc. VISAPP, pp. 484–491 (2011)
5. Loy, C.C., Hospedales, T.M., Xiang, T., Gong, S.: Stream-based joint exploration-exploitation active learning. In: Computer Vision and Pattern Recognition (CVPR), pp. 1560–1567 (2012)
6. Middlebury dataset, vision.middlebury.edu/flow/
7. MIT Traffic Data Set, http://www.ee.cuhk.edu.hk/xgwang/MITtraffic.html
8. Pachidis, T.: Pseudo Stereovision System (PSVS): A Monocular Mirror-based Stereovision System. In: Scene Reconstruction, Pose Estimation and Tracking, pp. 305–330. I-Tech Education and Publishing, Vienna (2007)
9. Pachidis, T.P., Lygouras, J.N.: Pseudo-Stereo Vision System: A Detailed Study. Journal of Intelligent and Robotic Systems 42(2), 135–167 (2005)
10. QMUL Junction Dataset, http://www.eecs.qmul.ac.uk/ccloy/downloads_qmul_junction.html
11. Wang, M., Wang, X.: Automatic Adaptation of a Generic Pedestrian Detector to a Specific Traffic Scene. In: IEEE Conference on Computer Vision and Pattern Recognition, Colorado Springs (2011)
12. Wei, Y., Dong, Z., Wu, C.: Depth measurement using single camera with fixed camera parameters. IET Comput. Vis. 6(1), 29–39 (2012)

Downloading and Analysing Images from the Internet in Order to Detect Special Objects

Mikołaj Leszczuk, Tomasz Piwowarczyk, and Michał Grega

AGH University of Science and Technology, al. Mickiewicza 30, PL-30059 Krakow, Poland
leszczuk@agh.edu.pl

Abstract. Along with all the positives brought by the Internet, the global network is also used for criminal purposes. The goal of the presented work was to create and optimize applications working in parallel with the search and illegal content analysis system (SWAT) created previously at the authors' university. The role of the SWAT system is to penetrate the Internet to search for images and provide links to the presented application. The presented application is able to detect various special objects, such as faces, symbols or child pornography. The use of bees algorithm-based optimization made it possible to increase the effectiveness of image analysis. With appropriate assumptions, the efficiency was increased by a factor of three times compared to the application without optimization. The efficiency of the optimization algorithm depends largely on the nature of the input data, the URL addresses.

Keywords: OpenCV, optimization algorithms, C$\sharp$, Python, Internet safety, Web Services.

1 Introduction

In the early days of the Internet, the global network was used only for essential business and communication matters. The Internet was appreciated for its speed and efficiency in the transmission of information. In time, when people began to fully appreciate the benefits brought by the global network, they started to their online activities, making the Internet present in all areas of human life. Today the Internet has become the most common source of information and data, at the same time fulfilling a role in entertainment, science, economics, and so on. In January 2013 the number of Internet users worldwide was estimated at more than 2 billion 406 million people (34.3% of the world population) [2]. In Europe, this percentage was 63.2%, while in Poland alone – 64.9%.

Unfortunately, along with all the benefits brought by the Internet, the global network is used for criminal purposes as well. Users, feeling anonymous and having easy contact with people from all over the world, commit all sorts of crimes, usually called "cyber-crime". The most popular "cyber-crimes" include:

- Internet fraud – extortion, fake online auctions, falsifying bank transfers,
- copyright infringement – sharing copyrighted multimedia content online,
- consolidation, distribution, download and storage of child pornography content,
- "Phishing" – impersonating well-known websites (e.g. banks) to fraudulently obtain sensitive information (passwords, codes),

A. Dziech and A. Czyżewski (Eds.): MCSS 2013, CCIS 368, pp. 130–143, 2013.

- distribution of "malware",
- sale of illegal goods and drugs.

The changing nature of crime brings new challenges for law enforcement. Having to deal with evidence in an electronic format requires that law enforcement personnel not only have a knowledge of forensics, but also an in-depth understanding of the "cyber-crime" techniques used. To be effective in the face of constant technological progress, investigators must constantly improve their techniques and develop new tools to enable them to fight against online offenders.

Methods for monitoring the content of Web pages are becoming an object of growing interest for law enforcement agencies on the Internet. Information providing evidence of criminal activity can be hidden from indexing systems, such as Google or Bing, by embedding it in multimedia materials (images or videos), since searching for such content poses a great challenge for modern criminal analysis. Help comes with systems specialized in extensive searches of online content (i.e. crawling) combined with tools for multimedia content analysis (detection of child pornography, dangerous symbols, etc.).

The notion of collection and analysis of images from the Internet seems to be simple and commonplace. However, a new concept combines highly efficient mechanisms to search the Internet with advanced tools for analysis of static images that can not only pose interesting academic problems but also help increase safety.

The aim of this work was to develop a system combining the search and content analysis system (SWAT) developed by the Department of Computer Science at the AGH University of Science and Technology [7,8] with static image analysis software developed as part of the INDECT project [3]. This combination will ultimately make it possible to search for illegal content on the Internet.

The SWAT crawling system [4], is designed to handle hundreds of millions of Web pages. It runs on a cluster of 10 computers and handles up to a few hundred pages per second. Performance of the system can be improved easily, by adding more computers to the cluster [7].

The SWAT system is used to search the Internet for multimedia content. The advantage of the system is its very high efficiency. This solution can analyse approx. 50 – 250 Web pages per second, returning found URLs to multimedia content (e.g. images). Software developed by the INDECT project analyses and detects specific static objects such as faces, certain symbols (such as the swastika) and child pornography.

The application developed in this study has two roles:

1. Buffer (queue) – because of the major differences in performance between searching for images for analysis and image analysis itself, we need a buffer which will store found URLs.
2. Optimization – thanks to a special algorithm, the system, based on the previous results of the analysis, increases the effectiveness of searching for specific objects by analysing images from more "promising" URLs.

The following sections provide a detailed description of the operation of the application. The structure of the paper is as follows. Section 2 describes the features of the application, its structure and operation. Section 3 describes the optimization algorithm and Section 4 tests its effectiveness. Finally we present a summary (Section 5) and bibliography.

2   The Structure and Operation of the Application

The structure and principles of operation of the application are described in this section. The overall structure of the system is presented first, followed by the system operation.

2.1   Application Structure

The main part of the application is a queuing system acting as a storekeeper for data sent from the SWAT system. Because of the considerable differences between the searching for URLs and the analysis performed on the images themselves, a buffer that holds the addresses provided by the SWAT system is used in this application. From the buffer, the URLs are selected for further processing using a specially-developed algorithm. During this search the algorithm used for image processing was face detection. However, it should be noted that any image processing algorithm can be used in its place, as the structure of the whole application consists of modules that can be freely exchanged.

The application uses FIFO for processing further packages of data sent from the SWAT system. After analysing the specific part of the addresses of the package, another package is analysed.

The applications second role is optimization. Because of the abovementioned performance differences, the natural conclusion is that not all of the URLs provided by the SWAT system will be analysed. To improve application performance – that is to detect more images of faces – an algorithm has been applied that allows predicting which URLs are more "useful". By this "usefulness" (or "relevance") we mean the probability of detecting a face in an image taken from a given address. Such optimization can be performed by separating the individual address domains and sorting domains based on their usefulness. By analysing the structure of websites, it can be concluded that some domains contain mostly images with specific characteristics (e.g., landscapes, people or vehicles). It follows that it makes the most sense to analyse the domains in which faces have been already detected.

Due to its SWAT availability, the application has an Internet (Web) format. Given the ease of implementation and independence from hardware platforms, the application works as a Web Service using the Simple Object Access Protocol (SOAP). The application (Web Service) was written in C♯ using the .NET Framework 3.5 platform.

Face detection uses a separate script (plug-in) written in Python launched from the Web Service application. All results of the analysis are stored in the resulting XML.

2.2 Application Performance

Basic scheme of the application is shown in Fig. 1.

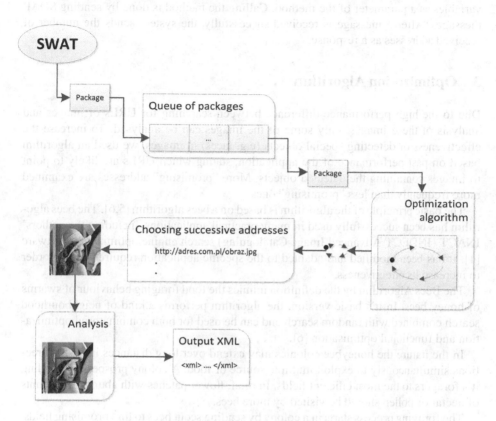

Fig. 1. Application diagram

The application works as follows:

1. Packages containing a fixed number of retrieved URLs are sent from the SWAT system to a Web service.
2. The received packages go to the FIFO, from which they are then taken for processing. The principle is that 10% of the package is processed, then the next package from the queue is analysed. The rest of the addresses go to the archival collection. If the queue is empty, archival addresses are processed until all the addresses are analysed or the next package arrives.
3. During the analysis of the package, addresses are grouped into domains, and during the concomitant algorithm optimization, other URLs for the analysis are chosen.
4. When a URL is selected, an image is retrieved from it and an analysis is performed using the image plug-ins. First, an image is subjected to filtering by structure (size, color) to exclude images that are not photographs. Face detection is performed next.
5. The result of image analysis is stored on a server in an XML format.

2.3 Using the Application

To send a package of URLs, SWAT uses the remote method, passing an array of string variables as a parameter of the method. Calling the method is done by sending SOAP messages. After a message is received successfully, the system sends the number of received addresses as a response.

3 Optimization Algorithm

Due to the high performance difference between searching for URLs of images and analysis of these images, only some of the images can be analysed. To increase the effectiveness of detecting special objects (e.g. faces) in images, we used an algorithm based on past performance of the application, stating which URLs are likely to point to images containing the detected objects. More "promising" addresses are examined more frequently than less "promising" ones.

The basic principle of the algorithm is based on a bees algorithm [5,6]. The bees algorithm has been successfully used in many practical applications, including the authors' INACT (INDECT Advanced Image Cataloguing) search engine optimization software [1]. It has been modified and adapted to the specific application requirements in order to increase its effectiveness.

The Bees Algorithm by the definition mimics the food foraging behaviour of swarms of honey bees. In it's basic version, the algorithm performs a kind of neighbourhood search combined with random search and can be used for both combinatorial optimization and functional optimisation [6].

In the nature the honeybee colonies may extend over long distances in many directions simultaneously to exploit multiple source of food. A colony prospers by sending it's foragers to the most efficient fields. In brief, flower patches with abundant amounts of nectar or pollen should be visited by more bees.

The foraging process starts in a colony by sending scout bees to find promising fields. Scout bees visit the following flower patches randomly. When they return to the hive, those bees that had found a patch rated above a certain quality threshold (measured as a combination of some ingredients, such as the level of sugar content) notify the colony of positions (direction and distance) and quality of the flower patches by a special dance (called waggle dance). This dance allows the colony to assess each field, and thus, to send a sufficient number of bees to harvest the food. Along with bees harvesting from a patch, more scout bees are being sent to promising fields. In this way the neighbourhood of the promising fields is also efficiently screened.

In order to improve "efficiency" of the URLs (i.e., the detection efficiency of the image indicated by the address), they were divided by domain. The term of a domain is the location of the file on the network, for example: Table 1.

In addition, using the domain hierarchy, the concept of the parent domain was introduced, for example: Table 2.

Table 1. Sample domains

URL	Domain
`http://kt.agh.edu.pl/_g/right_en.jpg`	`kt.agh.edu.pl/_g`
`http://kt.agh.edu.pl/loga_projektow/indect.png`	`kt.agh.edu.pl/loga_projektow`
`http://kt.agh.edu.pl/obraz.jpg`	`kt.agh.edu.pl`
`http://www.agh.edu.pl/files/header/naglowek-glowny-j.png`	`agh.edu.pl/files/header`
`http://www.agh.edu.pl/files/common/banerki-na-glownej/fundusze_euro.gif`	`agh.edu.pl/files/common/banerki-na-glownej`

Table 2. Sample parent domains

Domain	Parent domain
`kt.agh.edu.pl/_g`	`kt.agh.edu.pl`
`kt.agh.edu.pl`	`agh.edu.pl`
`agh.edu.pl/files/banner/small/`	`agh.edu.pl/files/banner`
`agh.edu.pl/files/header`	`agh.edu.pl/files`
`agh.edu.pl/files/common/banerki-na-glownej`	`agh.edu.pl/files/common`
`agh.edu.pl`	*N/A*
`google.pl`	*N/A*

While detecting the parent domain, the following functional Polish second-level domains were considered:

- com.pl,
- org.pl,
- net.pl,
- art.pl,
- edu.pl,
- aid.pl,
- agro.pl,
- atm.pl,
- auto.pl,
- biz.pl,
- chem.pl,
- gmina.pl,
- gsm.pl,
- info.pl,
- mail.pl,
- miasta.pl,
- media.pl,
- mil.pl,
- nom.pl,
- org.pl,
- pc.pl,
- powiat.pl,
- priv.pl,
- realestate.pl,
- rel.pl,
- sci.pl,
- sex.pl,
- shop.pl,
- sklep.pl,
- sos.pl,
- szkola.pl,
- targi.pl,
- tm.pl,
- tourism.pl,
- travel.pl,
- turystyka.pl.

These domains are not treated as separate, and are used only as second-level domains. For this reason, the domain **agh.edu.pl** does not have a parent domain.

The effectiveness of a given domain D_{Eff} is calculated using the formula:

$$D_{Eff} = \frac{F}{U} + \frac{1}{2}L_{Eff} + \frac{1}{4}P_{Eff} \tag{1}$$

where:

- F – the number of faces detected in images taken from addresses belonging to the domain
- U – the number of analysed addresses of the domain (where U is zero $\frac{F}{U}$ is also zero)
- L_{Eff} – the effectiveness of same-level domains, or domains with the same parent domain, calculated from the formula:

$$L_{Eff} = \frac{F_L}{U_L} \tag{2}$$

where:

- F_L – the number of faces detected in images taken from addresses belonging to same-level domains
- U_L – the number of analysed addresses of the domains on the same level (where U_L is zero $\frac{F_L}{U_L}$ is also zero)
- P_{Eff} – the effectiveness of the parent domain, calculated from the formula:

$$P_{Eff} = \frac{F_P}{U_P} \tag{3}$$

where:

- F_P – the number of faces detected in images taken from addresses belonging to the parent domain
- U_P – the number of analysed addresses from the parent domain (where U_P is zero $\frac{F_P}{U_P}$ is also zero)

Fig. 2 shows the diagram of the optimization algorithm.

We introduced four parameters corresponding to the numerical algorithm: *INIT*, *TOP*, *BEST*, and *RAND*. After downloading the address package from the queue, the following actions are performed:

1. From the list of domains, the domains with zero effectiveness and their parent domains are deleted (if not superior to other domains with non-zero efficiency).
2. Old URLs are archived.
3. New addresses are grouped by their domains and a paramount domain is assigned.
4. Successive phases follow:
   a *INIT* phase, during which the system learns. During this phase, a random domain is selected from all the domains of at least 10 addresses (the number of these domains is C). This phase is repeated n times, where $n = INIT \cdot C$.
   b *TOP* phase, during which the domain is chosen randomly from among the three domains with the highest coefficient of performance. This phase is repeated k times, where $k = TOP$.

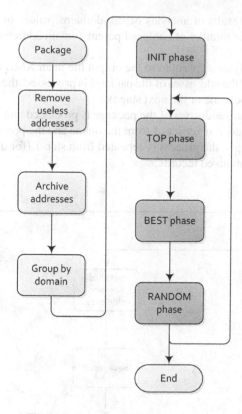

Fig. 2. Optimization algorithm – scheme

   c *BEST* phase, during which the domain with the highest coefficient of performance is selected. This phase is repeated *l* times, where *l* = *BEST*.

   d *RAND* phase, during which a random domain is selected. This phase is repeated *i* times, where *i* = *RAND*.

   e Back to the *TOP* phase (point b).

During each phase, a series of operations is presented in Fig. 3:

1. The domain is chosen; the mode of the choice is dependent on the phase (described above).
2. The random URL address is selected from the domain.
3. The address of the selected image is taken and then followed by the operation of image analysis plug-ins.
4. According to the result of the analysis of the domain, values of the number of detected faces and the number of addresses analysed (F and U) are updated.
5. According to the results of analysis of same-level domains, values of the number of detected faces and the number of analysed domain addresses on the same level (F_L and U_L) are updated.

6. According to the results of analysis of sub-domains, values of the number of detected faces and the number of analysed parent domain addresses (F_P and U_P) are updated.
7. Results of the analysis are written to the output file in an XML format.
8. If less than 10% of the addresses of the package is processed, the process is repeated from step 1 (for the same or the next stage).
9. If at least 10% of the addresses of the package is processed and the next package is waiting in the queue, it is retrieved from the queue and the process begins again.
10. If the queue is empty, the process is repeated from step 1 (for the same or the next phase) including archived records.

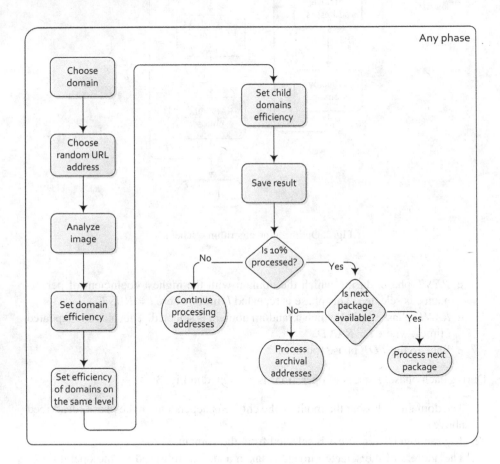

Fig. 3. Operations during the phase – scheme

The whole process is repeated until all the packages and archive addresses are processed.

4   The Effectiveness of the Optimization Algorithm

During the development of an optimization algorithm, its effectiveness was continuously measured in order to achieve the best results. The effectiveness of the algorithm is calculated as a percentage of detected faces among all the faces for a given address package. In the perfect scenario, 100% of the faces are detected; the worst scenario assumes 0% faces are detected. However, using a random selection method of addresses for the analysis, the average percentage of detected faces is as high as the percentage of addresses analysed (if 20% of the addresses of the package is analysed, an average of 20% of the faces are detected), therefore the minimum threshold will be taken.

The following results have been obtained for the form of the algorithm presented in Section 3:

Estimating the efficiency of both systems (SWAT and the presented application), it was assumed that 10% of the received URLs will be analysed. It was also assumed that the package will contain the addresses of 50,000 URLs – enough for the system to learn and use this knowledge when choosing the next address of the package.

4.1   Description of the Experiment

The optimization algorithm was tested using data obtained from the SWAT – 4 address packages (including 200,000 addresses). Packages were tested separately - i.e., after the analysis of each package, data on the effectiveness of each domain was deleted.

For each of the packages, all URLs were initially analysed to find out how many faces can be detected in images taken from the abovementioned addresses. Then, 10% of the addresses of the package (i.e. 5,000) was analysed and the number of detected faces was listed. Due to the random factors present during the optimization of the algorithm, tests were repeated five times.

Before the effectiveness of the algorithm for the next addresses package was measured accurately, the values for INIT, TOP, BEST, and RAND parameters were set. For different values of reasonable ranges, the effectiveness of the algorithm for one package was measured, and the best value of the abovementioned parameters was found. Subsequent studies have already been carried out for fixed values of these parameters.

In order to present the diversity of the data input into the system, Table 3 summarizes the address packages:

1. The total number of faces that can be detected by analysing all the URLs of the package.
2. The number of domains with URLs (without the parent domain).
3. The number of domains that contain at least 10 URLs – used in the INIT phase.

As can be seen, the data can be quite diverse – in the packages №1, №2 and №4, the numbers of domains are very similar (more than 11,000), while in the package №3, there are many more domains (over 15,000). A similar phenomenon can be observed by analysing domains with multiple addresses. In this case, package №4 differs from the "standard", as in this package there are approx. twice the number of domains containing URLs (at least 10) than in the other packages.

Table 3. Testing the effectiveness of the algorithm – packages information

Package of addresses	The total number of faces	Number of domains with URLs	Number of domains that contain at least 10 URLs
1	2 161	11 923	448
2	3 257	11 129	424
3	2 534	15 675	532
4	2 861	11 136	1 091

4.2   The Results of the Experiment

The following charts (Fig. 4 and Fig. 5) present the results of the search for the best INIT, TOP, BEST, and RAND parameters. The graphs show the number of detected faces (which translates into the effectiveness of the algorithm) according to one of the abovementioned parameters, while the other three are fixed.

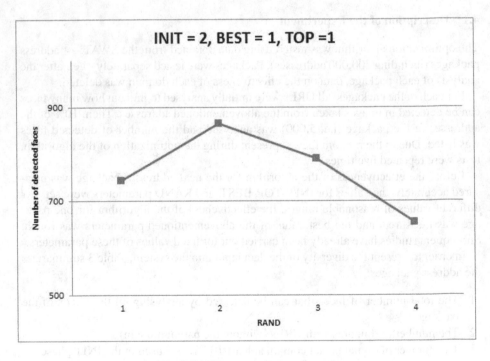

Fig. 4. RAND parameter search graph

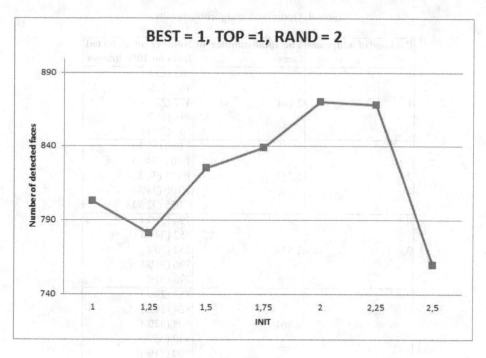

Fig. 5. INIT parameter search graph

After gathering all the results of searching for the best INIT, TOP, BEST, and RAND values, it was found that the effectiveness of the algorithm is the highest for the following values:

- $INIT = 2$
- $TOP = 1$
- $BEST = 1$
- $RAND = 2$

Algorithm performance test results for four packages are presented in Table 4.

As shown in the table, using the optimization algorithm, the application detects from 21% to 34% of all faces, processing only 10% of the images. It is clear that in relation to the effectiveness of the minimum threshold, which in this case is 10%, in the best case the result is improved over three times.

Results may vary depending on the type of data. The following can affect the results:

1. The total number of faces that can be detected in the package – the more images of faces, the more effectively this algorithm works. For the package №1, where the number of faces is approximately 4.3% of all URLs, the efficiency of the algorithm is the lowest, while for the package №2, when this number is approximately equal to 6.5%, the efficiency of the algorithm is the highest.

Table 4. Optimization algorithm results

Package of addresses	The total number of faces	Number of detected faces on 10% images
1	2 161	505 (23%) 463 (21%) 477 (22%) 498 (23%) 503 (23%)
2	3 257	1 066 (33%) 1 102 (34%) 1 103 (34%) 1 106 (34%) 1 055 (32%)
3	2 534	794 (31%) 852 (34%) 757 (30%) 796 (31%) 798 (31%)
4	2 861	833 (29%) 824 (29%) 908 (32%) 940 (33%) 900 (31%)

2. Correlating data – that is, the distribution of domain addresses. For example, if every address in the package belonged to another domain, the algorithm would have an efficiency of approx. 10% (the same as random selection).

It should be noted that it is impossible to accurately measure the effectiveness of the optimization algorithm because we cannot predict the input data structure. With some URL addresses the algorithm can work better than with others. By using several packages of addresses, we can only approximate the effectiveness value, although there is no doubt that the algorithm performs its function and can detect faces more frequently than a random selection of addresses for analysis.

In addition, while the application is running in a production environment, when the current data is transmitted from the SWAT system, we will not be able to determine the actual effectiveness of the algorithm, because it will not know the number of all possible faces to detect.

5   Conclusions and Future Work

The aim of this study was to develop and create an application combining the search and content analysis system (SWAT) developed by the Department of Computer Science at the AGH University of Science and Technology with software developed as part of the INDECT project for the analysis of static images. The application was developed and its performance was analysed. The use of bees algorithm-based optimization made it possible to increase the effectiveness of image analysis. With appropriate assumptions, plug-in efficiency was increased three times as compared to the application without optimization. However, it should be noted that the efficiency of the optimization algorithm depends largely on the nature of the input data, that is URL addresses.

Currently, the only plug-in which uses the application is face detection software. However, this is only the first step towards extending if by a further application of INDECT plug-ins, such as detection of child pornography, making it possible to detect dangerous content on the Web and empower law enforcement agencies.

Acknowledgements. The research leading to these results has received funding from the European Communitys Seventh Framework Programme (FP7/2007-2013) under grant agreement №218086 (INDECT) [3]. INDECT is a research project developing tools to fight terrorism and other criminal activities threatening the citizens of the European Union. The project involves the use of innovative methods to detect threats in both "real life" (smart cameras) and virtual (Internet) environments.

We also thank Wojciech Turek, PhD, from the Department of Computer Science at the AGH University of Science and Technology, for his support in connection with the SWAT application software.

References

1. Grega, M., Bryk, D., Napora, M., Gusta, M.: INACT — INDECT advanced image cataloguing tool. In: Dziech, A., Czyżewski, A. (eds.) MCSS 2011. CCIS, vol. 149, pp. 28–36. Springer, Heidelberg (2011), http://dx.doi.org/10.1007/978-3-642-21512-4_4
2. Group, M.M.: Internet world stats, http://www.internetworldstats.com/
3. INDECT: Welcome to INDECT homepage – INDECT-home, http://www.indect-project.eu/
4. Opaliński, A., Turek, W.: Information retrieval and identity analysis. In: Metody Sztucznej Inteligencji w Działaniach na Rzecz Bezpieczeństwa Publicznego, pp. 173–194. AGH University of Science and Technology Press (2009) No. 978-83-7464-268-2
5. Pham, D.T., Ghanbarzadeh, A., Koc, E., Otri, S.: Application of the bees algorithm to the training of radial basis function networks for control chart pattern recognition (2006)
6. Pham, D.T., Ghanbarzadeh, A., Koc, E., Otri, S., Rahim, S., Zaidi, M.: The bees algorithm, a novel tool for complex optimisation problems. In: Proceedings of the 2nd International Virtual Conference on Intelligent Production Machines and Systems (IPROMS 2006), pp. 454–459. Elsevier (2006)
7. Turek, W., Opalinski, A., Kisiel-Dorohinicki, M.: Extensible web crawler – towards multimedia material analysis. In: Dziech, A., Czyżewski, A. (eds.) MCSS 2011. CCIS, vol. 149, pp. 183–190. Springer, Heidelberg (2011), http://dx.doi.org/10.1007/978-3-642-21512-4_22
8. Wilaszek, K., Wójcik, T., Opaliński, A., Turek, W.: Internet identity analysis and similarities detection. In: Dziech, A., Czyżewski, A. (eds.) MCSS 2012. CCIS, vol. 287, pp. 369–379. Springer, Heidelberg (2012), http://dx.doi.org/10.1007/978-3-642-30721-8_36

Knife Detection Scheme Based on Possibilistic Shell Clustering

Aleksandra Maksimova

Institute of Applied Mathematics and Mechanics,
National Academy of Science of Ukraine, Donetsk, Ukraine
maximova.alexandra@mail.ru

Abstract. This paper deals with a novel method for knife detection in images. The special feature of any knife is its simple geometric form. The proposed knife detection scheme is based on searching object with corresponding form. Fuzzy and possibilistic shell clustering methods are used to find contours of objects in the picture. These methods give as a result a set of second-degree curves offered in analytical form. To answer the question whether there is a knife in the picture, the angle between two such curves is calculated and its value is estimated. A C++ program was developed for experiments allowing to confirm the suitability of the proposed scheme for knife detection. Robustness of possibilistic c quadric shell clustering to outlier points let us use this algorithm in real-life situations. The objective of research is to use the results for developing a system for monitoring dangerous situation in urban environment using public CCTV systems.

Keywords: fuzzy and possibilistic shell clustering, pattern recognition, knife detection, geometric approach.

1   Introduction

Automatic analysis of pictures in CCTV systems is a very important and challenging problem due to necessity to support the activities of the operator of such systems. It is known that operator's attention gets worse after an hour of continuous observation of several monitors (4, 9 and 16 monitors). The monitoring of dangerous situations is one of the operator's tasks. A knife in hand can serve as a sign of danger. So we solve the problem of knife recognition in the images from camera video sequence.

The knife detection problem is new and little studied. There are several approaches to its solution: using Haar cascades [1] and Active Appearance Model [2], which are learning-based. However, results shown in the publications use only for simple test examples, when the knife is clearly observed in the picture. So further research is going on for real-life situations.

The contour analysis methods are a basis for a lot of computer vision algorithms. Shell clustering algorithms are used to find the contours in a form of ellipses, rectangles, lines and second-degree curves in analytical form. Batch fuzzy and possibilistic shell clustering methods are related to alternating optimization clustering [3,4]. The

A. Dziech and A. Czyżewski (Eds.): MCSS 2013, CCIS 368, pp. 144–152, 2013.

fuzzy and possibilistic shell clustering algorithms give a set of contours prototypes, presented as second-degree curves in two-dimensional space as a result. The set of boundary pixels is obtained by special processing of the original picture. This set is an input for clustering algorithm. In this paper the possibility of using a similar approach for knife detection in the picture was analysed and some experiments with simple tests examples were conducted.

2   The Problem of Knife Detection

Let us discuss solving the pattern recognition problem for classes of objects «knives». The images are obtained from CCTV cameras. The picture is scanned with a window of size $W \times H$, so let us solve the problem for these $W \times H$ fragments of original picture. Let us speak about positive examples if there is a knife on the picture (Fig. 1 a), and about negative examples otherwise (Fig. 1 b).

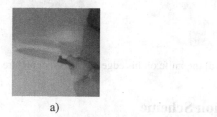

a)   b)

Fig. 1. Examples of the pictures: a) positive example, b) negative example

Since a knife grip is often in a hand of a criminal, let us consider the knife as an object consisting of two parts: the blade and the grip. A dangerous knife should have a blade end. This feature was also used in [2] to detect knife. Also the angle between the edge and the butt can`t be more than seventy degrees as per cold weapon classification. Knife blade has a special geometrical form and can be described with a pair of second-degree curves with constraints:

$$\begin{cases} F_1(x_1, x_2) = 0, x_1 \epsilon [w_{11}, w_{12}], x_2 \in [h_{11}, h_{12}] \\ F_2(x_1, x_2) = 0, x_1 \epsilon [w_{21}, w_{22}], x_2 \in [h_{21}, h_{22}] \end{cases} \qquad (1)$$

where F_1 и F_2 are the curves of the form $\boldsymbol{p}_i \boldsymbol{q} = 0$, $\boldsymbol{p}_i = [p_{i1}, ..., p_{i6}]^T$, i=1,2, $\boldsymbol{q} = [x_1^2, x_2^2, x_1 x_2, x_1, x_2, 1]$, $w_{11}, w_{12}, w_{21}, w_{22} \epsilon (1, W)$, $h_{11}, h_{12}, h_{21}, h_{22} \epsilon (1, H)$.

Let P be a bitmap of the picture $P = [P_{xy}], x = 1, ..., W, y = 1, ..., H$. Let us set a geometric form (1) describing the knife with the following required conditions:

(i) $[w_{11}, w_{12}] \cap [w_{21}, w_{22}] \neq \emptyset$
(ii) $[h_{11}, h_{12}] \cap [h_{21}, h_{22}] \neq \emptyset$
(iii) $\exists P(x^{(0)}, y^{(0)}): F_1(x^{(0)}, y^{(0)}) = F_2(x^{(0)}, y^{(0)})$.

where $(x^{(0)}, y^{(0)})$ is an intersection point.

A knife detection scheme is constructed with the help of an algorithm $D : D(P) = \alpha$, where $\alpha \in [0,1]$ is a degree of confidence estimating the presence of knife in the picture.

To solve the problem of knife recognition using a geometrical approach a number of task properties should be taken into account. The first problem is that a knife could be turned edgewise to the frame, which would change its appearance into a line (Fig. 2 a). This problem can be solved by analysing a sequence of images from surveillance cameras, which is not yet implemented at this stage of the research. The second problem is that the blade is highly reflective which leads to the appearance of highlights in the picture (Fig 2. b). This can be solved by installing polarizing filters on the camera lens or using highlights filtering software.

a)   b)

Fig. 2. The special cases: a) the knife on his edge b) lights in a picture

3   General Knife Detection Scheme

The proposed scheme of knife detection in the picture from surveillance camera is based on finding the geometrical forms corresponding to usual knife blade form using information about object contours. Images are filtered to determine the contours. Then the contours are described as second-degree curves in analytical form with constraints. The decision whether there is a knife in the image is based on the analysis of such contours. This approach can be used because the object «knife» has a simple geometric form, so let us call this approach geometric.

3.1   Main Stages of the Method

Let us break the algorithm D into four stages:

$$D(P) = (D_4 \circ D_3 \circ D_2 \circ D_1)(P) \tag{2}$$

where :

D_1 is filtration for border detection, D_2 is threshold filtration for special points preparing, D_3 is prototypes of borders detection, D_4 is making a decision about the presence of a knife in the picture, P is a bitmap of image.

On the first stage D_1 the colour P_{xy} in every pixel (x, y) of bitmap P is transformed from RGB into grayscale and then form a new image, where the colour value of the reference point with significant differences in brightness converge to white, and the value of the pixels located in areas of constant brightness (background) converge to black. The Sobel operator is a good choice for edge detection [5].

The second transformation D_2 is threshold filtration. As a result we receive a set of border points of the image $X = \{(x_{i,1}, x_{i,2}) | P_{xy}^{mod} > \lambda, \forall x, y, x_{i,1} = x, x_{i,2} = y\}_{i=1}^{n}$, where λ is a threshold of brightness selected individually for each case.

The result of the third stage D_3 is a set of contour prototypes $B = \{\beta_i\}_{i=1}^{c}$ in a form of second-degree curves in two-dimensional space. The number of prototypes c is different for each case. The prototypes β_i are represented by the parameter vectors $p_i = [p_{i1}, p_{i2}, ..., p_{i6}]^T$, which define the curve equation:

$$p_i q = 0 \tag{3}$$

where $q = [x_1^2, x_2^2, x_1 x_2, x_1, x_2, 1]$. The method of finding the coefficients of prototype curves will be discussed below. The constraints $[w_{i1}, w_{i2}]$ and $[h_{i1}, h_{i2}]$ describing an area on the bitmap containing pixels corresponding to β_i are calculated for prototype β_i. After that prototype $\hat{\beta}_i$ is a second-degree curve equation in a form (3) with constraints $[w_{i1}, w_{i2}]$ and $[h_{i1}, h_{i2}]$.

The last stage D_4 offers a method for deciding whether one of the pairs of curves with intersecting constraints can describe a blade shape. The inference method is discussed in detail in section 3.3. As a result we have an answer for a question whether there is a knife in the picture with some degree of confidence α.

The general scheme of the stages described is given in (Fig. 3).

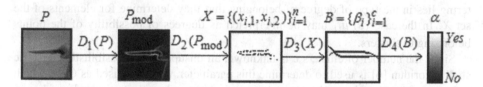

Fig. 3. The general scheme of knife detection method

3.2   Algorithm of Finding the Prototypes

Prototype-based fuzzy and possibilistic clustering algorithms are useful for solving the problem of finding the prototypes in the form (3). The fuzzy approach is used here because of its good characteristics, i.e. lower tendency to get stuck in local minima in comparison with hard versions [4].

Let us consider a fuzzy C quadric algorithm (FCQS) [6]. Let $x_j = (x_{j,1}, x_{j,2})$ be a point in two dimensional space. The prototypes β_i are represented by the parameter vectors $p_i = [p_{i1}, ... p_{i6}]^T$. We solve the following optimization problem:

$$J_Q(B, U) = \sum_{i=1}^{c} \sum_{j=1}^{n} (\mu_{ij})^m \, d_Q^2(x_j, \beta_i) \tag{4}$$

where $B = (\beta_1, ..., \beta_c)$, c is the number of clusters, n is the total number of points and $U = [\mu_{ij}]$ is the $c \times n$ fuzzy c–partition matrix that satisfies the following conditions.

$$\mu_{ij} \epsilon [0,1] \; \forall i, j, \; \sum_{i=1}^{c} \mu_{ij} = 1 \; \forall j, \; \sum_{j=1}^{n} \mu_{ij} < n \; \forall i \tag{5}$$

The algebraic distance d_{Qij}^2 from x_j to a prototype β_i:

$$d_{Qij}^2 = d_Q^2(x_j, \beta_i) = p_i^T M_j p_i \tag{6}$$

where $M_j = q_j q_j^T$, with $q_j^T = [x_1^2, x_2^2, x_1 x_2, x_1, x_2, 1]$.

To avoid the trivial solution we use a constraint that makes the distance invariant to translation and rotation [7]:

$$\left\| p_{i1}^2 + p_{i2}^2 + \frac{p_{i3}^2}{2} + \cdots + \frac{p_{i6}^2}{2} \right\|^2 = 1 \tag{7}$$

The constraint (7) is the best compromise between computational complexity and performance in the 2-D case.

The discussed FCQS algorithm is sensitive to outlier points. To overcome this difficulty a possibilistic variant of FCQS algorithm that is called possibilistic c quadric shell algorithm (PCQS) [8] is used. The minimizing functional for PCQS is (4). Let us search U as a possibilistic c −partition with constraints:

$$\mu_{ij} \in [0,1] \ \forall i,j, \ \sum_{i=1}^{c} \mu_{ij} \leq 1 \ \forall j, \ \sum_{j=1}^{n} \mu_{ij} < n \ \forall i \tag{8}$$

This means that the sum of degree of belonging to every cluster for a point is not necessarily equal to one. The difference between fuzzy and possibilistic approach to clustering lies in the type of degree of belonging that they determine for elements of the set X. In the case (8) μ_{ij} may be interpreted as degrees of possibility of the points belonging to clusters.

Since the number of clusters c is unknown, an unsupervised possibilistic c quadric shell algorithm [6] is used to determine this parameter. c is initialised as C_{max} which is known from practice to be about two times bigger than the estimated number of clusters.

3.3   Decision-Making Based on Analysis of Prototypes

Properties of geometric form of knife blade are the basis of decision making method. To check if the object is knife we have to calculate an angle between two curves in their intersection point. The first step is to sort out all possible pairs of prototypes that correspond to the model (1). Next we find the point of intersection $(x^{(0)}, y^{(0)})$ of curves F_1 and F_2 going through all possible candidates $x_1 \in [w_{11}, w_{12}] \cap [w_{21}, w_{22}], x_2 \in [h_{11}, h_{12}] \cap [h_{21}, h_{22}]$ provided that $(x_1, x_2) \in X \vee (x_1 \pm 1, x_2 \pm 1) \in X$ and put them into $F_1(x_1, x_2) = F_2(x_1, x_2)$. We calculate an angle between two second-degree curves in the point of intersection using derivatives. If $F_1(x, y^{(1)}) = 0$ and $F_2(x, y^{(2)}) = 0$ are equations of the first and the second curves in clockwise direction then:

$$\frac{dy}{dx}(x^{(0)}, y^{(0)}) = y_0 = \frac{2p_1 x^{(0)} + p_3 y^{(0)} + p_4}{2p_2 y^{(0)} + p_3 x^{(0)} + p_5}, \tag{9}$$

$$\phi = arctg\left(\frac{y_0^{(1)} - y_0^{(2)}}{1 - y_0^{(1)} y_0^{(2)}}\right) \tag{10}$$

where φ is the angle between curves F_1 и F_2, $y_0^{(1)}$, $y_0^{(2)}$ are values of the derivative $\frac{dy}{dx}$ in the intersection point $(x^{(0)}, y^{(0)})$.

Let us use the fuzzy inference rules to estimate a degree of confidence of figure described by two curves with angle φ between them in cross point. The reason for this is the following: there are many different types of knife; the different position of knife in the picture and knife blade can be rotated at different angles with respect to the surveillance camera. For different cases it is important to calculate a degree of certainty with which the observed pattern may be related to a class of objects knife. We will use the following fuzzy inference rule presented in general form:

$$IF\ Angle\ IS\ Typical\ for\ Knife\ THAN\ It\ is\ a\ knife\ (\alpha = \mu(\varphi)) \qquad (11)$$

Let us define a linguistic variable «Angle» on the universal set $U = [0,180]$. If the angle between edge and butt is more than seventy degrees, it is not a cold weapon, so this object cannot signify a danger. Therefore, one of the possible membership functions $\mu(\varphi)$ for the value of the angle «Typical for Knife» (Fig.4) is given by the equation:

$$\mu(\varphi) = \frac{1}{1+e^{-0.26(\varphi-7.5)}} \cdot \frac{1}{1+e^{1.6(\varphi-62.85)}}. \qquad (12)$$

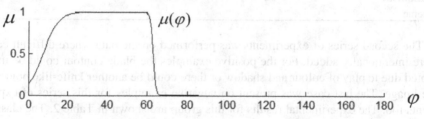

Fig. 4. Term «Typical for knife» for linguistic variable «Angle»

Of course, the angle is not the only parameter that can be used to estimate the shape of the figure given by the two curves on the domain. The length of lines could be estimated as well as the actual texture and pixel intensity inside the shape. In difficult cases we have to analyse the second part of figure, i.e. the knife grip and hand that holds it. But let us conduct the first group of experiments applying solely the rule (11).

4 Experiments Results

As a practical implementation of the methods offered a program KnifeDetection.exe, version 1 was developed. The input for program is a single test picture. The algorithm D (2) is implemented. Every stage of D can be inspected and its result can be visualized. The general result is a notification about knife detection in case it is found on the input picture. The special library FSC.dll was developed, where necessary filters, fuzzy and possibilistic shell clustering algorithms, the inference method of Sugeno were implemented.

The developed program KnifeDetection.exe was used for series of experiments. The initial data for this stage of the study were various simple pictures of knives obtained by a regular camera.

The experiments were conducted using fuzzy and possibilistic clustering algorithms. In the first case FCQS algorithm (fuzzy scheme) was used, and in the second case PCQS algorithm (possibilistic scheme) was used. Two groups of samples were selected for experiments. The first group dealt with so-called good cases. Photos with a knife placed on an almost homogeneous background without glare were used as a positive example. Pictures of background without objects that can be interpreted by the operator as a knife were used as negative examples. The experimental results for this group are shown in Table 1. Recognition quality for possibilistic scheme was slightly higher than for the fuzzy scheme and almost 98% which is an excellent result.

Table 1. Characteristic of the proposed geometric-based scheme for good examples

Method	Correctly classified positive examples (30 examples)	Correctly classified negative examples (60 examples)	Classification Accuracy
Fuzzy scheme	29	56	94,4%
Possibilistic scheme	30	58	97,7%

The second series of experiments was performed on the data where difficult cases were intentionally added. For the positive examples the blade contour could be interrupted due to play of colour and shadow or there could be another knife-like object on the image. The last case was present on negative examples for this series of experiments too. The experimental results for this group are shown in Table 2. The classification accuracy this time was lower, but the tendency for possibilistic scheme to be better presented itself similar to the first group of experiments.

Thus, possibilistic approach showed a higher level of recognition because of its lower sensitivity to outliers.

So, the proposed approach seems promising, but the practical implementation of this detection scheme requires a number of modifications that will be done in future work.

Table 2. Characteristic of the proposed geometric-based scheme for more difficult examples

Method	Correctly classified positive examples (30 examples)	Correctly classified negative examples (60 examples)	Classification Accuracy
Fuzzy scheme	25	45	77%
Possibilistic scheme	28	51	87%

5   Conclusion

The problem of detecting the knife in the picture, like most of the problems computer vision is challenging. The author considers the fuzzy approach to its solution to be very promising.

From the performed experiments the following conclusions can be drawn:

— the stage of model learning on the examples is absent, knowledge about the geometric form of object «knife» is used instead;
— the probabilistic clustering algorithm makes the detection scheme robust;
— the method is invariant to rotation of the object, which distinguishes it from some other methods, where an image fragment requires rotation and re-examination for each angle of rotation;
— the problem of knife position determination is solved automatically.

This paper presents a formal model of object "Knife" representation by a pair of second-degree curves. The basic characteristic of geometric form of knife is the angle between the blade and the butt of knife, which is the basis of the proposed detection scheme.

Errors of the method are mainly related to the play of light and shadow. This allows us to conclude that the success of solving this problem, unfortunately, depends heavily on the shooting conditions, i.e. lighting, equipment quality, camera resolution.

This paper deals with only one aspect of the problem of detecting the knife in the picture – a geometric approach to a knife as a figure. For a number of cases this approach has shown really good results, but there were certain images that did not seem to be difficult for recognition and where the algorithm failed nevertheless. This suggests that for best results we have to use complex methods, i.e. the combinations of different methods that are good for different subtypes of the problem and take into account some special feature of input image. Let us note that, since the computer vision problem lies in the sphere of artificial intelligence interests, the use of a complex approach corresponds to accumulation of experience by the operator.

Acknowledgements. The work has been co-financed by the European Regional Development Fund under the Innovative Economy Operational Programme, INSIGMA project no. POIG.01.01.02-00-062/09.

References

1. Żywicki, M., Matiolański, A., Orzechowski, T.M., Dziech, A.: Knife detection as a subset of object detection approach based on Haar cascades. In: Proceedings of 11th International Conference "Pattern Recognition and Information Processing", Minsk, Belarus, pp. 139–142 (2011)
2. Kmieć, M., Głowacz, A., Dziech, A.: Towards Robust Visual Knife Detection in Images: Active Appearance Models Initialized with Shape-specific Interest Points. In: Proceedings of th International Conference "Multimedia Communications, Services and Security", Krakow, Poland, pp. 148–158 (2012)

3. Krishnapuram, R., Frigui, H., Nasraoui, O.: Fuzzy and Possibilistic Shell Clustering Algorithms and Their Application to Boundary Detection and Surface Approximation Part 1& Part 2. IEEE Transactions on Fuzzy Systems 3(1), 29–60 (1995)
4. Klawonn, F., Kruse, R., Timm, H.: Fuzzy Shell Cluster Analysis. In: Della Riccia, G., Lenz, H.J., Kruse, R. (eds.) Learning, Networks and Statistics, pp. 105–120. Springer, Wien (1997)
5. Gonzales, R.C., Woods, R.E.: Digital Image Processing, 2nd edn. Prentice Hall, Upper Saddle River (2002)
6. Krishnapuram, R., Frigui, H., Nasraoui, O.: A Fuzzy Clustering Algorithm to to Detect Planar and Quadric Shapes. In: Proc. North American Fuzzy Information Processing Society Workshop (Puerto Vallarta, Mexico), pp. 59–68 (1992)
7. Bezdek, J.C., Keller, J.M., Krishnapuram, R., Pal, N.R.: Fuzzy Models and Algorithms for Pattern Recognition and Image Processing. Springer Science, New York (2005)
8. Krishnapuram, K., Keller, M.: A possibilistic approach to clustering. IEEE Transaction on Fuzzy Systems 1(2), 98–110 (1993)

3D Video Compression Using Depth Map Propagation

Sergey Matyunin and Dmitriy Vatolin

Department of Computational Mathematics and Cybernetics
Lomonosov Moscow State University
Moscow, Russia
{smatyunin,dmitriy}@graphics.cs.msu.ru

Abstract. We propose a method of 3D video compression based on 2D+depth representation. We use correlation between 2D video and depth map to reconstruct highly compressed depth map while decoding. Depth map is compressed with reduced spatial and temporal resolution. On decoding stage the algorithm restore original resolution using information from 2D video. We evaluated the influence of key frames' resolution, compression ratio and density on the performance of the algorithm. The proposed technique was compared to depth map compression using H.264 in compression pipeline for stereo video.

Keywords: Stereo image processing, video compression, three dimensional TV.

1   Introduction

This paper addresses the problem of stereoscopic video compression. Increasing demands to stereo content quality cause the need of the effective video compression algorithms development.

The simplest approach for stereo video coding is independent encoding of each view using conventional video codecs. The main disadvantage of this scheme is low compression performance and bad scalability for large number of views. To improve compression capabilities, most multiview coding schemes exploit interview redundancy of stereo or multiview video as well as temporal inter-frame redundancy [1,2]. This approach was applied in H.262/MPEG-2 [3] and H.264/MPEG-4 AVC [4] video coding standards. Compression with interview prediction improves compression capabilities however bitrate remains linearly proportional to the number of encoded views [5]. It makes multiview coding inefficient for content compression of modern autostereoscopic displays which require tens of views as input.

Another common approach to stereoscopic video compression is 2D-Plus-Depth or Multiview-Plus-Depth (MVD) format usage [5, 6]. Depth map is estimated for source multiview video on the encoder's side and encoded along with 2D view. On the decoder's side required number of views is synthesized from decoded video and depth map. This representation can't be used for correct processing of transparent objects and areas behind the objects. Nevertheless this representation is widely used in 2D-to-3D video conversion and as an internal format in a variety of TV's and monitors. 2D+depth format allows generation of arbitrary number of views in a displaying device and thus this format is suitable for multiview video coding and free viewpoint television.

A. Dziech and A. Czyżewski (Eds.): MCSS 2013, CCIS 368, pp. 153–166, 2013.

The simplest approach to the depth maps compression is using the traditional video codecs [7]. An important aspect here is determining a ratio between 2D and depth map bitrates that maximizes the resulting quality. Independent compression of depth maps using codecs developed for common video compression is ineffective.

2D video channel has high correlation with depth map so it can be used for depth map decoding and restoration. In [8] 2D image is used to increase frame rate and resolution of the depth map obtained using depth sensor. Modified cross-bilateral filtering is used to increase spatial resolution. Frame rate is doubled using temporal interpolation. The interpolation is based on motion vectors estimated from 2D video. In our approach we use more complex interpolation procedure so depth map restoration from sparse known key frames is possible.

In [9] joint compression of video and depth map is done using motion vectors estimated from the source video. Input scene is segmented. Extracted background is transmitted independently. Depth map is considered only for foreground objects. Additionally, motion in the third dimension is estimated and the obtained motion vectors are transmitted with the compressed video stream.

Another important aspect of the 3D video compression algorithms is quality measurement. Due to the complexity of stereoscopic perception there is no generally accepted method for quality measurement. Research in this direction is in progress [10,11]. The most common approach is to use conventional 2D quality metric. Direct measurements of depth map difference before and after compression is not relevant because depth map influences on synthesized views quality in a nontrivial way. Therefore 2D quality metrics are often applied to synthesized views [13]. We use the latter approach in our tests.

2   Proposed Scheme of Compression

The proposed algorithm uses 2D video and the corresponding depth map as input data. In our current research we don't consider 2D video compression. In all experiments we use uncompressed 2D video. Processing pipeline for depth map consists of the following steps:

1. Key frames are selected from input depth map at constant or variable intervals.
   (a) Constant intervals are 10, 20, 40 and 100 frames.
   (b) Variable intervals are selected adaptively to maximize the quality.
2. Key frames of input depth map are downsampled by constant factor k = 1 (without downsampling), 2 or 4.
3. Downsampled key frames are encoded using JPEG 2000 with a constant quality parameter q (64, 128, 256, 512). Size of compressed depth map is measured.
4. Full-resolution key frames are restored using YUVsoft Depth Upscale [14]. It provides better depth alignment to objects borders than conventional super-resolution methods. Additional color information from correspondent 2D frame allows improve quality of upscaled depth map.
5. Full depth map is restored from key frames using YUVsoft Depth Propagation [15]. Full-resolution depth key frames are used for restoration of depth map for non-key frames. Depth information is copied between frames according to motion and color restrictions extracted from 2D video. The algorithm is similar to the depth processing method described in [16].

Steps 1–3 correspond to encoding process, and steps 4–5 correspond to depth map decoding. The compression scheme was tested on a set of 9 sequences with different types of motion. Frame rate was assumed be equal to 30 frames/second.

3   Quality Evaluation

The proposed method was compared to the results of depth map compression using x264[1]. We measured the difference in quality for stereo video generated from compressed and original depth map.

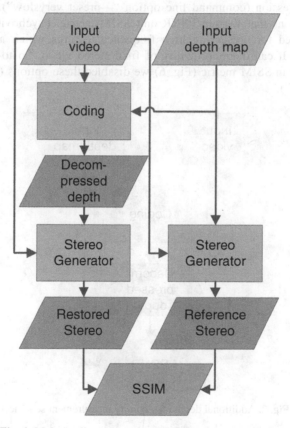

Fig. 1. Main quality measurement scheme for restored stereo

Methods of stereo reconstruction from 2D+depth don't provide per-pixel match to the original stereo [10]. Therefore the usage of per-pixel metrics doesn't provide appropriate comparison. Another problem of the 2D+depth representation is occlusion areas filling. Inpainting methods cannot fill large occlusions accurately. Extra

---

[1] x264 version is 0.122.2183.

information about occlusions should be encoded to provide good quality of restored stereo. We didn't use available original stereo footages in the comparison to eliminate the factors mentioned above. We compared synthesized stereo for depth map before and after compression (Fig. 1).

In addition we evaluated results using PSNR metric for decompressed depth map (Fig. 2). SSIM metric [12] was used for restored stereo. SSIM metric has higher correlation with human perception therefore we used it for evaluation of stereo quality. SSIM is not suitable for depth map quality assessment because depth map is not a visible decompressed video in the pipeline.

Initially we used the default x264 codec settings. Very slow preset was selected for better compression (command line option "—preset veryslow"). We also disabled optimizations that worsen PSNR and SSIM metric. Psychovisual optimizations are intended for preserving high frequency textures which are not typical for depth maps. It can degrade quality of final stereo video. So to maximize the quality of stereo in SSIM metric (Fig. 6) we disabled these options (command line option "--no-psy").

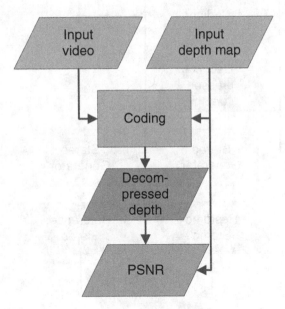

Fig. 2. Additional depth map quality measurement scheme

4   Description of the Experiments

We tested several aspects of the algorithm to achieve good compression. At first we tested two implementations of JPEG 2000 codec for key frames compression. Then we evaluated strategies of key frames selection.

4.1   Key Frames Compression Using JPEG 2000

We used two implementations of JPEG 2000 codec from FFmpeg[2] and from Image-Magick[3] packages for key frames compression. Codec from ImageMagick demonstrated better compression results both for PSNR and SSIM metrics (Fig. 3 and Fig. 4).

Compression with JPEG 2000 from ImageMagick yields low quality compression on high compression rates q and scale factor k. In this case codec gives single-colour grey image. It is displayed in Fig. 5 by significant quality loss for $k = 4$, $q = 256$ and $q = 512$.

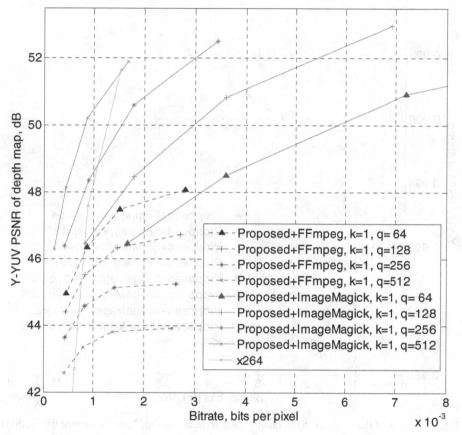

Fig. 3. Results of the restored stereo quality measurement for the "Lane" sequence[4] using PSNR metric. Each point on the proposed method lines corresponds to the certain value of the distance between key frames parameter. JPEG 2000 implementation from ImageMagick package demonstrated better compression performance.

---

[2]   FFmpeg version N-36088-gdd1fb65 built on Dec 22 2011 12:42:06 with gcc 4.6.2.
[3]   ImageMagick version 6.7.6-1 2012-03-14 Q16.
[4]   Source stereo sequence is provided by Alan Bovik's group.

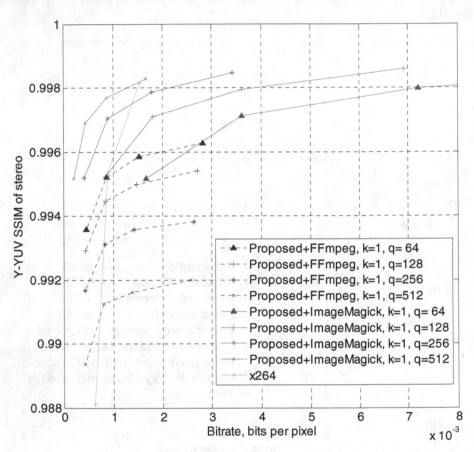

Fig. 4. Results of the restored stereo quality measurement for the "Lane" sequence using SSIM metric. Each point on the proposed method lines corresponds to the certain value of the distance between key frames parameter. JPEG 2000 implementation from ImageMagick package demonstrated better compression performance.

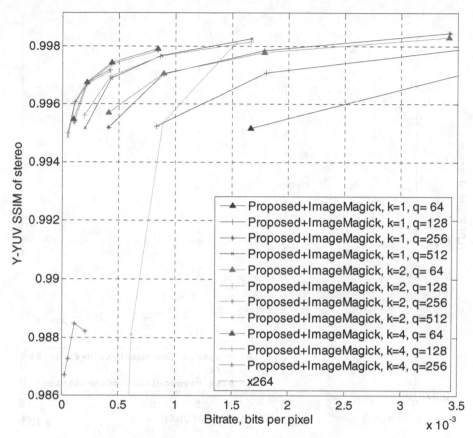

Fig. 5. Compression results for different JPEG 2000 parameter q and resolution factor k. Decreasing spatial resolution of depth map gives nearly the same effect as increasing JPEG 2000 compression.

4.2   Increase of Key Frames Density

We analyzed a relation between restored stereo quality and key frames density. Decreasing the distance between key frames down to encoding without depth propagation gives no gain over x264 (Fig. 6) due to independent depth map compression for key frames without motion compensation and interframe prediction. Higher key frames density yields SSIM increment, but quality gain is insignificant in comparison with bitrate growth.

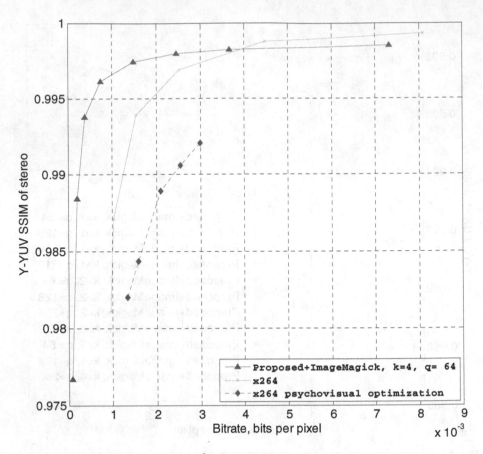

Fig. 6. Results for "Pirates" sequence[5]. Performance gain of proposed method decreases with increasing key frames density. Rightmost point of the red graph corresponds to compression without depth map propagation (compression of downsized depth map frames with JPEG 2000)

4.3   Adaptive Key Frames Placing

Initially key frames in the proposed method were selected at regular intervals. Obviously it is not an optimal strategy. We tested the approach of adaptive key frames selection. Static scenes require less key frames and dynamic scenes must be encoded using dense key frames to achieve acceptable quality.

As initial approximation we took a set of sparse equidistant key frames at the best parameter set (high scale factor, medium JPEG 2000 quality). Then key frames were added semi-automatically to maximize the metric. Example of per-frame SSIM of stereo for a part of "Basketball" sequence[6] is presented in Fig. 7. We tested automatic

---

[5]   The sequence is a part of official trailer of movie "Pirates of the Caribbean: On Stranger Tides".

[6]   Source stereo sequence is provided by Alan Bovik's group.

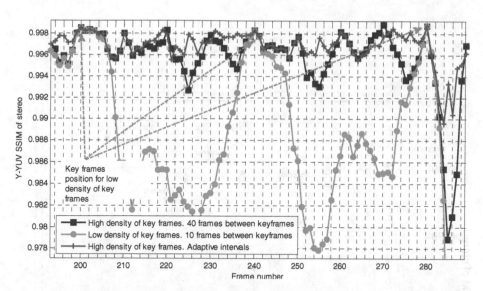

Fig. 7. Frame-by-frame metric values for a part of the "Basketball" sequence. The blue line corresponds to high key frames density. The green line corresponds to low key frames density. There is a significant decrease of the metric values between the key frames (frames No. 200, 240, 280). We added depth keyframes in the positions with the lowest metric values (red line). It yields quality gain and lower bitrate in comparison to dense keyframes configuration.

key frames placement to the minima of SSIM metric and to weighted minima. We didn't get significant compression enhancement and therefore we chose user-guided selection. More complex automatic criteria should be used to deal with complex scenes.

In addition we implemented P-frames analogue in our compression algorithm. While inserting new key frame between existing two we encoded only difference between predicted depth map (propagation results between existing key frames) and original depth map. Sometimes difference contains more high frequencies and requires more space than independent keyframe on the same position. In that case independent keyframe was inserted instead of P-frame.

Example of results for adaptive key frames selection is presented in Fig. 8. In this case we optimize SSIM for restored stereo. Visualization of the results is presented in Fig. 9 – Fig. 11.

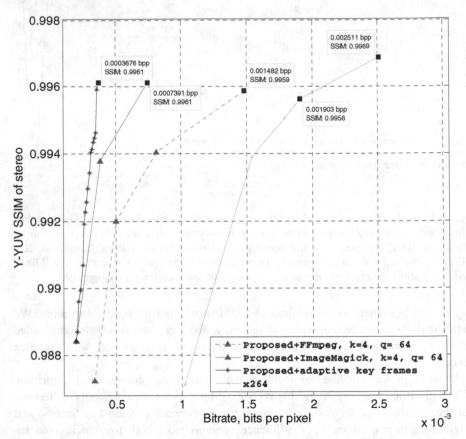

Fig. 8. Adaptive key frames distribution reduced the bitrate by 50% on the "Pirates" sequence leaving the SSIM metric values of the same level. The proposed method exceeds the x264 codec results more than 5 times. Each line for the proposed method corresponds to a certain set of the spatial resolution decrease and JPEG 2000 compression parameters (k and q respectively) values. Dots on the x264 line correspond to the different codec compression parameter (crf) values.

Fig. 9. Fragments of a view synthesized from original depth map (left) and original depth map (right). 16th frame of the "Statue" sequence [17].

Fig. 10. Fragments of synthesized view and SSIM metric visualization for 16th frame of the "Statue" sequence with constant key frames distribution. On the metric visualization lighter areas correspond to lower metric values. SSIM = 0.993088.

Fig. 11. Fragments of synthesized view and SSIM metric visualization for 16th frame of the "Statue" sequence with adaptive key frames distribution. Adaptive key frame choosing allows decreasing amount of the artifacts in the dynamic scenes when compressing with the same bitrate. SSIM = 0.994836.

5   Conclusions

We proposed a method of depth map compression for multiview video using 2D+depth representation. Only low resolution key frames of depth map are encoded. Depth for the whole video is restored on the decoding stage using information from 2D video. We found out that increased key frames density doesn't provide better compression ratio. Key frames must be selected adaptively to the properties of the depth map and the quality of the restored stereo. We tested several simple automatic approaches to key frames selection, but they were ineffective. We utilized user-guided key frames selection based on SSIM of the resulting stereo. We also implemented inter-frame prediction for intermediate key frames (analogue of P-frames) to improve compression ratio. The described improvements allowed reducing the bitrate up to 50% while preserving the same quality level.

Further quality improvements must include usage of quadro format to deal with occlusion areas. Uncovered regions must be encoded additionally to prevent artifacts in the areas where Inpainting of stereo generator doesn't provide good quality.

We also intend to implement more complex automatic approaches for key frames selection. They must consider scene changes and confidence metric of depth propagation to select appropriate places for key frames.

In the current part of the work we used constant quality for key frames compression. Another area of further research is optimal selection of key frames compression ratio.

Quality of depth propagation algorithm is very significant for the compression. The major drawbacks of the current version are forced depth boundaries alignment and depth leakage across objects borders. The first makes difference near objects borders larger if input depth map was not properly aligned to the source video. The second reduces the quality in the dynamic scenes. Eliminating of depth leakage is possible through additional detection and processing of occlusion areas.

Acknowledgements. This research was partially supported by grant 10-01-00697-a from the Russian Foundation for Basic Research and Intel-Cisco Video Aware Wireless Network Project.

References

1. Lukacs, M.E.: Predictive coding of multi-viewpoint image sets. In: International Conference on Acoustics, Speech, and Signal Processing (ICASSP), Tokyo, Japan, vol. 1, pp. 521–524 (1986)
2. Merkle, P., Muller, K., Smolic, A., Wiegand, T.: Efficient Compression of Multi-View Video Exploiting Inter-View Dependencies Based on H.264/MPEG4-AVC. In: Proc. IEEE International Conference on Multimedia and Expo., pp. 1717–1720 (2006)
3. ITU-T and ISO/IEC JTC 1, Final draft amendment 3, amendment 3 to ITU-T recommendation H.262 and ISO/IEC13818-2 (MPEG-2 Video), ISO/IEC JTC 1/SC29/WG 11 (MPEG) Doc. N 1366 (1996)
4. ITU-T and ISO/IEC JTC 1, Advanced video coding for generic audiovisual services, ITU-T Recommendation H.264 and ISO/IEC 14496-10, MPEG-4 AVC (2010)
5. Müller, K., Merkle, P., Wiegand, T.: 3D Video Representation Using Depth Maps. Proceedings of the IEEE, Special Issue on "3D Media and Displays" 99(4), 643–656 (2011)
6. Morvan, Y., de With, P., Farin, D.: Platelet-based coding of depth maps for the transmission of multiview images. In: Proc. Stereoscopic Displays and Applications, SPIE, vol. 6055, pp. 93–100 (2006)
7. Bosc, E., Jantet, V., Pressigout, M., Morin, L., Guillemot, C.: Bit-rate allocation for multiview video plus depth. In: Proc. 3DTV Conference The True Vision Capture Transmission and Display of 3D Video 3DTVCON, pp. 1–4 (2011)
8. Choi, J., Min, D., Sohn, K.: 2D-plus-depth based resolution and frame-rate up-conversion technique for depth video. IEEE Transactions on Consumer Electronics 56, 2489–2497 (2010)
9. De Silva, D.V.S.X., Fernando, W.A.C., Yasakethu, S.L.P.: Object based coding of the depth maps for 3D video coding. IEEE Transactions on Consumer Electronic 55, 1699–1706 (2009)
10. Kim, W.-S., Ortega, A., Lai, P., Tian, D., Gomila, C.: Depth map distortion analysis for view rendering and depth coding. In: Proc. International Conference on Image Processing, pp. 721–724 (2009)
11. Hewage, C.T.E.R., Martini, M.G.: Reduced-reference quality evaluation for compressed depth maps associated with colour plus depth 3D video. In: 17th IEEE International Conference on Image Processing, ICIP (2010)
12. Wang, Z., Bovik, A.C., Sheikh, H.R., Simoncelli, E.P.: Image quality assessment: From error visibility to structural similarity. IEEE Transactions on Image Processing 13(4), 600–612 (2004)
13. Lee, C., Jung, J.-I., Ho, Y.-S.: Inter-view Depth Pre-processing for 3D Video Coding. ISO/IEC JTC1/SC29/WG11, m22669, pp. 1–7 (November 2011)

14. YUVsoft Depth Upscale, http://www.yuvsoft.com/
    stereo-3d-technologies/depth-upscale/ (retrieved)
15. YUVsoft Depth Propagation, http://www.yuvsoft.com/
    stereo-3d-technologies/depth-propagation/ (retrieved)
16. Li, Y., Sun, L., Xue, T.: Fast frame-rate up-conversion of depth video via video coding. In: Proceedings of the 19th ACM International Conference on Multimedia, MM 2011, pp. 1317–1320. ACM, USA (2011)
17. Zhang, G., Jia, J., Wong, T.T., Bao, H.: Consistent depth maps recovery from a video sequence. IEEE Transactions on Pattern Analysis and Machine Intelligence 31(6), 974–988 (2009)

Using Sub-sequence Patterns
for Detecting Organ Trafficking Websites

Suraj Jung Pandey[1], Suresh Manandhar[1], and Agnieszka Kleszcz[2]

[1] University of York,
Heslington, York, YO10 5GH, UK
{suraj.pandey,suresh.manandhar}@york.ac.uk
[2] AGH University of Science and Technology, Al. A. Mickiewicza 30, 30-059 Krakow
agakleszcz87@gmail.com

Abstract. This paper presents a novel method for mining suspicious websites from World Wide Web by using state-of-the-art pattern mining and machine learning methods. In this document, the term "suspicious website" is used to mean any website that contains known or suspected violations of law. Although, we present our evaluation on illegal online organ trading, the method described in this paper is generic and can be used to detect any specific kind of websites. We use an iterative setting in which at each iterations we unearth both normal and suspicious websites. These newly detected websites are augmented in our training examples and used in next iterations. The first iteration uses user supplied seed normal and suspicious websites. We show that the accuracy increases in intial iterations but decreases with further increase in iterations. This is due to the bias caused by adding large number of normal websites and also due to the automatic addition of noise in training examples.

1 Introduction

Broadcasting information is becoming easier, effective and cheaper every passing day due to the availability of Internet. Websites can be created to advertise information about virtually anything. Unfortunately, websites can also be used to advertise criminal activities. For example, dealers selling drugs or weapons, or groups promoting terrorist activity, exchanging information and recruiting new members, or illegal organ trafficking.

It is necessary to collect information from the web to identify suspicious websites. The detection methods developed in the report can be employed by law enforcement agencies to narrow search pattern to aid an investigation.

In this paper, we describe a method that mines patterns from suspicious websites. The induced patterns then can be used to identify undetected suspicious websites from the World Wide Web. In this document, the term "suspicious website" is used to mean any website that contains known or suspected violations of law. In typical usage, a suspicious website could be a website that encourages violence, fraud, terrorist financing, and other crimes. However, the methods described in this report are generic and can be used to detect any specific kind of websites, for example, a website that discusses basketball and religion.

A. Dziech and A. Czyżewski (Eds.): MCSS 2013, CCIS 368, pp. 167–180, 2013.

We perform our evaluation on detecting illegal online organ trading. There are many websites that allow people to post advertisements to sell their organs. Most people willing to sell their organs volunteer due to their financial circumstances. At the present time, the demand for kidneys and other organs far exceeds the available supply. The reason is because of growing diabetes, high blood and heart problems throughout the world. People are desperate to find a kidney so they buy one from the black market. Officially, the trade in organs is illegal, and is punishable by law. There has been a dramatic increase in worldwide illegal organ trade. According to the World Health Organization (WHO), in 2010 about 10% of all transplant were performed illegally [1].

As buying and selling of human organs is illegal around the world, black market is created in order to meet the demand. Frequently, this black market consists of rich patients from developed countries using "brokers" to arrange for the purchase of organs from poor people in underdeveloped countries. Mostly the black market has centered on buying and selling of kidneys but there has also been extensive trading in other organs like liver, lung, eyeball or bone marrow. Websites that allows buying/selling of organs becomes easy medium for brokers to get in contact with donors.

There are many health risk associated with organ transplant for both the receiver and the donor. This is elevated in illegal trafficking due to lack of expert screening of both donors and recipients. Illegal organ trafficking is expected to become more severe in the future, due to increasing demand for organs. Therefore research into methods for tracking illegal organ trafficking websites is essential.

We extract patterns from organ trading websites, mine patterns and then identify new similar websites from World Wide Web. The classification of websites as either suspicious or normal is done using Support Vector Machine (SVM). The choice of SVM is due to its high performance in other text classification task [2].

The major contributions of this paper are:

- We devise an iterative algorithm which is used for unearthing suspicious websites from World Wide Web by using minimum number of seed websites. Seed websites are user collected websites of both suspicious and normal nature. At each iteration of our method we add new websites automatically to our suspicious and normal websites repository. This new knowledge obtained is used in next iterations for detecting new suspicious and normal websites.
- We show by evaluation that bootstrapping new websites by using seed websites works up to multiple level of iterations. The amount of noise added at each iterations will depend on the reliability of seed websites.
- We provide strong motivation for using sub-sequence as feature for text mining and classification.

2   Related Work

For text mining and classification methods, selection of features is an important step. The simplest feature for representing text is a *word* or a *term* or an *unigram*. A document can be represented by creating a vector where each component of the vector is a word/term from the document. Most earlier work in text mining use term based methods [3,4,5]. The major advantage of using terms as features for text mining is that the computation becomes very easy. Also the frequency of terms can be high within a document thus the problem of sparsity is also reduced. But terms in itself carries little contextual information and thus can retrieve lots of noise. To gather contextual information, phrases instead of terms can be used as features. An n-gram is a continuous sequence of n terms in a text. N-grams as features for text mining has been used to capture "semantic" information of keywords [6,7,8]. N-grams also have some distinctive disadvantages. Firstly, to better capture the context of any word n has to be high. Once the phrase is long, it becomes very sparse within the document collection. Secondly, n-grams only capture continuous adjacent phrases. This becomes problematic for detecting suspicious patterns where a suspicious patterns can be formed by combining words not adjacent to each other. Non-continuous phrases is captured by dependency parse phrase. A dependency parse phrase is constructed following a dependency path of given terms generated by a dependency parser. Dependency phrases have been successfully used in text classification [9]. To construct a dependency parse phrase each sentence is parsed using the Stanford dependency parser [10]. A dependency parse represents dependencies between individual words, in effect providing information about predicate-argument structure which are not readily available from phrase structure parses [11]. Although dependency parse phrases leads to compact phrases carrying contextual information, the computational overhead and reliability in accuracy of parsers makes them less appealing. An alternative to dependency parse can be sub-sequences. A sub-sequence is a sequence that is obtained by deleting one or more terms from a given sequence while preserving the order of the original sequence. Sub-sequences has been used extensively in the field of data mining/information mining– sentiment classification [12], web usuage mining [13,14] data mining [15,16]. The concept of sub-sequence mining was first used in [17] to mine sequential pattern over a database of customer transactions, where each transaction consists of customer-id, transaction time, and the items bought in the transaction. The advantage of using sub-sequence patterns over n-gram pattern is two fold (1) it captures contextual information of terms and (2) it is more compact and has less redundant terms.

Once patterns have been extracted it is necessary to weight and rank them for using in classification. Association mining has been used in Web text mining, which refers to the process of searching through unstructured data on the Web and deriving meaning from it [18,19]. The association between a set of keywords and a predefined category (e.g. suspicious websites) can be described as an association rule. The strength of the association can be computed using the hypothesis testing. Various methods like Chi-squared test and likelihood [20] ratios can be applied. Though this method can be used to find a large number of relevant patterns but one key disadvantage is that new patterns which do not co-occur with the seed pattern will not be identified.

Vector space model in conjunction with similarity calculation has been used successfully to measure semantic relationship between two terms [21].This concept can be used in our setting to measure the semantic relationship between two categories of websites. The similarity between two texts depends on the weights of coinciding terms in the two vectors. Similar method is also used in [22,23,24], all of them using TF-IDF (Term Frequency - Inverse Document Frequency) to weight the components of vectors. The term frequency for a word w_i is the number of its occurrences in the document. Inverse Document Frequency is the ratio of the total number of documents in which w_i appears to the number of documents in the corpus. If training data is available then then text classification can be achieved by using supervised machine learning models. SVMs are one of the most popular and reliable supervised learning methods that have been used in different tasks including text classification [2].

3   System Architecture for Detecting Suspicious Websites

This section presents the method for crawling websites for pattern mining, specifically websites that have possible criminal uses (e.g. illegal organ trading). The extracted patterns are then used to crawl other such websites. The specification of the iterative process is shown in Figure 1. As can be observed, the methodology consists of following main modules:

- Step 1: Pre-Processing:- In this step the input is tokenised, lemmatised, sentence boundaries are identified and stop words are removed. The preprocessed suspicious content is sent to Step 2 while normal content is sent to both Step 2 and Step 4 and Step 9.
- Step 2: Pattern Generation:- This module will take as input suspicious websites and normal websites and generate patterns from both. The patterns generated will be subsequences. The output patterns from suspicious websites and normal websites are both sent to Step 3 and Step 4 .
- Step 3: Classifier Training:- This module will take a labelled feature file (see Section 5.2) and use Support Vector Machine (SVM) to create a classifier to identify suspicious websites. The use of SVM classifier differentiates our system from a purely keyword matching system. A SVM classifier weights each term within a document according to its importance and makes decision based on sum of the weights of each terms.
- Step 4: Pattern Matching:- This module will match the patterns from both suspicious and normal websites and generate patterns unique to suspicious websites. The set of patterns selected by this method is termed as *initial pattern*. The initial patterns will be stored in a suspicious content repository.
- Step 5: Link Module:- The link module will take as input the patterns generated from pattern matching module. These patterns will be provided as input to a search engine to generate additional links to potentially suspicious websites. The generated links are passed to a crawling module.
- Step 6: Crawler:- A Web crawler is a software agent that starts with a list of seed URLs to visit. As the crawler visits these URLs, it identifies all the

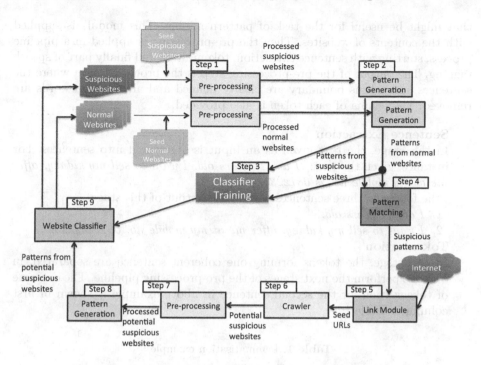

Fig. 1. Method specification for detecting suspicious website

hyperlinks in the page and adds them to the list of URLs to visit, called the crawler frontier. URLs from the frontier are recursively visited according to a set of policies. The purpose of the crawler is to find websites that are hyperlinked from potentially suspicious websites. The output of the crawler will include both the initial seed URLs and the hyperlinks URLs.

- Step 7: Pre-processing:- The additional new content generated by the crawler is preprocessed in this step (see Step 1).
- Step 8: Pattern Generation:- A set of *new patterns* are generated from the new suspicious content (see Step 2 for explanation of pattern generation).
- Step 9: Website classification:- The patterns generated from Step 9 is employed as features for classifier model generated by Step 3 to classify websites generated by crawler (Step 6).

The above steps are repeated. In each iteration a list of *suspicious* websites might be identified along with the suspicious patterns extracted from the pattern matching module.

3.1   Pre-processing

The aim of this module is to apply a set of pre-compiled NLP tools to the given unstructured text, so as to extract a set of contextual and syntactic features that might be useful for the task of pattern mining. This module is supplied with the contents of websites. Then the pre-processing is applied in a pipeline process, starting with sentence extraction, tokenisation and finally part of speech tagging. The output of the pre-processing step is the processed data where the sentences and tokens boundary are clearly defined and all the stop words are removed. The lemma of each token is also provided.

- **Sentence Extraction**
  In this stage, the text given as an input is segmented into sentences. For instance, given the text: *I am 27 years old. I want to sell my kidney, offer me at my mobile no. is 08122342434*
  , the following three sentences will be the output of this stage
  1. *I am 27 years old.*
  2. *I want to sell my kidney, offer me at my mobile no. 08122342434*
- **Tokenisation**
  In this stage, the tokens forming one coherent sentence are separated, in order to perform the next stages of the pre-processing pipeline. The outcome of tokenisation for the second sentence in above example is shown in first column of Table 1.

Table 1. Lemmatisation example

Token	Lemma
I	I
am	be
27	27
years	year
old	old

- **Lemmatisation**
  Lemmatisation refers to group together the different inflected forms of a given word and represent them by a common string, i.e. the lemma. Column 2 of Table 1 provide the lemmas of all the words of above example sentence.
- **Stop words**
  Stop words are words which are filtered out using a pre-defined list. For example, in our context, short function words, such as the, is, at, which and on are used as stop words.

3.2   Pattern Generation

Pattern Generation is the method to generate candidate patterns from the given document. Patterns are generated from both suspicious websites and normal

N-gram
1-gram :   "I" "want" "to" "sell" "my" "kidney " "offer" "me" "at" "my" "mobile" "no." "08122342434"
2-gram :   "I want" "want to" "to sell" "sell my" "my kidney" "kidney offer" "offer me" "me at" "at my" ...
3-gram :   "I want to" "want to sell" "to sell my" "sell my kidney" "my kidney offer" "kidney offer me" "offer me at"   "me at my "….
4-gram :   "I want to sell" "want to sell my " "to sell my kidney" "sell my kidney offer" "my kidney offer me" "kidney   offer me at"……
. . . .
13-gram :   "I want to sell my kidney offer me at my mobile no. 08122342434"

Fig. 2. N-gram sequences

websites. In the context of current work we use sub-sequences as patterns. A sub-sequence is a sequence that is obtained by deleting one or more terms from a given sequence while preserving the order of the original sequence. The advantage of using sub-sequence patterns over n-gram pattern is two fold (1) it captures contextual information of terms and (2) it is more compact and has less redundant terms.

If we consider that the pattern *sell-kidney-offer* suggests criminal behaviour in the sentence, "*I want to sell my kidney, offer me at my mobile no. 08122342434*". We can see from Figure 2 that it is not possible to extract the exact pattern *sell-kidney-offer* using any of the n-gram technique. Only when we set n greater or equal to 4 all of the words of the pattern occur in the same frame. Taking a long frame can hurt further search, since it will be hard to find a exact matching pattern for such lengthy frames. Search engines use frequency of match to extract websites. Using long frames will make features very sparse, thus we will miss out on desirable websites. In contrast to this, we can see in Figure 3 that one of the sub-sequences is *sell-kidney-offer* which is the pattern we want to extract. Also the probability of finding a sub-sequence *sell-kidney-offer* in a document about criminal activities can be considered high. Pseudo-code to extract all possible sub-sequences from a sentence is given in Algorithm 1:

3.3   Classifier Training

The training of our model and the classification is based on Support Vector Machines (SVMs). SVMs are one of the most popular and reliable supervised learning methods that have been used in different tasks including text classification [2], question classification [25], word sense disambiguation [26,27] and relation extraction [28].

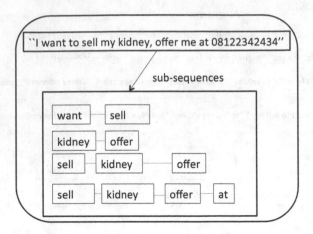

Fig. 3. Sub-sequences

Let us assume that we have a set of input vectors X_i (one vector for each document), while the target is to predict their labels, i.e. $Y_i = +/-1$ (suspicious or normal). The theoretical bounds on the generalization error specify the following:

- The upper bound on the generalization error does not depend on the dimensionality of the space.
- The bound is minimized by maximizing a quantity called the margin (Figure 4), i.e. the minimal distance between the hyperplane separating the two classes (1, -1) and the closest data points (support vectors) of each class.

A hyperplane can be written as a set of points x satisfying $w \cdot x - b = 0$, where w is a normal vector of weights perpendicular to the hyperplane and b is a constant. Note that $\cdot$ denotes the dot product. Maximizing the margin, i.e. the minimal distance between the hyperplane and the two classes (1,-1), is equivalent to minimizing $\frac{\|w\|}{2}$, subject to the constraint that $y_i \times (w \cdot x) - b \geq 1$.

$$W(\alpha) = \sum_{i=1}^{m} \alpha_i - \frac{1}{2} \sum_{i,j=1}^{m} a_i a_j y_i (x_i \cdot x_j) \qquad (1)$$

This constraint optimization problem can formulated as finding the optimum of a quadratic function 1, where α_i are Lagrange multipliers and m is the number of training pairs (x_i, y_i). Finally for binary classification the decision function is shown in Equation 2, where q is a new test instance.

$$D(q) = sign(\sum_{j=1}^{m} a_j y_j (x_j \cdot q) + b)) \qquad (2)$$

Using Equation 2, we can classify a given document as illegal or not.

```
 1  Define List¡String¿ subseq ;
 2  Define token[]=sentence.toTokens();
 3  for (int i = 0; i ¡ token.length; i++) do
 4      if (NOT(token[i] In subseq)) then
 5       |  Add token[i] to subseq;
 6      end
 7      String seq = token[i];
 8      for (int j = i + 1, l = i + 1; j ¡ token.length; j++) do
 9          seq = seq + " " + token[j];
10          if (NOT(seq In subseq)) then
11           |  Add seq to subseq;
12          end
13          if (j == token.length - 1) then
14           |   j = l;
15           |   l++;
16           |   seq = token[i];
17          end
18      end
19  end
```

Algorithm 1. Steps to generate all possible sub-sequence from a sentence

4 Pattern Matching

In this step we select patterns which show high association to suspicious websites than to normal websites. In many suspicious websites, the sentences containing messages to influence criminal activities are generally grouped within other normal sentences. For example, a suspicious websites can have many factual information and few suspicious lines. Thus, the patterns extracted from such suspicious websites are not all indicative of criminal activities. Most of these patterns will also occur in normal websites. To filter out such normal patterns we use a very simple approach. Once we generate patterns from both suspicious websites and normal websites. The patterns indicative of criminal activities are only those which are not present in normal websites. Thus, we select only patterns which are present in suspicious websites but not in normal websites. For example, from Table 2 we can see that except pattern *sell-kidney-offer* rest of the patterns are common in both suspicious and normal website. Thus, for this example we only choose pattern *sell-kidney-offer* to be used in next step.

Table 2. Possible patterns generated from suspicious and normal websites

Patterns from suspicious websites	Patterns from normal website
sell-kidney-offer	everest-mountain
everest-mountain	tall-mountain-world
tall-mountain-world	temperature-cold-winter

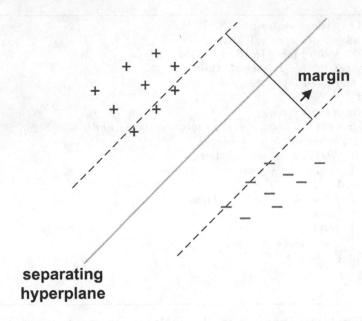

Fig. 4. Hyperplane separating 2 classes

4.1   Link Module

The link module will take as an input patterns from the pattern matching step. Given patterns will be used, as the keywords for the open search index API which will provide links to websites that are well known by the search engine. In this way seed set will contain as wide as possible coverage of start links which would prevent focusing crawling only to the limited number of domains.

4.2   Crawler

The purpose of the crawling module is to extract hyperlinks from the initial set of seed websites and maintain a crawling frontier. Adding a crawling module will help find new websites that are linked from current websites which otherwise would have been missed by the search engine.

A typical crawling software, at any given moment, maintains two important sets. The first set is the set of visited documents. These are the documents that the crawler downloaded and processed at a given moment. The second set is yet-to-be-visited nodes most of which are yet to be discovered by the crawler at any given moment. Crawler discovers new documents by extracting anchors from already processed documents.

Miniature Jack russel puppy for sale
West, Lincshire

Allen on 0345671235

Chinese teen sells kidney to purchase iPhone, iPad

4/6/2012

In an extreme case of gotta-have-it, a Chinese teen sold his kidney to get money to buy an iPhone and an iPad, Reuters reports. A group of five people who arranged the organ transfer, including a surgeon, have been charged with "illegal organ trading" and "intentional injury." They received roughly $31,500 for the kidney, while the teen got $3,500. The teen apparently admitted to his mom that he had sold the organ when she asked how he had gotten his shiny new Apple paraphernalia. He is now suffering from renal deficiency, and, sadly, his condition is reportedly deteriorating.

I am selling my mini jack russel pup, she is 6 months old and a great wee puppy, I have a 7 month old baby who she is great With, very sad sale as I really don't want to part with her but I cant cope and I want her to go to a good loving family. Please Genuine people only. 0345671235, £180 ONO.

|Ad ref 1234567 | Posted 21 minutes ago | Posting ads since August 2009

(a) News article about boy selling his kidney   (b) An advertisement about a dog

Fig. 5. Two different types of negative examples

5   Evaluation

In this section we present results of our evaluation. In the first section, we describe the evaluation setting and the dataset and then we present accuracy results on classification of suspicious websites.

5.1   Evaluation Setting

For the purpose of evaluation we collected websites that advertise buying and selling of human organs. The dataset consists of positive examples of websites selling/buying organs illegally and the negative examples of the normal websites.

The following is an example of a website advertising buying and selling of human organs:

I am 27 years old, healthy, I do not drink neither do i smoke. I want to sell my kidney, if interested offer me at 89073872924, India

In the above snippet, phone number and address are made up.

The negative examples are collected from two different kind of sources. The first source are articles on human organs and the second source are the advertisements of different product (e.g. cars, pets etc.) from various online shopping websites. These sources for negative examples helps make it a near match of positive examples which in turn can tune the classifier during training phase to make better distinction between near matches. For example, as we can see from Figure 5(a) and Figure 5(b) they both contain distinguishing keywords like "kidney", "sell", "contact number" but they are not advertising illegal organ selling. An Internet search with keywords "kidney-sell-offer" will result in websites with contents as shown in Figure 5. Thus, it is necessary to add such websites as negative training examples so that the classifier can make distinction between a normal shopping website or a news website and a website selling/buying organs illegally.

The dataset consists of 700 positive examples and 700 negative examples. For evaluation the dataset is divided into three folds. Each fold consists of 500 postive examples and 500 negative examples and remaining unique set from each fold is used as test data.

5.2 Classification Accuracy

The training of the classifier is done using LIBSVM [29]. Table 3 shows accuracy score on test data at each iteration and also the number of positive and negative examples used at each iterations. The first iteration is carried out with annotated data and then in each consecutive iteration websites classified by the classification module is added to the previous training set and the classifier is re-trained. We can observe that there is an increase in accuracy in first couple of iterations which shows that our method can correctly identify suspicious and normal websites. The decrease in accuracy at further iterations is due to the bias caused by addition of higher number of negative websites compared to the number of positive websites. The resulting incorrect classification causes addition of incorrect examples into training set.

Table 3. Classification accuracy on test data at each iteration

	Fold 1			Fold 2			Fold 3		
Iteration	Accuracy	#suspicious documents	#normal documents	Accuracy	#suspicious documents	#normal documents	Accuracy	#suspicious documents	#normal documents
1	75.3%	500	500	72.7%	500	500	69.50%	500	500
2	76.5%	740	15500	77.1%	680	14412	72.7%	686	15624
3	76.9%	2285	24336	60.16%	2936	20833	68.15%	1944	23323
4	52.3%	9627	33677	42.5%	9290	28960	46.8%	8565	32694
5	46.8%	16648	44025	38.12%	15781	38421	39.50%	15815	44037

6   Conclusion

This paper has presented a novel method for iteratively mining suspicious websites. Our background survey has shown that sub-sequence as feature works best for both text mining and classification. Standard language modelling methods have also been applied to generate patterns for querying World Wide Web.

In this paper, we have presented a methodology that aims to unearth websites that are involved in illegal organ trading. The method developed in this paper is generic and can be used for mining any specific topic from World Wide Web. We show that bootstrapping process works and is highly dependent on seed websites. The accuracy of the system increases during intial iterations but then decreases due to addition of higher number of incorrect examples to training set.

References

1. Heyes, J.D.: Global organ harvesting a booming black market business; a kidney harvested every hour, http://www.naturalnews.com/036052_organ_harvesting_kidneys_black_market.html(accessed January 30, 2013)

2. Joachims, T.: Text categorization with support vector machines: learning with many relevant features. In: Nédellec, C., Rouveirol, C. (eds.) ECML 1998. LNCS, vol. 1398, pp. 137–142. Springer, Heidelberg (1998), http://citeseer.ist.psu.edu/joachims97text.html
3. Baeza-Yates, R.A., Ribeiro-Neto, B.: Modern Information Retrieval. Addison-Wesley Longman Publishing Co. Inc., Boston (1999)
4. Li, Y., Zhang, C., Swan, J.: An information filtering model on the web and its application in jobagent. Knowledge-Based Systems 13(5), 285–296 (2000), http://www.sciencedirect.com/science/article/pii/S0950705100000885
5. Robertson, S., Soboroff, I.: The trec 2002 filtering track report. In: Text Retrieval Conference (2002)
6. Lewis, D.D.: Feature selection and feature extraction for text categorization. In: Proceedings of the Workshop on Speech and Natural Language, HLT 1991, pp. 212–217. Association for Computational Linguistics, Stroudsburg (1992)
7. Scott, S., Matwin, S.: Feature engineering for text classification. In: Proceedings of the Sixteenth International Conference on Machine Learning, ICML 1999, pp. 379–388. Morgan Kaufmann Publishers Inc., San Francisco (1999)
8. Sebastiani, F.: Machine learning in automated text categorization. ACM Comput. Surv. 34, 1–47 (2002)
9. Wang, Z., Zhang, D.: Feature selection in text classification via svm and lsi. In: Wang, J., Yi, Z., Żurada, J.M., Lu, B.-L., Yin, H. (eds.) ISNN 2006. LNCS, vol. 3971, pp. 1381–1386. Springer, Heidelberg (2006)
10. Klein, D., Manning, C.D.: Accurate unlexicalized parsing. In: Proceedings of the 41st Annual Meeting on Association for Computational Linguistics, ACL 2003, vol. 1, pp. 423–430. Association for Computational Linguistics, Stroudsburg (2003), http://dx.doi.org/10.3115/1075096.1075150
11. De Marneffe, M.C., Maccartney, B., Manning, C.D.: Generating typed dependency parses from phrase structure parses. In: LREC 2006 (2006)
12. Matsumoto, S., Takamura, H., Okumura, M.: Sentiment classification using word sub-sequences and dependency sub-trees. In: Ho, T.B., Cheung, D., Liu, H. (eds.) PAKDD 2005. LNCS (LNAI), vol. 3518, pp. 301–311. Springer, Heidelberg (2005)
13. Data mining for path traversal patterns in a web environment. In: Proceedings of the 16th International Conference on Distributed Computing Systems, ICDCS 1996, pp. 385–392. IEEE Computer Society, Washington, DC (1996)
14. Pei, J., Han, J., Mortazavi-Asl, B., Zhu, H.: Mining access patterns efficiently from web logs. In: Terano, T., Liu, H., Chen, A.L.P. (eds.) PAKDD 2000. LNCS (LNAI), vol. 1805, pp. 396–407. Springer, Heidelberg (2000)
15. Wu, S.-T., Li, Y., Xu, Y.: Deploying approaches for pattern refinement in text mining. In: Proceedings of the Sixth International Conference on Data Mining, ICDM 2006, pp. 1157–1161. IEEE Computer Society, Washington, DC (2006)
16. Jindal, N., Liu, B.: Identifying comparative sentences in text documents. In: Proceedings of the 29th Annual International ACM SIGIR Conference on Research and Development in Information Retrieval, SIGIR 2006, pp. 244–251. ACM, New York (2006)
17. Agrawal, R., Srikant, R.: Mining sequential patterns. In: Proceedings of the Eleventh International Conference on Data Engineering, ICDE 1995, pp. 3–14. IEEE Computer Society, Washington, DC (1995)
18. Feldman, R.: Mining associations in text in the presence of background knowledge. In: Proceedings of the Second International Conference on Knowledge Discovery and Data Mining, KDD 1996, pp. 343–346 (1996)

19. Holt, J.D., Chung, S.M.: Multipass algorithms for mining association rules in text databases. Knowl. Inf. Syst. 3, 168–183 (2001)
20. Dunning, T.: Accurate Methods for the Statistics of Surprise and Coincidence. Computational Linguistics 19(1), 61–74 (1993)
21. Buckley, C., Salton, G., Allan, J., Singhal, A.: Automatic Query Expansion Using SMART: TREC 3. In: TREC (1994)
22. Sahami, M., Heilman, T.: A web-based kernel function for matching short text snippets. In: International Workshop Located at the 22nd International Conference on Machine Learning (ICML), pp. 2–9 (2005)
23. Abhishek, V., Hosanagar, K.: Keyword generation for search engine advertising using semantic similarity between terms. In: Proceedings of the Ninth International Conference on Electronic Commerce, ICEC 2007, pp. 89–94. ACM, New York (2007)
24. Joshi, A., Motwani, R.: Keyword generation for search engine advertising. In: Sixth IEEE International Conference on Data Mining Workshops, ICDM Workshops 2006, pp. 490–496 (December 2006)
25. Moschitti, A., Quarteroni, S., Basili, R., Manandhar, S.: Exploiting syntactic and shallow semantic kernels for question answer classification. In: Proceedings of the 45th Annual Meeting of the Association for Computational Linguistics. Association for Computational Linguistics (2007)
26. Joshi, M., Pedersen, T., Maclin, R., Pakhomov, S.: Kernel methods for word sense disambiguation and acronym expansion. In: Proceedings of the 21st National Conference on Artificial Intelligence, vol. 2, pp. 1879–1880. AAAI Press (2006), http://portal.acm.org/citation.cfm?id=1597348.1597488
27. Lee, Y.K., Ng, H.T., Chia, T.K.: Supervised word sense disambiguation with support vector machines and multiple knowledge sources. In: Mihalcea, R., Edmonds, P. (eds.) Senseval-3: Third International Workshop on the Evaluation of Systems for the Semantic Analysis of Text, pp. 137–140. Association for Computational Linguistics, Barcelona (2004)
28. Zelenko, D., Aone, C., Richardella, A.: Kernel methods for relation extraction. J. Mach. Learn. Res. 3, 1083–1106 (2003), http://portal.acm.org/citation.cfm?id=944919.944964
29. Chang, C.-C., Lin, C.-J.: LIBSVM: A library for support vector machines. ACM Transactions on Intelligent Systems and Technology 2, 27:1–27:27 (2011), software available at http://www.csie.ntu.edu.tw/~cjlin/libsvm

Changing the Voice of a Subscriber on the Example of an Implementation of the PSOLA Algorithm for the iOS and Android Mobile Platforms

Zbigniew Piotrowski and Michał Ciołek

Military University of Technology, Faculty of Electronics,
gen. S. Kaliskiego 2 str., 00-908 Warsaw, Poland
zpiotrowski@wat.edu.pl,
michal.ciolek@student.wat.edu.pl

Abstract. This paper describes the implementation of the PSOLA algorithm for
two mobile platforms with embedded operating systems: Android and iOS. In
order to mask the voice identity of a telephony subscriber using a virtual voice,
a modification of the time scale of the utterance and of the pitch of the speaker
have been implemented, with the influence of these modifications on the recognition of the identity by listeners being studied. Mobile platforms were compared in terms of signal processing time, including the read and write times.

Keywords: voice impersonation, voice morphing, Android, iOS, smartphones,
PSOLA.

1   Introduction

Systems for masking the subscriber's voice and converting it into a voice that does not
exist in reality (a virtual voice), or for changing the voice to the voice of another
speaker, called morphing, are based on a technology for modifying prosodic features
of a speech signal and making them similar to the features of a different speaker [1-6].
The following are used in order to modify the prosodic features [7-8] of a voice: time
scale modification [9-10], pitch shifting [11-13] and, in particular, the PSOLA algorithm and its modifications [14 - 16]. An interesting example of the use of the PSOLA
algorithm is the digital watermarking of a speech signal [17] and the use of pitch
shifting for the synthesis of singing [18], modifications of selected frequency bands
are employed when implementing sound effects in DSPs [19]. This paper presents the
implementation of the PSOLA algorithm for mobile platforms: Android and iOS.
Smartphones are becoming an integral part of everyday life, so masking ones voice
identity and processing a subscriber's voice to a virtual voice may be useful in
helpline phone systems or police systems for recording witness statements or for receiving notifications of events.

A. Dziech and A. Czyżewski (Eds.): MCSS 2013, CCIS 368, pp. 181–193, 2013.

2   The Issue of Impersonation of a Subscriber's Voice in Telephony

In today's world telephony is the most popular medium for communication between people. In the years 2005–2011, the number of mobile subscribers worldwide increased from 2 million to over 6 million, equalling 86% of the world population [20]. A trend may be observed in recent years which might be called in short: "A new era of smartphones". According to statistics, smartphone sales in 2011 exceeded those of personal computers [21]. The expansion of mobile technology brings with it many benefits and risks. Mobile phones are no longer used just for talking, they now act as mobile computing platforms. At any given moment we can use a phone and its power to perform analyses, calculations and data processing.

The potential of these small devices is seen both by state institutions such as the judiciary and police, but also cybercriminals. Changing the voice identity profile to another, including a virtual, non-existent one, helps people calling helplines or people speaking in public (e.g. for broadcast reporting). The modification of a voice profile is also increasingly used in judiciary proceedings, where the testimony of witnesses can be of crucial importance. Most people in such situations are unwilling or afraid of disclosing their real voice as this could result in their identification.

Applying advanced speech processing algorithms to smart phones redefines the concept of cybercriminals. Voice impersonation makes it possible to conduct fraudulent actions, e.g. extortion through the so-called "grandchild method" (where an older person is manipulated into loaning money to persons pretending to be their grandchildren) [22].

3   Implementation of the PSOLA Algorithm for the iOS and Android Platform

The PSOLA method was presented in 1990 by E. Moulines [23]. It is based on the assumption that a speech signal is characterised by one basic parameter: the pitch. The PSOLA is a variant of the SOLA algorithm, with the difference being that speech signal processing is synchronous in relation to the pitch period. The point of this is to provide independent control over the duration of phonemes.

This requires pitch marking to be performed – determining whether a segment is voiced and measuring the pitch period. The pitch marking accuracy determines the correct functioning of the PSOLA algorithm. The best results are achieved when a laryngograph is used for recording the pitch directly. However, the use of this method is not possible due to technical limitations of a mobile device. It is therefore necessary to employ one of the methods that use the speech signal envelope. These algorithms can be divided into methods operating in the frequency domain, in the time domain, or hybrid methods. The AMDF algorithm was selected on the basis of [24] due to the low level of computational complexity. The basis for the implementation of the PSOLA algorithm was the proposal of Udo Zölzer [25].

Applications built for the Android platform use the Java programming language and a modified Java Virtual Machine (Dalvik) as a runtime environment. Such a solution, however, is not the most efficient one (e.g. lack of access to memory management) so as of system version 1.5 it is possible to run native C code. For this purpose an NDK was created that uses the Java Native Interface (JNI) to enable the running of libraries written in C from within Java. Unlike Android, iOS uses the Objective-C language which allows virtually transparent combining of languages from which it originates (C/C++).

The test of results over the PSOLA algorithm on mobile platforms consisted of three phases. The first one was a comparison of the performance of speech signal processing on the two most popular platforms using a proprietary "PSOLA BENCHMARK" application. In the second phase the feasibility of voice impersonation using the "PSOLA MORPHING" application was tested. The third phase consisted of "PSOLA VOIP" application tests to present the use of this algorithm by a VoIP subscriber.

3.1   Application 1 - PSOLA BENCHMARK

The first application was written in two versions: for the Android platform and for the iOS platform. The applications use the same implementation of the PSOLA algorithm written in C. The applications make it possible to conduct measurements of the speech signal processing time using a PSOLA implementation based on predefined input files. The applications use a simple interface presented in Fig. 1 that makes it possible to enter input parameters, such as:

- type of modification (time scale change or pitch shift)
- modification coefficient
- number of algorithm iterations.

Due to the time-consuming nature of the processing, algorithms are performed in secondary threads in order not to block the main thread and interaction with the user. In Objective-C this is implemented using the *dispatch_async* function that automatically creates a new thread and executes the dispatched block operation. Analogous steps are performed in Android using the *AsyncTask* class.

3.2   Application 2 - PSOLA MORPHING

Application 2 was created for iOS and its aim is to check the feasibility of removal of voice identity using the PSOLA algorithm. The program has three main functions: modifying the voice of 6 readers, playing them back to the listener and then filling out questionnaires. The modification of collected voice samples is performed using the PSOLA algorithm implementation from experiment 1. Playback is done using AVAudioPlayer. The questionnaire system is correlated with the playback, which enables the study participant to indicate recognised voices. The application interface is shown in Fig. 2.

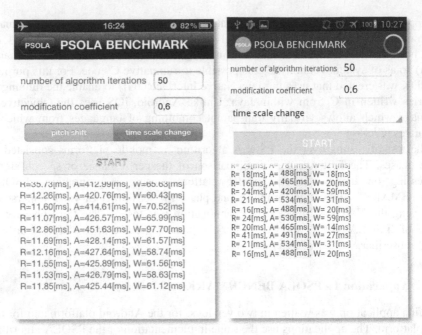

Fig. 1. User interface of the PSOLA BENCHMARK application - iOS on the left, Android – on the right

Fig. 2. PSOLA MORPHING application interface

3.3   Application 3 – PSOLA VoIP

At the moment there is no technical possibility to implement the PSOLA algorithm to modify a GSM audio stream (mobile operating systems do not provide handles for it). That is why application 3 uses a similar environment – Internet telephony. In order to implement the PSOLA algorithm a ready implementation of the SIP protocol was used, in the form of the open source Sipdroid application [26]. Sipdroid makes it possible to use an Android phone with any SIP provider. Connections can be made using a 3G network, as well as WiFi (with a wide range of audio codecs available). The application is integrated with the phone so it allows calls to be made easily.

Modifications that have been made to this application consisted in capturing the audio stream just before the coding stage and modifying it with use of the algorithm developed in experiment 1. The application allows the parameters of voice modification to be declared before the connection is established.

4   Test Results

The significant popularity of mobile devices has led to the creation of advanced operating systems with development kits that facilitate the creation of applications and increase in the efficiency of applications. This opens up new possibilities, such as the modification of a subscriber's voice using mobile devices. This chapter presents the implementation of the PSOLA algorithm in the two most popular systems: Android and iOS.

4.1   Features of the Measurement Platform

The hardware platform is the basis for the designed application. The measurement results are dependent on the appropriate choice of the platform. Comparing two different mobile operating systems, under certain conditions, leads to difficulties in picking the better system. This stems mainly from the closed nature of iOS, which is installed only on devices designed by Apple. It is not possible to run iOS and Android systems on one device. Therefore, the hardware platform consists of two devices: one running iOS and another running Android. This choice forced the most similar hardware specifications to be selected.

iOS is available for the following series of devices: iPhone (smartphone), iPod touch (music player) and iPad (tablet). Android, because of its open source nature, is used not only in phones and tablets, but also photo cameras, TVs and other everyday use devices. Smartphone type devices have been chosen due to such devices being best suited for speech processing.

There are 3 models of iPhones available on the market: iPhone 4, iPhone 4s, iPhone 5. Due to the best availability and greatest popularity the platform for testing the iOS apps will consist of the iPhone 4s. The Android device closest to the above, taking into account the previously mentioned factors, is the Samsung Galaxy SII.

Table 1. Technical parameters of the hardware platform [27] [28]

Device		Apple iPhone 4s	Samsung Galaxy SII GT-i9100
Launched		October 2011	May 2011
Operating system		iOS 5.1.1	Android 4.0.4
MPSoC	Name	Apple A5	Exynos 4210
	CPU	ARM Cortex-A9	ARM Cortex-A9
	ISA	ARMv7	ARMv7
	CPU clock	800 MHz	1200MHz
	Number of CPU cores	2	2
	Technological process	45 nm	45 nm
	RAM	512MB	1GB
	GPU	PowerVR SGX543MP2 (2 cores)	ARM Mali-400 MP4 (4 cores)
	Designer	Apple	Samsung
	Manufacturer	Samsung	Samsung

Tab. 1 presents the key technical parameters – those with the greatest impact on the obtained results. Both manufacturers used the same processing unit, but in a different configuration. Theoretically, the iPhone 4s has less computing power. In authors opinion Apple decided to lower the clock speed of the CPU to 800 MHz and use 512 MB in order to obtain better battery life.

In order to minimise the differences resulting from the higher CPU clock, the Samsung Galaxy SII was underclocked to 800MHz. This necessitated a modified kernel to be used. The most popular CyanogenMod 9[1] modification was employed for this paper. The process of smartphone software modification and installation of modifications has been described in [29].

4.2   Measurement Conditions

Many factors that affect the results must be taken into account when measurements are performed. This statement refers to experiment 1. Minimising the impact of external factors using mobile devices has imposed the need to meet the following conditions:

- compiling the program with the highest level of optimisation and using the latest compiler version
- running the testing program on the latest version of the operating system available for a particular device
- having a fully charged battery
- the device operating in flight mode
- programs running in the background turned off
- automatic sleep mode of the device turned off.

---

[1]   *CyanogenMod 9* – open source software based on the Android Ice Cream Sandwich operating system.

4.3   Experiments

Studies performed in the course of the presented research consist of three experiments. They are aimed at checking the feasibility of the implementation of the PSOLA algorithm on mobile platforms and its ability to mask voice identity.

Experiment 1 – Comparing the PSOLA Algorithm in the Android and iOS Systems. The first experiment was aimed at comparing the runtime of the PSOLA algorithm, written in C, on the following platforms: Android and iOS. The experiment consisted of multiple executions of the PSOLA algorithm in the same manner on both systems. The input file for the algorithm was a 19 second long audio file (mono, 44100 Hz, 16-bit, size: 1 585 KB, voices of 3 different readers). When the algorithm was executed, the following measurements were performed: input file read time from internal memory, algorithm execution time and output file write time to internal memory. The experiment was designed for 4 sets of parameters (Tab. 2).

Table 2. Sets of parameters for experiment 1

Set	Type of modification	Modification coefficient	Number of iterations
1.	time scale change	0.6	50
2.	time scale change	2	50
3.	pitch shift	0.6	50
4.	pitch shift	2	50

In order to compare two different systems, an Efficiency Coefficient (EC) was calculated expressed through equation 1:

$$EC = \sum_{i=1}^{m} 0.3 \cdot R_i + 0.4 \cdot A_i + 0.3 \cdot W_i \tag{1}$$

Legend:

  i - number of the next set of parameters

  m - number of parameter sets

  R_i - average input file read time in ms for set i

  A_i - average PSOLA algorithm execution time in ms for set i

  W_i - average output file write time in ms for set i

The results of the comparison performed in the second experiment are shown in Fig. 3. ECs calculated have been shown in Tab. 3.

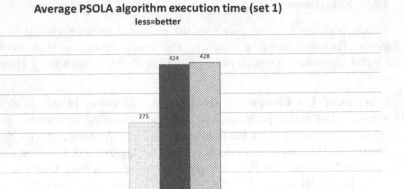

Fig. 3. Comparison of performance of the two platforms

Table 3. Efficiency Coefficients

Hardware platform	EC [pts] less = better
Galaxy SII 1200MHz	991
Galaxy SII 800MHz	1490
iPhone 4s	1634

The best result for the series of tests have been obtained by the Samsung Galaxy SII clocked at 1200 MHz. This result was due to the highest clock speed of the processor. When the same speeds are set for both smartphones, the results obtained by the algorithm are very similar. This demonstrates a comparable level of processing units used and a similar optimisation level of the systems (slightly in favour of Android).

The four sets of different parameters show the variation in how time consuming the speech signal processing is in relation to selected parameters. All sets were processed in real time (the maximum file processing time for a 19 second file was 1.5 seconds). This fact confirms that it is possible to use both platforms for real-time speech signal processing in telephone systems.

On the basis of an analysis of the results it is possible to notice a certain phenomenon: measurement results on the iOS platform are practically identical (the average deviation does not exceed 12 ms), while the average deviation in the Android system reaches a maximum of 64 ms. This confirms the distinctive way in which multitasking is implemented in iOS. In this system a "minimised" application can perform only certain tasks in the background (play or record audio, determine the location, send notifications) as opposed to Android (where applications can perform any task in their "minimised" state). Such an implementation of multitasking in iOS has its advantages (less intensive use of telephone resources, lower power consumption) but also some drawbacks (inability to perform multiple tasks simultaneously).

Particular attention should be paid to the speed of access to internal memory as shown in Tab. 4. It demonstrates that Samsung uses memory chips with a faster write speed than those in the iPhone 4s, while the iPhone 4s performs reads from internal memory faster than the Galaxy SII.

Table 4. Speed of access to internal memory

Hardware platform	Average read speed [MB/s]	Average write speed [MB/s]
Galaxy SII 1200MHz	126.9	49.3
Galaxy SII 800MHz	94.0	34.7
iPhone 4s	134.9	14.4

Experiment 2 - Speaker's Voice Recognition. In order to verify the correctness of the PSOLA algorithm an experiment was conducted consisting in speaker voice recognition. Sixteen students from the same training group took part in this experiment. They were divided into two groups: readers (6 men) and listeners (10 men). Samples of readers' voices, in the form of the following utterance: "The Minister of Foreign Affairs reminded..." have been modified using the PSOLA algorithm in the MORPHING application. Each voice was subject to one of six modifications with five intensity levels (from the most modified to unmodified) according to the following pattern:

1. reader 1 - time scale change - from increased to unmodified
2. reader 2 - time scale change - from lowered to unmodified
3. reader 3 - pitch shift - from raised to unmodified
4. reader 4 - pitch shift - from lowered to unmodified
5. reader 5 - combination of modifications 1 and 3
6. reader 6 - combination of modifications 2 and 4

For example, the first modification of the first reader is 100 percent slower, second modification is 80 percent slower, etc.

The group of listeners had the task to identify the speaker after listening to each of the 30 generated voice samples. Samples were played once on a continuous basis, from the most modified to unmodified. There was an interval between the samples necessary to record in the application the following: the data of the recognised person or a line if the speaker is not recognised. The listening was performed in a closed room with an iPhone 4s as the signal source and closed-end Creative Aurvana Live! headphones.

A chart of the effectiveness of reader voice identification was prepared on the basis of results collected from the MORPHING application (Fig. 4). The results of the experiment confirmed assumptions. The modified voice of reader 2 (time scale change - lowered) and voice of reader 1 (time scale change - increased) have proved to be the easiest to identify. The voice of reader 6, which was doubly modified (time scale change - lowered and pitch shift - lowered), proved the hardest to identify. This experiment shows that in order to hide the voice identity it is best to use a modified pitch or both modifications simultaneously. The results of the experiment confirm that there is a possibility of masking or changing the voice identity of the subscriber.

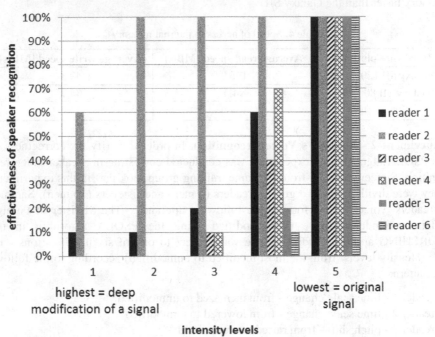

Fig. 4. Results of experiment 2 - effectiveness of speaker recognition

Experiment 3 - Checking the Implementation in the VoIP Client. The experiment consisted of five VoIP calls being made using the PSOLA VoIP application implemented on Android. The people to whom calls were made (five subscribers B) knew the person calling (one subscriber A). The voice of subscriber A was modified using the PSOLA algorithm. The modification parameters were selected on the basis of the second experiment (reduction of the pitch). Based on a 60-second utterance of subscriber A, the people who were called – subscribers B – were to recognise the identity of the caller. None of the subscribers B managed to recognise the voice of subscriber A. On the basis of results obtained using VoIP it has been concluded that there is a real possibility of employing the PSOLA algorithm in telephony systems when an audio stream is made available by mobile system developers.

5   Conclusions

This article was inspired by the growing popularity of mobile systems. It presents the feasibility of speech signal processing in the most popular mobile operating systems: Android and iOS.

The PSOLA algorithm has been implemented using the robust Xcode and Eclipse environments. Both tools differ significantly in terms of installation, configuration and use. The Xcode environment, despite having similar functionality as Eclipse, is decidedly more programmer-friendly. Its intuitive and powerful debugging system and tools for checking code optimisation significantly facilitated and accelerated the process of code implementation.

No performance problems were observed over the course of application testing. The created test applications have a simple user interface that enables inputting parameters for the PSOLA algorithm and playback of the input and output signals. Additionally, the Android application includes an implementation of the SIP protocol which is used to verify possibilities in real-world conditions. The ability of the PSOLA algorithm to change identity was confirmed in the first experiment.

The remaining two experiments were aimed at verifying mobile platforms in terms of real time signal processing capabilities. Experiment 1 was used to calculate the EC for the two platforms, on the basis of which it can be concluded that the effectiveness of the algorithm is to a large extent dependent on the CPU frequency. When considering these two different platforms with the same CPU clock speed, it is possible to notice that the obtained results are very similar. This indicates a similar level of optimisation of the two different operating systems. The implemented PSOLA applications, due to the obtained processing times, clearly show that the two platforms are predisposed for real-time speech signal processing.

The developed programs may form the basis for designing innovative applications. When creators of mobile operating systems make a handle for the GSM audio stream available, it will be possible to modify the caller's voice using the implemented PSOLA algorithm.

References

1. Hui, Y., Young, S.: Quality-enhanced voice morphing using maximum likelihood transformations. IEEE Transactions on Audio, Speech, and Language Processing 14, 1301–1312 (2006)
2. Hui, Y., Young, S.: High quality voice morphing. In: IEEE International Conference on Acoustics, Speech, and Signal Processing, vol. 1, pp. 9–12. IEEE Press, New York (2004)
3. Duxans, H., Bonafonte, A.: Residual Conversion Versus Prediction on Voice Morphing Systems. In: IEEE International Conference on Acoustics, Speech and Signal Processing, vol. 1. IEEE Press, New York (2006)
4. Ning, X., Xi, S., Zhen, Y.: A Novel Voice Morphing System Using Bi-GMM for High Quality Transformation. In: Ninth ACIS International Conference on Software Engineering, Artificial Intelligence, Networking, and Parallel/Distributed Computing, pp. 485–489 (2008)

5. Ning, X., Zhen, Y.: A precise estimation of vocal tract parameters for high quality voice morphing. In: 9th International Conference on Signal Processing, pp. 684–687 (2008)
6. Furuya, K., Moriyama, T., Ozawa, S.: Generation of Speaker Mixture Voice using Spectrum Morphing. In: IEEE International Conference on Multimedia and Expo, pp. 344–347. IEEE Press, New York (2007)
7. Drgas, S., Zamorski, D., Dabrowski, A.: Speaker verification using various prosodic kernels, Signal Processing Algorithms, Architectures, Arrangements, and Applications Conference Proceedings (SPA), pp. 1–5 (2011)
8. Drgas, S., Cetnarowicz, D., Dabrowski, A.: Speaker verification based on prosodic features, Signal Processing Algorithms, Architectures, Arrangements, and Applications (SPA), pp. 79–82 (2008)
9. Lopatka, K., Suchomski, P., Czyzewski, A.: Time-domain prosodic modifications for Text-To-Speech Synthesizer, Signal Processing Algorithms, Architectures, Arrangements, and Applications Conference Proceedings (SPA), pp. 73–77 (2010)
10. Kupryjanow, A., Czyzewski, A.: Time-scale modification of speech signals for supporting hearing impaired schoolchildren, Signal Processing Algorithms, Architectures, Arrangements, and Applications Conference Proceedings (SPA), pp. 159–162 (2009)
11. Yinqiu, G., Zhen, Y.: Pitch modification based on syllable units for voice morphing system. In: International Conference on Network and Parallel Computing Workshops, pp. 135–139 (2007)
12. Kumar, K., Jain, J.: Speech Pitch Shifting using Complex Continuous Wavelet Transform. In: Annual IEEE India Conference, pp. 1–4. IEEE Press, New York (2006)
13. Abe, M.: Speech morphing by gradually changing spectrum parameter and fundamental frequency. In: Fourth International Conference on Spoken Language, vol. 4, pp. 2235–2238 (1996)
14. Yifeng, S., Jia, J., Lianhong, C.: Detection on PSOLA-modified voices by seeking out duplicated fragments. In: International Conference on Systems and Informatics, pp. 2177–2182 (2012)
15. Wang, Y., Yang, S.: Speech synthesis based on PSOLA algorithm and modified pitch parameters. In: International Conference on Computational Problem-Solving, pp. 296–299 (2010)
16. Valbret, H., Moulines, E., Tubach, J.P.: Voice transformation using PSOLA technique. In: IEEE International Conference on Acoustics, Speech, and Signal Processing, vol. 1, pp. 145–148 (1992)
17. Celik, M., Sharma, G., Murat Tekalp, A.: Pitch and Duration Modification for Speech Watermarking. In: IEEE International Conference on Acoustics, Speech, and Signal Processing, vol. 2, pp. 17–20. IEEE Press, New York (2005)
18. Nakano, T., Goto, M.: Vocalistener2: A singing synthesis system able to mimic a user's singing in terms of voice timbre changes as well as pitch and dynamics. In: IEEE International Conference on Acoustics, Speech and Signal Processing, pp. 453–456. IEEE Press, New York (2011)
19. Lisiecki, B., Meyer, A., Dabrowski, A.: Implementation of sound effects on DSP platform, Signal Processing Algorithms, Architectures, Arrangements, and Applications Conference Proceedings (SPA), pp. 1–3 (2011)
20. Key Global Telecom Indicators for the World Telecommunication Service Sector, http://www.itu.int/ITU-D/ict/statistics/at_glance/KeyTelecom.html (accessed January 30, 2013)
21. Smart phones overtake client PCs in 2011, http://www.canalys.com/newsroom/smart-phones-overtake-client-pcs-2011 (accessed January 30, 2013)

22. Piotrowski, Z., Grabiec, W.: Voice trust in public switched telephone networks. In: Dziech, A., Czyżewski, A. (eds.) MCSS 2012. CCIS, vol. 287, pp. 282–291. Springer, Heidelberg (2012)
23. Moulines, E., Charpentier, F.: Pitch-synchronous waveform processing techniques for text-to-speech synthesis using diphones. Speech Communication 9(5/6), 453–467 (1990)
24. Verteletskaya, E., Šimák, B.: Performance Evaluation of Pitch Detection Algorithms, http://access.feld.cvut.cz/view.php?cisloclanku=2009060001 (accessed January 30, 2013)
25. Zölzer, U.: DAFX: Digital Audio Effects. Wiley, New York (2012)
26. http://code.google.com/p/sipdroid/ (accessed January 30, 2013)
27. http://www.ifixit.com/Teardown/iPhone+4S+Teardown/6610/2 (accessed January 30, 2013)
28. http://samsung.com/global/business/semiconductor/product/application/detail?productId=7644&iaId=844 (accessed January 30, 2013)
29. Tyler, J.: XDA Developers' Android Hacker's Toolkit: The Complete Guide to Rooting, ROMs and Theming. Wiley, New York (2012)

Use of the Bio-inspired Algorithms to Find Global Minimum in Force Directed Layout Algorithms

Patrik Dubec, Jan Plucar, and Lukáš Rapant

VSB-Technical University of Ostrava, 17. listopadu 15,
70833 Ostrava-Poruba, Czech Republic
{patrik.dubec,jan.plucar,lukas.rapant}@vsb.cz

Abstract. We present bio-inspired approach in a process of finding global minimum of an energetic function that is used in force directed layout algorithms. We have been faced with the issue of displaying large graphs. These graphs arise in the analysis of social networks with the need to view social relationships between entities. In order to find global minimum of an energetic function we employ two bio-inspired algorithms: Differential Evolution and Self-Organizing Migration Algorithm (SOMA). Differential evolution is inspired by crossbreeding of population whereas SOMA is inspired by migration of some species. In this article we will present basics of these algorithms, their results and comparison.

Keywords: Force-based layout algorithm, Differential evolution, Soma.

1   Introduction

In this article, we will discuss the enhancement of force directed layout algorithms. Force directed algorithms calculate the layout of a graph using only information contained within the structure of the graph itself. Graphs drawn with these algorithms tend to be easily readable, simple, intuitive and exhibit symmetries. However, there are also two distinctive disadvantages: poor local minima, high running time. The problem of calculating graph layouts arose in the Indect project when we tried to analyze data from social networks. From these data, we wanted to identify relationships between users of social networks, both obvious and indirect (for example, when two people share 5 common friends, the chances are that these two people know each other). Graph visualization and analysis could help us greatly with the task of relationship identification. We will visualize graph in a way, where the nodes represent individuals and edges represent relationships between each other. In this article we focus on the problem of finding the global minimum of an energetic function of these algorithms. To find the global minimum we will use two methods that belong to the bio inspired calculation class - Differential evolution and Soma. Both methods will be described in detail below.

A. Dziech and A. Czyżewski (Eds.): MCSS 2013, CCIS 368, pp. 194–203, 2013.
© Springer-Verlag Berlin Heidelberg 2013

2   State of the Art

When talking about force directed algorithms we can go back to 1984 where the spring layout method of Eades [1] and the algorithm of Fruchterman and Reingold [2] both rely on spring forces, similar to those in Hooke's law. In these methods, there are repulsive forces among all nodes, but also attractive forces between nodes which are connected by edge. Forces among the nodes can be computed based on their graph theoretic distances. They are determined by the lengths of the shortest paths between them. The algorithm of Kamada and Kawai [3] uses spring forces proportional to the graph theoretic distances. The utility of the basic force directed approach is limited to small graphs and results are poor for graphs with more than a few hundred vertices. The late 1990's saw the emergence of several techniques extending the functionality of force directed methods to graphs with tens of thousands vertices. One common thread in these approaches is the multi-level layout technique. Use of this technique is demonstrated in Gajer et al. [4] or Crawford [5]. Other approaches are more focused on aesthetic visualization than on performance. Examples of such approaches are Finkel and Tamassia [6], which use Bezier curves in order to improve angular resolution and edge crossing, and Chernobelskiy et al. [7], which use Tangent-Based Lombardi Spring Formulation.

3   Evolutionary Algorithms

A typical feature of evolutionary algorithms is that they are based on working with populations of individuals. We can represent the population as a matrix $M \times N$ where columns represent the individuals. Each individual represents a solution to the current issue. In other words, it is set of cost function argument values whose optimal number combination we are looking for. One of early evolutionary algorithms can be found in Price [11].

The main activity of evolutionary algorithms is the cyclic creation of new populations which are better than the previous ones. Better population is a population whose individuals have better fitness. If we are looking for global minimum, we can schematically describe it with following formula:

$$\forall\, indA, indB \in \mathbb{R}, f_{cost}(indA) < f_{cost}(indB) \Rightarrow F(indA) > F(indB)\,, \tag{3.1}$$

where $indA, indB$ are population members, f_{cost} is cost function and F is function computing fitness (it is transformed cost function in our case).

To create initial population we need to define a sample individual (specimen). This specimen is also used to correct individual parameters which are out of valid range. We can define specimen as a vector of parameters. These parameters are described using three constants: type of variable (Real, Integer) and two boundaries that constrain value of parameter (Lo – Lower boundary, Hi – High boundary). Example given: Integer,{Lo, Hi} – Integer,{1, 10}.

$$Specimen = \{\{Real, \{Lo, Hi\}\}, \{Integer, \{Lo, Hi\}\}, \dots, \{Decimal, \{Lo, Hi\}\}\} \tag{3.2}$$

Initial population P $_{(0)}$ is created using the specimen. Following formula guarantees that each individual of initial population will be randomly placed to space of possible solutions and its parameters will be inside of defined boundaries.

$$P_{i,j}^{(0)} = x_{i,j}^{(0)} = rand[0.1] \cdot \left(x_{i,j}^{(Hi)} - x_{i,j}^{(Low)} \right) + x_{i,j}^{(Low)}, \tag{3.3}$$

$$i = 1, \dots, M \quad , \quad j = 1, \dots, N$$

$$(x_{i,j} \text{ is a } j - \text{th parameter of } i - \text{th individual})$$

where rand[0.1] represents function that generates random real number drawn from uniform distribution on the open interval (0,1). The goal is to find a vector $X = (x_1, x_2, x_3, \dots, x_n)$ which minimizes our energetic function $f_{cost}(X)$ with regard to function and arguments restrictions. It is also necessary to ensure that all cost function argument values are from valid range while optimizing. We use very easy "individual returning" principle to manage that.

$$x'^{(EC+1)}_{i,j} = \begin{cases} rand[0.1] \cdot \left(x_{i,j}^{(Hi)} - x_{i,j}^{(Lo)} \right) + x_{i,j}^{(Lo)}, \\ if \left(x'^{(EC+1)}_{i,j} > x_{i,j}^{(Hi)} \right) \vee \left(x'^{(EC+1)}_{i,j} < x_{i,j}^{(Lo)} \right), \\ x'^{(EC+1)}_{i,j}, else \end{cases} \tag{3.4}$$

where $x_{i,j}$ is a j-th parameter of i-th individual and EC is a general expression that represents evolution cycle .

3.1   Differential Evolution (DE)

Differential evolution has proven to be an efficient method for optimizing real-valued functions. DE is trying to breed as good population of individuals as possible in loops called "generations" [12].

The very first step is defining constants affecting behavior of evolution algorithm. Those constants are crossover probability (CR) which influences probability of choosing a parameter of the mutated individual instead of the original one, mutation constant (F) which determines volume of mutation of the mutated individual, population size (NP) and finally trial specimen. Now we have a specimen and we are able to create initial population vector X.

Whenever we have initial population prepared so called generation loop begins. In each generation cycle nested loop is executed. This loop is called evolution cycle. Each individual from current generation is bred to have better characteristic using mutations in evolution cycle.

Algorithm finishes either if a solution is good enough (individual) or after defined number of generation loops had been executed.

For our purposes the DE/rand/1 algorithm mutation is the best choice. The notation DE/rand/1 specifies that the vector v to be perturbed is randomly chosen and the perturbation consists of one weighted vector.

$$v = x_{r1,j}^G + F \cdot \left(x_{r2,j}^G - x_{r3,j}^G \right) \tag{3.5}$$

Due to this mutation, new individuals are not affected by the temporary best individual from generation and space of possible solutions is searched through uniformly. More detailed description of Differential Evolution can be found in Price [9, 12].

Pseudo code (DE/rand/1)

```
Input parameters:
  X: initial population (vector)
  f_cost: function returning fitness of current solution
  NP: population size
  F: mutational constant
  CR: Crossover threshold
  Specimen: trial specimen


for I < Generation do begin
  for J < NP do begin
    Select J individual
    Select three random individuals from population
    Compute the new individual fitness
    Choose a better one from both individuals to new pop-
ulation
  end
end;
```

3.2   Self-Organizing Migration Algorithm (SOMA)

SOMA is a stochastic optimization algorithm that is using social behavior of co-operating individuals. Although the SOMA is not typical representative of evolution algorithm class because it is not creating new children while executing, it has very similar features as DE algorithm. SOMA is based on vector operations and evolutionary loops called *migration loops*.

Whenever we specify control parameters and create a specimen we will randomly distribute all individuals of initial population over the search space. Each specimen computes its own fitness and the best individual becomes a *Leader*.

Within each migration loop, all individuals travel certain distance of defined length (PathLength) towards the Leader making specified number of steps of certain length (Steps). Direction of these steps is however progressively deformed by perturbation vector (PRT). This vector forces specimen to explore larger area and avoid local minima. Each individual computes its fitness on each step position and at the end of the migration loop it returns back to the best path position.

Once we find acceptable solution (diversity between the worst and the best specimens is lower than a defined value) the SOMA ends. More detailed description of SOMA can be found in Zelinka [8].

Pseudo code (All to One)

```
Input parameters:
  X: initial population (vector)
  f_cost: function returning fitness of current solution
  PathLenght - length of individual's way to Leader
  Step - density of individual's steps on way to Leader
  PRT - perturbation vector affecting the direction of
  way to Leader
  PopSize - population size
  Migration - number of generations
  MinDiv - minimal diversity
  Specimen: trial specimen
```

```
for I < Migration do begin
  Choose the best specimen as the Leader

  for J <= PopSize do
    select J specimen
    //compute f_cost at the new position
    store the best found solution of the path to the
population
  end

  if MinDiv < |best_specimen - worst_specimen| then
    begin
      stop SOMA
    end
  end if
end;
```

4   Results and Their Discussion

Our proposed methods were implemented in Matlab programming language and tested on two random graphs, one with twenty vertices and one with hundred vertices. We have used energy function of the force directed approach as an objective function of both Soma and Differential evolution. Variables governing these optimization methods were determined experimentally by testing these methods on a random graph with 20 vertices. We have tried various different configurations for parameters perturbation in case Soma and crossbreeding threshold a mutation constant in case of differential evolution. We have chosen the best values of these constants based on the best minimum found by using various configurations of surveyed parameters. These values are shown in the Figures 1, 2 and 3. These graphs are depicting dependency of the minimum on chosen parameter. Other parameters like number of generations and population size for both methods were determined from the literature [8] [10].

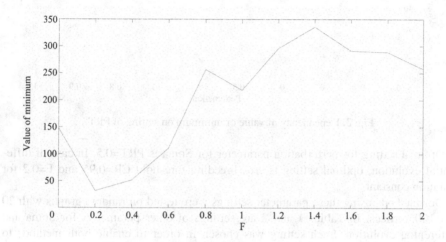

Fig. 1. Dependency of value of minimum on setting of F

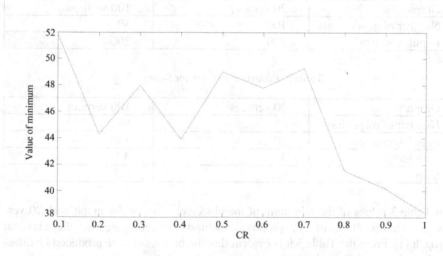

Fig. 2. Dependency of value of minimum on setting of CR

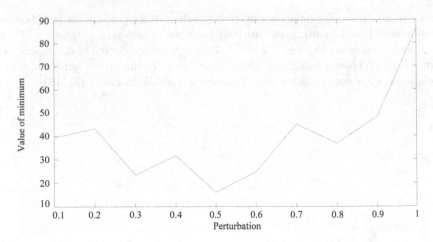

Fig. 3. Dependency of value of minimum on setting of PRT

Optimal setting for perturbation parameter for Soma is PRT=0.5. In case of differential evolution, optimal setting is crossbreeding threshold CR=0.95 and F=0.2 for mutation constant.

Our methods using these parameter settings were tested on random graphs with 20 and 100 vertices. In Tables 1 and 2 are settings of other parameters for Soma and differential evolution. Such setting was chosen in order to enable both methods to have similar number on objective function evaluation.

Table 1. Parameter settings for differential evolution

Graph	20 vertices	100 vertices
Number of generations	100	50
Population size	200	2000

Table 2. Parameter settings for Soma

Graph	20 vertices	100 vertices
Number of migrations	68	65
Population size	20	100
Path length	3	3
Step	0.2	0.2

In Table 3 values of the minimum of the objective function for graph with 20 vertices are shown. Both of our proposed methods are compared to the classical approach [1]. From the Table 3 it is evident that the best results are produced by differential evolution, followed by classical approach and Soma. However, even Soma found an acceptable minimum. Table 3 also shows the results for the graph with 100 vertices. Here Soma clearly dominates over the differential evolution. The reason for this is that the parameters are determined for the graph with 20 vertices and differential evolution is more sensitive to their setting. This can be solved by some form of optimization of parameters done prior using differential evolution. This is, however, very time demanding in case of larger graphs and slows down the algorithm. Classical approach is unusable here as it diverges and is not able to find the minimum. Results of these algorithms for graph with 100 vertices are shown in the Figures 1 and 2.

Table 3. Minimums of the energetic function found on experimental graphs by compared algorithms

Graph	20 vertices	100 vertices
Soma	16.5994	699.3705
Classical approach	13.6005	-
Differential evolution	12.654	1866.6

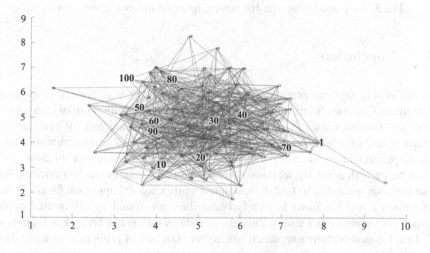

Fig. 4. The graph layout with 100 vertices based on Soma approach

Value of the minimum is well represented in the drawings as graph based on Soma calculation has all the properties of Force directed algorithm. Graph based on differential evolution has much lower degree of these properties.

In terms of speed, both proposed algorithms have similar performance. This speed is not optimal as difficulties with evaluation of the objective function arise, especially in case of the larger graph. Calculating forces among so many vertices is very demanding and slows down the algorithms as objective function has complexity of n2. This is combined with relatively high number of evaluations of the objective function which is required by both of our proposed methods. However, this problem can be easily solved by parallelization of the computation objective function as well as optimizations. This will be a subject of our future study.

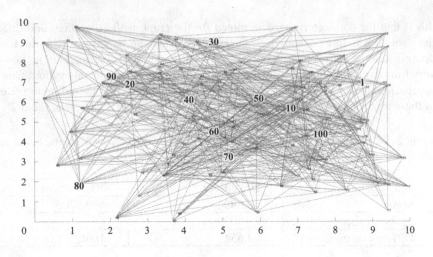

Fig. 5. The graph layout with 100 vertices based on differential evolution approach

5 Conclusion

In this article we have proposed alternative variants of force directed graph drawing algorithm. One uses Soma approach for calculation of the minimum of energetic function and the other uses differential evolution for the same task. When tested on a graph with 20 vertices, proposed methods were able to find similar minimum as classical approach at worst as it can be seen in Table 3. Differential evolution performs even better with correctly set parameters. In case of a graph with 100 vertices, both of our methods were able to find the minimum while classical approach failed. However, minimum found by Soma is clearly better than one found by differential evolution which is evident from Table 3. This also translates into graph layouts in Figures 4 and 5. Graph based on Soma approach has higher standard of properties of force directed layout. This is clearly due to sensitivity on parameter setting of differential evolution as we have used settings optimized for graph with 20 vertices. In current state of our algorithms, such optimization for a graph with 100 vertices would be very time demanding. Comparing both of our proposed methods differential evolution performs better than Soma, but is more sensitive to the parameters setting and requires some form of their optimization. The most notable weakness of our approaches is their speed, but this problem will be addressed in our future work by their parallelization using CUDA.

Acknowledgements. The research leading to these results has received funding from the European Community's Seventh Framework Programme (FP7/2007-2013) under grant agreement no. 218086.

References

1. Eades, P.: A heuristic for graph drawing. Congressus Numerantium 42, 149–160 (1984)
2. Fruchterman, T., Reingold, E.: Graph drawing by force-directed placement. Softw. – Pract. Exp. 21(11), 1129–1164 (1991)
3. Kamada, T., Kawai, S.: An algorithm for drawing general undirected graphs. Inform. Process. Lett. 31, 7–15 (1989)
4. Gajer, P., Goodrich, M.T., Kobourov, S.G.: A multi-dimensional approach to force-directed layouts of large graphs. Computational Geometry 29(2004), 3–18 (2004)
5. Crawford, C.: A Multilevel Force-directed Graph Drawing Algorithm Using Multi-level Global Force Approximation. In: 2012 16th International Conference on Information Visualisation, IV (2012)
6. Finkel, B., Tamassia, R.: Curvilinear Graph Drawing Using the Force-Directed Method. In: Pach, J. (ed.) GD 2004. LNCS, vol. 3383, pp. 448–453. Springer, Heidelberg (2005)
7. Chernobelskiy, R., Cunningham, K.I., Goodrich, M.T., Kobourov, S.G., Trott, L.: Force-Directed Lombardi-Style Graph Drawing. In: Speckmann, B. (ed.) GD 2011. LNCS, vol. 7034, pp. 320–331. Springer, Heidelberg (2012)
8. Zelinka, I.: SOMA – Self Organizing Migrating Algorithm. In: Babu, B.V., Onwubolu, G. (eds.) New Optimization Techniques in Engineering. STUDFUZZ, vol. 141, pp. 167–218. Springer, Heidelberg (2004)
9. Price, K., Storn, R.: Differential Evolution – A simple evolutionary strategy for fast optimization. Dr. Dobb's Journal 264, 18–24 and 78 (1997)
10. Price, K.: Differential evolution: a fast and simple numerical optimizer. In: Proc. 1996 Biennial Conference of the North American Fuzzy Information Processing Society, pp. 524–527. IEEE Press, New York (1996)
11. Price, K.: Genetic Annealing. Dr. Dobb's Journal, 127–132 (October 1994)
12. Price, K.: An Introduction to Differential Evolution. In: Corne, D., Dorigo, M., Glover, F. (eds.) New Ideas in Optimization, pp. 79–108. McGraw-Hill, London (1999)

Neural Network Regression of Eyes Location in Face Images

Krzysztof Rusek and Piotr Guzik

AGH University of Science and Technology,
Department of Telecommunications, Krakow, Poland
krusek@agh.edu.pl, guzik@kt.agh.edu.pl
http://kt.agh.edu.pl

Abstract. Automatic eye localisation is a crucial part of many computer vision algorithms for processing face images. Some of the existing algorithms can be very accurate unfortunately at the cost of computational complexity. In this paper the new solution to the problem of automatic eye localisation is proposed. Eye localisation is posed as a nonlinear regression problem solved by standard feed-forward multilayer perceptron (MLP) with two hidden layers. Additionally the procedure for artificial training samples generation is proposed.

The input feature vector is constructed from coefficients of two dimensional discrete cosine transform(DCT) of a face image. Both, the feature extraction and neural network prediction have known efficient implementations, thus the entire procedure can be very fast.

Obtained results indicate that the accuracy of the proposed approach is comparable or better than existing ones.

Keywords: eye localisation, neural network, DCT, computer vision.

1 Introduction

The problem of automatic eye localisation had arised several years ago, along with the invention of automatic facial recognition algorithms. In fact it was the facial recognition research that motivated the development of eye localisation algorithms. It was quickly realised that the accuracy of most of facial recognition algorithms strongly depends on appropriate alignment of the detected face. This problem was broadly investigated in [11]. Sometimes satisfactory results can be obtained without face alignment [12]. Having said that it is reasonable to assume, that additional alignment can only improve the accuracy. The face alignment with use of the position of eyes seems to be a natural choice here.

Although the automatic eye localisation problem has been investigated for a few decades now, its performance still is not as good as one would need. The main problem with this task is a variability of eye appearance. The eye appearance on an image not only depends on a personal differences but also on the lighting conditions, pose, expression, etc.

A. Dziech and A. Czyżewski (Eds.): MCSS 2013, CCIS 368, pp. 204–212, 2013.

In this article we present another approach to the problem of eye localisation with the problem stated as a regression one. DCT coefficients are proposed as a feature vector and artificial neural network is used to find regression parameters.

The rest of the paper is organised as follows. The section 2 describes the related work on eye localisation, in 3 our solution is presented. Results are discussed in section 4. Finally, section 5 concludes the paper.

2 Related Work

The problem of finding eyes (or any part of the face) location in face image can be posed as a classification or a regression problem. In classification approach a classifier is trained to recognize whether a given part of an image contains an eye. Such classifier is then applied to sliding window at different scales. The combined results from neighbouring windows and scales define the final rectangle containing the eye. Any classifier can be used but since the algorithm is repeated many times, its speed is an important factor.

The most common approach is to use AdaBoost algorithm with Haar or LBP features. Exactly this technique is used in popular computer vision library OpenCV in an implementation of eye detection algorithm. All algorithms using template matching also fall into this category.

While the classification approach is much more common, the problem was also stated as a regression one [5]. In this formulation the eyes locations are estimated from the feature vector x extracted from the face image.

Everingham and Zisserman limited their analysis to kernel regression model and subset of pixels being the features. In this paper we use the similar approach but instead of using a subset of image we reduced the dimensionality by taking most important DCT coefficients as a feature vector. Having performance, accuracy and model simplicity under consideration we decided to use an artificial neural network for regression. Similar approach was presented in [8] where authors suggested using MLP with DCT from YCbCr planes for classification.

3 Proposed Approach

Following Everingham and Zisserman [5] we formulate the problem of finding the eye location as a multinomial regression problem. Having a feature vector x we want to predict the output vector y representing coordinates of both eyes. This is the standard regression problem and variety of solutions were proposed to deal with that. Among them, artificial neural networks and support vector regression (SVR) are state-of-the-art nonlinear regression algorithms. Since SVRs are commonly defined only for one dimensional predicted variable they would require four independent models, one for each component. Thus, we used neural networks. In such a case the single model gives multidimensional prediction. Furthermore it is significantly more compact, and hence faster to evaluate, than a support vector machine having the same generalization performance [2]. Usefulness of a neural network for such task is presented in [9], where authors used neural network to refine eye location indicated by different algorithm.

3.1 Features Selection

When it comes to image processing, pixel intensities are the obvious candidates for features. However they are highly dimensional, thus the model gets complicated and hard to train. One can reduce the dimensionality by resizing the image but in such a case, some useful information about the face is lost. The other problem with resizing the image is that the estimated eyes coordinates have to be scaled to the coordinates of the original image. Due to this scaling, the regression error is also scaled and it grows linearly with the scale.

All those problems vanish if the proper features are selected. Coefficients of two dimensional discrete cosine transform(DCT) B_{pq} of a square image A_{mn} of size N given by equation (1) appear to have all the properties required to construct the feature vector.

$$B_{pq} = \alpha_p \alpha_q \sum_{m=0}^{N-1} \sum_{n=0}^{N-1} A_{mn} \cos\left(\frac{\pi(2m+1)p}{2N}\right) \cos\left(\frac{\pi(2n+1)q}{2N}\right) \quad (1)$$

$$\alpha_p = \begin{cases} \sqrt{\frac{1}{N}} & p = 0 \\ \sqrt{\frac{2}{N}} & p \neq 0 \end{cases} \qquad \alpha_q = \begin{cases} \sqrt{\frac{1}{N}} & q = 0 \\ \sqrt{\frac{2}{N}} & q \neq 0 \end{cases}$$

They contain all the information stored in the original image but in DCT domain it is much easier to remove unimportant details with shape information being preserved.

Eyes location is determined by the orientation and shape of the head. Since we are processing images coming from the face detector, the largest object on the image is the head. Thus only some small number of low frequency DCT coefficients are enough to contain all the information about head location and orientation(see Figure 1). This gives the possibility to reduce the dimensionality of a feature vector.

Fig. 1. 64 × 64 Face image before (left) and after(right) removing small DCT coefficients. Only 210 coefficients are remained nonzero.

Another property of DCT coefficients is that they are not invariant under rotation nor translation. What might be a problem for some tasks is well expected in eyes location task since faces are often translated and rotated. DCT coefficients are affected not only by the geometrical transformation. Different lighting conditions result in substantially different coefficients of DCT transform. To make the algorithm resistant against such changes some processing is required. In the proposed algorithm we applied histogram equalisation and obtained results proved to be quite satisfactory.

3.2   Neural Network Regression

For the regression we used standard feed-forward multilayer perceptron with two hidden layers. Second hidden layer increases accuracy without noticeable memory consumption during training phase compared to larger network with single hidden layer. The architecture is presented in Figure 2. Each unit in the hidden layer has tansig (2) activation function while the output layer is pure linear.

$$tansig(n) = \frac{2}{1 + e^{-2n}} - 1 \tag{2}$$

In order to make neural network training more efficient a pre-processing was performed on inputs and targets [7]. Inputs (DCT coefficients) were normalized to have zero mean and unit variance while the outputs (eyes coordinates) were normalized in such a way, that the lower left corner of an image had coordinates $(\frac{1}{N}, \frac{1}{N})$, where N is image size(it is not $(0,0)$ because in Matlab indexes start from 1). The top right corner is at $(1,1)$.

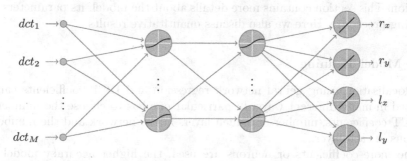

Fig. 2. Neural network structure. Hidden layers have tansig activation function and output layer is pure linear.

Neural Network just like any other supervised learning algorithm requires labelled training examples. The bigger the training set is, the more complex network can be fitted. However one has to be careful with designing very complex models, since neural networks are prone to overfitting in such a case.

Fortunately there is an easy way to multiply the amount of training examples by a factor of few hundreds. For each image in the database and associated eye coordinates we can apply affine transforms to get the new training examples.

Not all of the transforms are valid. Some of them may introduce such a deformation of the face that the resulting image would be unrealistic. Therefore we permitted only *translation* by a vector (b_1, b_2), *rotation* by an angle θ and *scaling* by a scale parameter a. All allowed transforms of a two dimensional vector x can be expressed in matrix notation as

$$x' = a \begin{bmatrix} \cos(\theta) & -\sin(\theta) \\ \sin(\theta) & \cos(\theta) \end{bmatrix} x + \begin{bmatrix} b_1 \\ b_2 \end{bmatrix}. \tag{3}$$

By varying parameters a, b_1, b_2 and θ, we can generate as many examples as needed from a single labelled image. The parameters have to be chosen carefully to generate plausible images i.e. such as one would expect at the output from face detector.

With this artificial training examples it is possible to train the larger network with the higher generalization power compared to the network trained on the original database. However, the examples generated by this procedure cannot span the entire feature space since no out of plane rotations are involved. That is the reason why quite large labelled training dataset like [1] is still needed.

4   Numerical Experiments

The previous section describes the problem and the concept of the proposed solution. This section contains more details about the model, its parameters and training procedure. Here we also discuss quantitative results.

4.1   Model Training

Eye localisation using neural network regression and DCT coefficients can be realized in many different ways. In particular one has to choose the number M of DCT coefficients, number of hidden layers in the network and the number of neurons in each layer.

The more coefficients or neurons are used, the higher accuracy model can be obtained. However, large number of parameters implicate large number of training samples to avoid overfitting. This can be problematic even when the previously described training samples generation procedure is applied. The second problem is that large training set requires large amount of memory (quite often few dozens of GB is required) during training phase.

With all this restrictions in mind, one need to find the parameters that result in quite accurate model with reasonable training set size. The first parameter to tune is the number of DCT coefficients. We found that 210 coefficients chosen in zig-zag order is enough to correctly localize eyes by a human. That is apparent in Figure 1. Such number of features is used as an input to the neural network.

Having the features dimensionality selected, it is possible to experiment with different topologies of the neural network. After some trials we have found that fully connected 2 hidden layer network with 18 neurons in each layer gives satisfactory results. Obviously such a solution is sub-optimal and it is possible to find another one that will got a bit better accuracy. We have found, that the network with two hidden layers has better accuracy compared to the network with single layer. Additionally, less memory is required for training such network than for a network with a single layer and 36 neurons. Thus we end up with the network shown in Figure 2.

As it was mentioned earlier, there is a need for appropriate number of training examples. The rule of thumb is to have about ten times more training samples than number of parameters in the considered model. The network from Figure 2 has about 4000 parameters, thus 40000 training samples is a must. We decided to increase this number to $\sim$ 100000 samples because 30% of them are used as test and validation sets during neural network training phase.

Typical face database with labelled eye positions contains about thousand images. Therefore from each image in the database one hundred examples have to be generated. We picked hundred random transformations of type (3) for every training image. The parameters of the transformations were uniformly distributed in the following ranges $a \in (0.8, 1.2)$, $\theta \in (-\frac{\pi}{16}, \frac{\pi}{16})$, $b_1, b_2 \in (-15, 15)$.

4.2   Model Validation

Usually, the eye localisation algorithm is supposed to be working on images obtained from the face detector. In particular, cascade-based face detector such as the one implemented in popular computer vision library OpenCV. In order to make the validation images as close as possible to the real input images, face regions were selected by the cascade classifier *haarcascade_frontalface_alt.xml* with min size (50,50), scale 1.1 and min neighbors 2. If the cascade found no face or more than one, such example was removed.

After this procedure we got 1430 images from BioID database [1] All detected faces were randomly divided into two sets. The first 451 images were used only for validation, while remaining 979 served as templates for training samples.

Validation set was never used for training its only purpose is to measure accuracy of eye localisation. The accuracy can be describe quantitatively in many different ways. The simplest measure is the mean squared error given by neural network training tool. Unfortunately this measure is not normalized. Therefore we used instead normalized eye localization error proposed in [9], which is defined in terms of the eye centre positions according to

$$d_{eye} = \frac{\max(d_l, d_r)}{\|C_l - C_r\|}, \tag{4}$$

where C_l and C_r are the ground-truth positions and d_l and d_r are the Euclidean distances between the detected eye centres (left and right respectively) and their ground-truth positions. The accuracy of eye localisation algorithm is measured by the fraction of training samples with normalized error less than 0.1 or 0.25. The histogram of normalized error for neural network regression is shown in Figure 3. Its empirical CDF is shown in Figure 4. One may notice, that the most

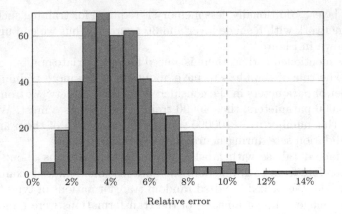

Fig. 3. Histogram of the relative error

probable value of normalized relative error is ~ 0.04. We are dealing with images of size 64x64 px on which the eyes are usually more or less 25 px apart, thus the reported value of the normalized error corresponds to ~ 1 px. We did not note any single example with normalized error larger than 0.14.

The final results and comparison to the other eye localisation methods are collected in Table 1. The results described as 'Neural network regression' were derived from 451 testing images that were not used in a process of additional samples generation. 'Neural network regression (full)' are the results obtained with use of all 1430 images from BioID database. Neither of those images was used in training phase, however large part of them (979) were used as a reference images in a generation of artificial samples.

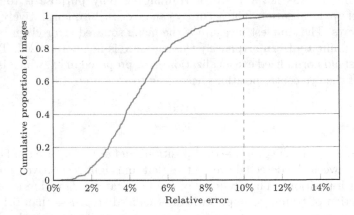

Fig. 4. Empirical cumulative distribution function of the relative error

Table 1. Eye localisation accuracy for BioID database

Method	d_{eye}	per-centage
HPF [15]	0.25	94.81%
Isophote curvature [13]	0.1	90.9%
scale Eyes + mouse [3]	0.1	93.2%
Multiscale sparse dictionaries [14]	0.1	95.5%
Multi-scale LBP [10]	0.1	97.9%
Neural network regression	**0.1**	**98%**
Neural network regression	**0.25**	**100%**
Neural network regression (full)	**0.1**	**98.3%**
Neural network regression (full)	**0.25**	**99.9%**

5   Conclusion

Artificial neural network can be used for accurate eye localisation in face image. Since neural network can be implemented in efficient way, the proposed solution may be used in large-scale multimedia systems like OASIS Archive [4,6].

In contrast with typical classification models, in this paper the regression model is proposed. Such a model gives the final eyes coordinates in a single evaluation step. It does not require extensive searching with sliding window mechanism.

Use of discrete cosine transform coefficients as the features allows to reduce the network size while retaining most of the information stored in the image. This property, combined with powerful artificial training samples generation procedure gives possibility to train an accurate and efficient regression model. The accuracy of the proposed model evaluated on the standard database BioID, is comparable with state-of-the-art techniques.

Acknowledgment. This work has been performed in the framework of the EU Project INDECT (*Intelligent information system supporting observation, searching and detection for security of citizens in urban environment*) – grant agreement number: 218086. This research was supported in part by PL-Grid Infrastructure.

References

1. BioID face database, http://www.bioid.com
2. Bishop, C.: Pattern Recognition and Machine Learning. Information Science and Statistics. Springer (2006)
3. Campadelli, P., Lanzarotti, R., Lipori, G.: Precise eye and mouth localization. International Journal of Pattern Recognition and Artificial Intelligence 23(03), 359–377 (2009)

4. Enge, J., Głowacz, A., Grega, M., Leszczuk, M., Papir, Z., Romaniak, P., Simko, V.: OASIS archive – open archiving system with internet sharing. In: Mauthe, A., Zeadally, S., Cerqueira, E., Curado, M. (eds.) FMN 2009. LNCS, vol. 5630, pp. 254–259. Springer, Heidelberg (2009)
5. Everingham, M., Zisserman, A.: Regression and classification approaches to eye localization in face images. In: Proceedings of the 7th International Conference on Automatic Face and Gesture Recognition, pp. 441–448 (2006)
6. Głowacz, A., Grega, M., Leszczuk, M., Papir, Z., Romaniak, P., Fornalski, P., Lutwin, M., Enge, J., Lurk, T., Šimko, V.: Open internet gateways to archives of media art. Multimedia Tools Appl.
7. Hudson Beale, M., Hagan, M.T., Demuth, H.B.: Neural Network Toolbox User's Guide. MathWorks, Natick (2012)
8. Ioannou, S., Kessous, L., Caridakis, G., Karpouzis, K., Aharonson, V., Kollias, S.: Adaptive on-line neural network retraining for real life multimodal emotion recognition. In: Kollias, S., Stafylopatis, A., Duch, W., Oja, E. (eds.) ICANN 2006. LNCS, vol. 4131, pp. 81–92. Springer, Heidelberg (2006)
9. Jesorsky, O., Kirchberg, K.J., Frischholz, R.W.: Robust face detection using the hausdorff distance. In: Bigun, J., Smeraldi, F. (eds.) AVBPA 2001. LNCS, vol. 2091, pp. 90–95. Springer, Heidelberg (2001)
10. Kroon, B., Maas, S., Boughorbel, S., Hanjalic, A.: Eye localization in low and standard definition content with application to face matching. Comput. Vis. Image Underst. 113(8), 921–933 (2009)
11. Riopka, T., Boult, T.: The eyes have it. In: Proceedings of ACM SIGMM Multimedia Biometrics Methods and Applications Workshop, pp. 9–16 (2003)
12. Rusek, K., Orzechowski, T., Dziech, A.: LDA for face profile detection. In: Dziech, A., Czyżewski, A. (eds.) MCSS 2011. CCIS, vol. 149, pp. 144–148. Springer, Heidelberg (2011)
13. Valenti, R., Gevers, T.: Accurate eye center location and tracking using isophote curvature. In: IEEE Conference on Computer Vision and Pattern Recognition, CVPR 2008, pp. 1–8 (June 2008)
14. Yang, F., Huang, J., Yang, P., Metaxas, D.: Eye localization through multiscale sparse dictionaries. In: 2011 IEEE International Conference on Automatic Face Gesture Recognition and Workshops (FG 2011), pp. 514–518 (March 2011)
15. Zhou, Z.H., Geng, X.: Projection functions for eye detection. Pattern Recognition 37(5), 1049–1056 (2004)

People Detection and Tracking from a Top-View Position Using a Time-of-Flight Camera

Carsten Stahlschmidt, Alexandros Gavriilidis, Jörg Velten,
and Anton Kummert

Faculty of Electrical Engineering and Media Technologies
University of Wuppertal, D-42119 Wuppertal, Germany
{stahlschmidt,gavriilidis,velten,kummert}@uni-wuppertal.de

Abstract. This paper outlines a method for the detection and tracking of people in depth images, acquired with a low-resolution Time-of-Flight (ToF) camera. This depth sensor is placed perpendicular to the ground in order to provide distance information from a top-view position.

With usage of intrinsic and extrinsic camera parameters a ground plane is estimated and compared to the measured distances of the ToF sensor in every pixel. Differences to the expected ground plane define foreground information, which is used as regions of interest (ROIs). These regions are analyzed to distinguish persons from other objects by using a matched filter on the height-segmented depth measurements of each ROI. The proposed method separates crowds into individuals and facilitates a multi-object tracking system based on a Kalman filter.

Experiments have proven the applicability of the system for different crowding scenarios but also revealed inaccuracies of the detection of people in special cases.

Keywords: people detection, top-view, people tracking, time-of-flight, matched filter.

1 Introduction

Surveillance camera systems in public areas become more and more important in order to increase people safety and security.

Particularly, observation of dense crowds got in the focus of research. Every year, crowd disaster occur many times in different areas of the world [10]. Disasters as the Love Parade catastrophe in Duisburg, Germany, 2010, where 21 people died and more than 500 got injured, show the importance of surveillance systems that help to indicate and avoid potentially dangerous situations. Crowd panics often arise in areas where many people accumulate and form a dense crowd [16]. These areas must be analyzed for risks.

Expert reports regarding the Love Parade disaster outline the importance of crowd monitoring systems [10,16] in order to gain knowledge about the people and analyze the crowding situation. Therefore information about the number of people in an area, flow rates or densities of people within a crowd are useful.

A. Dziech and A. Czyżewski (Eds.): MCSS 2013, CCIS 368, pp. 213–223, 2013.

The proposed system in this paper describes a method for the detection of individuals within a dense crowd, which enables the analysis of every person's movement in contrast to the movement within the entire group. With knowledge about individuals, the crowding situation can be characterized.

A ToF camera, which provides depth and gray-scale images of a scene, is mounted perpendicular to the ground for the detection of people. This enables an easier separation and tracking of people, because people do not overlap much in the dimension normal to the ground [9].

Instead of calculating a plan-view projection of the scene from an eye-level or high-angle positioned camera, the sensor is applied directly to the so called "top-view" position. This saves computational costs and reduces loss of depth information for occluded persons from different camera angles.

The used ToF camera is specified in [12]. In this paper, image processing is restricted to the detection and tracking of human persons merely using depth images. Comparable systems also use Kalman filters for people tracking, but the detection of people in plan-view images varies. Idealized shapes for people detection [17] are as well used as Gaussian blobs [2,3] and adaptive templates with a support vector machine to identify people in depth images [8].

The proposed system in this paper is based on usage of a scaled matched filter in combination with height-segmented foreground information. The advantage of this method is the ability to distinguish individual persons from a dense crowd, in contrast to systems where people need to enter the scene separately [2,17].

Thus method enables a multi-object tracking of persons and their differentiated movement analysis in contrast to the behavior of the crowd.

This paper is organized as follows. Section 2 outlines the basic Time-of-Flight principle. In Section 3 the algorithm is described, partitioned in preprocessing, people detection, and people tracking. Section 4 is used to show and discuss experimental results. Finally, Section 5 draws conclusions.

2   Time-of-Flight Camera Principle

Camera-based Time-of-Flight sensors are relatively new camera systems, which provide depth images of a scene at a high frame-rate. Distance information are captured and provided as optical signals, where each pixel on the CMOS imager describes the distance from the camera to the corresponding point in the real world.

As it is outlined in [14], ToF cameras are based on the principle of pulse modulation. Distances are calculated from a light reflecting object to the sensor by measuring the phase delay between the incoming infrared light and a reference signal directly in each pixel. Therefore, most cameras are equipped with active illumination units. The phase of an incoming signal is calculated by

$$\Phi = \arctan\left(\frac{A_1 - A_3}{A_2 - A_4}\right). \tag{1}$$

Here, A_1, A_2, A_3, A_4 are four samples of the signal, each shifted by $90°$. The distance d is proportional to phase Φ and calculated by using signal frequency f_{mod} and speed of light c by

$$d = \frac{c\Phi}{4\pi f_{mod}}. \tag{2}$$

By measuring d in every pixel of the sensor, a depth signal is generated.

This measurement principle is of importance due to the fact that it defines the maximum distance to be measured without phase ambiguity [7]. This constraint in the maximum distance is depending on modulation frequency f_{mod} and calculated by $d_{max} = \frac{c}{2f_{mod}}$. ToF cameras assume a maximum $\Phi = 2\pi$ that limits every modulation frequency to a d_{max}. For real distances in the scene farther away than d_{max}, this results in a wrong measured distance d. For the proposed system ,the camera was placed below d_{max} in order to avoid phase ambiguity.

Due to the method of illuminating the entire scene with modulated infrared light and measuring the phase delay in every pixel of the PMD sensor individually, rather than using a single scanning laser beam to estimate distances, a much higher frame-rate of gathering depth maps can be accomplished [13]. In contrast to common gray-scale cameras, camera-based ToF sensors measure not only the distances from the camera to an object in the scene, but can also provide gray-scale values of every pixel in an intensity image. In the following sections,

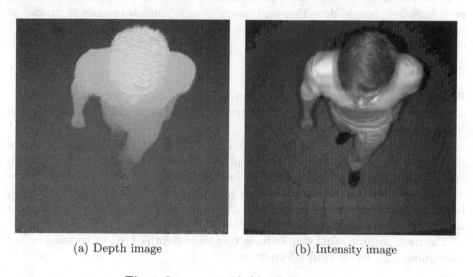

(a) Depth image   (b) Intensity image

Fig. 1. Images provided by ToF camera

$$f(\mathbf{n}) = f(n_t, n_x, n_y) \tag{3}$$

with $\mathbf{n} = (n_t, n_x, n_y)'$ denotes a distance value in pixel (n_x, n_y) at a particular time n_t. $f(\mathbf{n})$ can be interpreted as one depth image from a sequence of depth images, defined by measurements of the ToF camera for $\mathbf{n} \in \mathcal{D}$ with

$$\mathcal{D} = \left\{ \mathbf{n} \in \mathbb{Z}^3 | 0 \leq \mathbf{n} \leq \mathbf{N} \right\}, \tag{4}$$

where $\mathbf{N} = (N_t, N_x, N_y)'$. $\mathbf{N}$ describes the number of points in each dimension. An arbitrarily shaped subset $\mathcal{R} \subseteq I$ of an image, with

$$\mathcal{I} = \left\{ \begin{pmatrix} m_x \\ m_y \end{pmatrix} = \mathbf{m} \in \mathbb{Z}^2 \middle| 0 \leq m_x \leq N_x, 0 \leq m_y \leq N_y \right\} \tag{5}$$

is denoted as region of interest (ROI) within $\mathcal{I}$. In this paper, the signal $f(\mathbf{n})$ describes an $N_x \times N_y$ image containing depth information in N_t frames.

Figure 1 shows the difference between depth and intensity images. Depth images provide range information from camera to real world. Bright pixel indicate reflecting objects located nearer to the camera than dark pixel. Intensity images correspond to $f(\mathbf{n})$ but provide gray-scale information of the scene in each pixel. The corresponding intensity image is of the same size as the depth image.

3   Algorithm

The people detection algorithm is divided into several components regarding preprocessing, people detection and assignment of measurements to tracks as described in the following subsections.

3.1   Preprocessing

Preprocessing of depth data is necessary in order to reduce noise from considerably noisy pixel, estimate regions of interest and segment measured depths into height segments.

Depth measurement errors arise from different sources [4] and affect the posterior height segmentation process. The proposed method uses a straightforward spatial neighborhood filter, sufficient for the system to decrease depth measurement errors. A static ground plane $g(n_x, n_y)$ is defined as described in [5], based on extrinsic camera parameters. Hence, expected distances from camera to ground are specified when no obstacles reflect the camera beam.

The next preprocessing step reduces measured depths $f(\mathbf{n})$ to an image $F(\mathbf{n})$ containing only foreground information, by

$$F(n_t, n_x, n_y) = f(n_t, n_x, n_y) - g(n_x, n_y), \tag{6}$$

where n_t denotes the n_tth image. In other words, measured depths from an empty room lead to an $F(\mathbf{n}) = 0$.

When objects are present, $F(\mathbf{n})$ contains depth values that define the foreground. If one object exists, one associated local region is estimated that defines the ROI of the depth image. In cases of more objects present in $F(\mathbf{n})$, the number of ROIs can alter between one and the number of objects. In cases where several objects are closely spaced and an erosion process fails to differ these, one ROI can contain more than one object.

The depths values of ROIs $\mathcal{R}_i$ of one or more (if overlapping or nearby) objects are sliced into height segments, where $\mathcal{R}_i \subseteq \mathcal{I}$ and $\mathcal{R}_i \cap \mathcal{R}_j = \emptyset$, for $i \neq j$. Individual segmentation of depths in each region $\mathcal{R}_i$ reassigns the measured depth values to segmentation levels $S_{i,l}$, where l denotes the level number and i the index of the belonging region. By using

$$S_{i,step} = \frac{F(n_t, \mathbf{m}_{max}) - F(n_t, \mathbf{m}_{min})}{c}, \tag{7}$$

$$S_{i,l} = \left\lfloor \frac{d - F(n_t, \mathbf{m}_{min})}{S_{i,step}} \right\rfloor + 1, \tag{8}$$

$$F(n_t, \mathbf{m}_{max}) = max(F(n_t, \mathbf{m})) \forall \mathbf{m} \in \mathcal{R}_i, \tag{9}$$

$$F(n_t, \mathbf{m}_{min}) = min(F(n_t, \mathbf{m})) \forall \mathbf{m} \in \mathcal{R}_i, \tag{10}$$

increment $S_{i,step}$ and segmentation levels $S_{i,l}$ are determined. d denotes the measured depth of the processed pixel, $F(n_t, \mathbf{m}_{max})$ and $F(n_t, \mathbf{m}_{min})$ denote the extremes. The proposed system clusters depths of every region in a static number c of steps. Depth data is segemented to an image $\widehat{F}(\mathbf{n})$ with

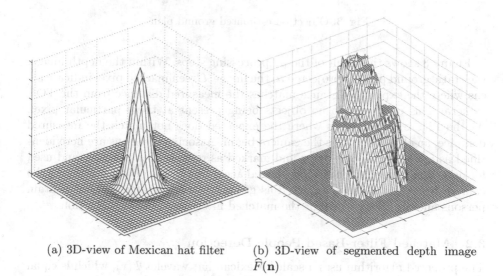

(a) 3D-view of Mexican hat filter   (b) 3D-view of segmented depth image $\widehat{F}(\mathbf{n})$

Fig. 2. Matched filter and segmented depth image

$$\widehat{F}(n_t, n_x, n_y) = \begin{cases} S_{i,l} \text{ , if } \mathcal{R} \in \mathcal{R}_i \\ 0 \text{ , else} \end{cases} \tag{11}$$

for every n_tth image.

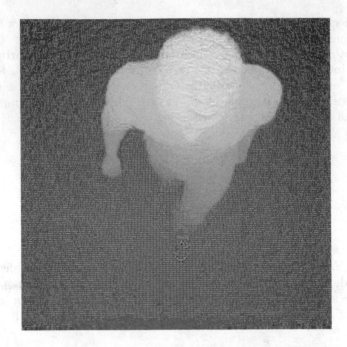

Fig. 3. Object on estimated ground plane

Figure 3 shows the result of the preprocessing steps. Within the depth image, the static ground plane is projected to the image. Green marked pixel indicate areas where the expected distance matches the measured distance from the TOF camera. This concludes to no objects being present at these particular pixel. As the Figure shows, areas where the expected does not match the measured distance, an object occupies the camera beam. Associated regions are here identified as non-ground plane areas and marked as regions of interest $\mathcal{R}_i$ and used for detection of people. Each $\mathcal{R}_i$ is shaped according to the object occupying the camera beam. Image areas, marked as ground plane, therefore cannot contain persons and are disregarded for the matched filter-based people detection.

3.2   Matched Filter-Based People Detection

The proposed algorithm uses a scaled Mexican hat wavelet $\Psi(\mathbf{r})$, which is equal to the second derivative of a Gaussian [11]. It is used as a matched filter to distinguish people from different objects in $\widehat{F}(\mathbf{n})$. The normalized Mexican hat wavelet, given by

$$\Psi(\mathbf{r}) = \frac{2}{\sqrt{3}\sigma\pi^{1/4}} \left(1 - \frac{\mathbf{r}^2}{\sigma^2} \right) \exp\left(-\frac{\mathbf{r}^2}{2\sigma^2} \right) \tag{12}$$

with $\mathbf{r} = (x, y)'$. $\Psi(\mathbf{r})$ is scaled according to the expected size of silhouettes of persons, that depends on the positioned height of the camera above ground level.

If the camera is positioned lower above ground level, people appear larger within the image. A high positioned camera results in a larger field of view that results in people appearing smaller.

The Mexican hat wavelet is used as impulse response $\Psi(\mathbf{r})$. Due to its resemblance with upright standing people, it is used here as a generalized depth silhouette for people. This silhouette approaches the depth information of upright standing persons in a way where the orientation of the person in the field of view is of no importance.

(a) Gray-scale image   (b) Segmented depth image   (c) Correlation Matrix

(d) Gray-scale image   (e) Segmented depth image   (f) Correlation Matrix

Fig. 4. Correlation procedure visualized by gray-scale image, segmented depth image $\widehat{F}(\mathbf{n})$ and resulting correlation matrix $\mathcal{C}$ with a marker defining the position $\mathbf{z}$ of detected persons for different crowding scenarios

Figure 2(a) shows the 3D-view of a Mexican hat filter used as a generalized depth silhouette for people detection, 2(b) the segemented depth image calculated from Figure 1(a). In a preprocessed image $\widehat{F}(\mathbf{n})$, a detected ROI $\mathcal{R}_i$, containing the foreground object, is segmented in c ascending depth levels. The ground level equals $S_{1,0}$.

The 2D cross correlation, with respect to variables n_x and n_y at time n_t, is calculated by $\mathcal{C}(n_t, n_x, n_y) = \widehat{F}(n_t, n_x, n_y) * \Psi(\mathbf{r})$ of preprocessed depth images $\widehat{F}(\mathbf{n})$ with matched filter $\Psi(\mathbf{r})$. In image processing,

$$C(n_t, n_x, n_y) = \frac{1}{N_x N_y} \sum_{k_x=0}^{N_x-1} \sum_{k_y=0}^{N_y-1} \widehat{F}(n_t, k_x, k_y) \Psi(n_x + k_x, n_y + k_y) \qquad (13)$$

calculates the correlation signal C [6].

High values in C denote similarity with matched filter $\Psi(\mathbf{r})$ in a ROI $\mathcal{R}_i$ of image $\widehat{F}(\mathbf{n})$, that may indicate a person. In other words, positions of peaks in C define the location in $\widehat{F}(\mathbf{n})$ where the matched filter is alike to the silhouette of a human person. Also objects similar $\Psi(\mathbf{r})$ result in high values in C.

The correlation results are independent from the absolute height of a person due to the prior height segmentation.

Taking into consideration that a region $\mathcal{R}_i$ contains more than one person, several peaks in regions are feasible. The combination of a peak finding algorithm using the extended h-maxima transform and a thresholding procedure for a further analyzis of peaks is then used to distinguish people in region $\mathcal{R}_i$ from different objects. Extended h-maxima transform suppresses regional maxima, whose peak is less than a given threshold [15].

Remaining peaks after the thresholding process indicate an upright standing person. Their location is used for the Kalman-filter based tracking procedure. Figure 4 outlines the people detection algorithm for different crowding scenarios. Images 4(a)-4(c) show the detection process for a moderate crowding scene where three persons are present. Images 4(d)-4(f) contain five persons. Depth image 4(b) is partitioned into two regions $\mathcal{R}_i$, one in the upper part containing two persons, the other one in the lower part of the image.

These regions are segmented in height into segmentation levels to normalize the measured depths and achieve independence from the measured height of a person. This is needed for a reliable detection of children or small people.

3.3   Track Assignment

The assignment of measurements $z(n_t)$ to tracks is based on the people detection algorithm that provides $\mathbf{z}_i = [x_i, y_i, d_i]'$. The coordinates (x_i, y_i) of measured depth d_i describe object i. Each image $\widehat{F}(\mathbf{n})$ contains $i = 0, \ldots, O$ detected objects identified as a person, where O defines the number of detections in frame n_t.

A new track is initialized if $\mathbf{z}_i$ cannot be assigned to an existing track. The state of a track is defined as state vector $\mathbf{x}_i(n_t) = [x_i, y_i, \dot{x}_i, \dot{y}_i, d]'$, where $(\dot{x}_i, \dot{y}_i)$ is the velocity and used to improve the definition of the state of a person.

Time update and measurement update are defined analogously to [1] as

$$\mathbf{x}(n_t + 1) = \mathbf{A}\mathbf{x}(n_t) + \mathbf{v}(n_t) \qquad (14)$$

$$\bar{\mathbf{z}}(n_t + 1) = \mathbf{H}(n_t + 1)\mathbf{x}(n_t + 1) + \mathbf{w}(n_t + 1), \qquad (15)$$

where $\bar{\mathbf{z}}$ is the measurement prediction error and $\mathbf{v}(n_t)$ is a sequence of zero-mean white Gaussian process noise with covariance $E[\mathbf{v}(n_t)\mathbf{v}(n_t)'] = \mathbf{Q}(n_t)$. Sequence

$\mathbf{w}(n_t)$ is also of zero-mean white Gaussian measurement noise with covariance $E[\mathbf{w}(n_t)\mathbf{w}(n_t)'] = \mathbf{R}(n_t)$. System matrix $\mathbf{A}$ with assumption of constant velocity is used as

$$\mathbf{A} = \begin{bmatrix} 1 & 0 & \Delta n_t & 0 & 0 \\ 0 & 1 & 0 & \Delta n_t & 0 \\ 0 & 0 & 1 & 0 & 0 \\ 0 & 0 & 0 & 0 & 0, \end{bmatrix} \tag{16}$$

where Δn_t denotes the time difference between two frames.

Assignment of measurements to tracks is performed by usage of a gating process, using the well-known Mahalanobis distance. Tracks taken into account by the previous step selected. This gaiting process is followed by an association process that finally assigns measurements to known or new tracks by applying a nearest-neighbor procedure.

4   System Setup and Experiments

Our test environment is a hallway equipped with a ToF camera, positioned in a hallway normal to entrance of a room at a height of 2.8 meters

The used ToF camera provides a resolution of 200×200 pixel with a frame-rate up to 40 fps, a field of view of $40° \times 40°$ and a standard measurement range up to 7 meter. Figure 5 shows images of detected and tracked persons. Red crosses define the positions of measurements from each frame, combined to a tracking path showing the movement of each person. The connectivity of measured positions identifies the successful tracking of a person. Numbers beside the tracking path define the tracking identification number that increases by one for each new track.

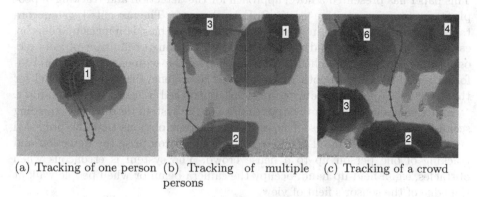

(a) Tracking of one person   (b) Tracking of multiple persons   (c) Tracking of a crowd

Fig. 5. Tracking of people in different crowding scenarios

The proposed algorithm is fully implemented in MATLAB and has been tested for different crowding scenarios. The sequences used for experiments are up to thousand frames in length and consist of up to eight persons simultaneously.

Experiments for different crowding scenarios on real data have demonstrated the applicability of the system as shown in Figure 5.

Problems with people detection occur in cases where a person is not fully present in the camera's field of view, but at the edge. This is called "body in the pyramid effect" [17] that describes the body shape which comes closest to the shape from top-view position. In this case, a person is not fully visible but partially by crossing the camera's beam. A person not fully visible, but detected as a person is shown in Figure 4 in track 3.

If a person walks at the edge of the sensor's beam and alters between providing sufficient and insufficient shape and height information, this person may not be detected certainly while residing in the field of view. As a consequence, the person can be considered a new track multiple times. As long as a person provides sufficient shape and height information it maintains its logical identity in the scene.

As a result of a generalized depth silhouette, experiments have shown that the orientation of a captured person within the image is of no importance. This means, walking direction and angle to the camera do not affect the detection result of a person. Based on the usage of one matched filter, the detection algorithm is adapted to upright standing or walking persons. Currently, the system's reaction for people in wheelchairs, wearing hats or walking ducked has not been tested.

Experiments were conducted offline and show the applicability of the system to detect and track persons from the described top-view position, even in cases with many people forming a dense crowd.

5   Conclusions

This paper has presented a novel approach for the detection and tracking of people from a top-view position using a ToF depth sensor. The presented system contains procedures to determine foreground information based on measured depths, estimated ground-plane and the detection and tracking of multiple-objects recognized as people. A matched filter is applied to the segmented foreground information of measured depth images, scaled as a generalized depth model for the detection of persons. Detected persons are tracked by using a Kalman-filter.

Experiments have shown the applicability of the system for different crowding scenarios of people in real sequences. It has become obvious that the proposed system works reliable in all tested scenarios, which comprise the detection and tracking of one person up to a dense crowd. The system is erroneous when obstacles, e.g. a held-up hand, occupy the camera beam or when people walk at the edge of the sensor's field of view.

We believe that such erroneous people detections can be improved by the fusion with a classifier trained on gray-scale images from this top-view position.

Acknowledgements. The research leading to these results has received funding from the European Community's Seventh Framework Programme (FP7 / 2007 - 2013) under grant agreement no. 218086.

References

1. Bar-Shalom, J., Rong Li, X., Kirubarajan, T.: Estimation with Applications to Tracking and Navigation. John Wiley & Sons (2001)
2. Bevilacqua, A., Di Stefano, L., Azzari, P.: People tracking using a Time-of-Flight depth sensor. In: IEEE Fifth International Conference on Advanced Video and Signal Based Surveillance (2006)
3. Beymer, D., Konolige, K.: Tracking People from a Mobile Platform. In: Siciliano, B., Dario, P. (eds.) Experimental Robotics VIII. STAR, vol. 5, pp. 234–244. Springer, Heidelberg (2003)
4. Foix, S., Alenyá, G., Torras, C.: Lock-in Time-of-Flight (ToF) Cameras: A Survey. IEEE Sensors Journal 11(9), 1917–1926 (2011)
5. Gavriilidis, A., Schwerdtfeger, T., Velten, J., Schauland, S., Hohmann, L., Haselhoff, A., Boschen, F., Kummert, A.: Multisensor data fusion for advanced driver assistance systems - the Active Safety Car project. In: International Workshop on Multidimensional Systems (nDs), vol. 7, pp. 1–5 (2011)
6. Gonzalez, R.C., Woods, R.E.: Digital Image Processing, 2nd edn. Prentice Hall International, Boston (2001)
7. Hansard, M., Lee, S., Choi, O., Horaud, R.P.: Time of Flight Cameras: Principles, Methods, and Applications. Springer Briefs in Computer Science. Springer (2012)
8. Harville, M.: Stereo person tracking with short and long term plan-view appearance models of shape and color. In: Proceedings of International Conference on Advanced Video and Signal based Surveillance (AVSS), vol. 1, pp. 511–517. Santa Fe (2005)
9. Harville, M., Li, D.: Fast, Integrated Person Tracking and Activity Recognition with Plan-View Templates from a Single Stereo Camera. In: IEEE Conference on Computer Vision and Pattern Recognition, Washington (2004)
10. Helbing, D., Mukerji, P.: Crowd Disasters as Systemic Failures: Analysis of the Love Parade Disaster. Tech. rep., ETH Risk Center, Zürich (2011)
11. Mallat, S.: A Wavelet Tour of Signal Processing. Academic Press (1998)
12. PMD Technologies, PMD vision CamCube 3.0 Specsheet - High resolution 3D video camera. Tech. rep., PMD Technologies GmbH (2010)
13. Reynolds, M., Dobos, J., Peel, L., Weyrich, T., Brostow, G.: Capturing Time-of-Flight Data with Confidence. In: Proc. of IEEE Conference on Computer Vision and Pattern Recognition, CVPR (2011)
14. Ringbeck, T.: A 3D Time of Flight Camera for Object Detection. In: Optical 3-D Measurement Techniques (2007)
15. Soille, P.: Morphological Image Analysis: Principles and Applications. Springer (1999)
16. Still, G.K.: Duisburg - July 24, 2010, Love Parade Incident, Expert Report. Tech. rep., Bucks New University (2011)
17. Tanner, R., Studer, M., Zanoli, A., Hartmann, A.: People Detection and Tracking with TOF Sensor. In: IEEE Fifth International Conference on Advanced Video and Signal Based Surveillance (2008)

Video Analytics-Based Algorithm
for Monitoring Egress from Buildings

Maciej Szczodrak and Andrzej Czyżewski

Multimedia Systems Department,
Faculty of Electronics, Telecommunications and Informatics,
Gdansk University of Technology
Narutowicza 11/12, 80-233 Gdansk, Poland
{szczodry,andcz}@multimed.org

Abstract. A concept and practical implementation of the algorithm
for detecting of potentially dangerous situations of crowding in passages
is presented. An example of such situation is a crush which may be
caused by obstructed pedestrian pathway. Surveillance video camera signal analysis performed on line is employed in order to detect hold-ups
near bottlenecks like doorways or staircases. The details of implemented
algorithm which uses optical flow method combined with fuzzy logic are
explained. The implementation details are introduced with focus on the
computing platform and parallel processing. The experiments were carried out on the set of gathered video recordings from the surveillance
camera installed in the campus of Gdansk University of Technology. The
results of experiments performed on gathered video recordings show that
efficiency of the algorithm is high.

Keywords: Crowd, Crowd behavior, Egress monitoring.

1 Introduction

Gathering of large number of people in confined area may be the source of dangerous events. Participants of concerts, sport games and other similar ceremonies
are imposed to serious physical injuries, and in the worst case they might even
lose life. The emergency situations occurred many times in the history [1][2][3].
One of the dangerous situations is a crush which may be caused by obstructed
pedestrian pathway. Obstruction of passages or exits may occur during crowd
events, where many people are gathered on a small area. Such a situation may
take place i.e. in a sport object or an entertainment hall during a football game,
a concert, etc. in the moment when every participant intends to leave the building. Regardless of existence of multiple exits in building people tend to choose
their known way, for example the way they entered the facility. This may result
in raising of a significant slowdown or formation of blockages in places such as
passages, halls near door or elevators. Nowadays in such objects monitoring systems are commonly used. In parallel with popularization of monitoring systems,
a continuous process of refining surveillance algorithms can be observed not only

A. Dziech and A. Czyżewski (Eds.): MCSS 2013, CCIS 368, pp. 224–232, 2013.

for video but also often for audio processing algorithms [4]. Conventional video surveillance systems employ object detection and tracking in order to extract the moving people or cars from the background. Research subjects range from algorithms [5] to complete video monitoring systems like a system for event detection in underground stations [6]. Analysing of crowded scenes is much more complex when compared to the non crowded ones due to problems of detection and tracking of individuals. Various subjects of video analysis of crowd are undertaken by scientists. For example crowd behavior detection and classification are made as normal or abnormal, including opposite movement in crowd, division, fighting, by finding corresponding motion attributes [7][8]. Another work focus on estimation of crowd density using diverse methods, like recognition of the head contour using Haar wavelet transform (HWT) and support vector machines (SVM) [9], or image texture statistical analysis [10]. As an alternate example a system can serve for detection overcrowding in underground station platform [11]. In this paper a video analytics algorithm for monitoring egress from buildings or rooms is proposed. The main focus is put on detection of blocking of pedestrian flow near bottlenecks such as door or narrow corridors. State of pedestrian flow in a given area is determined by examining the rates of movement of pedestrians and their density, obtained by video analysis algorithms. Determination of flow velocity of the crowd does not require detection and tracking of individuals, and even that would be cumbersome to implement. For this purpose a method based on optical flow combined with fuzzy logic is utilized. Average velocity of flow is calculated in a selected points in the frame, according to the direction of movement of people. Estimation of the state of congestion is performed by fuzzy logic. For example, if the observed velocity at checkpoints is decreasing and the occupancy of the area is large, a lock of the area is probable. Automatic recognition of the degree of congestion at critical points allows detecting the lock and respond appropriately, for example, by identifying other exit paths. Processing of the video signal in nearly real time is required to provide a practically usable solution. Therefore the supercomputer was employed to provide the hardware base for performing the calculations on the video streams. The management of the resources of the cluster during acquisition and processing of multimedia data is supported by the dedicated platform called KASKADA engineered at Gdansk University of Technology [12].

2   Algorithm

Crowding detection is realized in several stages. In the initial phase *optical flow field* is determined for estimating the speed and direction of movement of pedestrians. The input for the algorithm performing this task are always two consecutive image frames. The next step is to analyze the traffic by calculating the average velocity of the stream of pedestrians in each of the previously defined checkpoints. The next step is to determine the occupation of area by the method of image background subtraction. The obtained information is provided to the input the of fuzzy logic system, whose task is to give the final result of determining the state of congestion of the analyzed area. Illustration of the concept of the detector is shown in Fig. 1. The assumption is made that no other objects apart from people appear in the investigated area. Therefore, additional recognition of object type is not required. The control lines k_i are perpendicular to the exit path and defined separately for each camera. The average speed of people $v_{k,i}$ obtained by the optical flow method is determined for vectors crossing each control line. The speed vectors $v_{k,i}$ are calculated synchronously in each image frame.

2.1 Motion Detection

The method based on calculation of the optical flow was utilized for detecting of crowd motion speed and direction. The algorithm utilized for obtaining the optical flow field is employing CLG (Combined Local Global) method [13]. Similarly to characteristic for optical flow algorithms coarse-to-fine strategy, this algorithm uses a multigrid approach, where estimates of the flow are passed both up and down the hierarchy of approximations. The algorithm combines the advantages of the global Horn-Schunck approach [14] and the local LucasKanade method [15]. Moreover, it was the best-performing algorithm according to the comparison study [16].

The CLG method computes the optical flow field $(u(x,y), v(x,y))^\mathsf{T}$ of image sequence $f(x,y,t)$ at instant t by solving a system of the partial differential equations. The solution is found by the multigrid methods [17][18]. The smallest density of grid is determined by *max_level* parameter and the largest depends on *start_level* parameter. The density of each intermediate grid between the sparsest and the densest doubles.

2.2 Pedestrian Flow Analysis

Obtained continuous flow field (motion direction and velocity determined for each pixel) is sampled in fixed spatial density $(\Delta x, \Delta y)$. Vectors extracted in this way intersect with control lines. During processing of subsequent image

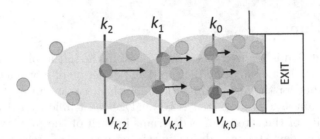

Fig. 1. The concept of clogging detector: k_0, k_1, k_2–control lines, $v_{k_0}, \ldots$–pedestrian flow speed

frames m and $m + 1$, having defined the number of control lines K, we obtain sets of vectors representing instantaneous velocity $v_{m,k,i}$,

where: k – control line number, $k = 1...K$,
$i = 1...I$, I – number of vectors which intersect control line k.

Motion velocity in each control line k is calculated according to equation:

$$v_{m,k} = \frac{1}{N_k} \sum_i v_{m,k,i} \tag{1}$$

where N_k means number of vectors intersecting control line. The final value of velocity v_k is found as a result of temporal averaging of speed ((1)) in a defined M frames period

$$v_k = \frac{1}{M} \sum_{m=1}^{M} v_{m,k} \tag{2}$$

Parameter z which represents occupancy of area is obtained with use of the background subtraction method [19] as defined in equation:

$$z = \frac{P_{FG}}{P_{TOTAL}} \tag{3}$$

where: P_{FG} – number of pixels not qualified as background, P_{TOTAL} – total number of pixels in image.

The fuzzy logic is employed for making an assessment of the state of pedestrian flow [20] [21]. Determined in previous stages of processing velocity and area occupancy parameters constitute the input data to the decision-making system. Mamadanis method was used as fuzzy inference technique. Membership functions defined for parameters v_k and z defined by equations (2) and (3), named *Speed{k}* and *Occupancy*, have triangle shape. For fuzzy OR and AND rules evaluation fuzzy union and intersection operators are applied. In defuzzification procedure, the centroid method is utilized.

The main rules utilized in the system with 3 control lines are as follows:

```
if Speed0 is LOW and Speed1 is LOW and
   Speed2 is LOW and Occupancy is LOW
   then Clogging is NONE
if Speed0 is LOW and Speed1 is LOW and
   Speed2 is LOW and Occupancy is HIGH
   then Clogging is HIGH
```

2.3   System Architecture

The architecture of the system is shown in Fig. 2. Input video signal is acquired by the set IP camera installed in various locations in the campus of Gdansk

University of Technology. The data from each camera is transmitted to the supercomputer and connected to KASKADA platform. The discussed platform introduces a convenient solution for the processing multimedia in the nearly real-time on the supercomputer. In case of video processing, the running algorithm provides output which consists of the video stream and optional messages which are managed by the message server. The latter allows for sending the analysis outcome outside the KASKADA platform. The system can be easily enhanced with elements such as displays providing dynamically updated information for pedestrians about possible pathways.

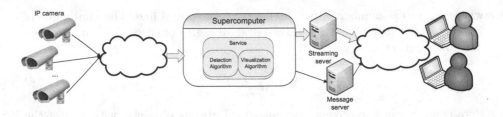

Fig. 2. System architecture

2.4   Application of Parallel Processing in Clogging Detector

The most computationally complex element of the discussed algorithm is computation of the optical flow. It requires solving of elliptic partial differential equations involving the application of multigrid methods. The idea behind the multigrid is to use a sequence of coarse grids as a means to accelerate the problem solving on the finest grid. This is performed by recursive algorithms application such as V-cycle or W-cycle, which traverse between fine and coarse grids. Moreover, the result calculation of a new pixel value depends on its neighbors state. In this case a convenient method of parallel processing, based on an assignment of the incoming video frames to the individual threads, was utilized. The performance of the clogging detection algorithm was described by the popular measure, namely the number of frames processed in one second. The aim of the experiments was the determining of the effective fps of the output stream. Various number of parallel threads was employed for the image processing – 8, 12 and 24. The performance was also investigated for *start_level* parameter values of 0 and 1.

The gathered recordings were processed with various combinations of parameters having a significant influence on the performance, namely number of threads and *start_level*. The investigation was performed for 2 test recordings, which parameters are presented in Table 1.

The recordings varied with motion intensity. Each measurement was repeated 10 times and an average value of the obtained fps was calculated. The tests were preliminarily conducted on a single node of the KASKADA platform (cluster Galera+) containing 12 cores. The results of measurements are shown in Table 2.

Table 1. Characteristics of test video recordings for performance evaluation

Num.	resolution	fps	frame count	description
1	704×576	25	5749	Auditorium L, large number of people
2	704×576	25	5454	Auditorium R, small number of people

Table 2. Performance of image processing (fps) for one node of Galera+ cluster

	Recording 1	Recording 2
num. of threads	704×576	704×576
start_level 0		
8	6.74	7.14
12	8.32	8.91
24	8.39	8.96
start_level 1		
8	19.97	20.13
12	23.62	23.92
24	24.39	24.75

The presented measurement results show that one node of the cluster is needed for processing of one 704×576 stream. Assuming that the video streams originating from a monitoring system in a large building are analysed, the use of supercomputer is thereby justified. Moreover, in such an approach the computational resources are used efficiently. The value of parameter *start_level* has a significant influence on the processing time, particularly in case of 0 what means that calculations are performed on the image of original resolution (not scaled down). In order to achieve a better performance, the service which allows for employing more than one node was also implemented.

3   Experiments

The experiments were carried out on the set of gathered video recordings from the surveillance camera installed in the campus of Gdansk University of Technology. Two cameras mounted in the lecture hall near a building exit were utilized for gathering the test material. The camera view and the corresponding video processing result are presented in Fig. 3. Experimental material consisted of 60 recordings. Two types of egress were recorded, namely a normal where people flow is fluent and an obstructed one. The efficiency of the algorithm was determined by comparing the algorithm outcomes to the reference data prepared manually by an expert. The recordings content presents people exiting from the lecture hall and the reference data describe the degree of crowding near the door which was prepared for each frame of the video. The degree of crowding can be regarded as a function of two variables

$$R(t) = f(s, d, t) \tag{4}$$

where: s – speed of pedestrian flow, d – density of the crowd in the area adjacent to the door, mean d is defined as ratio of number of pixels belonging to pedestrians to number of pixels in the area of interest.

The preparation of the reference data by the expert was based on the analysis of the number of people and their movement speed on the way leading towards the exit, according to guidelines [22]. Annotation is based on a textual description of degree of crowding categorized as follows: low, medium, high, very high. 'Low' means normal situation (undisturbed flow). Each category i can be regarded as a range described by two numbers which represent its minimum and maximum ($L_{i,min}$ and $L_{i,max}$). The measure of algorithm quality (Q) is defined as the ratio of number of algorithm results matching the expert indication (R) to the total number of results (N).

(a) Image recorded by camera   (b) Processing result, control lines and motion map are visible

Fig. 3. Experiment results: recorded image (a) and processing outcome (b)

$$r_{i,t} = \begin{cases} 1 & L_{i,min} \le R_t < L_{i,max} \\ 0 & otherwise \end{cases} \tag{5}$$

$$R = \sum_{t=0}^{T} \sum_{i=1}^{4} r_{i,t} \tag{6}$$

$$Q = \frac{R}{N} \tag{7}$$

A series of experiments was carried out with regards to two situations near exit door from Auditoriums L and P. The average quality calculated for situations of crowding is 0.86 and for the normal exit is 0.83. These results were obtained for *start_level* parameter value equal to 1. The outcomes of algorithm representing typical two situations for the recording are presented in Fig. 4.

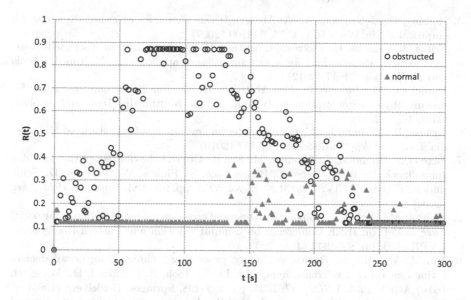

Fig. 4. Comparison of algorithm output for normal egress and overcrowding for Auditorium L

4 Conclusions

The concept, the implementation and the practical utilization of the algorithm for the detecting of potentially dangerous situations in crowd were presented. Based on example experiment results shown in the paper, a conclusion can be made that proposed algorithm is sufficient for detecting pedestrian clogging near passage bottlenecks. In the future some enhancements of the system can be done, for example adding messages sending by a common short message system. Moreover, a connection of multiple cameras to the system can provide a route prediction for pedestrians in large buildings correlated to the present situation.

Acknowledgments. Research funded within the project No. POIG.02.03.03-00-008/08, entitled "MAYDAY EURO 2012 - the supercomputer platform of context depended analysis of multimedia data streams for identifying specified objects or safety threads". The project is subsidized by the European regional development fund and by the Polish State budget.

References

1. Taylor, P.: The Hillsborough Stadium disaster, inquiry by the Rt Hon Lord Justice Taylor : interim report. Her Majesty's Stationery Office (April 15, 1989)
2. Grosshandler, W.L., Bryner, N., Madrzykowski, D., Kuntz, K.: Report of the technical investigation of the station nightclub fire. In: NIST NCSTAR 2. National Institute of Standards and Technology, Gaithersburg (2005)

3. Helbing, D., Johansson, A., Al-Abideen, H.Z.: Dynamics of crowd disasters: An empirical study. Phys. Rev. E 75, 046109 (2007)
4. Kotus, J., Lopatka, K., Czyzewski, A.: Detection and localization of selected acoustic events in acoustic field for smart surveillance applications. Multimedia Tools and Applications, 1–17 (2012)
5. Hammami, M., Jarraya, S., Ben-Abdallah, H.: On line background modeling for moving object segmentation in dynamic scenes. Multimedia Tools and Applications, 1–28 (2011)
6. Krausz, B., Herpers, R.: Metrosurv: detecting events in subway stations. Multimedia Tools and Applications 50, 123–147 (2010)
7. Saxena, S., Brémond, F., Thonnat, M., Ma, R.: Crowd behavior recognition for video surveillance. In: Blanc-Talon, J., Bourennane, S., Philips, W., Popescu, D., Scheunders, P. (eds.) ACIVS 2008. LNCS, vol. 5259, pp. 970–981. Springer, Heidelberg (2008)
8. Mehran, R., Oyama, A., Shah, M.: Abnormal crowd behavior detection using social force model. In: IEEE Conference on Computer Vision and Pattern Recognition, CVPR 2009, pp. 935–942 (June 2009)
9. Yin, J., Velastin, S., Davies, A.: Image processing techniques for crowd density estimation using a reference image. In: Li, S., Teoh, E.-K., Mital, D., Wang, H. (eds.) ACCV 1995. LNCS, vol. 1035, pp. 489–498. Springer, Heidelberg (1996)
10. Marana, A., Velastin, S., Costa, L., Lotufo, R.: Automatic estimation of crowd density using texture. Safety Science 28(3), 165–175 (1998)
11. Lo, B., Velastin, S.: Automatic congestion detection system for underground platforms. In: Proceedings of 2001 International Symposium on Intelligent Multimedia, Video and Speech Processing, pp. 158–161 (2001)
12. Krawczyk, H., Proficz, J.: Kaskada - multimedia processing platform architecture. In: SIGMAP, pp. 26–31 (2010)
13. Bruhn, A., Weickert, J., Schnörr, C.: Combining the advantages of local and global optic flow methods. In: Van Gool, L. (ed.) DAGM 2002. LNCS, vol. 2449, pp. 454–462. Springer, Heidelberg (2002)
14. Horn, B., Schunck, B.: Determining optical-flow. Artificial Intelligence 17(1-3), 185–203 (1981)
15. Lucas, B., Kanade, T.: An iterative image registration technique with an application to stereo vision. In: Proceedings of the 7th International Joint Conference on Artificial Intelligence, IJCAI 1981, pp. 674–679 (April 1981)
16. Baker, S., Scharstein, D., Lewis, J., Roth, S., Black, M., Szeliski, R.: A database and evaluation methodology for optical flow. In: IEEE 11th International Conference on Computer Vision, ICCV 2007, pp. 1–8 (October 2007)
17. Wesseling, P.: An Introduction to Multigrid Methods. John Wiley & Sons, Chichester (1992)
18. Briggs, W., Henson, V., McCormick, S.: A Multigrid Tutorial, 2nd edn. SIAM Books, Philadelphia (2000)
19. Kaewtrakulpong, P., Bowden, R.: An improved adaptive background mixture model for realtime tracking with shadow detection. In: Proc. 2nd European Workshop on Advanced Video Based Surveillance Systems, AVBS 2001, Video Based Surveillance Systems: Computer Vision and Distributed Processing. Kluwer Academic Publishers (2001)
20. Kosko, B.: Fuzzy engineering. Prentice-Hall, Inc., Upper Saddle River (1997)
21. Zadeh, L.A.: Fuzzy logic, neural networks, and soft computing. Commun. ACM 37(3), 77–84 (1994)
22. Polus, A., Schofer, J., Ushpiz, A.: Pedestrian flow and level of service. Journal of Transportation Engineering 109(1), 46–56 (1983)

Risk Assessment for SWOP Telemonitoring System Based on Fuzzy Cognitive Maps*

Piotr Szwed, Pawel Skrzynski, and Pawel Grodniewicz

AGH University of Science and Technology
{pszwed,skrzynia}@agh.edu.pl, grodniewicz@gmail.com

Abstract. For various IT systems security is considered to be a key quality factor. In particular, for health care systems security is of uttermost importance, as it is related to patients' health and safety. Risk assessment is an important activity in security management; it aims at identifying assets, threats and vulnerabilities, analysis of implemented countermeasures and their effectiveness in mitigating risks. This paper discusses a new risk assessment method, in which risk calculation is based on Fuzzy Cognitive Maps (FCMs) approach. FCMs are used to capture dependencies between assets and FCM based reasoning is applied to aggregate risks assigned to lower-level assets (e.g. hardware, software modules, communications, people) to such high level assets as services, maintained data and processes. An application of the method is studied on an example of e-health system providing remote telemonitoring, data storage and teleconsultation services. Lessons learned indicate, that the proposed method is an efficient and low-cost approach, giving instantaneous feedback and enabling reasoning on effectiveness of security system.

Keywords: security, risk assessment, telemedicine, fuzzy cognitive maps.

1 Introduction

In the area of health information systems security is an important factor that should be taken into consideration during design, implementation and deployment of the system. According to [14,16] *security* is the protection afforded to information system in order to preserve integrity of data and system functions, its availability, authenticity and confidentiality.

Security of services and medical data maintained by health information systems is of uttermost importance, as it is directly related to the patients' health and safety. Various regulations make requirements to treat them as sensitive resources, at the level comparable to the one, which is used in financial institutions.

* This work is supported by the National Centre for Research and Development (NCBiR) under Grant No. NR13-0093-10.

A. Dziech and A. Czyżewski (Eds.): MCSS 2013, CCIS 368, pp. 233–247, 2013.
© Springer-Verlag Berlin Heidelberg 2013

Risk assessment is a key process in the management of IT systems security. It can be considered as an extensive study of assets, threats and vulnerabilities, likelihoods of their occurrences, potential losses and theoretical effectiveness of security measures [14]. Several risk assessment processes are defined by over 15 standards or methods [2], including most popular: ISO/IEC 27005 [19], NIST 800-30 [27] and CRAMM [1]. The standards, apart of defining risk scoring methods, specify organizational foundations for performing risk assessment in the broader context of IT security risk management. It can be observed, that a risk assessment performed strictly in compliance with a selected standard can be a large and costly endeavor.

This paper proposes a new *lightweight* risk assessment method, in which risk calculation is based on Fuzzy Cognitive Maps (FCMs) approach. FCMs are used to capture dependencies between assets and FCM based reasoning is applied to aggregate risks assigned to lower-level assets (e.g. hardware, software modules, communications, people) to such high level assets as services, maintained data and processes. An application of the method is studied on an example of e-health system providing remote telemonitoring, data storage and teleconsultation services.

The paper is organized as follows: in Section 2 we provide an overview of risk assessment methods. Section 3 introduces Fuzzy Cognitive Maps, followed by Section 4, in which risk assessment methodology is described. Further, in Section 5 the analyzed system is presented, then in Section 6 application of the proposed risk assessment method is discussed. Finally, Section 7 gives concluding remarks.

2   Related Works

Risk assessment has its roots in the nuclear power industry, where probabilistic models were built to analyze potentially catastrophic faults in nuclear power facilities [16]. In 1979 National Bureau of Standards proposed the Annual Loss Expectancy (ALE) metric [18] being applicable for non safety-critical systems. It defined risk as a sum of products of *frequencies* of a harmful events and induced *losses* expressed in dollars. This approach to risk characterization influenced many methodologies, e.g. CRAMM [1] or recently NIST 800-30 [27]. In some frameworks the statistical term *frequency* is replaced by *likelihood* or *probability*, *loss* by *impact*. Furthermore, difficult to estimate absolute values are often mapped on ordinal scales (low, medium, high) defining coarse levels of probabilities and losses. In spite of popularity of ALE metric, its application to risk assessment is considered problematic due to cognitive bias in estimating likelihoods of threats [17], lack of statistical data, difficulties in calculating losses and extremely high costs of the whole process.

Recent practical approaches to implementation of risk assessment and management include *Integrated Business Risk-Management Frameworks* that make attempt to ignore technical details and embed IT security within holistic business risk management context (SABSA [28]), *Valuation-Driven Methodologies* ignoring difficult to assess likelihoods and recommending safeguards using as a sole criterion estimated values of assets, *Scenario Analysis Approaches*, which focus on eliciting and evaluating scenarios compromising security or *Best Practices* that rely on standardized lists of safeguards eligible for given types of assets.

In parallel to the business practice, there can be observed ongoing (mainly academic) efforts aiming at building risk models going beyond ALE and applying them to real or hypothetic systems. In several case they were followed by proposals of methodologies proposed or guidelines, often with dedicated interactive software packages. Furthermore, these guidelines are frequently combined with modeling techniques that are widely applied in reliability and safety engineering, such as Fault Trees, Event Trees, Markov Chains, and FMEA (Failure Mode Effects Analysis) [32,7,29]. These techniques provide a representation of system operations and undesirable events and validation of system safety level [12,24,8,30,9].

Han, Yang and Chang described an expansible vulnerability model in order to qualitatively assess security of active network and active nodes, aiming at solving the problem that it is more apt for active network, than traditional network [15]. Eom, Park and Han introduced a risk assessment method based on asset valuation and quantification [13]. Baudrit and Dubios proposed a risk assessment method of node transmission and possibility exposure [6]. Sun, Srivastava, and Mork introduced a risk assessment system model based on DS evidence reasoning [31]. Disadvantages of all those methods are related to strong subjectivity of premises. Hence, Chen put forward quantitative hierarchical threat assessment model and corresponding quantitative calculation method that exploits statistics of system attacks that occurred in the past [10]. Wang et. al. analyze the network security by using probable attack graph generated on the basis of security case reasoning, carrying out qualitative risk assessment to the network system mainly from the attack perspective [33].

Within last couple of years, risk assessment techniques evolved towards integrating real time and intelligent functions. In particular, wide attention was paid to artificial immunology due to such its advantages as self-organization, self-adaptability, diversity and self-learning. Although research results have been applied only to invasion detection and fault detection, the application in information security risk assessment has just began [11,26].

Information security risk assessment model and a corresponding risk calculation method, which are based on danger theory was introduced in [34]. The approach addresses the problem of the strong subjectivity and aims at improving accuracy and real time performance of current information security risk assessment systems, by reference to dynamic response characteristic of danger theory in immunology.

An application of a new method of risk analysis to an e-health system of monitoring vital signs was discussed in [23]. The method utilized CRAMM approach for identifying and valuating assets, threats, and vulnerabilities. The system was considered as safety-critical and for calculation of risks a Bayesian Network model, which presented concisely all interactions of undesirable events in the system was developed.

3   Fuzzy Cognitive Maps

Cognitive maps were first proposed by Axelrod [5] as a tool for modeling political decisions, then they were extended by Kosko [21] by introducing fuzzy values. A large number applications of FCM were reported, e.g. in project risk modeling, crisis management and decision making, analysis of development of economic systems, introduction of new technologies [20], ecosystem analysis, signal processing and decision support in medicine. A survey on Fuzzy Cognitive Maps and their applications can be found in [3] and [25].

FCMs are directed graphs whose vertices represent concepts, whereas edges are used to express causal relations between them. A set of concepts $C = \{c_1, \ldots, c_n\}$ appearing in a model encompasses events, conditions or other relevant factors. System state is an n-dimensional vector of concept activation levels ($n = |C|$) that can be real values belonging to $[0, 1]$ or $[-1, 1]$.

Causal relations between concepts are represented in FCM by edges and assigned weights. A positive weight of an edge linking two concepts c_i and c_j models a situation, where increase of the level of c_i results in growing c_j; a negative weight is used to describe opposite rapport. In the simplest form of FCM, values from the set $\{-1, 0, 1\}$ are used as weights. They are graphically represented as a minus $(-)$ sign attached to an edge, absence of edge or a plus $(+)$ sign. While building FCM models, more fine-grained causal relations can be introduced. They are usually specified as linguistic values, e.g.: *strong_negative, negative, medium_negative, neutral, medium_positive, positive, strong_positive* and in a computational model mapped on values uniformly distributed over $[-1, 1]$.

Causal relations between concepts in FCM can be represented by $n \times n$ influence matrix $E = [e_{ij}]$, whose elements e_{ij} are weights assigned to edges linking c_i and c_j or have 0 values, if there is no link between them.

Reasoning with FCM consist in building a sequence of states: $\alpha = A(0), A(1), \ldots, A(k), \ldots$ starting form an initial vector of activation levels of concepts. Consecutive elements are calculated according to the formula (1). In $k + 1$ iteration the vector $A(k)$ is multiplied by the influence matrix E, then the resulting activation levels of concepts are mapped onto an assumed range by means of an *activation* (or *splashing*) function.

$$A_i(k + 1) = S_i(\sum_{j=1}^{n} e_{ij} A_j(k)) \tag{1}$$

Selection of activation function depends on assumptions regarding the calculation model, in particular selected range and the decision of using continuous or discrete values. Multiplication of n-dimensional square matrix E, both containing elements, whose absolute values are bounded by 1, results in a vector having elements in $[-n, n]$. Values from this interval should be mapped by an activation function into the range $[-1, 1]$ (or $[0, 1]$) preserving monotonicity and satisfying $S(0) = 0$ (or $S(0) = 0.5$ in the second case.)

In the further analysis two activation functions were used

$$S_{cut}(x) = \begin{cases} -1, & \text{if } x < -1 \\ x, & \text{if } x \geq -1 \text{ and } x \leq 1 \\ 1, & \text{if } x > 1 \end{cases} \qquad (2)$$

$$S_{exp}(x) = \begin{cases} 1 - \exp(-mx), & \text{if } x \geq 0 \\ -1 + \exp(-mx), & \text{if } x < 0 \end{cases} \qquad (3)$$

Basically, a sequence of consecutive states $\alpha = A(0), A(1), \ldots, A(k), \ldots$ is infinite. However, it was shown that after k iterations, where k is a number close to the rank of matrix E a steady state is reached or a cycle occurs. Hence, a stop criterion for the reasoning algorithm in the k step:

$$\exists j < k \colon d(A(k), A(j)) < \epsilon, \qquad (4)$$

where d is a distance and ϵ a small value, e.g. 10^{-2}.

A sequence of states α can be interpreted in two ways. It can be treated as a representation of a dynamic behavior of the modeled system. In this case there exist implicit temporal relations between consecutive system states, and the whole sequence describes an evolution of the system in the form of a *scenario*. Under the second interpretation the sequence represents a non-monotonic fuzzy inference process, in which a selected elements of a steady state are interpreted as reasoning results. An occurrence of a cycle can be treated as a form of undecidability.

In this paper FCMs are considered to be a tool for risks modeling and the focus is put on the second approach.

4   Methodology of Risk Assessment

The methodology for risk assessment comprises of the basic steps common to various standards and guidelines, see [14,19,27,22]. The salient difference is using in calculations FCM based model of influences between assets, allowing to track their dependencies during risk aggregation.

4.1   Conceptual Model

In the assumed conceptual model (Fig. 1) we assign *utility value* to *assets* and organize assets into *added value tree*, a hierarchical structure, in which components of lower level deliver value to parent elements. The top of the tree is occupied by processes; they are identified according to business drivers. Utility of processes depend on data and services. Various data sources: users, sensors and external data providers contribute to the utility of data. Services depend on software, hardware and communication, but also involved staff, physical infrastructure (buildings, rooms, electricity) and external services (e.g. Public Key Infrastructure).

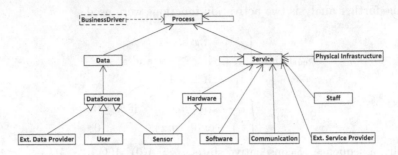

Fig. 1. Classes of assets appearing in an added value tree

Utility values assigned to assets can be interpreted as aggregations of various quality attributes: security, reliability, usability, etc. Changes of utility values assigned to lower level assets influence higher level components that use them. It should be observed that the tree structure of dependencies between classes of assets results in a lattice of dependencies between instances of assets, e.g. data analysis, data storage and access services depend on the database (software).

The risk model assumes that a utility of an asset can be compromised by a threat, which decreases its value. In the presented approach we opt for asset-based identification of threats in opposition to approaches focused on adversarial actions or threat agents.

An influence of a threat on an asset can be compensated by an appropriate countermeasure. Moreover, in case of presence of internal company policies or regulatory requirements, some countermeasures can be obligatory, e.g. auditing data access in case of system storing medical documentation.

Finally, it arises a problem of defining risk in this setting. In many areas of security and safety analysis, risk assessment is correlated with possible financial losses. However, for many IT systems it is difficult to estimate financial loss caused by potential failures, as it requires the specification of a business environment, in which the system is deployed.

For the evaluation purposes we define

- *utility* assigned to assets as a value from range $[0, 1]$ or $[-1, 1]$
- *risk* related to an asset as negative difference between assumed utility and the value calculated at the end of reasoning process.

The reasoning process takes into account influence of threats and countermeasures directly linked to assets, but also changes in utility resulting form added value tree.

4.2   Risk Assessment Process

The risk assessment process comprises six stages.

1. *Identification of assets.* The input for this step are existent documents specifying system vision, operational concept and architecture, but also interviews

with designers and development teams. The outcome is a list of assets identifying key processes, services, data, software modules, hardware, communication, providers of external data and services, involved people and physical premises.

2. *Building added value trees.* The step aims at making assessment, how lower level assets contribute to higher level, e.g. hardware, software and communication channels to services, data and services to processes. Influences are expressed by linguistic values, which are assigned during interviews with software developers and brainstorming sessions.

3. *Establishing threats.* For this purpose a general taxonomy of threats, e.g. an available ontology can be used and customized to the analyzed case. We use asset based model of threats, i.e. identify threats that are related to a particular asset.

4. *Performing first stage of risk assessment for individual assets.* As a basic tool we use a questionnaire, in which various involved stakeholders reply to questions concerning applied countermeasures. The outcome of this phase is an assignment of risk values (negative real numbers) to assets.

5. *Performing reasoning with FCM and interpreting results.* Reasoning with FCM approach aims at establishing how risks assigned to low level assets accumulate to yield risk profiles of high level assets. This step involves required preparations, e.g. normalization of FCM influence matrix.

6. *Issuing recommendations.* In particular, this step may include a *what if* analysis consisting in assuming application of additional countermeasures at various levels of individual assets and repeating the step 5.

5   Presentation of the SWOP System

SWOP is an e-health system dedicated to patients suffering from chronic conditions (*SWOP* is an acronym of the Polish name *System Wspomagania Opieki Przewlekłej*). The main goal of the system is to help patients in self-management of chronic disease through monitoring of symptoms, self-assessment, informing about necessary actions when symptom levels indicate a problem, as well as interactions with health care professionals.

On a regular basis patients manually or automatically send results of self-observations or self-measurements specific for their chronic disease e.g. hypertension, asthma, diabetes, osteoarthritis. A set of implemented communication modules provide a great flexibility at configuring the parameters, operational modes of sensors and communication channels (WiFi, WAN, GPRS).

Medical staff is also provided with configuration tools allowing to configure certain parameters used in medical analyzes. The system offers also capabilities of asynchronous communication between patients and personnel providing support to them (virtual carers, leading physicians or other health professionals). If needed, an assistance of specialist may be asked. Moreover, the system offers an option of transferring patients' data from an external HL7-compliant health information systems.

The architecture of the system is presented in Fig. 2. Personal Telemonitoring Devices (sensors) (1) gather raw medical data and transmit them via Bluetooth interface to Mobile Client Application on Patient's Smartphone (2). After initial validation health parameters are sent to the SWOP Server. Data are filled out in medical questionnaires, available on Patient's Smartphones or in Browser Based Clients and then transmitted to the server using SSL encrypted connection. Certification Server based on Nginx Server (3) receives data and routes them to one of the Application Server instances. The Application Server, (4) is the component, where main system logic resides; it is written in Python programming language and served via WSGI interface by Gunicorn Server. Application Server is responsible for authorization, data validation, generation of notifications, as well as communication with the Database (5) and the Data Analysis (6) servers. The Database, hosted on two independent servers in master-slave configuration, is designed to securely store critical patients' data. The Data Analysis Server is responsible for identification of trends in disease course.

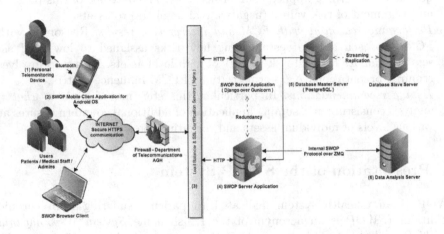

Fig. 2. Architetcure of the SWOP system

6   Risk Analysis for the SWOP System

Selecting the scope of the risk analysis we decided to include three areas: *IT security* understood as protection against adversarial actions and accidental leak of sensitive data, *business continuity* that can be mapped on such quality attributes as reliability and availability of services and protection against *operational incidents*, as errors in entered data or process execution. For a telemedicine system, they can stem from low patient skills, low quality of sensors and not motivated or untrained staff.

6.1   Assets and Added Value Tree

In the assessment we considered the following assets:

1. Processes: Telemonitoring, Storing medical records, Access to medical records, Teleconsultation,
2. Services: data storage and retrieval, data transfer, analysis, SMS and e-mail notification,
3. Data: measurements, medical records and configuration data,
4. Software modules: Nginx Proxy, SWOP Application, SWOP database, SWOP mobile application, Sensor software and SWOP Data Analysis,
5. Hardware modules: Proxy firewall server, Application server, DB server, Data Analysis Server, Smartphones and Sensors
6. Communication: External network https over WLAN, LAN and GPRS, Internal network (HTTP) and Bluetooth for sensor to smartphone connection,
7. People: patients, medical and technical staff,
8. Infrastructure provided by third party (communications, electricity).

The above listed elements constitute a network of dependent elements, i.e. processes depend on services that are provided by software and hardware modules and refer to data, which are stored and exchanged within the system.

Influences between the assets were established based on architectural views and during interviews with software architects and developers. They were, then described in form of FCM influence matrix, using the following linguistic values: *high, significant, medium, low* and *none*.

To give an example, the utility of *Telemonitoring process* is *highly* influenced by the *Data storage* and *Data transfer* services, *significantly* influenced by the *Data analysis* service and utility of *Measured data*, influenced at *medium* level by *SMS notification* and *E-mail notification* services and at *low* level by *Configuration data*.

Analogous statements were made for all assets. In most cases positive influences were assigned, however in special cases negative values were used to indicate, that one asset can be replaced by another, e.g: *SMS notification* and *e-mail notification* services were linked with *medium* negative influences.

6.2   Threats

Identification of threats was based on available sources, e.g. [14,27,22], as well as previous experience. The elicited list of threats to be considered in vulnerability analysis was comprised of 58 elements grouped in eleven families corresponding to classes of assets.

The families include: *Process* (e.g bad design), *Software* (e.g. quality failures, lack of maintenance, malware), *Hardware* (quality failures, resource exhaustion), *Communications* (protocol weakness, service disruption), *Data* (confidentiality or integrity breach), *External services* (loss of PKI, SMS gate, PaaS, SaaS), *External data providers* (errors in HL7 interfaces), *Physical infrastructure* (premises, electricity, air condition), *People* (including threats related to patients, medical and technical staff), *Natural disasters, Medical decision, Economical conditions* and *Legal*.

6.3   Risk Assessment for Individual Assets

This step in the risk assessment process combines two activities identified in various methodologies, namely: the analyzes of vulnerabilities and of effectiveness of countermeasures. Technically, an assessment is performed using questionnaires, in which answers reflecting best practices are attributed with weights describing their influence on a risk profile.

In the case of SWOP system, we used a questionnaire comprised of about 140 questions divided into 11 groups of threats and countermeasures.

A logical structure of a sample questionnaire related to mobile application is presented in Table 1. For each question (a security feature), at most three answers (ratings) are defined. Answers are attributed with weights $e_{ij} \in [0,1]$ that can be interpreted as their impact on the asset's risk profile. Moreover, influences of features can be differentiated with weight w_i shown in the last column of the table. (These weights are not visible for interrogated members of development team, software architects and other involved stakeholders).

It should be observed, that a questionnaire defines in fact a structure of a Fuzzy Cognitive Map, in which weights express influences. Moreover, they were selected in a voting process, what is typical practice of FCM construction.

Risk $R_a(s)$ for an asset s is calculated with the formula (5) based on values of answers a_{ij} to questions Q_i, $i = 1, \ldots, k$. Values 1 and 0 are used for positive and negative answers.

$$R_a(s) = \frac{w_i}{W} \sum_{j=1}^{3} a_{ij}e_{ij}, \text{ where } W = \sum_{i=1}^{k} w_i \tag{5}$$

The normalization factor W in the formula (5) plays analogous role as activation function in (1).

To illustrate the calculations we marked in Table 1 obtained answers to the questionnaire by using underlined, bold font. Application of the formula (5) yields the value 0.38, which indicates that threats can not be fully neutralized by countermeasures (what would hold, if the calculated value were equal to 0). The

Table 1. Risk assessment questionnaire related to mobile application

Question Q_i	$Answer_1$	e_{i1}	$Answer_2$	e_{i2}	$Answer_3$	e_{i3}	w_i
Does mobile application store user name and/or password in the local memory/database?	yes, as not encoded data	1.0	no	**0.0**	as encoded data	0.5	1.0
Has the application code used to build the executable version been obfuscated?	yes	0.2	no	**0.8**			0.6
Does the communication with the middleware involve third party proxy server?	yes	0.9	no	**0.1**			0.7
Is the app available at official distribution channel (ex. Google Play, AppStore)?	yes	0.2	no	**0.8**			0.4
Does the communication use SSL?	yes	**0**	no	1	no verification of SSL certificate	0.5	1.0
Is antivirus software installed on the mobile device?	yes	0.1	no	0.9	lack of information	**0.5**	0.4

obtained values (their negations) are used in the next step aiming at calculation of aggregated risk with FCM.

6.4   Calculation of Aggregated Risk with FCM

The calculation of aggregated was preceded by a normalization of matrix of influences. While preparing the matrix we used four linguistic variables to describe influence: *high, significant, medium, low* and *none*. Then, they were mapped to weights $\{1.0, 0.75, 0.5, 0.25, 0\}$ and for each row $i = 1, \ldots, n$ normalized values of influences were calculated according to formula (6).

$$\bar{e}_{ij} = \begin{cases} 0, & \text{if } e_{ij} = 0 \\ \exp(m \cdot e_{ij})/Z_i, & \text{if } e_{ij} \geq 0 \end{cases}, \tag{6}$$

where $Z_i = \sum_{\substack{j=1 \\ e_{ij} \neq 0}}^{n} \exp(m \cdot e_{ij})$ and m is a positive constant.

Such normalization gives a probability distribution. Motivation for assuming such distribution stems from the Game Theory. Suppose, that a high-level asset a_h depends on low-level assets $a_{l_1}, \ldots, a_{l_k}$, with influences $e_{hl_1}, \ldots, e_{hl_1}$. If a *threat agent* treated as an adversarial player is to select a low-level asset to launch an attack on, it should choose an element a_{l_m} giving the highest influence e_{hl_m} on the risk profile of a_h. However, the player can make errors in estimation of influences. Resulting probability of an adversarial actions depends on distribution of errors, which, in general case, is difficult to track. However, assuming a double exponential distribution of errors, we arrive to a *logit* model [4] given by the formula (6).

For the final calculation of aggregated risks two sequences of vectors were constructed:

$$\alpha^{nr} = A^{nr}(0), \ldots, A^{nr}(k), \ldots \text{ and } \alpha^r = A^r(0), \ldots, A^r(k), \ldots$$

by successively applying FCM state equation (1).

The *no-risk sequence* α^{nr} starts with a vector $A^{nr}(0)$, in which all elements expressing the utility of assets are set to 1. For the risk sequence α^r the initial vector $A^r(0)$ is a sum of vectors of asset utilities $A^{nr}(0)$ and individual risks R_a established in the previous phase using the formula (5): $A^r(0) = A^{nr}(0) + R_a$.

Finally, by subtracting corresponding elements of α^{nr} and α^r we obtain the sequence of aggregated risk values $R(0), \ldots, R(k), \ldots$, where $R(i) = A^{nr}(i) - A^r(i)$. This sequence converges to values that express aggregated risks for all assets at different levels of added value tree.

Fig. 3 shows results of risk calculations for three groups of assets in SWOP system: data, services and processes. Diagrams show results obtained by applying activation functions *cut* (left) and *expcut* (right) defined by formulas (2) and (3). The comparison indicate, that qualitative results for both functions are identical.

While interpreting the results of the calculation, there appears an issue of converting them back to linguistic values, e.g. low, medium, high, often expected

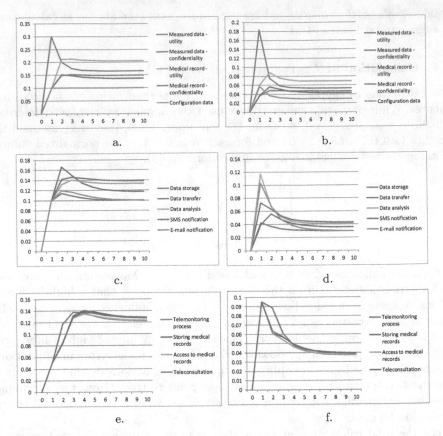

Fig. 3. Reasoning about risks related to: data (a-b), services (c-d) and processes (e-f). Activation functions: cut (a,c,e), exp-cut (b,d,f)

stakeholders responsible for decision making. To support such conversion, we established values of two thresholds: $LM = 0.26$ and $MH = 0.52$ by making simple experiments: calculating risks for absence and presence of all safeguards. The resulting interval $[0.07, 0.86]$ was uniformly divided into three intervals corresponding to low, medium and high risk levels. The obtained thresholds pertain to *cut* activation function, for *expcut* they are about three times smaller.

6.5   Results of Assessment

Our findings indicate low level of aggregated risks related assets placed at top of the utility tree (processes, data and services). Medium risk for compound assets, e.g. mobile application presented in the example in Section 6.3, is caused by the fact that a prototype, still not deployed in production environment, was evaluated. We assume, that for a target deployment, several safeguards will be activated, e.g. using trusted Certificate Authority, official distribution channels for the mobile application, UPS, regular backups, access control to physical premises, etc.

Our attention was attracted by relatively higher risks for utility of medical records and measured data. In general, these risk are rather operational, than related to IT security. They are caused by threats falling into the category *People*, i.e. Low skill level, Subjective selfobservation, Low selfdiscipline and Technology related anger for patients and Low attention level, Epidemic illness, Staff turnover, Lack of professional behavior for staff. Such risks can be partly mitigated by providing training, but also by implementing still absent reminders notifying patients about the necessity of feeding data.

7 Conclusions

This paper presents a new method for risk assessment of IT systems based on FCMs. The method include steps present in various standards and methodologies: identification of assets, threats, analysis of vulnerabilities and effectiveness of countermeasures, however, it relies on FCM reasoning to calculate risks. A cornerstone of the proposed method is *added value tree* expressing dependencies between assets. A salient feature of the method is, that it uses an abstract term *utility* (and a loss of utility caused by a threat) in place of financial loss. This makes the method applicable for IT system, for which financial loss is difficult to estimate. Moreover, at lower level of assessment the method incorporates the widespread *Best Practices* approach to IT security, representing them by questionnaires.

We study the method on example of the SWOP e-health system and describe its stages: preparing lists of assets based on architectural views and interviews, building influence matrix reflecting an added value tree, identifying threats, calculating non-aggregated risks related to assets with use of questionnaires based on best practices and finally performing reasoning with FCM techniques.

The proposed method can be considered as a *lightweight* approach to risk assessment, suitable for small and medium size systems. In the case of SWOP system, the data was collected during three interviews and brainstorming sessions, in the meantime questionnaires used in previous analyzes by the assessment team were adapted to reflect specific assets and threats.

Lessons learned indicate, that the proposed method is an efficient and low-cost approach, giving instantaneous feedback and enabling reasoning on effectiveness of security system. It can be considered as an alternative to heavy assessment processes defined by standards.

References

1. CRAMM, http://www.cramm.com/ (last accessed Januay 2013)
2. Inventory of risk management / risk assessment methods,
   http://rm-inv.enisa.europa.eu/methods/rm_ra_methods.html (last accessed January 2013)
3. Aguilar, J.: A Survey about Fuzzy Cognitive Maps Papers (Invited Paper). International Journal 3(2), 27–33 (2005)

4. Anderson, S., De Palma, A., Thisse, J.: Discrete Choice Theory of Product Differentiation. MIT Press (1992)
5. Axelrod, R.M.: Structure of Decision: The Cognitive Maps of Political Elites. Princeton University Press (1976)
6. Baudrit, C., Dubois, D., Guyonnet, D.: Joint propagation and exploitation of probabilistic and possibilistic information in risk assessment. Trans. Fuz. Sys. 14(5), 593–608 (2006)
7. Birolini, A.: Reliability engineering: theory and practice, 3rd edn. (2000)
8. Bowles, J.B., Wan, C.: Software failure modes and effects analysis for a small embedded control system (2001)
9. Cervesato, I., Meadows, C.: Fault-tree representation of NPATRL security requirements (2003)
10. Chen, X.Z.: Hierarchical threat assessment and quantitative calculation method of network security threatening state. Journal of Software 17(4), 885–897 (2006)
11. Chiang, F., Braun, R.: Self-adaptability and vulnerability assessment of secure autonomic communication networks. In: Ata, S., Hong, C.S. (eds.) APNOMS 2007. LNCS, vol. 4773, pp. 112–122. Springer, Heidelberg (2007)
12. Craft, R., Vandewart, R., Wyss, G., Funkhouser, D.: An open framework for risk management, vol. 1 (1998)
13. Eom, J.-H., Park, S.-H., Han, Y.-J., Chung, T.-M.: Risk assessment method based on business process-oriented asset evaluation for information system security. In: Shi, Y., van Albada, G.D., Dongarra, J., Sloot, P.M.A. (eds.) ICCS 2007, Part III. LNCS, vol. 4489, pp. 1024–1031. Springer, Heidelberg (2007)
14. Guttman, B., Roback, E.A.: An introduction to computer security: The NIST handbook. Security 800(12), 1–290 (1995)
15. Han, Y.J., Yang, J.S., Chang, B.H., Na, J.C., Chung, T.M.: The vulnerability assessment for active networks; model, policy, procedures, and performance evaluations. In: Laganá, A., Gavrilova, M.L., Kumar, V., Mun, Y., Tan, C.J.K., Gervasi, O. (eds.) ICCSA 2004. LNCS, vol. 3043, pp. 191–198. Springer, Heidelberg (2004)
16. Hoo, K.J.S.: How much is enough? A risk-management approach to computer security. In: Economics and Information Security, pp. 1–99. U.C. Berkeley, CA (2000)
17. Hubbard, D., Evans, D.: Problems with scoring methods and ordinal scales in risk assessment. Journal of Research and Development 54(3), 1–10 (2010)
18. Institute for Computer Sciences and Technology: Guideline for automatic data processing risk analysis. National Bureau of Standards, Institute for Computer Sciences and Technology (1979)
19. ISO/IEC: Information technology – security techniques – information security risk management, ISO/IEC 27005:2011. Tech. rep., International Organization for Standardization (2011)
20. Jetter, A., Schweinfort, W.: Building scenarios with Fuzzy Cognitive Maps: An exploratory study of solar energy. Futures 43(1), 52–66 (2011)
21. Kosko, B.: Fuzzy Cognitive maps. International Journal of Machine Studies 24, 65–75 (1986)
22. Landoll, D.J.: The Security Risk Assessment Handbook: A Complete Guide for Performing Security Risk Assessments. Auerbach Publications (2005)
23. Maglogiannis, I., Zafiropoulos, E., Platis, A., Lambrinoudakis, C.: Risk analysis of a patient monitoring system using bayesian network modeling. J. of Biomedical Informatics 39(6), 637–647 (2006)
24. Modarres, M., Kaminskiy, M., Krivtsov, V.: Reliability engineering and risk analysis

25. Papageorgiou, E.I.: Learning Algorithms for Fuzzy Cognitive Maps - A Review Study. Construction, 1–14 (2011)
26. Peng, L.X., et al.: Model danger theory based network risk assessment (2007)
27. Ross, R.S.: Guide for conducting risk assessments, NIST SP - 800-30rev1, vol. 85. NIST Special Publication (September 2011)
28. Sherwood Applied Business Security Architecture: SABSA, http://www.sabsa-institute.org/the-sabsa-method (last accessed January 2013)
29. Stamatis, D.H.: Failure mode and effect analysis: FMEA from theory to execution. ASQ Quality Press, Milwaykee (2003)
30. Stathiakis, N., Chronaki, C., Skipenes, E., Henriksen, E., Charalambus, E., Sykianakis, A., Vrouchos, G., Antonakis, N., Tsiknakis, M., Orphanoudakis, S.: Risk assessment of a cardiology eHealth service in HYGEIAnet (2003)
31. Sun, L., Srivastava, R.P., Mock, T.J.: An information systems security risk assessment model under the Dempster-Shafer theory of belief functions. J. Manage. Inf. Syst. 22(4), 109–142 (2006)
32. Vesely, W.E., Goldberg, F.F., Roberts, N.H., Haasl, D.F.: Fault Tree handbook, Technical Report NUREG-0492 (1981)
33. Wang, Y., et al.: Research on and application of the analyzing method of network security based on security case reasoning. Minitype Computer System 24(12), 2082–2085 (2003)
34. Zhuang, Y., Li, X., Xu, B., Zhou, B.: Information security risk assessment based on artificial immune danger theory. In: Proceedings of the 2009 Fourth International Multi-Conference on Computing in the Global Information Technology, ICCGI 2009, pp. 169–174. IEEE Computer Society, Washington, DC (2009)

Application of New ATAM Tools to Evaluation of the Dynamic Map Architecture*

Piotr Szwed, Igor Wojnicki, Sebastian Ernst, and Andrzej Głowacz

AGH University of Science and Technology
{pszwed,wojnicki,ernst,aglowacz}@agh.edu.pl

Abstract. The paper reports an application of Architecture-based Tradeoff Analysis Method (ATAM) for early evaluation of the Dynamic Map architecture. The Dynamic Map is a complex information system, composed of spatial databases, storing static and dynamic data relevant for urban traffic, as well as a set of software modules responsible for data collection, interpretation and provision. Due to the complexity of the system, its size and key importance of its services to other subsystems, we decided to perform architecture evaluation using the ATAM method. To facilitate the task new tools supporting ATAM based assessment are proposed: Scenario Influence Matrix and Architectural Decision Matrix. Taking as example an excerpt from the system architecture, we present how they were used during the architecture evaluation. The gathered experience confirm usefulness of the tools, enabling ATAM to help detecting real flaws in a design and identify potential risks.

Keywords: dynamic map, ATAM, architecture, evaluation.

1   Introduction

Development of complex information systems is a difficult process, and the success of the outcome is largely dependent on appropriate decisions made early in the design process. Features such as diversity of data models, platform heterogenity, performance (e.g. real-time) requirements and the need for interoperability make it even more complicated.

The Dynamic Map is one of the key subsystems of the INSIGMA project [1].It can be considered a complex information system, composed of spatial databases, storing static and dynamic data related to urban traffic, as well as a set of software modules responsible for data collection, interpretation and provision to clients. The data originates from a network of sensors, both fixed (e.g. video detectors, acoustic sensors, inductive loops) and on-board GPS receivers installed in vehicles. Clients of the Dynamic Map include various software modules performing such tasks as visualization, route planning, traffic optimization, object tracking and threat detection.

* Work has been co-financed by the European Regional Development Fund under the Innovative Economy Operational Programme, INSIGMA project no. POIG.01.01.02-00-062/09.

A. Dziech and A. Czyżewski (Eds.): MCSS 2013, CCIS 368, pp. 248–261, 2013.
© Springer-Verlag Berlin Heidelberg 2013

The paper reports the experiences gained by using the Architecture-based Tradeoff Analysis Method (ATAM)[12] for early evaluation of the Dynamic Map architecture. The main contribution of this paper is an extension of ATAM through introduction of additional supporting tools, as well as adaptation of the method to fit the characteristics of the Dynamic Map.

The paper is organized as follows. A more detailed description of the INSIGMA Project, the concept of the Dynamic Map and challenges related to the design process are given in Section 2. It is followed by an introduction to the ATAM method (Section 3). Application of the proposed approach is given in Section 4. Section 5 presents the actual subset of the INSIGMA system under consideration, its architecture, scenarios and architectural decisions. It also describes the results of ATAM analysis. Finally, conclusions and observations are given in Section 6.

2 Motivation

The INSIGMA project aims at development and implementation of an advanced information system for optimizing road traffic. While more and more cities now are facing the problem of traffic jams and worsening ecological conditions, INSIGMA will provide tools for efficient traffic control and threat detection. In case of existing solutions for map creation and traffic management, the main problem is related to the lack of efficient tools that enable conversion of object location and audiovisual data into dynamic maps. In practice, traffic control is often based on low-frequency components of traffic dynamics. Thus, in case of road accidents or other threats, these systems are incapable of fast response. In such scenarios, traffic problems can be first detected after 30 minutes. Another issue is the limited area of the managed region. Traffic detectors are mostly deployed in major highways but in limited scope in access roads.

On the other hand, vehicle users demand efficient route planning and optimization. Existing navigation solutions consist in analysis of static parameters (e.g. total route length or road type), and even recent solutions rarely use statistical data (e.g. maximum driving speed in selected hours). The dynamic traffic component still remains unaddressed and relevant traffic conditions need to be personally recognized by the user in advance or, worse, in the place of event. Thus, in case of a jammed metropolis, the efficiency of route optimization is far from what is expected. This is particularly important in daily operations of emergency services, fire brigades, police, etc.

The first and foremost feature of INSIGMA is analysis of traffic parameters and further processing on basis of dynamic maps. *Dynamic map* can be viewed as a set of data describing the state of the road infrastructure. This corresponds to dedicated system services. In the INSIGMA project, these include: route planning, navigation, traffic control or crisis management. Managed data consists of: specifics of road infrastructure, current traffic conditions and preferences.

The road infrastructure is defined by the road network (road locations, connections, lanes and points of interest) with information about organization of traffic, which contains traffic signs, lights, temporary exclusions (e.g. road repairs) or detours.

The traffic conditions include monitored traffic density and atmospheric phenomenons such as rain or snow, icing, etc. It is also important to consider extraordinary events, e.g. traffic accidents or other dangerous situations.

The scope described above is supplemented by the preferences which correspond to specific needs of particular system. For example, route planning for transport of dangerous materials can operate on reduced map containing only main highways. On the other hand, emergency service may require fastest navigation through jammed city – using all possible connections (also against one-way streets).

Thus, the Dynamic Map can be perceived as a representation of the road transport infrastructure combined with up-to-date information about traffic intensity and historical traffic data. Such a combination includes information stored in a database and map visualization, which can be presented to the end user via a network or mobile interface. Algorithms for dynamic route optimization are applied to the system; they aid traffic control systems and are particularly useful in urban environments.

There are several factors that influence the design of the Dynamic Map. They include the expected performance, flexibility concerning representation of processed information and seamless integration of various types of sensors, including those already present in the urban traffic infrastructure.

Due to the complexity of the system, its size and key importance of its services to other subsystems, we decided to perform architecture evaluation at an early system development stage to identify and correct potential design flaws and limitations, as well as to mitigate the risks of not meeting functional and non-functional requirements. The ATAM[12], was selected for this purpose, as it is considered a mature, efficient and non-costly method which can be applied to various types of architectural designs.

Faced with the task of applying the ATAM to Dynamic Map architecture assessment, we realized that the method provides excellent guidelines on how to organize the entire process and how to specify requirements and describe the outcomes. However, due to its generic character, the ATAM lacks supporting tools and techniques which would allow to describe the impacts of scenarios on particular components and to collect various properties (design decisions) of architectural elements.

During the assessment, we developed and used two such tools: the Scenario Influence Matrix (SIM) and the Architectural Decision Matrix (ADM), which extended the architectural views described in the ArchiMate [17] language.

This paper discusses the key elements of the adopted approach in a case study reduced to just few of the high priority requirements (scenarios) and a limited number of components and architectural decisions. Due to the high number of components of the Dynamic Map, a presentation of the full analysis would have exceeded the expected volume of the paper. For the analyzed scenarios, the outcomes (sensitivity points, tradeoffs, risks and recommendations) have been listed.

3 The ATAM Method

The goal of software architecture evaluation methods is to assess whether a system meets or will meet certain requirements concerning quality characterized as *quality attributes*. A standardized list of quality attributes is published in ISO/IEC 9126-1 [7] and ISO/IEC 25010 [8] standards, which define nine attribute categories, e.g. Functionality, Reliability, Usability, Efficiency, Maintainability, Modifiability and Portability.

Architecture evaluation methods may bring the greatest benefits to software development if applied early in the software lifecycle, as identified flaws in system design can be corrected at a lower cost [14]. Typically, an assessment is conducted based on the specification of the software architecture (architectural views) and use other sources of information, such as interviews with various stakeholders such as owners, future users, architects and development teams.

The ATAM was developed at the Software Engineering Institute (SEI) in 2000 [12], [4]. Its goal is to evaluate architectural decisions against specific quality attributes and to detect: *risks* – architectural decisions that may cause problems to assure some quality attributes, *sensitivity points* – decisions related to components or their connections that are critical for achieving required level of a quality attribute and *tradeoffs* – decisions that increasing one quality attribute have negative impact on others.

ATAM uses a quality model called the *utility tree*. At the root of the utility tree, an abstract concept *Utility* is placed. Its child nodes are annotated with general quality attributes, which can be decomposed into more specific attributes at the next level; finally, scenarios are placed at leaves.

The advantage of using scenarios is that they turn somehow vague expectations into verifiable requirements. ATAM distinguishes three types of scenarios: use case, growth and exploratory.

Use case scenarios define the expected interactions between users and an implemented system. Most often, they are assigned in the utility tree to such quality attributes as: performance (response time, throughput), usability (a user can easily perform a specific task) or reliability (actions to be taken in case of failures or exceptional conditions).

Growth scenarios capture anticipated future changes in the system. Scenarios belonging to this group usually fall into such categories as modifiability, scalability, interoperability or portability.

Exploratory scenarios are not likely to occur. However, they can be identified and analyzed to detect implicit assumptions and communicate to the stakeholders limits in the architectural design.

There are reports on successful applications of ATAM to assessment of a battlefield control system [10], wargame simulation [9], product line architecture [5], control of a transportation system [3] and credit card transactions system[13]. Recently, a few extensions of ATAM were proposed, including combination with the Analytical Hierarchy Process [18] and APTIA [11].

4   Supporting Tools for the ATAM Method

The ATAM has many obvious benefits: it precisely defines the quality model based The on the utility tree, enumerates the expected outcomes, indicates the participants and provides an organizational framework for the evaluation.

Nevertheless, due to its generic character, the method can cause problems related to gathering and representing information that can be used for an architecture assessment. When preparing the assessment of the Dynamic Map according to ATAM, we realized that architectural views that can be the input to the ATAM do not provide constructs do describe the influence of a given scenario on a particular component. This regards in particular growth scenarios, achievement of which may require modifications, redesign of components, but may also increase resource utilization or generate demand on data capacity.

We have decided to design and develop two specifications (artifacts) that helped us conduct the evaluations: the Scenario Influence Matrix and the Architectural Decision Matrix.

4.1   Scenario Influence Matrix

The Scenario Influence Matrix (SIM) describes an influence of a scenario on components using a standard set of values defined in a vocabulary established for evaluation purposes. At this point, a remark should be made. Typically, an architecture description encompasses components and their connections. In most cases we omit connections during analysis, because in the architectural view we used ArchiMate [17] diagrams, which distinguish an *Interface* from a module providing it. The interface specification (e.g. a Web Service interface) very often decides on the nature of a connections that use it. Typically, an interface can be realized by a Façade – a module responsible for its implementation.

The Scenario Influence Matrix is defined as a partial function that assigns actions or influences to scenarios and components:

$$SIM : S \times C \to Mod \times Act \cup Inf, \tag{1}$$

where: S – is a set of scenarios, C – is a set of components, Mod – is an access mode $Mod = \{M, A\}$, where M stands for manual and A for automatic, Act – is a set of actions on components, Inf – is a set of influences.

The vocabulary of actions Act used in the evaluation is as follows:

- AC: adding a dedicated component,
- UF: using a function of a component,
- $MStr$: modifying a component structure,
- MF: modifying a component function,
- RC: remove component,
- CC: cloning a component,
- PC: partitioning component,
- MS: modify component state,

- CD: creating data managed by a component,
- RD: reading component data,
- MD: modifying data,
- DD: deleting data.

For Inf (influences) three values were used: IRU: increase resource utilization, ICP: increase capacity and ICL: influence component's logic.

For evaluation purposes, the SIM matrix was represented by a spreadsheet with scenarios placed at rows and components (including interfaces) at columns. The vocabulary of possible actions and influences was selected to fit the particular task of Dynamic Map evaluation. For other applications, it can be extended according to particular needs.

4.2 Architectural Decision Matrix

The second artifact prepared as an input for evaluation is the Architectural Decision Matrix (ADM). Its goal is to assign design approaches or decisions to each component. Filling the ADM is an important step of evaluation, as it helps to ask questions about certain decisions that can be perceived as important to reach expected scenario responses.

The Architectural Decision Matrix is defined as a partial function that assigns sets of possible decision values to pairs of decisions and components under consideration. The mapping is defined in (2) as follows. For each design decision $d \in D$, the function $ADM(d)$ assigns a set of possible decisions to a component. The whole mapping is a sum of $ADM(d)$ mappings for individual decisions corresponding to rows of an ADM matrix.

$$ADM = \bigcup_{d \in D} ADM(d), \text{ where } ADM(d) : C \to 2^{V(d)} \qquad (2)$$

Examples of design decisions from the set D and their values are:

1. Platform (PostgreSQL, Linux, IIS, Glassfish,..., choice<$list\ of\ platforms$>)
2. Component logic (fixed, customizable)
3. Query granularity (bulk, low, medium, high, flexible)
4. Transaction distribution (no, over<$list\ of\ components$>)
5. Use of web services (REST, SOAP, RPC, document, encoded, literal)
6. Communication type (synchronous, asynchronous)
7. Buffering (yes, no)
8. Security method (https, WS Security, XML Encryption, XML Signature...)
9. Separation of concerns (coupled with <$component\ name$>)
10. Use of ontologies (structure definition, integration, semantic querying)

We do not claim that the above list is either complete or general enough to be applied to any architectural design. However, it reflects some salient questions that emerged during the assessment of the Dynamic Map architecture. We treat the lists of decisions and their values as a flexible mean to collect and describe those properties of the design which are missing in architectural views.

As ATAM-based evaluation should be conducted at an early stage of a software lifecycle, it may frequently occur that particular design decisions have not been made or some specification is missing. In this case, we use the values *not decided* or *not specified* (e.g. a platform is not decided, the logic of a component is not specified).

We consider ADM a useful tool, which provides an overview of the map of architectural decisions and helps detect white spots (e.g. decisions that have not been made), which can introduce a substantial risk during future development. Beyond the assessment task, ADM provides a useful background reference supplementing the architectural views, therefore we decided to maintain it during system development.

5   Evaluation of the Dynamic Map

ATAM-based evaluation of the Dynamic Map was performed in accordance to the general method guidelines, with some minor deviations. The INSIGMA system is being developed by several distributed teams and it was extremely difficult to gather all stakeholders to participate in the brainstorming sessions. Direct communication was replaced by teleconference and wiki-based voting.

5.1   Architecture

The architecture of the Dynamic map is functionally decomposed into three subsets of components: the Static Map, the Traffic Repository and the Event Repository (the top layer). These subsets are collections of active components and interfaces grouped around databases.

1. The Static Map is responsible for storing information about road connections and other objects appearing on the map. These data originate from Open Street Map project [2] and have similar representation. The Static Map also contains information about traffic organization and uses additional structures: Lanes, Turns and Crossroads.
2. The Traffic Repository adopts a simple data model: it stores *Types* of monitoring parameters, typed *Instances* linked indirectly to locations on the map and roads and current *Values*. Traffic Repository has two functions coupled in one database: it provides a discoverable directory of monitoring parameters and the storage supporting high volume of feeds and queries about values of instances. The design of the Traffic Repository is general enough, to integrate various types of sensors. This approach was positively verified while integrating video detectors [6].
3. The Event Repository follows the approach taken for the Traffic Repository, it defines various types of events (e.g. traffic jams, accidents, weather conditions) and information on their occurrences.

Such approach defines clear separation of concerns. However, certain queries are distributed between databases; that may introduce performance risks. It should also be mentioned that all data structures, including dictionaries representing types of monitoring parameters and events, are defined using ontologies which were used at the development stage to model the domain [15] and provide further semantic reference to support integration [19,16].

The Static Map architecture is given in Fig. 1. It consists of a relational database (DB Static Map) with an SQL-based interface (OSM SQL interface). It also provides an interface façade: IMS (Insigma Map Static) Facade. The Façade is used by two separate interfaces: IMS.Query and IMS.Management for querying and managing Static Map data respectively.

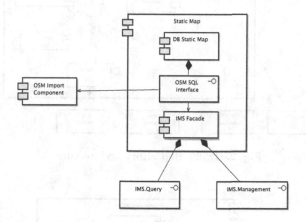

Fig. 1. Static Map architecture

The Traffic Repository architecture (Fig. 2) introduces several new components. The External Subscriber Façade allows to subscribe to chosen traffic parameter data feeds and therefore have such information delivered as soon as it is available in the repository. The RT Event Interpreter analyzes traffic parameters and infers events that are caused by them. The repository is fed with data through the Feed Interface from diverse sensors.

The Event Repository architecture (Fig. 3) consists of a database, native SQL-based interface and several façades with corresponding interfaces (IMD stands for Insigma Map Dynamic). It also introduces a discovery interface which enables to identify what kind of events are actually stored in the repository. Since events are geo-localized the Query Facade and the Event Reporting Facade utilize the Static Map interfaces (OSM SQL interface, IMS.Query).

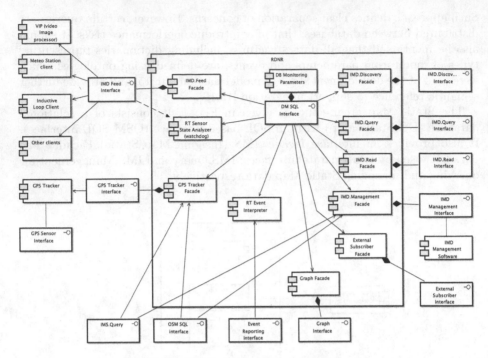

Fig. 2. Traffic Repository architecture

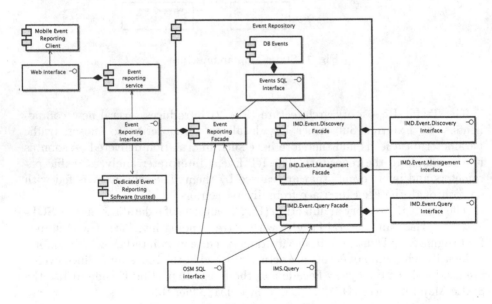

Fig. 3. Event Repository architecture

5.2 High Priority Scenarios

High priority scenarios, which are usually identified in a brainstorming session, were elicited in a few sessions performed with smaller teams, documented on the project wiki pages and submitted to voting. Their list is presented below. The related quality attributes are marked in parentheses.

1. New sensor types and sensor processing software will be integrated in <6 days> (Modifiability)
2. Dynamic Map will be capable of accepting feeds from up to 1000 sensors occurring every <60> sec (Performance)
3. Dynamic Map will be capable of processing up to <200> read queries per second (Performance)
4. New map features can be introduced and made discoverable with built-in functionality (Usability).
5. Updating of data defining the road network can cause a loss of at most 10 values of a single monitoring parameter (Reliability).
6. Sensor failures will be detected in a configurable period ranging from 3 to 20 minutes (Reliability).
7. New event types and corresponding customizable detection routines can be introduced in 1 day (Modifiability)
8. System will be able to accommodate and interpret location data from 5000 GPS tracker units updated every 5 sec (Performance).
9. A Dynamic Map component can be ported to another platform within 20 days (Portability)

5.3 Results of Evaluation and Mitigation Strategies

The input for the architecture evaluation were two matrices: the SIM and ADM discussed in Section 4.

Table 1 representing SIM specifies influence of scenarios (listed in rows) on architecture components (table columns). Cells of the table are filled with actions defined in Section 4.1.

For ADM shown in Table 2 column headers contain architecture components, row headers types of architectural decisions. Cells define assignments of decision values to particular components.

The contents of the presented matrices are excerpts from the specifications that are a few times larger. For better readability, just a subset of the defined scenarios (see Section 5.2) and decisions (see Section 4.2) is chosen.

Further part of the section presents results of evaluation for two selected scenarios.

Scenario #1: New Sensor Types and Sensor Processing Software Will Be Integrated in <6 Days>. The goal of the scenario is to integrate a new sensor, e.g. a videodetector, within the Dynamic Map, with developed and tested processing software capable of calculating several types of traffic parameters.

Table 1. Scenario Influence Matrix. Used acronyms: A – automatic, M – manual, MD – modifying data, MF – modifying a component function, ICP – increase capacity, IRU – increase resource utilization, CD – creating data managed by a component, UF – using a function of a component, RD – reading component data, ICL – influence component's logic.

Scenario	DB Static Map	OSM import component	IMS facade	DB Monitoring Parameters	Monitoring Parameters Ontology	IMD.Feed facade	RT Sensor State Analyzer	RT Event Interpreter	IMD.Discovery facade	IMD.Query facade	DB Events	Event Reporting Facade	IMD.Event Discovery Facade	Event Subscribe	Graph Interface
1 New sensor types and sensor processing software will be integrated in <6 days>				A: MD	M: MD	IRU	IRU	M: MF	ICP	ICP					ICP
2 Dynamic Map will be capable of accepting feeds from up to 1000 sensors occurring every <60> sec				A: CD		A: UF	A: UF	A: UF				A: MD A: CD	A: UF	A: UF	ICP
4 New map features can be introduced and made discoverable with built-in functionality	A: CD	A: UF	A: UF		A: RD										A: UF
5 Updating of data defining the road network can cause a loss of at most 10 values of a single monitoring parameter	A: MD	A: UF	M: MD						ICL						ICL

Table 2. Architectural Decision Matrix. Used acronyms: ND – not decided, Nd – not defined, SD – structure definition, RD – reference data, Pg – PostgreSQL, Lin – linux, Sc – script, Gs – Glassfish, IIS – Internet Information Services, SP – stored procedure, RB – rule-based (rule expression language), B – bulk, F – flexible, H – high, Fi – fixed.

Decision	SM database	OSM Import Component	IMS Facade	DB Monitoring Parameters	Monitoring Parameters Ontology	IMD Feed Facade	RT Sensor State Analyzer	RT Event Interpreter	IMD Discovery Facade	IMD Query Facade	DB Events	Event Reporting Facade	IMD.Event Discovery Facade	Event Subscribe	Graph Interface
Data objects	OSM Lane Turn Crsd.	OSM	OSM Lane Turn Crsd.	Snsr. Type Inst. Value	All	Inst. Value	Snsr. Inst. Value	Value Event	Type Inst.	Inst. Value	Event Occr.	Occr.	Event Occr.	Event	OSM Lane Turn Crsd.
Use of ontologies	SD	ND	yes				RD	RD	RD		SD	RD	RD	RD	
Use of web services		ND	yes SOAP		yes SOAP	yes SOAP			yes SOAP	yes SOAP		yes SOAP	yes SOAP	ND	ND
Communication type			syn		syn	syn ND			syn	syn		asyn ND	syn	syn or poll	
Platform	Pg	Lin Sc	Nd IIS Gs		Gs	Nd IIS Gs	Nd IIS Gs SP	Nd IIS Gs RB	Nd IIS Gs	Nd IIS Gs		Nd IIS Gs	Nd IIS Gs	Nd IIS Gs	
Query granularity		B	F		H F	H F			H F						
Component logic		Fi			Fi	F	F	ND	ND		Fi	ND	ND	ND	

It is assumed that the sensor software will be augmented by a ready-to-use communication component using a web service interface over a SSL-secured network.

Introduction of a new sensor type may result in adding descriptions of a sensor and measured parameters into the system ontology, inserting new values to the dictionaries and the directory of sensors and instances in the TM database. Adding a new sensor indirectly increases the required capacity of components that store or allow access to instances of measured parameters and their values.

- *Sensitivity point*: definitions of monitoring parameter types appear in the ontology and dictionaries within the TM database.
- *Tradeoff*: coupling of directory and storage functions within the TM database is a tradeoff between performance and modifiability. While feeding values, their ranges are to be checked within real-time constraints. This precludes examining the directly the ontology, due to the lack mature of Semantic Web tools at .NET platform. Access to the ontology is wrapped by a web service, what would introduce an overhead influencing the performance. On the other hand, the directory in TM database has a fixed structure, what may hinder changes.
- *Risk*: there is a potential risk of loosing cohesion between the ontology and dictionaries as no decision is made concerning the rules for updating the dictionaries within TM database to reflect changes in the ontology.
- *Non-risk*: data structures and interfaces are designed to support seamless integration.
- *Recommendation*: Make a decision on the ontology storage and define a workflow for updating the dictionaries based on ontology.

Scenario #2: Dynamic Map Will Be Capable of Accepting Feeds from up to 1000 Sensors Occurring Every <60> Sec. The scenario specifies a typical performance requirement. The approach taken assumes that a single sensor can feed multiple values of monitoring parameters (typically 20) at time using a synchronous web service that place them into a common memory buffer. Values collected in memory are entered to the database by bulk queries executed by a periodical process.

- *Sensitivity points*: query granularity, use of synchronous web services and buffering
- *Non-risk*: the initial tests of the communication overhead and data base performance indicate that there is no substantial risk to achieving the scenario response. Data originating from the assumed number of sensor can be published in the database with the latency limited to 10 seconds (assuming 5 second period of a thread executing bulk inserts of maximum 20000 values)

6   Conclusions

Experience gathered during theanalysis of the Dynamic Map architecture indicates that ATAM is a valuable method, as it helps to detect real flaws in the design and identify potential risks. We did not use ATAM to gain a false conviction that the system is optimally designed, but to collect requirements that were not expressed earlier, which represent expectations of various stakeholders, and to assess that they can be satisfied with the proposed system architecture (including adaptations and changes at limited costs). The presented list of risks and recommendations proves that the initial system architecture was not perfect in every detail and several issues were detected by applying ATAM.

A significant contribution of this paper is development and application of two supporting tools for ATAM: the Scenario Influence Matrix (SIM) and the Architectural Decision Matrix (ADM).

SIM is used to collect information on the impact of a scenario on particular components. Obviously, for use case scenarios, e.g. related to performance, message sequence charts are a more natural way to represent the communication flow. However, for growth scenarios, there is no appropriate language to represent their impact on components.

ADM provides a centralized view on properties and decisions related to components (and in some cases, connections). Maintaining such a view is of high importance for a large project being developed by independent teams working in different locations, because many implicit decisions are made locally and are difficult to track.

References

1. INSIGMA project, http://insigma.kt.agh.edu.pl (last accessed January 2013)
2. OpenStreetMap wiki, http://wiki.openstreetmap.org/wiki (last accessed January 2013)
3. Boucké, N., Weyns, D., Schelfthout, K., Holvoet, T.: Applying the ATAM to an architecture for decentralized control of a transportation system. In: Hofmeister, C., Crnković, I., Reussner, R. (eds.) QoSA 2006. LNCS, vol. 4214, pp. 180–198. Springer, Heidelberg (2006)
4. Clements, P., Kazman, R., Klein, M.: Evaluating Software Architectures: Methods and Case Studies. Addison-Wesley Professional (2001)
5. Ferber, S., Heidl, P., Lutz, P.: Reviewing product line architectures: Experience report of ATAM in an automotive context. In: van der Linden, F.J. (ed.) PFE 2002. LNCS, vol. 2290, pp. 364–382. Springer, Heidelberg (2002)
6. Głowacz, A., Mikrut, Z., Pawlik, P.: Video detection algorithm using an optical flow calculation method. In: Dziech, A., Czyżewski, A. (eds.) MCSS 2012. CCIS, vol. 287, pp. 118–129. Springer, Heidelberg (2012),
http://dx.doi.org/10.1007/978-3-642-30721-8_12
7. ISO/IEC: ISO/IEC 9126. Software engineering – Product quality. ISO/IEC (2001)
8. ISO/IEC: ISO/IEC CD 25010.3: Systems and software engineering - Software product Quality Requirements and Evaluation (SQuaRE) - Software product quality and system quality in use models. ISO/IEC (2009)
9. Jones, L.G., Lattanze, A.J.: Using the architecture tradeoff analysis method to evaluate a wargame simulation system: A case study. Technical Report CMU-SEI2001TN022 Software Engineering Institute Carnegie Mellon University Pittsburgh PA, 33 (December 2001)

10. Kazman, R., Barbacci, M., Klein, M., Carriere, S.J., Woods, S.G.: Experience with performing architecture tradeoff analysis. In: Proceedings of the 21st International Conference on Software Engineering, ICSE 1999, pp. 54–63 (1999)

11. Kazman, R., Bass, L., Klein, M.: The essential components of software architecture design and analysis. Journal of Systems and Software 79(8), 1207–1216 (2006)

12. Kazman, R., Klein, M., Clements, P.: ATAM: Method for architecture evaluation. Tech. rep., Carnegie Mellon University, Software Engineering Institute (2000)

13. Lee, J., Kang, S., Chun, H., Park, B., Lim, C.: Analysis of VAN-core system architecture- a case study of applying the ATAM. In: Proceedings of the 2009 10th ACIS International Conference on Software Engineering, Artificial Intelligences, Networking and Parallel/Distributed Computing, SNPD 2009, pp. 358–363. IEEE Computer Society, Washington, DC (2009)

14. Roy, B., Graham, T.C.N.: Methods for evaluating software architecture: A survey. Computing 545(2008-545), 82 (2008)

15. Sliwa, J., Gleba, K., Chmiel, W., Szwed, P., Glowacz, A.: IOEM - ontology engineering methodology for large systems. In: Jędrzejowicz, P., Nguyen, N.T., Hoang, K. (eds.) ICCCI 2011, Part I. LNCS, vol. 6922, pp. 602–611. Springer, Heidelberg (2011), http://dx.doi.org/10.1007/978-3-642-23935-9_59

16. Szwed, P., Kadluczka, P., Chmiel, W., Glowacz, A., Sliwa, J.: Ontology based integration and decision support in the insigma route planning subsystem. In: Ganzha, M., Maciaszek, L.A., Paprzycki, M. (eds.) FedCSIS, pp. 141–148 (2012)

17. Van Den Berg, H., Bosma, H., Dijk, G., Van Drunen, H., Van Gijsen, J., Langeveld, F., Luijpers, J., Nguyen, T., Oosting, Gerand Slagter, R., et al.: Archimate made practical. Work (2007)

18. Wallin, P., Froberg, J., Axelsson, J.: Making decisions in integration of automotive software and electronics: A method based on ATAM and AHP. In: Fourth International Workshop on Software Engineering for Automotive Systems, SEAS 2007, p. 5 (2007)

19. Wojnicki, I., Szwed, P., Chmiel, W., Ernst, S.: Ontology oriented storage, retrieval and interpretation for a dynamic map system. In: Dziech, A., Czyżewski, A. (eds.) MCSS 2012. CCIS, vol. 287, pp. 380–391. Springer, Heidelberg (2012), http://dx.doi.org/10.1007/978-3-642-30721-8_37

Detection of Moving Objects in Images Combined from Video and Thermal Cameras

Grzegorz Szwoch and Maciej Szczodrak

Gdansk University of Technology, Multimedia Systems Department
Narutowicza 11/12, 80-233 Gdansk, Poland
{greg,szczodry}@sound.eti.pg.gda.pl

Abstract. An algorithm for detection of moving objects in video streams from the monitoring cameras is presented. A system composed of a standard video camera and a thermal camera, mounted in close proximity to each other, is used for object detection. First, a background subtraction is performed in both video streams separately, using the popular Gaussian Mixture Models method. For the next processing stage, the authors propose an algorithm which synchronizes the video streams and performs a projective transformation of the images so that they are properly aligned. Finally, the algorithm processes the partial background subtraction results from both cameras in order to obtain a combined result, from which connected components representing moving objects may be extracted. The tests of the proposed algorithm confirm that employing the dual camera system for moving object detection improves its accuracy in difficult lighting conditions.

Keywords: object detection, background subtraction, thermal images, video surveillance.

1   Introduction

Object detection is a procedure that is commonly performed within the frameworks for the automatic analysis of camera images in surveillance systems [1]. This procedure is performed at the earliest stage of the processing chain and is composed of an optional image preprocessing, a background subtraction, morphological cleaning and extraction of connected components. After the background subtraction, a binary mask of foreground and background pixels is obtained. Errors in background subtraction may result from numerous factors: objects color similar to the background, existence of shadows, bright lights, snow flakes, etc. These errors limit the accuracy of object detection and, in consequence, of further analysis stages, e.g. the event detection [1]. The main drawback of the currently used systems based on standard cameras is inability to detect objects with a satisfactory accuracy in difficult conditions, such as low light (e.g. night scenes), strong sunlight (presence of strong shadows), fog, etc.

Recently, thermal cameras began to be used in monitoring systems because of their ability to detect the moving objects (mostly humans) and the decreasing price. Although these devices, equipped with an uncooled microbolometer sensor, are greatly

A. Dziech and A. Czyżewski (Eds.): MCSS 2013, CCIS 368, pp. 262–272, 2013.

simplified compared with the 'true' thermal cameras, they are useful for monitoring purposes. However, there are some problems with this type of cameras, mainly related to a limited resolution and frame rate and to the fact that they provide an image that is not always informative. Nevertheless, thermal cameras are useful for the automatic image analysis.

Extensive studies related to use of such acquisition devices have been recently conducted. Detection of humans in the infrared image from camera mounted in a vehicle was presented by Bertozzi et al. [2]. Another group of applications focus on improving the face recognition by connecting two modalities of visible and thermal images [3, 4, 5]. A fusion of both sources is applied for enhancing the robustness of video surveillance systems. In the recent work [6], a statistical method (a Bayesian model) and a gait pattern analysis are used for pedestrian tracking in visual and thermal images. Davis et al. [7] propose a contour extraction based technique using thermal and visible imagery for object detection. Han et al. [8] describe a hierarchical genetic algorithm-based two-modal image registration approach and show an improvement of human silhouette extraction performance with fused image over the separate modalities. However, the experiments involve only indoor scenarios.

Fusion of infrared and visual images is a potential solution to improve person detection and tracking performance. Using only visual image for this purpose is challenging due to occurrence of shadows, light reflections, darkness, and luminosity changes. Thermal image is characterized by low susceptibility to ambient illumination changes and provides possibility of object detection in various lighting conditions including total darkness.

In order to improve the accuracy of moving object detection in difficult conditions, we propose an algorithm that combines the background subtraction results from two cameras – the thermal and the standard one – mounted in close proximity and monitoring the same area. The idea is that in difficult conditions, at least one of these cameras will be able to provide sufficiently accurate data for object detection. First, a method of synchronizing the video streams and performing a fusion of the images from both cameras is presented. Next, an algorithm which processes the masks of moving objects obtained from the separate cameras is presented. The proposed approach is tested in various conditions and the results are provided and discussed.

2   Description of the Algorithm

The structure of the algorithm is shown in Fig. 1. First, a background subtraction is performed in separate images from the video and thermal cameras. The results of analysis are cleaned morphologically. Next, both video streams are synchronized, then the images are aligned using a homographic transformation. Once the background subtraction masks are in the same coordinate system, a morphological processing of mask corresponding to the same scene content is performed in order to improve the accuracy of extraction of the connected contours during the next stage.

2.1   Background Subtraction

Background subtraction is a process that separates the image pixels belonging to moving objects from those belonging to a stable background. The Gaussian Mixture Model (GMM) algorithm is one of the most widely used approaches [9, 10]. In this section, application of the GMM algorithm to the background subtraction in a single-channel image from a thermal camera is briefly presented. The thermal camera used for the experiments was equipped with an uncooled microbolometer sensor, sensitive to an infrared radiations. Information processed by the thermal sensor is converted to an image using a procedure which maps the amount of radiation measured by a sensor cell to a color or grayscale intensity. For the background subtraction purposes, a standard *white-hot* mapping in which the black and white colors represent the lower and the higher temperature, respectively, is used. The mapping may be linear or non-linear (if an equalization is turned on in the camera settings) and the gain of the mapping function is also adjustable. Other mappings available in the camera produce an image in which different temperatures are represented by different colors are not suitable for background subtraction.

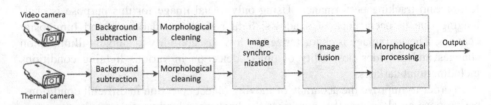

Fig. 1. Block diagram of the proposed algorithm for object detection in combined images from the video and thermal cameras

A thermal image obtained using the white-hot mapping is a single-channel, grayscale one, usually encoded using 8 bits. Processing of such images with the GMM algorithm is as follows. Each pixel in the thermal image is represented as a weighted mixture of K Gaussians, representing different modes of the background. Each Gaussian η is represented by a weight w, a mean μ and a standard deviation σ. Therefore, the probability of observing the current pixel value x at the time t is given by [9]:

$$P(x_t) = \sum_{k=1}^{K} w_{i,t} \cdot \eta\left(x_t, \mu_{i,t}, \sigma_{i,t}\right). \tag{1}$$

Usually, for three-channel images, $K = 5$ is used, but the background in thermal images is more uniform, so we observed that a lower number of Gaussians is sufficient, which reduces the memory usage and the computation time. Therefore, we set $K = 3$.

For the first image frame, one of the Gaussians is initialized by setting its mean to the pixel value, its standard deviation to a high value and the weight to unity. For each successive image, the values of image pixels are compared with their Gaussians in the model, ordered by a descending w/σ ratio. The first Gaussian with a distance between its mean and the current pixel value lower than 2.5 times the standard deviation is marked as a matching one. Next, weights of all Gaussians are updated using a running average and the mean and the variance of the matched Gaussian only is updated [1, 9]. If none of the Gaussians matched, the one with the lower weight is replaced by a new one, initialized by the current pixel value and a high variance.

One important modification had to be made to the original GMM algorithm. If the standard deviation of the Gaussian is constantly updated, it will eventually fall to a very small value. As a result, even small deviations from the mean will result in not being able to find a matching Gaussian, so the pixel will not be assigned to the background. In order to prevent this effect, a limit was imposed on a minimum allowable value of standard deviation. If the value falls below the threshold, it is readjusted.

The background subtraction result is a binary mask of the foreground and background pixels. This mask is usually distorted by noise and gaps, so it is processed using the morphological operations. First, a morphological opening (the erosion followed by the dilation) is performed for removing the isolated pixels, then a morphological closing (a dual operation) is used for filling small gaps [14].

2.2   Image Synchronization and Fusion

Before the object detection is performed, the images from both cameras have to be combined. This operation requires first selecting two camera images representing the same moment and then transforming the images so that they overlap each other. Both operations are not trivial. For the purpose of video stream synchronization, each image frame obtained from the cameras is time-stamped. However, the timestamps do not represent the actual acquisition time. Time differences between the video streams from both cameras depend on many conditions, including different frames per second (fps) ratios, fps jitter, different times needed for image encoding and transmission, etc. The proposed synchronization method is based on comparing the results of background subtraction. For each processed image, a differential image is computed by finding pixels that were marked as a foreground in the current frame, but were assigned to the background in the previous frame. A number of such images is stored in the buffers, separately for each camera. Synchronization is done by comparing the timestamps of the images and then by finding a pair of differential images from both buffers that yields the best match, i.e. the number of non-zero pixels in an image computed as a logical product of two differential images is the largest.

Once the synchronization is done, a fusion of a pair of matched images has to be performed. A proper solution to this problem requires a camera calibration procedure that estimates both the intrinsic and extrinsic camera parameters [11]. However, in our experiments we used a simplified procedure which does not take distortions of the optical systems of the camera into account. We only search for parameters of a perspective transformation between two camera images. We found that such a simplified approach is sufficient for our purpose. However, a full calibration procedure may also be used if necessary. Since the resolution of the thermal image is lower than that of the video camera, it is recommended to transform the latter into the pixel coordinates of the former. Such a transformation is described by a homography [12]:

$$s_i \begin{bmatrix} x_i' \\ y_i' \\ 1 \end{bmatrix} = \mathbf{H} \begin{bmatrix} x_i \\ y_i \\ 1 \end{bmatrix} \tag{2}$$

where $\mathbf{H}$ is the 3×3 homography matrix which transposes image coordinates (x, y) into distorted coordinates (x', y'), with a scaling factor s. In order to find the elements of $\mathbf{H}$, we determined the coordinates of a number of corresponding points in both camera images by reviewing the recorded material, using clearly visible parts of moving objects as the fusion markers. We found out that such a simplified procedure yields sufficiently accurate results. Once the calibration points are determined, the $\mathbf{H}$ matrix may be found using e.g. the Least-Median of Squares (LMedS) method [13]. After the calibration, coordinates of the transformed image may be calculated as:

$$x_i' = \frac{h_{11}x_i + h_{12}y_i + h_{13}}{h_{31}x_i + h_{32}y_i + h_{33}}, \quad y_i' = \frac{h_{21}x_i + h_{22}y_i + h_{23}}{h_{31}x_i + h_{32}y_i + h_{33}} \tag{3}$$

The result of background subtraction in the video camera images (a binary image) is transformed into coordinates of the thermal camera image, using the nearest neighbor interpolation method. The camera image may be transformed using the same matrix $\mathbf{H}$, but the bilinear interpolation should be used in this case.

2.3   Object Detection in the Combined Images

Once both images are in the same coordinate systems, the results of background subtraction from two cameras may be combined. Ideally, both masks should be identical and they should correspond to the actual foreground image (the ground truth). In practical situations, both masks are affected by undetected pixels (the false negatives) and the pixels wrongly assigned to the foreground (the false positives). We observed that the number of incorrect results increases in suboptimal conditions and that the type of errors is different in each camera. For example, false positives in the video camera were related to shadows, vehicle lights, reflections, etc. The false negatives occurred if the color of the moving object was similar to the background. In the thermal camera, mostly the false negatives were observed when parts of the moving objects were cooler than the rest (e.g. backpacks) or the objects did not emit a sufficient amount of radiation (e.g. a recently started vehicle). Generally, none of the two cameras provided a satisfactory percentage of correct results in varying conditions. Therefore, we aim to combine the results of background subtraction from two cameras in order to improve the quality of moving objects detection at the next processing stage.

In the approach described here, we utilized a concept of morphological reconstruction [14]. Let $\mathbf{V}$ and $\mathbf{T}$ denote binary images containing the background subtraction results from the video and thermal camera images, respectively. First, we treat $\mathbf{V}$ as the mask and $\mathbf{T}$ as the marker, and we perform the geodesic dilation:

$$\mathbf{R}_1 = (\mathbf{T} \oplus \mathbf{S}) \cap \mathbf{V} \tag{4}$$

where **S** is the structuring element of size $n \times n$ and disk shape. The thermal result **T** is dilated by **S** and then the intersection with **V** is found. This way, fragments of moving objects that were detected in the video image but not in the thermal image are reconstructed. The size n determines how large are the reconstructed fragments. Next, a similar procedure is applied to **V** as the marker, this time using **T** as the mask:

$$\mathbf{R_2} = (\mathbf{V} \oplus \mathbf{S}) \cap \mathbf{T} \tag{5}$$

using the same structuring element. This operation reconstructs fragments of objects visible only in the thermal images, e.g. object parts with color similar to the background. Finally, the result is obtained as a sum of these two partial results:

$$\mathbf{R} = \mathbf{R_1} + \mathbf{R_2} \tag{6}$$

In the next processing stage, connected components are extracted from the **R** mask. We used the border following algorithm proposed by Suzuki [15] to extract the contours from the binary image. The extracted components are then filtered by size in order to remove small objects (noise, separate fragments, etc.) and too large objects (e.g. large areas of image incorrectly assigned to the foreground because of sudden changes in scene lighting or camera readjustment). The remaining contours may be used in further analysis stages, including object tracking, object classification and automatic event detection [1].

3   Experiments and Results

The proposed algorithm was validated using a setup of two cameras. The video device was the Axis P1346 Network Camera, with original image resolution 2048 × 1536 pixels. A 640 × 480 pixels section was cropped from this image for the analysis. The second device was the Axis Q1910 Thermal Camera, providing an image with an original (not scaled) resolution of 384 × 288 pixels. Exposure setting of the thermal camera were set to a linear gain control, with maximum gain of 6 dB and automatic exposure zones. Since the frame rate of the thermal camera was limited to 8.33 fps, the frame rate of the video camera was set to the same value. Both cameras were mounted at the same location and the cropped video image covered a scene similar to the one observed by the thermal camera (Fig. 2).

(a)   (b)   (c)

Fig. 2. An example of image fusion: (a) video camera image, (b) thermal camera image, (c) aligned images. White circles show the positions of fusion points.

Image fusion was performed off-line by taking the corresponding images from both cameras and finding coordinates of pixels representing the same points in the observed space. Features that were clearly visible in both camera images (e.g. feet of walking persons, parts of passing vehicles) were manually selected as the fusion points. A total of 48 points were selected (Fig. 2). The homography matrix was found using the LMedS algorithm [12], the mean square error was 5.52 px^2. Observation of the fusion results (Fig. 2c) indicated that the proposed method allows for aligning the images with a satisfactory accuracy for the purpose of the described algorithm.

Five recordings from both cameras were made in various conditions in order to evaluate the algorithm performance. Unfortunately, we were unable to test even more difficult conditions such as a thick fog or an unlit night scene, because such conditions did not occur during the tests. Each pair of recordings was processed by the proposed algorithm and the output masks of the moving objects were recorded at the algorithm output, as well as after processing the images from a single camera. For the evaluation, a representative image frame was selected from each recording and the ground truth data (the mask of the actual moving objects) were created manually for a reference. The processing results were compared with the ground truth data and the pixels assigned correctly to the foreground and the background were counted as true positive (TP) and true negative (TN) results, respectively. Pixels assigned incorrectly to the foreground or the background were counted as false positive (FP) and false negative (FN) results, respectively. With these results, the following performance measures were obtained:

$$precision = \frac{TP}{TP + FP} \tag{7}$$

$$recall = \frac{TP}{TP + FN} \tag{8}$$

$$accuracy = \frac{TP + TN}{TP + TN + FP + FN} \tag{9}$$

The results of the algorithm evaluation for each recording and the overall result for all test scenarios are presented in Table 1 and the obtained background subtraction masks are shown in Fig. 3. The results obtained for a single camera may be treated as a reference, for a comparison of the proposed algorithm (video and thermal camera) with the existing approaches that use a single camera type. The results obtained for different conditions were as follows.

- *Cloudy* – normal, stable lighting conditions.
- *Sunny* – in the scene brightly lit by the sun, long shadows significantly reduce the precision and accuracy of the video camera. The thermal camera performs better, as the shadows are not detected by this camera type. With the proposed method, a higher recall is obtained at the cost of reduced recall, because some parts of the shadows were retained because of morphological operations.

- *Snow* – in this scene, precision for video camera was very low. The proposed algorithm improves the precision compared with the video camera. The accuracy is similar to that of the thermal camera, while the recall is higher and the precision is lower.
- *Dusk* – in this low-light scene, the proposed algorithm has best recall of all three methods, but the precision is lower than for the thermal camera. The accuracy of all three algorithms is high and very similar.
- *Night* – in the scene lit by streetlights, the video camera has a very low precision (because of detecting the vehicle headlights as moving objects) and high recall, while for the thermal camera the situation is opposite – a low recall value is caused by inability to detect the vehicle because of its relatively low temperature. The proposed algorithm balances these two effects, providing the recall and accuracy values comparable to the best results and the precision situated between the results obtained for the single cameras.

Frame	**Video**	**Thermal**	**Combined**

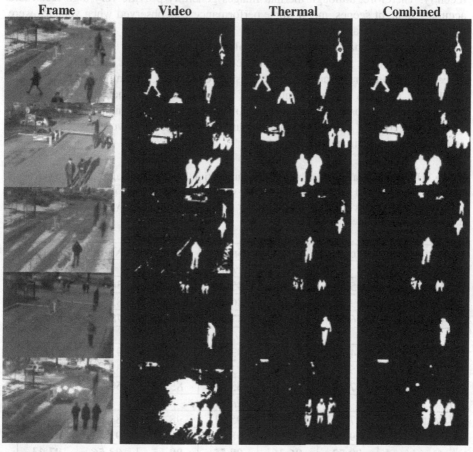

Fig. 3. Results of background subtraction: video camera frames, the results obtained from separate camera images and from the combined images, with the proposed algorithm. Test scenarios, top to bottom: cloudy, sunny, snow, dusk, night.

The overall results indicate that the proposed algorithm has accuracy similar to the thermal camera analysis, the recall is much higher and the precision is significantly lower. Compared with the video camera analysis, the accuracy is better, the recall is slightly lower because of problems with the night scene and the precision is significantly improved.

It may be observed that the proposed algorithm achieves better results than the video camera alone in all cases except the recall for the night scene, where the thermal image results were not accurate enough to achieve an improvement with the morphological operations. The cause of this situation was that it was not possible to separate the vehicle silhouettes from the background in thermal images. It was possibly caused by configuration of the camera used in the experiments which adjusted the sensor sensitivity so that objects with higher temperature (persons) were clearly visible. Since the camera used a microbolometer sensor with a limited dynamic range, moving vehicles blended into the background, especially in case of vehicles that were started recently. Therefore, although thermal images generally provide very high recall and accuracy in night scenes, much worse performance was observed when vehicles were present in the camera view.

Compared with the thermal camera, analysis of the combined images generally improves the recall, at the cost of a decreased precision. However, as far as the object detection by contour extraction in the mask is concerned, the improved recall is desired, as it prevents the fragmentation of detected objects. Since the precision observed for the proposed algorithm does not fall below 77%, a higher number of FPs does not deteriorate the object detection unless the objects move very close to each other, which results in merged objects.

Table 1. Results of evaluation of background suntraction in separate images from the video and thermal cameras, and in combined images with the proposed algorithm. The values of precision, recall and accuracy are presented for each source type (only video, only thermal and a combined video + thermal images).

Algorithm	Cloudy	Sunny	Snow	Dusk	Night	Overall
Precision						
Video	95.53	62.22	45.26	84.39	34.61	51.30
Thermo	99.16	90.32	86.40	98.66	82.13	91.72
Combined	**96.26**	**79.91**	**77.44**	**90.34**	**78.37**	**83.73**
Recall						
Video	74.38	78.46	83.34	66.94	93.37	81.21
Thermo	95.33	89.23	71.05	80.10	32.77	71.81
Combined	**97.04**	**92.06**	**85.03**	**85.43**	**50.93**	**80.10**
Accuracy						
Video	97.93	91.91	95.71	98.38	81.34	93.05
Thermo	99.61	97.62	98.53	99.25	92.42	97.48
Combined	**99.52**	**96.36**	**98.55**	**99.15**	**93.56**	**97.43**

4   Conclusions

The results of evaluation of the proposed algorithm indicate that background subtraction in combined images from thermal and video cameras resulted in obtaining the masks of moving objects that facilitate a more accurate object detection for the purpose of further processing, including the automatic event detection. The proposed algorithm allows for synchronization and fusion of images from both cameras using a simple yet effective approach. The main problem is that vehicles (mostly these recently started) are not detected by the thermal camera, so only the video camera detects such objects and there is not enough data for the morphological processing to mark these object with a sufficient accuracy. Therefore, the future work will focus on improving the algorithm so that the vehicles detected by the video camera only will be included in the final result, without spoiling it with unwanted elements such as shadows or headlights. The proposed algorithm, together with a simple dual-camera setup, may be used in an automated video surveillance system for detection of important security threats that would be undetected when using only the video camera.

Acknowledgements. Research is subsidized by the European Commission within FP7 project INDECT, Grant Agreement No. 218086.

References

1. Czyżewski, A., Szwoch, G., Dalka, P., et al.: Multi-Stage Video Analysis Framework. In: Lin, W. (ed.) Video Surveillance, pp. 147–172. InTech, Rijeka (2011)
2. Bertozzi, M., Broggi, A., Grisleri, P., Graf, T., Meinecke, M.: Pedestrian Detection in Infrared Images. In: Proc. IEEE Intelligent Vehicles Symposium, Columbus, pp. 662–667 (2003)
3. Friedrich, G., Yeshurun, Y.: Seeing People in the Dark: Face Recognition in Infrared Images. In: Bülthoff, H.H., Lee, S.-W., Poggio, T.A., Wallraven, C. (eds.) BMCV 2002. LNCS, vol. 2525, pp. 348–359. Springer, Heidelberg (2002)
4. Wang, J., Liang, J., Hu, H., Li, Y., Feng, B.: Performance Evaluation of Infrared and Visible Image Fusion Algorithms for Face Recognition. In: Proc. International Conf. Intelligent Systems and Knowledge Engineering, ISKE 2007, Chengdu, China, pp. 1–8 (2007)
5. Krotosky, S.J., Cheng, S.Y., Trivedi, M.M.: Face Detection and Head Tracking Using Stereo and Thermal Infrared Cameras for "Smart" Airbags: A Comparative Analysis. In: The 7th Int. IEEE Conf. on Intelligent Transportation Systems, San Diego, pp. 17–22 (2004)
6. Leykin, A., Ran, Y., Hammoud, R.: Thermal-Visible Video Fusion for Moving Target Tracking and Pedestrian Classification. In: IEEE Conf. on Computer Vision and Pattern Recognition, Minneapolis, pp. 1–8 (2007)
7. Davis, J., Sharma, V.: Fusion-Based Background-Subtraction using Contour Saliency. In: IEEE Computer Society Conference on Computer Vision and Pattern Recognition, San Diego (2005)
8. Han, J., Bhanu, B.: Fusion of Color and Infrared Video for Moving Human Detection. Pattern Recognition 40, 1771–1784 (2007)

9. Stauffer, C., Grimson, W.E.L.: Adaptive Background Mixture Models for Real-time Tracking. In: Proc. of IEEE Conference on Computer Vision and Pattern Recognition (CVPR), pp. 246–252 (1999)

10. Zivkovic, Z., Van der Heijden, F.: Efficient Adaptive Density Estimation per Image Pixel for the Task of Background Subtraction. Pattern Recognition Letters 27, 773–780 (2006)

11. Zhang, Z.: A Flexible New Technique For Camera Calibration. IEEE Transactions on Pattern Analysis and Machine Intelligence 22, 1330–1334 (2000)

12. Hartley, R., Zisserman, A.: Multiple View Geometry in Computer Vision, pp. 32–33. Cambridge University Press, Cambridge (2003)

13. Rousseeuw, P.: Least Median of Squares Regression. Journal of the American Statistics Association 79, 871–880 (1984)

14. Gonzalez, R.C., Woods, R.E.: Digital Image Processing, 3rd edn. Pearson Prentice Hall, Upper Saddle River (2008)

15. Suzuki, S., Abe, K.: Topological Structural Analysis of Digitized Binary Images by Border Following. Computer Vision, Graphics, and Image Processing 30, 32–46 (1985)

INDECT Security Architecture

Manuel Urueña[1], Petr Machník[2], Marcin Niemiec[3], and Nikolai Stoianov[4]

[1] Universidad Carlos III de Madrid, Department of Telematics Engineering,
Avda. Universidad 30, 28911 Leganés (Madrid) Spain
muruenya@it.uc3m.es
[2] VSB-Technical University of Ostrava, Department of Telecommunications,
Listopadu 15, 708 33, Ostrava, Czech Republic
petr.machnik@vsb.cz
[3] AGH University of Science and Technology, Department of Telecommunications,
Mickiewicza 30 Ave., 30-059 Krakow, Poland
niemiec@kt.agh.edu.pl
[4] Technical University of Sofia, INDECT Project Team,
8, Kliment Ohridski St., 1000 Sofia, Bulgaria
nkl_stnv@tu-sofia.bg

Abstract. In order to carry its duties to serve and protect, the Police must deploy new tools and applications to maintain the pace of technology evolution. The INDECT project is developing such novel investigation tools for European Police forces. However Police ICT systems have stringent security requirements that may delay the deployment of these new applications to first implement the required security measures. This paper presents an integrated security architecture that is able to provide common security services to both, novel and legacy ICT applications, while fulfilling the high security requirements of Police forces. By reusing the security services provided by this architecture, new systems do not have to implement custom security mechanisms themselves, and may be easily integrated into the existing Police ICT infrastructure. The proposed INDECT security architecture features state-of-the-art technologies, like encrypted communications at network and application levels, or multi-factor authentication based on certificates stored in Smart Cards.

Keywords: INDECT Project, Police ICT systems, Security.

1 Introduction

The continuous evolution of Information and Communication Technologies (ICT) has brought enormous changes to the world, where the Internet is a prime example of this progress. However organized crime has also embraced these new technologies and is increasingly employing them to perform criminal activities, in order to be one step ahead of the Law Enforcement Agencies (LEAs) that pursue them. Therefore Police forces must not lose the pace of technology evolution, and have to employ new tools to fight those new high-tech crimes, as well as to leverage ICT technologies to improve their investigations.

A. Dziech and A. Czyżewski (Eds.): MCSS 2013, CCIS 368, pp. 273–287, 2013.
© Springer-Verlag Berlin Heidelberg 2013

INDECT [1] (*Intelligent information system supporting observation, searching and detection for security of citizens in urban environment*) is a research project funded by the EU 7th Framework Program that is developing cost-effective tools for helping European Police services to enforce the law and guarantee the protection of their citizens. Thus the so-called INDECT system is composed by a set of novel applications and ICT services designed to help Police forces in their current investigations, as well as to fight new forms of cyber-crime.

Therefore Police forces are very interested in deploying these new tools as soon as possible in order to do not lag behind in the continuous arms race with organized crime. However, since the information handled Police forces during their investigations is extremely sensible (e.g. names of informants, protected witnesses, etc.), any new system to be deployed inside Police's ICT infrastructure must fist fulfill a stringent set of security requirements [2]. Therefore it is quite common that new tools must implement additional security mechanisms, which are usually custom made. This process may greatly delay the deployment of these new tools, and there is a important risk that those custom-made security mechanisms, added in a later stage of the development process, do not provide the adequate protection. Moreover, Police administrators have to manage a set of heterogeneous ICT systems with fairly different security mechanisms that cannot be easily integrated with other legacy applications or even into their normal operations (e.g. user management), which have to be modified to include each new application, further increasing the deployment delay.

In order to solve these problems, and given that there are no works in the public literature dealing with these problems with Police ICT systems, this paper presents an integrated security architecture in order to provide common security services (i.e. authentication, authorization, confidentiality, integrity, non-repudiation, auditing, etc.) for Police ICT systems, and thus being implemented with state-of-the-art security technologies. Although this architecture has been designed for the systems being developed inside the INDECT Project, it can be also employed for other Police ICT applications, including legacy ones.

2   INDECT Security Architecture

The proposed INDECT security architecture provides a set of common security services, which were previously defined in [2]. The set of common services provided by the INDECT Security Architecture include Authentication, Authorization (Access Control), Non-Repudiation, Privacy/Auditing, Communication Security, Data Confidentiality and Integrity. Other security services such as Efficiency, Reliability and Availability or common ICT security best practices are out of the scope of this paper because they greatly depend on the ICT environment they will be deployed in.

Although each INDECT application has its own security needs and characteristics, the proposed architecture includes a number of security infrastructures [3] that provide common security services using standardized protocols and mechanisms. Those security services are provided by means of a combination of novel and standard security protocols and mechanisms. Figure 1 shows a simplified view of the integrated INDECT Security Architecture for Police ICT systems.

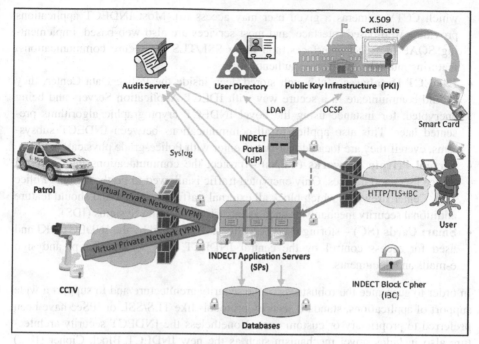

Fig. 1. INDECT Security Architecture

The main components of proposed INDECT Security Architecture are:

- **Public Key Infrastructure (PKI)** – to issue, mange, store and revoke X.509 certificates used in system. Certificates are issued to all INDECT users and ICT systems to authenticate them as well as to secure their communications.
- **LDAP User Directory** – to store all users' contact data and credentials for legacy systems that do not support certificate-based authentication. The user directory also stores general authorization information, such as the users' clearance level or the specific applications they can access to.
- **Audit Server** – all relevant user actions (e.g. accessing an application or requesting classified information) are logged both locally and in a secure centralized system. These logs are constantly being reviewed by security personnel and Police auditors in order to detect suspicious behaviours.
- **INDECT Portal** – is the homepage of Police users. It allows them to access the different services and applications available to them, according to particular scenarios (e.g. in a crisis). The INDECT portal will also act as the Identity Provider (IdP) of INDECT Federated-enabled systems. User authentication is based on X.509 certificates and/or user credentials stored at the LDAP User Directory.
- **INDECT Application Servers** – execute the different services, applications and tools being developed by the INDECT project. They may act as Federated Service Providers (SP), authenticating the users through the INDECT Portal (IdP) although they may also handle application-specific user's authorization attributes (e.g.

which CCTV cameras a given user may access to). Most INDECT applications provide a web-based interface, and most services are also web-based, implementing SOAP or REST interfaces, and using SSL/TLS for secure communications, featuring mutual client-server authentication.

- **INDECT Databases** – although stored deep inside the Police Data Center, they should communicate in a secure way with IDECT Application Servers and being encrypted, for instance using the novel INDECT cryptographic algorithms presented later. This also applies to all communications between INDECT subsystems, even if they are located in a Data Center with Police-grade physical security.
- **Virtual Private Networks (VPNs)** – protect the communications with external Police users and devices. Only encrypted traffic is allowed to go through the Police Data Center firewalls, which block all external traffic by default and should feature additional security mechanisms such as Intrusion Detection Systems (IDS).
- **Smart Cards (SC)** – storing users' certificates are issued by the INDECT PKI and used for access control by the central INDECT web portal, encrypt and sign e-mails and documents.

In order to guarantee the robustness of the security architecture and to support a wide support of applications, standard security protocols like TLS/SSL or IPSec have been preferred to proprietary or custom ones. Nonetheless the INDECT security architecture also includes novel mechanism such as the new INDECT Block Cipher (IBC) that may be employed to encrypt TLS/SSL sessions and VPN tunnels.

For a complete description of the proposed INDECT Security Architecture, the reader is referred to [4].

2.1   LDAP User Directory

Although it is recommended that all INDECT applications are based on the proposed Federated Identity Management, where the INDECT Portal acts as the Identity Provider (IdP) and thus authenticates all users, it is still possible that some applications, including legacy Police systems, do not implement Federated ID management or even certificate-based authentication. Therefore the INDECT Security Architecture also includes a LDAP Directory Service that stores users' information, including user credentials (i.e. login/password) for such legacy applications. A LDAP-based directory service has been selected because nowadays it is commonly employed by enterprises, including Law Enforcement Agencies, for user management (e.g. Windows Active Directory is based on LDAP). The proposed INDECT LDAP schema has been designed to be as standard as possible in order to be easily integrated in existing LDAP systems.

LDAP User Directory contains the information about all INDECT applications and users. This way it is possible to specify, in a centralized way, which applications can be accessed by each user, as well as to specify common authorization attributes of users. Legacy applications can then query the INDECT User Directory by means of

LDAP commands in order to: (i) verify whether a user has access to that application or not, (ii) validate the authentication credentials provided by the user, and (iii) check the user's authorization attributes to enable only the allowed actions.

2.2 Audit Server

Given the sensitive information that Law Enforcement Agencies (LEAs) handle, and in order to protect the privacy of citizens, the operations of LEA agents are continuously monitored by a specialized department of auditors. However, the complexity of INDECT system would require LEA auditors and security personnel to check the logs of a huge number of systems and applications. Therefore the proposed INDECT security architecture also includes a centralized Audit Server that aggregates the logs of all INDECT subsystems. This way, LEA auditors and ICT security personnel only have to monitor a single log stream, with the additional benefit of easing the correlation of events from different systems, which could be easily missed with separated logs.

This centralized log server also provides benefits from a security point of view, because logs are stored in two places, locally at the Application Server and remotely at the Audit Server, which can only be accessed by LEA auditors and that does not support deleting log records. This way, even if a server is compromised and the attacker is able to erase its actions from the local log, by then they would be already stored at the Audit server and thus subject to auditors scrutiny. Therefore all relevant INDECT user actions and system events must be logged locally by the Application Server, as well as be sent to the centralized Audit Server. This also applies to remote applications, that may use VPN tunnels to send its log events to the Audit Server, either directly or through an INDECT Application Server acting as proxy.

For especially sensible operations (i.e. authorizing the wiretap of a suspect) and/or due to regulatory requirements, just logging those operations may be not enough. The details of such sensible operations must be cryptographically signed by the officer requesting/approving it for proper authorization and to ensure non-repudiation.

3   INDECT Cryptographic Algorithms

This section presents new cryptographic solutions that have been developed by the INDECT project. Currently, two novel symmetric ciphers (block and stream) as well as a hash function are ready to be used by end-users. Additionally, new high-level security methods for quantum cryptography have been proposed. These solutions are the significant part of INDECT security architecture.

3.1   INDECT Block Cipher (IBC)

Encryption of confidential data is the most important task of cryptography. It relies on transforming plain data into another encrypted form, unreadable to anyone except of those possessing the cryptographic key, by using an appropriate algorithm, called cipher.

Nowadays, there are many different ciphers. A well-known example is Advanced Encryption Standard (AES) that encrypts data using simple functions: substitutions with a single S-box, permutations, and adding the key. The INDECT project has further developed these ideas: employing more substitution boxes (S-boxes), using a cipher with dynamic structure, etc.

In general, the new cipher, called INDECT Block Cipher (IBC), consists of nonlinear transformations, which are dependent on the key [5]. This feature ensures a higher level of security. Additionally, the large number of secure S-boxes makes each encryption highly unique. The construction of this cipher is based on substitution and permutation functions that are used in each round of the IBC cipher. This structure ensures a good performance and a fast data encryption.

The IBC algorithm is a block cipher. Each 256-bit block of data is divided into 64 sub-blocks. Each sub-block is transformed by the appropriate substitution box and output values are concatenated into one 256-bit block. At the end of the round, the permutation function based on S-box, further modifies the 256-bit block of data. These steps are repeated for a number of iterations (e.g. a minimum of 8 times).

The novel idea of the IBC cipher is unique approach to key. The key is still a pseudo-random sequence, however it is used to create new S-boxes. These substitution boxes are based on the AES S-box, and ensure the same level of security. In this way, we can create about $5.35 \cdot 10^{18}$ new S-boxes from a single AES S-box. All new S-boxes represent a unique non-linear transformation: substitution or permutation. Because of S-box size, the cryptographic keys of IBC cipher must be a multiple of 64 bits. Four key lengths have been chosen for practical use:

- **128 bits** where two S-boxes are used: one for substitution and another for permutation. For 128-bit keys, eight rounds of cipher are proposed.
- **192 bits** where three S-boxes are used: two for substitution and one for permutation. For 192-bit keys, ten iterations of the cipher are proposed.
- **320 bits** where five S-boxes are used: four for substitution and one for permutation. For 320-bit keys, twelve rounds of the cipher are proposed.
- **576 bits** where nine S-boxes are used: eight for substitution and one for permutation. For 576-bit keys, fourteen rounds of the cipher are proposed.

3.2   INDECT Stream Cipher (ISC)

Stream ciphers are able to encrypt a single bit (or byte) of data using a generated key. They are a class of symmetric ciphers that are based on the one-time pad principle. The main difference is that in one-time pad ciphers the key length must be equal to the message length, while stream ciphers employ a key with a much smaller length.

The INDECT Stream Cipher (ISC) provides two encryption modes: a keystream generation based on Linear Feedback Shift Registers (LFSRs), and a symmetric stream cipher based on the IBC cipher.

The keystream generator based on LFSRs uses 16 binary registers and one additional operating in the integer domain. All registers are initialized at the beginning of the encryption process with the provided key. Since the size of registers varies, the provided key is truncated each time before initialization in order to fit in a given register. The key size required for this encryption mode must be 256 bits long.

The stream cipher based on IBC is the solution where a block of data is encrypted by the IBC algorithm using two operation modes: Output Feedback (OFB) and Cipher Feedback (CFB), which may operate over bit or byte streams.

3.3   INDECT Hash Function (IHF)

Hash functions are a group of transformations where variable length data are transformed into a small, fixed-length digest. This transition must be one-way only and part of the original information is lost. Although these functions have a small probability of collision (i.e. when two different input data produce the same output) is almost impossible in practice.

A new hash function, called INDECT Hash Function (IHF), has been created by INDECT project. The hash function has a structure of substitution-permutation network, with different key lengths and different number of rounds. Therefore, this hash function provides different security levels. The design of IHF is based on the IBC algorithm using the CBC-MAC chaining mode. Thus, the key sizes and number of rounds proposed for the INDECT Hash Function are the same as in IBC.

3.4   Quantum Cryptography Methods

Quantum Cryptography (QC) is a new way of solving the key distribution problem for symmetric ciphers. It provides a secure key distribution service by means of the laws of quantum mechanics:

- any measurement modifies the state of the transmitted *qubit* (quantum bit) and this modification can be discovered by end-users,
- it is not possible to clone an unknown qubit (it is not possible to measure the quantum state and simultaneously send a cloned qubit to the real receiver).

Some new high-level quantum cryptography methods have been proposed [6] by the INDECT project, including the verification of the described solutions. This study is based on both theoretical analyses, as well as in a custom-developed simulator (the QKD Protocol Simulator) [7].

The new QC methods are based on the idea of measuring the security level during the QBER estimation and privacy amplification processes. Two new functions were proposed: a measure of security and entropy of security. They define the average security of the key when we uncover and compare a part of the exchanged key. Using these functions we can specify the security levels in a QC system. We propose two security levels: basic and advanced security. Thanks to these security levels we can personalize the security for specific end-users and services. Also, we have verified the methods by means of simulations, and have distributed a questionnaire of interest among potential end-users of QC systems.

4   INDECT Public Key Infrastructure (PKI)

A Public Key Infrastructure (PKI) is a common way to solve the problems related to the distribution of public keys, because it offers the scalability that is required for big communication and information infrastructures. A PKI is usually used to create policies, and mechanisms for asymmetric key management, where public keys are distributed in the form of the so called digital certificates. However in INDECT the information that is included in certificates is more than just a public key since they are also employed for authentication and authorization purposes. Certificates are digitally signed to ensure the integrity and validity of the contained information [8].

4.1   Digital Certificates

A digital certificate is a representation of the link between the identity of a person or device and its corresponding digital information. This digital cryptographic information is comprised by the public keys of the subject. The digital certificate also contains other information related to people or devices, and this information is independently signed by the so-called Certification Authority (CA).

The basic elements of the INDECT PKI infrastructure are:

- **Root CA server** – is based on a self-signed (root) certificate, and it is always offline because it only issues the certificates of its Sub-CAs..
- **Users CA** (Subordinate certificate authority for users) – manages all certificates related to users. These certificates are stored on smart-cards to enable two-factor authentication.
- **Devices CA** (Subordinate certificate authority for devices) – manages all system certificates issued for devices. In the INDECT architecture devices could be: Servers, CCTVs, Users' PCs, Tablets, Smartphones, communication devices, etc.
- **Users RA** (Registration authority for users) - generates certificates from PKCS#10 requests, generates PKCS#12 for the end user, performs key recovery of the users' key (if requested using PKCS#12), edits users, revokes certificates, renews the certificates of existing users, generates a key storage for existing users, etc. The Users RA is operated by the EJBCA software package [9].
- **Devices RA** (Registration authority for devices) - generates certificates for devices, edits devices profiles, revokes certificates, renews certificates for existing devices. The Devices RA is also operated using the EJBCA software.
- **PKI Backup/Log Server** – for disaster-recovery procedures and for auditing the processes of certificate management. PKI logs are also copied into the global INDECT Audit Server.

The architecture of the deployed INDECT PKI infrastructure is shown in Figure 2.

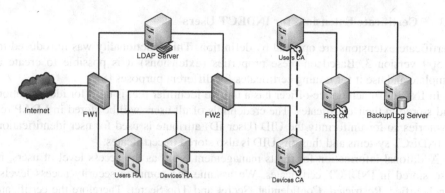

Fig. 2. INDECT Public Key Infrastructure (PKI)

The process for requesting and issuing certificates through a RA are as follows:

1. A certificate request is sent to the RA by a user.
2. The certificate request is checked and verified by the RA and stored locally.
3. The CA is waiting for certificate requests and periodically checks the RA database.
   It processes the request by issuing a certificate and stores it back to the RA's DB.
4. The RA periodically looks for new certificates issued by the CA.
5. The RA sends the new certificate to the user after processing it.

4.2   Certificate Revocation List (CRL)

Often some certificates must be revoked before certificates' validity periods expire, for instance if its private key is somehow compromised. In this case the CA must create a list of revoked certificates, called Certificate Revocation List (CRL). This list includes the serial number of the revoked certificate and the reason for its revocation. Up to date information about revoked certificates is critical for a healthy PKI system. Therefore, the proposed update time for the CRLs of the INDECT PKI is 5 minutes. Four settings should be also configured on EJBCA [9] (the CA software employed for managing certificates) to define how CRL generation is done:

- CRL Expire Period: This is the validity period of the generated CRL. It is set to 24 hours.
- CRL Issue Interval: This is the interval when the new CRL will be issued. For INDECT PKI it is set to 0, meaning that new CRL will be issued after old CRL is expired (24 h).
- CRL Overlap Time: This setting defines the time when the new CRL should be issued before the old CRL is expired. For INDECT PKI, the CRL Overlap Time is set to 10 minutes.
- Delta CRL Period: This setting defines the amount of time a Delta CRL (i.e. differences with a previous CRL) is valid after being issued.

4.3   Certificate Extensions for INDECT Users

Certificate extensions are optional by definition. This functionality was introduced in X.509 version 3. Based on these properties (extensions) it is possible to create a template and use it for issuing certificates for different purposes [8].

In INDECT each police-officer has a unique identifier that is used for identification and stored in their certificates. The credentials of all users will be stored in LDAP repositories so for uniformity the UID (User ID) attribute is used for user identification in INDECT systems and thus this UID is also stored in certificates.

Additional information for rights management, such as the access level of users, is also stored in INDECT certificates. We assume the common security access levels: Unclassified, Restricted, Confidential, Secret and Top Secret. Therefore the certificate has an additional extension that stores the maximum access level of the user as follows:

- Unclassified access level: 0.
- Restricted access level: 1.
- Confidential access level: 2.
- Secret access level: 3.
- Top Secret access level: 4.

5   INDECT Communications Security

Given the distributed nature of the INDECT system, one of the main components of the secure communication infrastructure is a Virtual Private Network (VPN) framework that will enable the secure communication among multiple remote nodes and servers interconnected over public networks [4]. Nowadays VPNs are mostly based on two different technologies – SSL (Secure Socket Layer) and IPsec (Internet Protocol Security).

5.1   SSL VPNs

The best open-source SSL VPN solution is the OpenVPN software package [10]. OpenVPN can be installed in computers with most of current operating systems. OpenVPN is a very flexible and scalable VPN software. The advantages of OpenVPN SSL VPNs are as follows [11]:

- OpenVPN can be installed on various platforms – computers with Linux, Windows, or Mac OS X operating systems; smartphones with Windows Mobile, or Android (using CyanogenMod firmware) operating systems.
- OpenVPN offers two basic modes that run either as a layer 2 or layer 3 VPN. For example, OpenVPN layer 2 tunnels are able to transport Ethernet frames. Because of this ability, OpenVPN behaves more as an IPsec VPN, than a typical SSL one, which is mainly used for a secure web communication.
- Once OpenVPN has established a tunnel, the central firewall in the Police headquarters can protect the client device, even though it is not a local one.

- OpenVPN can use either TCP or UDP transport protocols and can work as a server or client. To improve the security level, a server can accept only connections initiated by clients within the specific virtual private network.
- Since OpenVPN 2.0, a special server mode allows multiple incoming connections on the same TCP or UDP port, while still using different configuration for every single connection. Thus, only one port in the firewall has to be opened.
- OpenVPN has no problems with Network Address Translation (NAT) and hence can be employed in networks with private IP addresses.
- OpenVPN offers many possibilities to start individual scripts during connection setup. These scripts can be utilized for a great variety of purposes like authentication or failover.
- Both tunnel endpoints can have dynamic IP addresses.

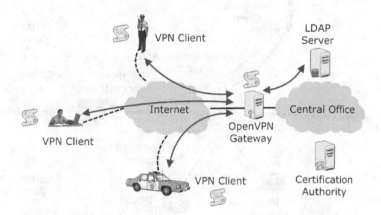

Fig. 3. Example of an OpenVPN network

Within the INDECT system, users will employ mainly OpenVPN to securely communicate between their remote terminals (desktop, laptop, tablet, smartphone, etc.) and servers located in the police headquarters (see Fig. 3). The INDECT Devices CA will be employed to authenticate the individual terminals.

To improve the security, so-called two-factor authentication mechanism can be employed. In that case, the user certificate is stored in a smart card or USB cryptographic token. Such a solution provides a strong user authentication, because the user needs to have the authenticator (smart card or USB token) and, concurrently, needs to know the password which protects the stored certificate from misusage.

To use these advanced authentication mechanisms, two open-source software packages exist that enable working with them – OpenSC and OpenCT. OpenSC [12] provides a set of libraries and utilities to work with smart cards and USB tokens. Its main focus is on authenticators that support cryptographic operations, and facilitate their use in security applications such as authentication, mail encryption and digital signatures. OpenSC implements the PKCS#11 API, so applications supporting this API (such as Mozilla Firefox and Thunderbird) can use it. On the card side, OpenSC implements the PKCS#15 standard and aims to be compatible with every software or card that does so too. OpenCT [13] implements drivers for several smart card readers and USB tokens. OpenCT also has a primitive mechanism to export smart card readers to remote devices via TCP/IP.

5.2   IPsec VPNs

The StrongSwan software package [14] provides an open-source IPsec VPN solution. StrongSwan is intended primarily for Linux devices. It is fully compatible with other standard IPsec VPN implementations, and thus can be used in networks with mixed equipment (see Fig. 4).

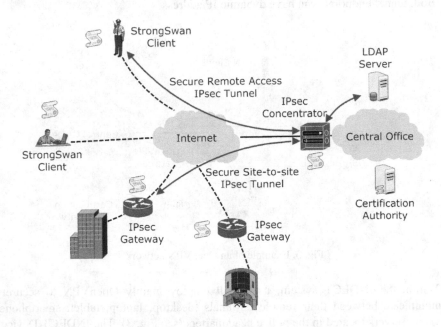

Fig. 4. IPsec VPN with StrongSwan clients

The main benefits of StrongSwan IPsec VPNs are as follows:

- StrongSwan supports various popular platforms – computers with Linux, Mac OS X, or FreeBSD operating systems; smartphones with the Android operating system.
- StrongSwan implements both IKEv1 and IKEv2 (Internet Key Exchange) protocols, and it fully supports IPv6.
- StrongSwan enables dynamic IP addresses and interface updates with IKEv2 Mobility and Multihoming Protocol, and IKEv2 Multiple Authentication Exchanges.
- It allows the automatic insertion and deletion of IPsec policy-based firewall rules.
- StrongSwan supports NAT-Traversal via UDP encapsulation and port floating.
- The XAUTH functionality is based on IKEv1 Main Mode authentication.

- The device authentication is based on X.509 certificates or pre-shared keys.
- StrongSwan enables secure IKEv2 EAP (Extensible Authentication Protocol) user authentication.
- RSA private keys and certificates can be stored on smart cards or USB tokens supporting the PKCS #11 interface.

5.3   Future Work

The next step to achieve secure data communication via VPNs within the INDECT system is to evaluate the security and reliability of the proposed solutions in specific cases. Further, it is necessary to assess the compatibility of the proposed solutions in relation to the current solutions that are employed by the end users of the INDECT project (e.g., compatibility tests of IPsec tunnels based on StrongSwan and implementations based on commercial products). We also need to test cooperation of VPNs with other components of the INDECT Security Architecture in different situations and under different conditions.

6   Federated Identity Management

Federated ID management could greatly simplify all user-related security issues, such as authentication, authorization and auditing, by providing a common user management service to a set of cooperating organizations, usually called *circle of trust*.

In a Federated ID management system, all user-related information is centralized in the Identity Provided (IdP), so the Service Providers (SPs) does not have to manage any user information but just authenticate their users and obtain user information through the Identity Provider. This process is more secure, since users only need a single set of credentials. Moreover, it also enables the so called Single Sign-On (SSO), since users only have to authenticate once with the trusted IdP and then they can access any Federated Service Provider immediately, without any further authentication.

The proposed INDECT Security Architecture also includes Federated ID management functionalities, by means of the INDECT Portal that will act as the Identity Provider of INDECT users. Since all users have X.509 certificates (issued by the INDECT PKI and stored in Smart Cards), and the INDECT Portal is a secure (i.e. HTTPS) web server, users can securely log into the INDECT Portal using the TLS/SSL mutual authentication mechanisms, and therefore employing a secure two-factor authentication process.

Web-based applications can then act as Federated Service Identity Providers, and authenticate their users though the INDECT Portal (i.e. Identity Provider). For legacy applications that do not support Federated ID management, an LDAP user directory has been also deployed, which stores the credentials (i.e. login/password) and additional information of all Police users to ease its management.

Although Federated ID Management may also enable inter-organization cooperation, in this case the INDECT Security Architecture only applies to a single LEA. Given the different national legislations and specific LEA regulations, inter-LEA cooperation is not just a technical issue but a procedural one, and thus is out of the scope of this paper.

7   Conclusions

This paper has presented an integrated security architecture to allow European Law Enforcement Agencies (LEAs) to employ the novel tools and applications being developed by the INDECT project in a secure and reliable way. By providing common security services such as Federated ID management, it will be much easier to integrate new investigation tools into existing Police ICT systems, since it is only necessary to integrate the appropriate security service, instead of adapting each separate application. It is also worth noting that the proposed INDECT Security Architecture also considers legacy applications, which enables current Police ICT systems to be integrated into the proposed security architecture.

In particular, this paper has studied in detail the different security infrastructures, mechanisms and protocols that provide the main security services of such architecture. For instance, it has overviewed the novel cryptographic algorithms developed by INDECT project: the INDECT Block Cipher (IBC), the INDECT Stream Cipher (ISC), the INDECT Hash Function (IHF), as well as an analysis of the security level provided by quantum key distribution protocols.

One of the key characteristics of this architecture is the widespread usage of digital certificates to authenticate users and devices and to establish secure communications among them. Therefore the INDECT Public Key Infrastructure (PKI) is one of the main components of this solution. The INDECT PKI has a hierarchical structure with cross-certification, which enables all INDECT users and devices to be securely associated with an asymmetric key pair by means of digital certificates. Moreover, multi-factor authentication is supported by storing users' certificates in Smart Cards.

Secure communications are implemented by means of standard security protocols such as Virtual Private Networks (VPNs), supporting both SSL- and IPSec-based VPNs, and Transport Layer Security (TLS) that also leverages the digital certificates issued by the INDECT PKI for mutual authentication. The proposed INDECT Security Architecture also considers Federated ID Management. The INDECT Portal will act as the Identity Provider (IdP) of all INDECT users, while federated-enabled INDECT subsystems will act as Service Providers (SPs), benefiting from a centralized and secure user authentication, as well as Single Sign-On (SSO) capabilities.

Acknowledgements. This work has been funded by the EU Project INDECT (Intelligent information system supporting observation, searching and detection for security of citizens in urban environment) — grant agreement number: 218086.

References

1. INDECT Project, http://www.indect-project.eu (accessed: February 1, 2013)
2. Urueña, M., Machník, P., Martínez, M.J., Niemiec, M., Stoianov, N.: INDECT Advanced Security Requirements. In: IEEE Multimedia Communications, Services and Security, MCSS 2010, Krakow, Poland, May 6-7 (2010)
3. Stoianov, N., Urueña, M., Niemiec, M., Machník, P., Maestro, G.: Security infrastructures: Towards the INDECT system security. In: Dziech, A., Czyżewski, A. (eds.) MCSS 2012. CCIS, vol. 287, pp. 304–315. Springer, Heidelberg (2012)
4. INDECT Consortium. D8.7: Definition of mechanisms and procedures for the security and privacy of the exchanged information (January 2013)
5. Niemiec, M., Machowski, Ł.: A new symmetric block cipher based on key-dependent S-boxes. In: International Congress on Ultra Modern Telecommunications and Control Systems, ICUMT 2012, Saint Petersburg, Russia, October 3-5 (2012)
6. Niemiec, M., Pach, A.R.: The measure of security in quantum cryptography. In: IEEE Global Telecommunications Conference, GLOBECOM 2012, Anaheim, USA, December 3-7 (2012)
7. Niemiec, M., Romański, Ł., Święty, M.: Quantum cryptography protocol simulator. In: Dziech, A., Czyżewski, A. (eds.) MCSS 2011. CCIS, vol. 149, pp. 286–292. Springer, Heidelberg (2011)
8. Adams, C., Lloyd, S.: Understanding PKI: Concepts, Standards, and Deployment Considerations, 2nd edn. Addison Wesley (2002) ISBN: 0-672-32391-5
9. EJBCA PKI, http://ejbca.org (accessed: February 1, 2013)
10. OpenVPN, http://openvpn.net/index.php/open-source.html (accessed: February 1, 2013)
11. Failner, M., Graf, N.: Beginning OpenVPN 2.0.9. Packt Publishing, Birmingham (2009)
12. OpenSC, https://github.com/OpenSC/OpenSC/wiki (accessed: February 1, 2013)
13. OpenCT, https://github.com/OpenSC/openct/wiki (accessed: February 1, 2013)
14. StrongSwan, http://www.strongswan.org (accessed: February 1, 2013)

Comparison of Different Feature Types
for Acoustic Event Detection System

Eva Kiktova, Martin Lojka, Matus Pleva,
Jozef Juhar, and Anton Cizmar

Technical University of Kosice
Dept. of Electronics and Multimedia Communications, FEI TU Kosice
Park Komenskeho 13, 041 20 Kosice, Slovak Republic
{eva.kiktova,martin.lojka,matus.pleva,jozef.juhar,anton.cizmar}@tuke.sk
http://kemt.fei.tuke.sk

Abstract. With the increasing use of audio sensors in surveillance or
monitoring applications, the detection of acoustic event performed in a
real condition has emerged as a very important research problem. This
paper is focused on the comparison of different feature extraction algorithms which were used for the parametric representation of the foreground and background sounds in a noisy environment. Our aim was to
automatically detect shots and sounds of breaking glass in different SNR
conditions. The well known feature extraction method like Mel-frequency
cepstral coefficients (MFCC) and other effective spectral features such
as logarithmic Mel-filter bank coefficients (FBANK) and Mel-filter bank
coefficients (MELSPEC) were extracted from an input sound. Hidden
Markov model (HMM) based learning technique performs the classification of mentioned sound categories.

Keywords: Feature extraction, acoustic event detection, SNR, HMM.

1 Introduction

The acoustic event detection is currently a very attractive research domain. It
used knowledge from different scientific areas such as pattern recognition, machine learning, signal processing, artificial intelligence, etc. The term of acoustic
event denotes the specific sound category, which is relevant for the particular
task. It usually has a rare occurrence and it is hard to predict when and whether
it occurs. This paper is focused on two sound classes, i.e. gun shot and breaking
glass. These sounds are relevant for security applications and they belong to the
foreground sounds, which appointed to an abnormal situation. In normal conditions, the foreground sounds do not occur, but when they occur, it probably
determines some criminal activity. The intelligent security (or surveillance) system works according to the given instructions and it is not influenced or limited
by various factors, not as a human. It should work autonomously and generate
alert only when some dangerous situation is detected. It should also provide a
constantly support for a police operator. The detection of acoustic events is a
partial task in the complex security system [1].

A. Dziech and A. Czyżewski (Eds.): MCSS 2013, CCIS 368, pp. 288–297, 2013.

As was indicated in previous paragraph, the detection of acoustic event in real condition is a challenging task [2], [3], [4]. An unstable background sound, different weather conditions, changing values of SNR and many similar noisy non-event sounds (like trucks, trams, etc.) limit the performance of each security system. In this paper we investigated the impact of very important limiting factor- the noise level measured as Signal-to-Noise-Ratio (SNR).

Different types of audio features (MELSPEC, FBANK and MFCC) [5] and HMM prototypes (different number of states) were tested and finally we identified the suitable parametric representation. Events and background sounds were modeled using well known Hidden Markov Models (HMMs). Their number of states and topology (mainly ergodic) were based on the experiments.

The rest of the paper has the following structure: Section 2. presents the motivation and related works. Section 3. gives information about applied feature extraction methods and Section 4. gives information about the used part of sound database. Section 5. describes performed experiments and Section 6. summarizes obtained results, then follows the conclusion is Section 7.

2   Motivation and Related Works

Many algorithms can be used for the extraction of relevant features [6], [9]. They describe the nature of input sounds in the time, spectral, cepstral or some other transformation domain. MPEG-7 descriptors [8], speech inspired features [11], [12] are used very often. Some works contain the description of the acoustic event detection for surveillance applications, e.g. [2], [3].

Our previous works are focused on the feature extraction, which combines different approaches with the respect to the on-line applicable post-processing of features [6], [7] or another work which describes the long term monitoring performed by our own detector, which is based on the modified approach to detection of decision point, when it is located inside decoder (without any dependency on the front-end) [4].

Our proposed solution of the intelligent audio surveillance system has a promising results for a long-term audio-events monitoring application.

3   Feature Extraction

The feature extraction is a crucial aspect for each detection system, because the recognition performance depends on the quality of extracted feature vectors. In this work Mel-frequency cepstral coefficients (MFCC), Log Mel-filter bank coefficients (FBANK) and Mel-filter bank coefficients (MELSPEC) were used [11], [12]. Their computation process is described below.

The ear's perception of frequency components in the audio signal does not follow the linear scale, but rather the Mel-frequency scale which should be understood as a linear frequency spacing below 1 kHz and logarithmic spacing above 1 kHz. So filters spaced linearly at a low frequency and logarithmic at high frequencies can be used to capture the phonetically important characteristics. The relation between the Mel-frequency and the frequency is given by the formula:

$$Mel(f) = 2595 \times log_{10}\left(1 + \frac{f}{700}\right) \tag{1}$$

where f is frequency in Hertz. MFCC, FBANK and MELSPEC coefficients are computed according to the Fig. 1.

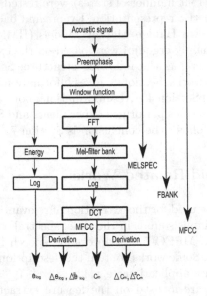

Fig. 1. Principial block scheme of MELPSEC, FBANK and MFCC coefficients

Normally, signal is filtered using preemphasis filter then the 25ms Hamming window method was applied on the frames. Then, they are transformed to the frequency domain via the discrete Fast Fourier Transform (FFT), and the magnitude spectrum is passed through a bank of triangular shaped filters. After this step we have MELSPEC features. The energy output from each filter is then log-compressed and represent FBANK features. Finally MFCC coefficients were obtained after the transformation to the cepstral domain by the Discrete Cosine Transform (DCT).

As it was described earlier the MELSPEC coefficients represent linear Mel-filter bank channel outputs and FBANK coefficients are logarithmic Mel-filter bank channel outputs. Mentioned features are computed during the extraction of popular MFCC coefficients.

4   Acoustic Event Database

The extended acoustic events database JDAE TUKE [10] used in this work involved the gun shot recordings with 463 realisations of shots from commonly used weapons, breaking glass recordings with 150 realizations of broken glass and background recording (traffic sounds) with the duration of 53 minutes.

SNR influence was investigated on the recordings with different levels of SNR (Signal Noise Ratio). Nine new recordings (approximately 53 min) with different SNR i.e. -3dB, 0dB, 3dB, 6dB, 8dB, 11dB, 14dB, 17dB, 20dB were created and used in the training process. In the testing phase 33 min recordings with different SNR were recognised. They contained two series of continuous gun shots and two series of continuous breaking glass events. Shots and breaking glass sounds formed one class i.e. the acoustic events class, so they were evaluated together.

Background recordings include traffic sound, car honks, singing birds, and other loud sounds. All recordings have wav format with 48 kHz sampling frequency, resolution 16 bits per sample. They were cut and manually labeled using Transcriber[1].

5 Description of Experiments

Many internal experiments with speech based features such as Mel-Frequency Cepstral Coefficients (MFCC), Perceptual Linear Prediction (PLP), Linear Prediction Coefficients (LPC) and Linear Prediction Cepstral Coefficients (LPCC) were done. Relatively good results were obtained by MFCC coefficients, which achieved better recognition performance than the rest of the mentioned parametrization approaches. Features were extracted with 25 ms of Hamming window and 10 ms of frame step. 22 Mel-filter were used and the final number of coefficients was set to 12 (or 13 when using also energy or zero cepstral coefficient). Each acoustic HMM model was evaluated by the classifier based on the Viterbi decoder. Experiments presented in this paper were performed in HTK (Hidden markov model ToolKit) environment [5].

For this reason we decided to investigate MFCC approach more precisely. We evaluated different settings of MFCC with, zero cepstral coefficient (0), energy (E), delta (D), acceleration (A) coefficients and with or without cepstral mean normalisation (Z).

Generally the presence of energy E or 0th coefficient brought significant improvement in the relatively quiet environment without any louder sounds and with stable value of SNR. But, it is very difficult to restrict louder sounds and to have appropriate level of SNR in a real environment.

First and second time derivations of the baseline coefficients expanded feature vectors from 12 to 36 coefficients (or 13 to 39). The derivated coefficients had positive impact for each tested scenario. Generally speaking, also HMMs with higher number of PDFs achieved significant improvements.

Acoustic models trained with MFCC_EDA or MFCC_0DA features have in a testing process low detection performance because tested input sound had SNR ratio between -3dB and 20dB. These models were successfully applied only for particular SNR value of analysed audio signals.

---

[1] http://trans.sourceforge.net/

Cepstral mean normalisation (CMN) [5], [9] is very effective for the recognition performed in a noisy environment and it is de facto standard operation for most large vocabulary speech recognition systems. The CMN algorithm computes a long-term mean value of the feature vectors and subtracts the mean value from the all feature vectors. CMN reduces the variability of the data and allows simple but effective feature normalization. CMN in HTK is realized by the optional value "Z" [5].

On the basis of promising results with MFCC_DAZ, we decide to investigate also features, which were obtained before final feature set. Therefore MEL-SPEC_DAZ and FBANK_DAZ were extracted too.

In this work, two different system architectures were analysed. First is based on the HMM models for shots, glass and several backgrounds, see Fig. 2. We used a separate background model for each SNR value. In these experiments ergodic HMMs from one to four states and from 1 to 1024 Probability Density Functions (PDFs) were trained and evaluated in offline tests.

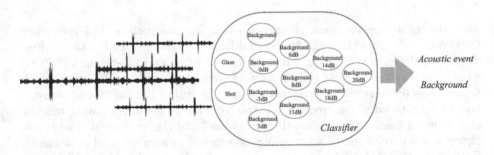

Fig. 2. Description of first detection system scheme

We considered also the second system architecture, which is based only on the one HMM for background. The rest of background models were not applied in the testing process. Models for shots and glass were the same. The principal scheme of this approach is depicted in the Fig. 3.

6   Results of Experiments

Three types of features MELSPEC_DAZ, FBANK_DAZ and MFCC_DAZ were used for the evaluation of the proposed robust system. We supposed that several background models will by more suitable for recognition of acoustic events in different SNR conditions. The testing set consisted from 9 recordings, more details are available in the Section 4. Obtained results of experiments is depicted in the Fig.4, where the results were averaged for each model type using widely used Accuracy measurement technique [5], [6].

The approach based on the MFCC_DAZ parametrization achieved results higher than 75% only in the two cases, i.e. ACC = 76,67% was achieved by four states HMM with 1 PDF (HMM_4_1) and ACC = 75,56% with HMM_3_1.

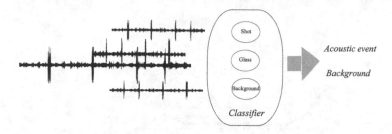

Fig. 3. Description of second detection system scheme

FBANK_DAZ features obtained promising results. The accuracy higher then 75% were achieved nine times. The highest value of ACC=87,78% was reached by HMM_1_32, second best results ACC=86,67% belonged to HMM_3_1.

Like a previous case, MELSPEC_DAZ features were evaluated by the same way. Four times ACC higher then 75% were yielded. The best MELSPEC models HMM_1_64 achieved 80% ACC.

Generally suitable results were yielded by FBANK features, otherwise MFCC features seem to be the less appropriate. As it was mentioned, the results from Fig. 4 are averaged.

More detailed information about SNR impact for selected best models that yielded three highest ACC [%] (based form Fig. 4) will be presented in details for first system architecture in Fig. 5 and for second architecture in Fig.6.

The Fig.5 depicted the obtained results for system with several background models and Fig.6 refers to the system with one background model.

As you can see in the Fig.5 and Fig.6 many models had the same performance. From this point of wiev the presence of several models was not as important as we supposed. The CMN operation as a partial operation in the feature extraction process fixed the SNR problem very effective way.

- **The first system architecture with several SNR background models (Fig.5)**
  Perfect recognition results only for MELSPEC_DAZ were reached. Recordings with SNR 20dB, 17dB, 14dB were recognised overall seven times with ACC = 100% with using HMM_1_32, HMM_1_64 PDFs and HMM_1_128 PDFs. In the cases of very noisy conditions (SNR = -3 dB, 0dB) one state MELSPEC_DAZ models failed. These models achieved the lowest values of ACC = 40%. FBANK_DAZ models detected events in range of 80% to 90% of ACC. MFCC_DAZ models achieved lower ACC values.

- **The second system architecture with one background model (Fig.6)**
  The proposed system worked similarly as in the case of several background models. The perfect recognition result of ACC=100% was achieved nine times only for MELSPEC_DAZ approach. HMM_1_64 correctly recognised testing recordings with SNR 11dB, 14dB, 17dB and 20dB. Good performances were achieved also by MELSPEC_DAZ HMM_1_32 for recordings with SNR 14dB, 17dB, 20dB and HMM_1_128 for SNR 17dB and 20dB.

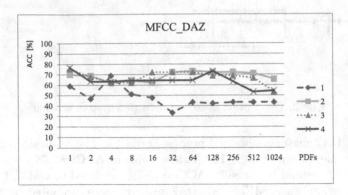

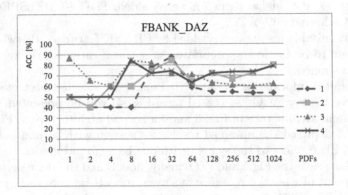

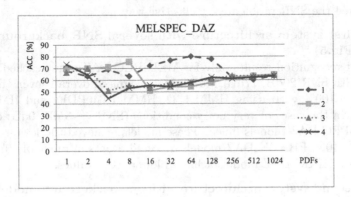

Fig. 4. The recognition results of average ACC [%] for each parametrization, (number of HMM states is depicted in legend)

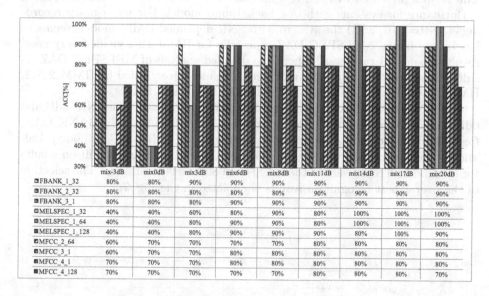

	mix-3dB	mix0dB	mix3dB	mix6dB	mix8dB	mix11dB	mix14dB	mix17dB	mix20dB
FBANK_1_32	80%	80%	90%	90%	90%	90%	90%	90%	90%
FBANK_2_32	80%	80%	80%	80%	80%	90%	90%	90%	90%
FBANK_3_1	80%	80%	80%	90%	90%	90%	90%	90%	90%
MELSPEC_1_32	40%	40%	60%	80%	90%	80%	100%	100%	100%
MELSPEC_1_64	40%	40%	80%	90%	90%	80%	100%	100%	100%
MELSPEC_1_128	40%	40%	80%	90%	90%	90%	80%	100%	90%
MFCC_2_64	60%	70%	70%	70%	70%	80%	80%	80%	80%
MFCC_3_1	60%	70%	70%	80%	80%	80%	80%	80%	80%
MFCC_4_1	70%	70%	70%	80%	80%	80%	80%	80%	80%
MFCC_4_128	70%	70%	70%	70%	70%	80%	80%	80%	70%

Fig. 5. The recognition results of ACC [%] for selected HMMs (several background models)

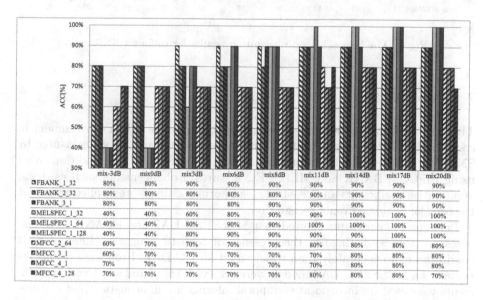

	mix-3dB	mix0dB	mix3dB	mix6dB	mix8dB	mix11dB	mix14dB	mix17dB	mix20dB
FBANK_1_32	80%	80%	90%	90%	90%	90%	90%	90%	90%
FBANK_2_32	80%	80%	80%	80%	80%	90%	90%	90%	90%
FBANK_3_1	80%	80%	80%	80%	90%	90%	90%	90%	90%
MELSPEC_1_32	40%	40%	60%	80%	90%	90%	100%	100%	100%
MELSPEC_1_64	40%	40%	80%	90%	90%	100%	100%	100%	100%
MELSPEC_1_128	40%	40%	80%	90%	90%	90%	90%	100%	100%
MFCC_2_64	60%	70%	70%	70%	70%	80%	80%	80%	80%
MFCC_3_1	60%	70%	70%	70%	70%	70%	80%	80%	80%
MFCC_4_1	70%	70%	70%	70%	70%	70%	80%	80%	80%
MFCC_4_128	70%	70%	70%	70%	70%	80%	80%	80%	70%

Fig. 6. The recognition results of ACC [%] for selected HMMs (one background model)

The results presented in the Fig.5 and the Fig.6 appointed better recognition performance for systems with one background model. For more noisy recordings (SNR= 6dB, 8dB) the system with SNR depended HMM models seems to be slightly better. MELSPEC_DAZ especially for HMM_1_64 yielded very good results when SNR ratio was higher. The detailed analysis of MELSPEC_DAZ results showed that other perfect recognition results were yielded by HMM_2_512, HMM_2_1024 and HMM_3_512 for SNR= 3dB, 6dB and 8dB.

Other MELSPEC_DAZ models reached usually ACC=40% for SNR -3dB and 0dB, therefore we analysed other approaches (MFCC_DAZ and FBANK_DAZ) for finding the most suitable models regarding to the SNR (-3dB and 0dB). Balanced results were achieved by the FBANK_DAZ where the recognition results for low and high SNR were in the range from 80% to 90% of ACC. The selection of the overall best recognition results is depicted in the Fig. 7.

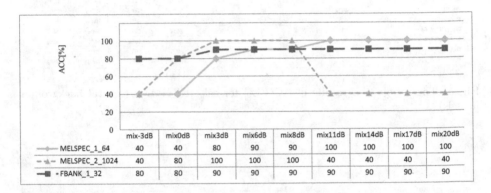

	mix-3dB	mix0dB	mix3dB	mix6dB	mix8dB	mix11dB	mix14dB	mix17dB	mix20dB
MELSPEC_1_64	40	40	80	90	90	100	100	100	100
MELSPEC_2_1024	40	80	100	100	100	40	40	40	40
FBANK_1_32	80	80	90	90	90	90	90	90	90

Fig. 7. The best achieved recognition results for different SNR ratio

7   Conclusion

This paper evaluated the acoustic event detection in the urban environment in consideration of the very important limiting factor - the noise level measured by SNR. We analysed the detection performance for different SNR conditions with using MFCC, FBANK and MELSPEC features. Enhancements such as delta, acceleration coefficients and cepstral mean normalisation were applied as robust features for acoustic events recognition.

Performed experiments showed that MELSPEC_DAZ and FBANK_DAZ features are able to distinguish the presence of acoustic events in different SNR conditions more accurately than widely used MFCC_DAZ. Promising results especially for MELSPEC_DAZ models were achieved. Delta and acceleration coefficients were used for incorporate temporal information in acoustic event features and cepstral mean normalisation contributed apparently to the robustness of created acoustic models.

Acknowledgments. This work has been performed partially in the framework of the EU ICT Project INDECT (FP7 - 218086) and by the Ministry of Education of Slovak Republic under research VEGA 1/0386/12 and under research project ITMS-26220220155 supported by the Research & Development Operational Programme funded by the ERDF.

References

1. INDECT project homepage, http://www.indect-project.eu/
2. Clavel, C., Ehrette, T., Richard, G.: Events Detection for an Audio-Based Surveillance System. In: IEEE International Conference on Multimedia and Expo. 2005, pp. 1306–1309 (2005)
3. Atrey, P.K., Maddage, N.C., Kankanhalli, M.S.: Audio Based Event Detection for Multimedia Surveillance. In: IEEE International Conference on Acoustics, Speech and Signal Processing 2006, vol. 5, pp. 813–816 (2006)
4. Pleva, M., Lojka, M., Juhar, J., Vozarikova, E.: Evaluating the Modified Viterbi Decoder for Long-Term Audio Events Monitoring Task. In: 54th International Symposium Croatian Society Electronics in Marine - Elmar, pp. 179–182 (2012)
5. Young, S., et al.: The HTK Book, p. 368. Cambridge University (2006)
6. Vozarikova, E., Lojka, M., Juhar, J., Cizmar, A.: Performance of Basic Spectral Descriptors and MRMR Algorithm to the Detection of Acoustic Events. In: Dziech, A., Czyżewski, A. (eds.) MCSS 2012. CCIS, vol. 287, pp. 350–359. Springer, Heidelberg (2012)
7. Vozáriková, E., Juhár, J., Čižmár, A.: Acoustic Events Detection Using MFCC and MPEG-7 Descriptors. In: Dziech, A., Czyżewski, A. (eds.) MCSS 2011. CCIS, vol. 149, pp. 191–197. Springer, Heidelberg (2011)
8. Kim, H.G., Moreau, N., Sikora, T.: MPEG-7 audio and beyond: Audio content indexing and retrieval, p. 304. Wiley (2005)
9. Toh, A.M., Togneri, R., Nordhoolm, S.: Investigation of Robust Features for Speech Recognition in Hostile Environments. In: Asia-Pacific Conference on Communications 2005, pp. 956–960 (2005)
10. Pleva, M., Vozarikova, E., Dobos, L., Cizmar, A.: The joint database of audio events and backgrounds for monitoring of urban areas. Journal of Electrical and Electronics Engineering 4(1), 185–188 (2011)
11. Psutka, J., Müller, L., Psutka, J.V.: Comparison of MFCC and PLP parametrizations in the speaker independent continuous speech recognition task. In: Eurospeech 2001, pp. 1813–1816 (2001)
12. Wong, E., Sridharan, S.: Comparison of linear prediction cepstrum coefficients and mel-frequency cepstrum coefficients for language identification. In: International Symposium on Intelligent Multimedia, Video and Speech Processing, pp. 95–98 (2001)

New Robust Video Watermarking Techniques Based on DWT Transform and Spread Spectrum of Basis Images of 2D Hadamard Transform[*]

Jakob Wassermann

Dep. of Electronic Engineering
University of Applied Sciences Technikum Wien
Hoechstaedplatz 5, 1200 Wien
jakob.wassermann@technikum.at

Abstract. This paper presents a new approach for watermarking of digital video providing robustness against MPEG compression. The initial video is decomposed by one-dimensional 2 Level Wavelet Transform. The low pass filtered LL video stream is used for embedding the procedure. Every frame of this sequence undergoes a 16x16 block wise DCT before the embedding procedure is applied on selected coefficients of the spectrum. The embedding algorithm itself is realized by spread spectrum techniques. The watermark bits are substituted by a set of 16 basis images of 2D-Hadamard Transform of the block size 8x8. Instead of embedding 1 or 0 of the watermark the corresponding pattern of basis images are embedded by spread spectrum routine into the selected coefficients of DCT spectrum. The experimental results show that this method seems to be very robust against MPEG compression, adding noise and obtaining low degradation of the host sequence.

Keywords: Videowatermarking, DWT, Hadamard Transform, DCT, Spread Spectrum.

1 Introduction

Rapid development of internet and social networks like Facebook or Flickr give rise to the challenge how to protect intellectual properties of multimedia data against illegal usage or tempering. Copyright protection and content authentication are now a day one of the most important issues of Multimedia Industry. Two main technologies have been established to reach these goals: cryptology and watermarking. In the cryptographic approach the multimedia data are encrypted and only a holder of valid key is able to access them. One big disadvantage of this technology is the fact that when data have been encrypted, there is no way to track their distribution and reproduction.

---

[*] This research was supported by European Commission FP7Grant INDECT Project. No.FP7-218086.

A. Dziech and A. Czyżewski (Eds.): MCSS 2013, CCIS 368, pp. 298–308, 2013.

The watermark technology can avoid these disadvantages [1],[2]. The main problem of watermarking consists of the ability to embed the watermark into host signal in such way that it will be invisible or at least will not produce serious degradation of the host. The second important property of the watermarking system should be the robustness against any manipulation of the host signal. The watermark should be able to survive any attacks like compression, scaling, noise, compression etc.

To realize such properties there are two strategies how the embedding procedure should be done. One strategy is oriented in the embedding watermarks into the spatial and the other into the frequency domain. In the spatial domain the Quantization Index Modulation (QIM) method [3] is very popular and in spectral domain the spread spectrum technology [4]. As a transform domain the DCT is well established [5] but also other transforms like wavelet have been investigated [6].

In this paper a new scheme for watermarking based on Discrete Wavelet Transform (DWT)for video sequencesis introduced, where the embedding procedure of watermarks is realized by using basis images of Hadamard transform and spread spectrum Modulation.

2   Basis Images of Orthogonal Transform

Every orthogonal transform possesses so called basis functions. In case of 2D transform they are called basis or eigen images. An example ofbasis images of the block size 4x4 is depicted in Figure 1.

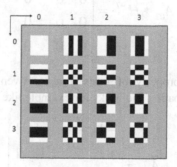

Fig. 1. Basis images of 2D (4x4) Walsh-Hadamard Transform

These basis images are orthogonal to each other and their numerical representation could be generated from 1D Hadamard matrix (1).

$$H = \begin{pmatrix} 1 & 1 & 1 & 1 \\ 1 & -1 & 1 & -1 \\ 1 & 1 & -1 & -1 \\ 1 & -1 & -1 & 1 \end{pmatrix} \tag{1}$$

The corresponding matrix of the basis image A_{02} is depicted in the Figure 2.

$$A_{02} = \begin{pmatrix} -1 & -1 & 1 & 1 \\ -1 & -1 & 1 & 1 \\ -1 & -1 & 1 & 1 \\ -1 & -1 & 1 & 1 \end{pmatrix}$$

Fig. 2. Numerical and visual representation of the basis Image A_{02} of Hadamard Transform

The 2D Hadamard Transform of basis image A_{02} delivers a spectrum C where only the coefficient C_{02} is unequal to zero ($|C_{02}| = 16$).

$$C = H * A_{02} * H^{-T} = \begin{pmatrix} 0 & 0 & -16 & 0 \\ 0 & 0 & 0 & 0 \\ 0 & 0 & 0 & 0 \\ 0 & 0 & 0 & 0 \end{pmatrix} \tag{2}$$

This is the orthogonal property of basis images. Even if the basis image A_{02} is corrupted by some perturbation and looks for example like

$$\tilde{A}_{02} = \begin{pmatrix} -1 & -1 & -1 & 1 \\ -1 & 1 & 1 & 1 \\ -1 & -1 & 1 & 1 \\ 1 & -1 & 1 & 1 \end{pmatrix}$$

the absolute value of C_{02}($|C_{02}| = 10$) remains the biggest between the other spectral coefficients of C.

$$C = H * \tilde{A}_{02} * H^{-T} = \begin{pmatrix} 2 & -2 & -10 & 2 \\ -2 & -6 & 2 & -2 \\ -2 & -2 & -2 & 2 \\ -6 & -2 & 2 & 6 \end{pmatrix}$$

Fig. 3. Hadamard Transform of corrupted Matrix $\tilde{A}_{02}$

This fact can be utilized to create a new scheme for watermarking of an embedding procedure that could be more robust against different kinds of perturbations. In this case the Hadamard Transform conduces as an error correcting code.

3 Application of Basis Images in the Embedding Procedure of Watermarks

The fact that the spectrum of basis images is robust against the noise can be utilized for the embedding procedure of watermarking. For example following set up for the watermarking coding could be used: watermark value "1" can be dedicated to the basis image A_{01} and the watermark value "0" to the basis image A_{10}. Such code book is depicted in Table 1. Such scheme seems to be uneconomic, because to embed one bit of watermark requires spending 16 bits of the host image. To make it work more efficiently all 16 basis images of the Hadamard transform can be used. But in this case the increasing numbers of basis images will reduce the robustness and increase the sensitivity towards noise and other perturbations of the system. This fact is well known as a Hamming distance in the information theory.

Table 1. Simple Code Book for Watermarking

Watermark	Basis Image
1	
0	

The optimal code book will be a compromise between robustness and efficiency. In this paper the presented results have been done with 8 instead of 16 possible basis images of 4x4 Hadamard Transform. In this case 3 bits are coded with one basis image. The corresponding code book is depicted in Table 2.

Table 2. The 3 Bit Code Book with Basis Images

Watermark	Coefficientsof Hadamard Matrix	Basis Image
000	C_{02}	
Watermark	Coefficientsof Hadamard Matrix	Basis Image
001	C_{20}	
010	C_{01}	
011	C_{10}	
100	C_{12}	
101	C_{21}	
110	C_{13}	
111	C_{31}	

4   Proposed Watermarking Scheme

The proposed method combines the previously described coding of watermark bits with basis images ofHadamardTransform with Discrete Wavelet Transform (DWT) of video sequences. The luminance channel of the original video stream is decomposed by one dimensional 2 Level DWT into the low pass filtered LL video and two additional streams. The low pass filter is a simple averaging procedure and the high pass filter builds the difference between the frames.

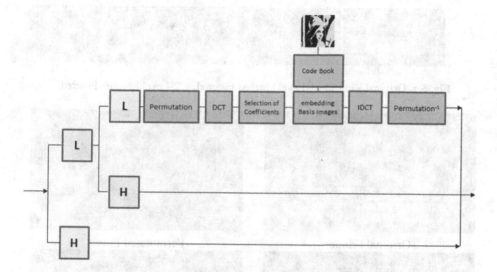

Fig. 4. Overall Watermarking Encoding Scheme with Basis Images

The LL low pass filtered stream is used for the watermarking embedding scheme. At the beginning every frame of this sequence is permutated before it undergoes block wise DCT. After this procedure special coefficients are selected from the DCT spectrum and the embedding procedure of the basis images is applied on them. It is done by modulation of the LSBs of spectral coefficients with values of basis images. In Figure 4 the whole encoding scheme is depicted. The 1- level and 2-level low pass video streams are shown in Figure 5.

The dedication between the watermarks and the basis images is done in the code book unit. The IDCT and inverse permutation complete the hiding procedure of the watermark in the LL lowpass video stream. Appling the inverse DWT on these three streams generates a watermarked video sequence.

The permutation has a big influence on the DCT spectrum and can increase the number of significant coefficients [6]. In Figure 6 this influence is illustrated. Without permutation the spectrum of the original frame has a visible structure. It is even possible to discover the outlines of the original image. In contrast the DCT spectrum ofpermutated frame looks like noise. The coefficients are distributed uniformly and they have more or less the same absolute values.

Fig. 5. a. Original Video, b. 1-Level lowpass Filtered, c. 2-Level lowpass Filtered.

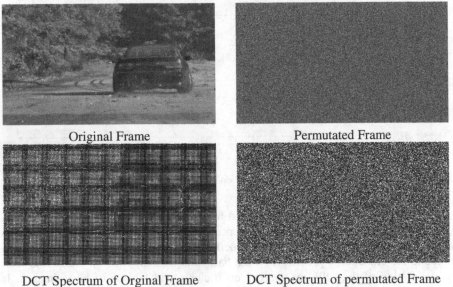

Original Frame   Permutated Frame

DCT Spectrum of Orginal Frame   DCT Spectrum of permutated Frame

Fig. 6. Block wise DCT Spectrum of Original and Permutated Frame

On the decoder´s side the received video undergoes the 2-level DWT Transform in order to get the 2-level lowpass filtered video stream. The further extraction procedures are depicted in Figure 7.

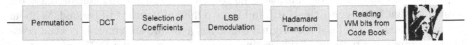

Fig. 7. Extraction Procedure

After a permutation and the block wise DCT the proper coefficients with the embedded information are selected. By demodulating their LSBs the values of the basis images are detected. Their identification is done by the Hadamard Transform coefficients. Afterwards the code book gives the information of the watermarks bit.

Selection of the Embedding Coefficients

To realize the watermarking embedding procedure some coefficients from the block wise DCT spectrum of the LL-filtered video frame should be selected. Because of the permutation, which is applied before DCT, the spectral significant coefficients are distributed uniformly(see Figure 6), actually they can be chosen freely. The experimental results show, that the best performance could be achieved with coefficients from the grey area (Coefficients Nos.:2,9,10, 17, 18: see Figure 8)

1	9	17	25	33	41	49	57
2	10	18	26	34	42	50	58
3	11	19	27	35	43	51	59
4	12	20	28	36	44	52	60
5	13	21	29	37	45	53	61
6	14	22	30	38	46	54	62
7	15	23	31	39	47	55	63
8	16	24	32	40	48	56	64

Fig. 8. The Ordering Structure of DCT Coefficients

The number of embedded coefficients determines the embedding data rate but impairs the quality of the image. The tradeoff between capacity and quality lies by two coefficients per block of 8x8 pixels(see chapter Results).

Quantization Procedure

To make the embedding procedure more robust against distortions and attacks the following quantization algorithm is proposed. Is the embedded value of the watermark "one" then the last 7 bits of the selected coefficientsare substituted by value 32. In case the watermark value is "zero" the last 7 bits of the selected coefficientsare substituted by value 96. The corresponding decoding process is very simple. By selecting the embedded coefficients out of the DCT spectrum, the last 7 bits are investigated. If the calculated value is inside the interval [0-64], "one" is detected. Otherwise (interval [65-128]) the detected value is "zero". The sign and the MSB of the selected coefficients were preserved.

5   Results

The investigation was done with raw video format and the resolution of 640*360 and 25fps. The watermarking processing was performed only for a luminance channel (after converting RGB into YCrCbcolorspace), because it is more robust against distortions, than any other channels. It was investigated the robustness against compression attacks. The degradation of the watermarked output video was measured with SSIM (Structural Similarity) index. SSIM is based on the human eye perception and so the expressiveness about distortion is better than in the traditional methods like PSNR (Peak Signal to Noise Ratio) or MSE (Mean Square Error) [8].

In Table 3 the results of capacity and robustness measurements are presented. The original video sequence "drift.avi" has a data rate of 10 Mbit/s in moving JPEG format (MJPEG). It was embedded with watermark data rate of 33.75 Kbit/s. This sequence was compressed by H.264 Codec with different compression ratios. Even by compression ratio of 1:10 (data rate 1 Mbit/s) the watermarks can be completely extracted with SSIM index of 1. The embedded video shows hardly any visible degradations and has SSIM of 0.8843. The artefacts are mostly induced by the compression itself rather than through embedding procedure (see Figure 10).

Table 3. Results of Robustness and Capacity investigation

Format	Video Data Rate	Number of Blocks per Frame	Number of embedded Coefficients	Embedded Data Rate	SSIM Video	SSIM Water-marking
MJPEG	10Mbit/s	3600	2	33.75Kbit/s	0.9843	1
H.264	1 Mbit/s	3600	2	33.75Kbit/s	0.8843	1
H.264	0.5Mbit/s	3600	2	33.75 Kbit/s	0.9012	0.8796

Fig. 9. Original Frame with 10 Mbit/sand Detailed View

Fig. 10. Embedded and compressed with H.264: 1 Mbit/s

Fig. 11. Embedded and compressed with H.264: 0.5 Mbit/s

The extracted watermarks from MJPEG and H.264 1Mbit/s streams are completely recovered without any errors. The watermark of H.264 stream of 0.5 Mbit/s is impaired by the compression procedure but is still well visible (see Figure 12).

MJPEG 10 Mbi	H.264 1Mbit/s	H.264 0.5 Mbit/s

Fig. 12. Extracted Watermarks after Compression

6   Conclusion

A new method for embedding watermarking into video sequences based on Discrete Wavelet Transform and basis images of Hadamard Transform was introduced. The robustness of this system was tested by compression attacks of H.264 codec. The embedded watermark data rate is 33.35 kBit/s. These data can be extracted completely from a 1 Mbit/s H.264 video stream. The embedded video has still a good quality with a SSIM value of 0.8843. By increasing the compression ratio to 1:20 (0.5 Mbit/s) the watermark can still be extracted with small degradations (SSIM 0.8796).

The method seems to be very promising, especially by introducing higher Level DWT decompositions and 3D basis images of Hadamard Transform the robustness could be further increased.

References

1. Hartung, F., Kutter, M.: Multimedia Watermarking Techniques. Proceeding of IEEE 87, 1079–1107 (1999)
2. Swanson, M.D., Kobayashi, M., Tewfik, A.H.: Multimedia Data-Embedding and Watermarking Technologies. Proceeding of IEEE 86, 1064–1087 (1998)
3. Chen, B., Wornell, G.W.: Quantization Index Modulation for Digital Watermarking and Information Embedding of Multimedia. Journal of VLSI Signal Processing 27, 7–33 (2001)
4. Cox, I.J., Killian, J., Leighton, F.T., Shammon, T.: Secure Spread Spectrum Watermarking for Multimedia. IEEE Transactions on Image Processing 6, 1673–1687 (1997)
5. Benham, D., Memon, N., Yeo, B.-L., Yeung, M.M.: Fast Watermarking of DCT-based compressed images. In: Proceeding of International Conference and Imaging Science, Systems and Applications, pp. 243–252.
6. Zhao, D., Chen, G., Liu, W.: A Chaos-Based Robust Wavelet-Domain Watermarking Algorithm. Chaos, Solutions and Fractals 22, 792 (2004)
7. Moulin, P., O'Sullivan, A.: Information-Theoretic Analysis of Information Hiding. IEEE Transaction of Information Theory 49(3), 563–593 (2003)

Practical Implementation of Visual Hash Functions for CCTV Footage Authentication

Katarzyna Żarnowiec, Paweł Korus, Andrzej Dziech, and Andrzej Głowacz

AGH University of Science and Technology
al. Mickiewicza 30, 30-059 Kraków, Poland
katarzyna.zarnowiec@gmail.com, {pkorus,aglowacz}@agh.edu.pl,
dziech@kt.agh.edu.pl

Abstract. This paper deals with practical implementation of semi-fragile watermarking for CCTV footage authentication. Despite the variety of available literature, certain important aspects remain unaddressed. The existing schemes are mostly evaluated against purely academic attacks, and the most practical attacks on information trust remain unaddressed. In this paper, we focus on the collage and the visually insignificant changes attacks, which are of critical importance in the video surveillance scenario. Based on a well-known robust hash function, we design three variants of a digital image authentication scheme. We show that the choice of the watermark embedding technique, although unaddressed in the literature, has critical influence on the tampering detection accuracy. Based on the performed evaluation, we also propose small modifications of the original algorithm, which lead to further improvement of the classification performance.

Keywords: image authentication, semi-fragile watermarking, video surveillance.

1 Introduction

Apart from purely functional requirements like usability or availability, trust is one of the most fundamental features of a video surveillance system. It determines the possibility of using the recorded footage as evidence. It is also one of the most elusive requirements as the prospective content forgeries are aimed at imitating the original content. Hence, the ability to authenticate the content of the captured footage is one of key features of a modern video surveillance system. The necessary law regulations which address the use of anti-tampering measures have already started to emerge. In Great Britain public CCTV cameras are required to protect their streams using digital watermarking [1, 16].

It is of high importance to start the protection process as close to information source as possible. Due to the fact that the transmitted footage is likely to undergo further processing, it is beneficial to employ authentication techniques which can discriminate between the allowed (e.g., compression) and disallowed processing (e.g., content replacement). This requirement is addressed by robust hash functions, which aim to capture the actual content represented by the

A. Dziech and A. Czyżewski (Eds.): MCSS 2013, CCIS 368, pp. 309–323, 2013.
© Springer-Verlag Berlin Heidelberg 2013

signal. The resulting hashes are usually calculated for individual image blocks in order to provide tampering localization capabilities. In practice, robust hash functions are often used in conjunction with traditional cryptographic hashes to further improve the tampering detection reliability. There also exist content reconstruction schemes, which allow for approximate recovery of the original appearance from before the malicious modifications [8, 13, 22]. Although due to limited embedding capacity of lossy-compressed media such schemes are often not used in practice, some early efforts in this direction have been made. The recently emerging flexible schemes are capable of high-quality reconstruction if the tampering affects only small image area [23]. Alternative adaptive schemes allow for high-quality reconstruction of selected image fragments, at the cost of the fidelity of the remaining background content [12].

The problem of content authentication has been widely addressed by the research community, and it is difficult not only to enumerate the existing schemes but even to provide a concise summary of available distinct approaches. A recent attempt to survey the existing techniques is available in [9]. Despite this huge amount of available publications, practical application of the described authentication schemes is still a daunting task. Even though many necessary algorithms are readily available, there is still a fair amount of design decisions which have not been addressed, especially with respect to integration issues. An additional problem is that very often the described algorithms are tested only against typically academic attack, many of which are not representative for practical use cases of the technology at hand.

The goal of this paper is to provide a case study of implementing robust hash functions for CCTV footage authentication. We consider the protection of a Motion JPEG stream, which is a common output format for many digital CCTV cameras. First, we briefly review the available robust hash functions. Then, based on a selected one, we develop three image authentication algorithms which represent different design decisions, which are not addressed in the available literature. We show that, apart from the utilized hashing algorithm, the choice of the watermark embedding function has significant impact on the authentication efficiency.

The performed evaluation focuses on two types of attacks, aiming at imitating legitimate surveillance footage, i.e., object removal, and modification of cars' license number plates. The latter is particularly important since it dramatically changes the semantics of the content, and can be virtually unnoticeable, both for a human eye, and for automatic number plate recognition software.

This paper is organized as follows. Section 2 summarizes the approaches of existing robust hash functions. Section 3 describes practical implementations of an authentication systems based on a selected robust hash function. The emphasis is on the design decisions that need to be made for their successful implementations. Section 4 discusses the considered attacks, and describes the evaluation scenario. Experimental evaluation results are presented and discussed in Section 5. Finally, we conclude in Section 6.

2   Overview of Robust Hash Functions

A general approach to content authentication is to calculate either cryptographic or robust hashes for individual blocks of the image. This hash is then either directly used as a digital watermark, or serves as a basis for its generation. At the decoder side, the hashes are recomputed and compared with the embedded ones, either via the introduced bit errors or by dedicated watermark detection functions.

Common use of block-based authentication schemes stems from the security concerns with respect to pixel-wise authentication [3, 10]. For authentication of video surveillance footage, the tampering identification accuracy on the level of individual image blocks is usually sufficient. In this section, we briefly review the available algorithms for calculation of robust visual hash functions. We aim to present the most diverse approaches. Then, based on a selected algorithm, we will develop a functional content authentication scheme.

In the robust hash function from [21], first a discrete wavelet transform (DWT) of the whole image is computed, then each subband is divided into small random rectangular tiles. In the next step, either their variances or mean values are computed, depending on the subband. In the final step, randomized rounding is performed on the statistics of each tile, and the hash value is obtained by feeding the randomized statistics to a decoder of an error correction code.

In [20] the authors propose a hashing algorithm, in which the original image is low-pass filtered and scaled to a specified size. After histogram equalization, a Fourier transform is calculated and translated to polar coordinates. A feature vector is formed by summing polar coefficients along consecutive azimuths. Unnecessary high frequency components are discarded, and the resulting feature vector is quantized and compressed to obtain the final, key dependent, robust hash.

In the algorithm from [17], the host image is randomly divided into blocks, and each block is then decomposed with a DWT. Significant regions are then determined by thresholding. Iterative filtering is applied to discard the regions with geometrically weak components and enhance the regions with geometrically strong components. Binary representations of the resulting blocks are randomly ordered into 1-dimensional vectors, and concatenated together. Finally, random projection of the vector is performed to yield the final robust hash.

The Fridrich-Goljan algorithm [5–7] is based on an observation that it is not possible to change visual content of the image without affecting significantly the magnitudes of low frequency DCT coefficients. The image is dived into 64×64 px blocks, and N random matrices $P_{64x64}^{(n)} \leftarrow U(0,1)$ are drawn from a uniform distribution on the range $(0, 1)$. Generation of the pseudo-random numbers is controlled by a secret key K. The resulting random patterns are then low-pass filtered, and the mean value is subtracted. The N bits of the robust hash, for each block B, are obtained by random projection of B on the random pattern $P^{(n)}$ $(1 \leq n \leq N)$. Absolute values of the projections are then compared with a threshold Th:

$$b_n = \begin{cases} 0 & \text{if } |BP^{(n)}| < Th \\ 1 & \text{if } |BP^{(n)}| \geq Th \end{cases}$$

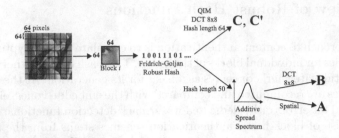

Fig. 1. The use of the robust hash by the considered variants of the authentication algorithm: A and B use spread spectrum embedding, C and C' use QIM

To achieve the highest information content of the hash, the threshold should be chosen to ensure a balance between the resulting zeros and ones.

All of the reviewed algorithms are robust to common image processing operations, such as JPEG compression, adding uniform noise, contrast and brightness enhancements, sharpening, blurring, histogram equalization, etc. Unfortunately, none is robust against geometric distortions such a rotation, cropping, shearing and shifting [5–7, 17, 20, 21].

3 Image Authentication Schemes

When implementing robust content authentication in a working system, there is a number of design decisions that need to be made in order to obtain a fully functional solution. Most of the decisions stem from the necessity to integrate different system components. It is important to ensure that the utilized information embedding algorithm has minimal impact on the hash calculation procedure. The choice of the watermarking algorithm will also impact the number of hash bits than should be produced.

We base the considered authentication scheme on the robust hash function by Fridrich and Goljan [6–8]. It is one of the best known algorithm for this purpose. Despite being thoroughly studied in independent research, some of the aspects of its practical implementation are still unaddressed. As a result, it is sometimes used in a suboptimal way, e.g., [4] uses a globally-determined threshold Th, which along with an insufficiently long (16-bit) hash vector, is responsible for the obtained suboptimal performance. Although most of the papers use 64×64 px blocks and 50-bit hash vector, there is no universal answer whether this is the optimal value. In general, longer hash vectors are preferred to short ones, yet the final value depends, among other factors, on the utilized embedding scheme. In our study, we use 64×64 px blocks and 50 or 64 bits of the hash vector.

The considered robust hash function does not prefer any particular information embedding technique. The algorithm provides both a binary feature vector and a Gaussian sequence generation procedure. No recommendation, however, is made in this respect. On the one hand, it allows for certain flexibility in the design of the most appropriate image authentication scheme. On the other hand, some of the algorithms deliver visibly worse performance than others. This aspect has not been addressed in the available literature so far.

In our study, we consider four variants of the image authentication scheme. All of them use a locally determined threshold Th and differ mainly in the utilized watermark embedding scheme. We consider three embedding schemes (Fig. 1). Scheme A uses additive spread spectrum watermarking in the spatial domain. The watermark is a 4096-element Gaussian sequence w generated from a 50-bit hash vector. The detector regenerates a new Gaussian sequence w' and attempts to detect it using the correlation coefficient [3]. The traditional watermark detection hypotheses, i.e., H_0 for the absence and H_1 for the presence of the watermark are then fully equivalent to the tampered and authentic hypotheses in the discussed application.

Scheme B differs from scheme A only with respect to the watermarking domain and the utilized detector. The watermark is generated in the same manner, but is embedded int the DCT domain, calculated block-wise on 8×8 px blocks. The transform coefficients are modified with additive spread spectrum embedding, and the detection is performed using an asymptotically optimal detector for the DCT domain [18]. Following [14] we use constant parameters for the detector. We use the shape parameter $\gamma = 0.6$.

The last of the considered embedding schemes is the quantization index modulation (QIM) [2]. It is the basis for the remaining two variants: scheme C and scheme C', both of which directly embed the binary robust hash. We have used the 8×8 px DCT spectrum as the embedding domain. In order to adapt to the resulting block structure, a 64-bit hash vector is used. Hence, a single 8×8 px image block carries a single bit of the watermark payload. The watermark bit is embedded into a single selected low-frequency AC coefficient. The watermark detection procedure consists in extracting the embedded feature vector, and the decision is based on a threshold on the obtained bit error rate (BER).

Scheme C' is an improved version of scheme C. It uses additional filters prior to hash extraction. Problems with scheme C can be encountered when dealing with flat image blocks. Due to block-wise choice of the threshold Th, the resulting hash bits cannot be properly balanced. The problematic flat blocks, are detected by examining the difference between the highest and the lowest pixel value within a block. If the difference does not exceed an established threshold, the block is assumed to be flat. In order to capture the average block intensity, the information about the median gray level is extracted, and an artificial binary hash sequence is computed, with a proper balance between 1s and 0s. The artificial hash is randomly permuted, with the seed obtained from the key K, the median gray level of the block, and the block position i.

4   Attacks on Information Trust in Video Surveillance

In this study, we focus on the attacks on information trust, in which the forgeries aim at perfect imitation of the authentic content. Most of existing publications focus on trivial attacks, like content removal or obvious content replacement, which are not considered in this study. Two fundamental attacks on information trust can be distinguished, i.e., the collage, and the visually insignificant semantic changes attacks. Both of them are of critical importance in the CCTV scenario, due to the abundant amounts of historical video footage, which can be easily exploited to prepare a perfect forgery.

While the collage attack is widely recognized in the scientific community, the visually insignificant semantic changes are usually not addressed. In the described experiments, both attacks are implemented in a more sophisticated scenario, compared to the traditional formulation of these attacks in the literature. The pixels in the tampered blocks are replaced only if the difference between the original and the desired counterfeit intensity exceeds a certain threshold.

In the performed experiments, we also evaluate the considered schemes with respect to their receiver operation characteristics (ROC), which serve as a measure of generic authentication performance. Discrimination between authentic and tampered image blocks is formulated in terms of traditional hypothesis testing, where the watermark presence hypothesis (H_1) corresponds to the block being authentic. The decision threshold is derived from the general ROC evaluation as the threshold, which corresponds to the closest point to $(0,1)$ in a false positive vs. false negative coordinate system.

4.1   Data Sets

The performed experiments are carried out on two separate data sets. The ROC evaluation is performed on the uncompressed colour image database (UCID) of Austin University [19]. Obtained ROC curves are in full correspondence with previously reported results [4], both experimental and theoretical ones.

The application specific evaluation is performed on a dedicated data set, which consists of sample CCTV images and attack definition files. The images were obtained from recordings from a running CCTV system monitoring the entrance for the vehicles to the area of our university [11, 15]. The owners of the cars have given written consent, which allows for using the recorded material for testing and publication purposes. The images are RGB color images with resolution 1280×720 and were extracted from HD720p video sequences, recorded as 5.6 - 10 Mbps H.264 streams. Selected images are shown in Fig. 2.

4.2   Test Scenarios

This section provides a detailed description of the considered test scenarios. The performed evaluation covers both general authentication performance, expressed by means of receiver operation characteristic (ROC), and targeted attacks on information trust. The latter include object removal by means of collage, and license number plate tampering, which constitutes a visually insignificant semantic change of the content.

Receiver Operation Characteristic. The purpose of this test is to evaluate the ROC of the inspected authentication schemes. The characteristic is obtained

Fig. 2. Sample images from the CCTV test set

from a set of 100 randomly chosen images from the UCID data set. Authentication is performed on both unwatermarked and watermarked images.

In addition to the standard ROC evaluation, we also focus on the assessment of its behavior under varying conditions. Firstly, we evaluate the authentication efficiency, i.e., the achievable ROC performance for various embedding strengths. This experiment allows to answer an important question, i.e., how are different embedding methods efficient in exchanging the introduced distortion for the tampering classification accuracy.

The second aspect of the considered ROC behavior evaluation is the impact of lossy JPEG compression on the achievable performance. The test-scenario has been extended to include JPEG compressed images with quality levels between 50 and 100.

Collage Attack. The second test scenario aims to validate the sensitivity to the collage attack. The attack is performed with the use of historical frames to aid removal of selected objects from the scene. The tampering area is defined by a simple mask, but the pixels are modified only when needed, i.e., when the difference in pixel values exceeds a predefined threshold. In total, the test consists of 109 independent tampering attempts. Exemplary forgeries are shown in Fig. 3: (a) and (b) show the original image, and the tampering source, respectively. The actually replaced pixels are shown in (c).

Visually Insignificant Semantic Changes. This attack reflects one of the most challenging problems with robust hash functions. Visually insignificant changes are able to introduce critical changes in the meaning of the content. We consider a license number plate tampering attack. A new license number plate is doctored, and overlaid on the original image. The forgeries have been prepared

Fig. 3. Sample images used in the collage attack: (top left) original image, (top right) previous frame with marked tampering region (bottom left) actually replaced pixels, (bottom right) resulting forgery.

to alter various number of the letters or digits. In order to minimize the amount of introduced modifications, the pixels are replaced only if the difference between the original and the tampered values exceeds a predefined threshold. An example forgery is shown in Fig. 4. In total, 100 images were tested.

5   Evaluation Results

The implemented authentication schemes differ with respect to the detector response domain which are $\mathbf{R}$, $\mathbf{R}^+$ and $\{0, \ldots, N\}$ for the A, B and C schemes, respectively. For convenience, the results for scheme B will be presented using the logarithm of the detector's responses. Fig. 5abc show example histograms of detector responses for both of the considered hypotheses. The overlap between these two distributions contributes to the classification errors. Changes in the decision threshold control the trade-off between the false positive and false negative errors. The resulting ROC curve represents the performance of the authentication system for a given watermarking-inflicted image distortion. By modifying the embedding strength, we obtain a family of ROC curves. Fig. 6 illustrates the impact of the embedding strength on the authentication efficiency, expressed in terms of integrated ROC curves.

The standard ROC analysis does not address the authentication performance degradation caused by lossy image compression. The additional distortion introduced during this process scatters the detector responses, most intensely for the authentic block hypothesis (H_1). Fig. 5d-i show the histograms for JPEG-compressed images for low and high embedding strengths. The range of the considered quality levels is 50-100.

Fig. 4. Visually insignificant semantic change: a cropped fragment of the original image (left), and the tampered image (right)

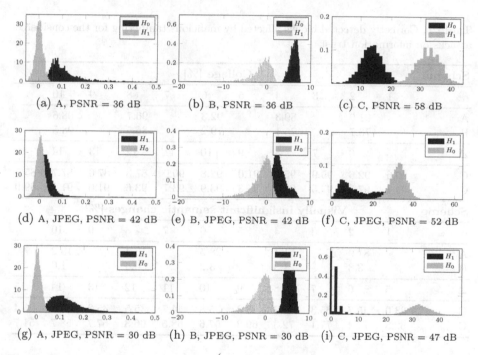

Fig. 5. Histograms of watermark detection responses for the three considered schemes: (a) - (c) uncompressed images, (d) - (e) JPEG-compressed images with low embedding strength, (f) - (g) JPEG-compressed images with high embedding strength

Considering both the standard ROC evaluation, and its counterpart for compressed images, the best efficiency is achieved by schemes C and C', which are based on QIM embedding. The second best is scheme B, which is based on spread-spectrum embedding in the DCT domain. The worst results were obtained for scheme A with spatial domain watermarking. Both the efficiency, and the tolerance for JPEG compression are worse than for schemes B and C.

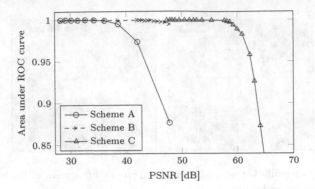

Fig. 6. Impact of the embedding strength on the authentication performance

Table 1. Correctly detected blocks affected by malicious tampering for the considered attacks on information trust

Scheme	Collage [%]									
α	1	2	3	4	5	6	7	8	9	10
A		91.0		89.3		92.3		96.7		98.6
B		73.7		75.1		79.2		86.5		98.5
Δ	5	6	7	8	9	10	11	12	13	14	15
C	90.6	92.6	95.9	95.6	91.0	92.8	90.0	87.8	87.6	87.7	85.1
C'	94.8	97.7	97.5	96.4	95.3	93.9	93.7	93.6	91.0	91.1	89.0
Scheme	**Visually insignificant semantic changes [%]**									
α	1	2	3	4	5	6	7	8	9	10
A		81.9		51.4		28.5		18.4		15.2
B		3.8		1.3		3.2		0.6		1.6
Δ	5	6	7	8	9	10	11	12	13	14	15
C	33.0	45.7	65.3	64.7	46.0	55.8	44.7	35.5	35.2	34.6	23.4
C'	62.8	77.4	77.1	72.3	69.2	67.6	68.5	66.3	57.7	58.7	51.7

Fig. 7 and Fig. 8 show the histograms of the obtained detector responses for the collage, and the visually insignificant changes attacks. The charts illustrate both the detection statistics, and the corresponding scatter-plots of the detector response vs. the fraction of actually modified pixels. The figures show the results for the embedding strength, which leads to the highest observed classification accuracy, provided that the distortion level is acceptable. This corresponds to embedding strengths $\alpha = 6$ for schemes A and B, and $\Delta = 6$ and $\Delta = 7$ for schemes C and C', respectively.

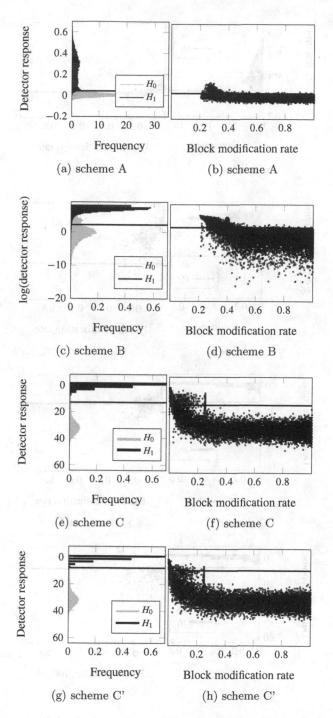

Fig. 7. Histograms of the detector responses, and the corresponding scatter plots vs. the actual pixel modification rate for the collage attack

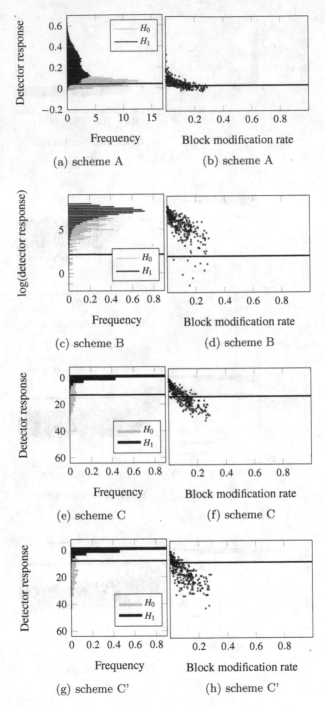

(a) scheme A   (b) scheme A

(c) scheme B   (d) scheme B

(e) scheme C   (f) scheme C

(g) scheme C'   (h) scheme C'

Fig. 8. Histograms of the detector responses, and the corresponding scatter plots vs. the actual pixel modification rate for the visually insignificant semantic changes attack

In order to ensure proper operation of the schemes, the decision thresholds in the experiments with malicious tampering are selected based on the performed ROC evaluation. The thresholds are chosen by minimizing the distance of the corresponding ROC points to the (1,0) point in a true positive vs. false positive coordinate system. This ensure good overall classification accuracy.

For each of the considered schemes, it is possible to find a threshold on the pixel modification rate, above which practically all forgeries were correctly detected. For the collage attack this threshold is 48%, 52%, 16% and 14% for the schemes A, B, C and C' respectively. Significantly greater values for schemes A and B partially stem from the higher distortion introduced by the spread spectrum embedding procedure. This phenomenon is clearly visible on the scatterplots in Fig. 7ab, where a gap of approx. 20% can be observed in the achievable modification rates. Below the described modification rate threshold, it is possible to determine the percentage of misclassified forgeries. The fraction of undetected forgeries is 7.5% in case of scheme A, 20.8% in case of scheme B, 6.3% in case of scheme C, and 2.3% in case of scheme C'. This performance changes with the embedding strength. Table 1 collects the percentage of correctly detected maliciously tampered blocks for different embedding strengths.

For the collage attack, the best performance, in terms of both the detection accuracy and the embedding-inflicted distortion, it obtained for scheme C'. The schemes based on spread-spectrum embedding can achieve comparable performance only for prohibitively large distortion, i.e., $\alpha > 8$ where the PSNR is around 30 dB. Interestingly, the spatial domain spread-spectrum scheme provides significantly better performance than its DCT domain counterpart, which performs particularly poorly for small block modification rates. This is best visible for the visually insignificant changes attack, where the modification rates do not exceed 30%. Scheme B failed to detect practically all of the visually insignificant forgeries. The maximum achieved percentage of correctly classified tampered blocks is 77.4% for scheme C' and 81.9% for scheme A.

6   Conclusions

In this paper we presented an extensive experimental evaluation of the authentication performance of robust visual hash functions in the context of video surveillance systems. Based on a selected robust hash, we designed and evaluated four variants of a complete image authentication scheme. The considered schemes represent three popular choices with respect to the information embedding approach.

Based on the presented results, we can conclude that the utilized embedding technique impacts the achievable authentication performance. While it is not possible to correctly detect all modifications, especially for small block modification rates, the considered schemes were able to detect up to approx. 80% of blocks affected by visually insignificant tampering. In case of more visible changes, e.g., removal of whole objects from the image, the achievable false negative classification rate drops to 2.3%. Hence, in our opinion, such performance suffices to justify the application of robust hash function for CCTV footage authentication. However, an additional protection mechanism should also be considered to further improve the reliability of the system.

Acknowledgment. The research leading to these results has received funding from the European Regional Development Fund under INSIGMA project no. POIG.01.01.02-00-062/09.

References

1. British Security Industry Association: Code of practice for digital recording systems for the purpose of image export to be used as evidence (October 2005), http://www.ipusergroup.com/upload/BSIACodeofPractice.pdf
2. Chen, B., Wornell, G.W.: Quantization index modulation: a class of provably good methods for digital watermarking and information embedding. IEEE Transactions on Information Theory 47(4), 1423–1443 (2001)
3. Cox, I., Miller, M., Bloom, J., Fridrich, J., Kalker, T.: Digital Watermarking and Steganography, 2nd edn. Morgan Kaufmann Publishers Inc., San Francisco (2007)
4. Domínguez-Conde, G., Comesaña, P., Pérez-González, F.: Performance analysis of fridrich-goljan self-embedding authentication method. IEEE Transactions on Information Forensics and Security 4, 570–577 (2009), http://dl.acm.org/citation.cfm?id=1651180.1651206
5. Fridrich, J.: Robust bit extraction from images. In: IEEE International Conference on Multimedia Computing and Systems (ICMCS), pp. 536–540 (1999)
6. Fridrich, J.: Robust hash functions for digital watermarking. In: International Conference on Information Technology: Coding and Computing (ITCC), pp. 178–183 (2000)
7. Fridrich, J.: Visual hash for oblivious watermarking. In: Wong, P.W., Delp, E.J. (eds.) Security and Watermarking of Multimedia Contents II. Proceedings of SPIE, vol. 3971, pp. 286–294. SPIE, San Jose (2000)
8. Fridrich, J., Goljan, M.: Images with self-correcting capabilities. In: Proc. of IEEE International Conference on Image Processing, vol. 3 (1999)
9. Haouzia, A., Noumeir, R.: Methods for image authentication: a survey. Multimedia Tools Appl. 39, 1–46 (2008), http://dl.acm.org/citation.cfm?id=1380735.1380744
10. Holliman, M.J., Memon, N.D.: Counterfeiting attacks on oblivious block-wise independent invisible watermarking schemes. IEEE Transactions on Image Processing 9(3), 432–441 (2000)
11. Janowski, L., Kozowski, P., Baran, R., Romaniak, P., Glowacz, A., Rusc, T.: Quality assessment for a visual and automatic license plate recognition. Multimedia Tools and Applications, pp. 1–18 (2012), http://dx.doi.org/10.1007/s11042-012-1199-5
12. Korus, P., Dziech, A.: A novel approach to adaptive image authentication. In: Proc. of IEEE International Conference on Image Processing (2011)
13. Korus, P., Dziech, A.: Efficient method for content reconstruction with self-embedding. IEEE Transactions on Image Processing 22(3), 1134–1147 (2013)
14. Kwitt, R., Meerwald, P., Uhl, A.: Lightweight detection of additive watermarking in the dwt-domain. IEEE Transactions on Image Processing 20(2), 474–484 (2011)

15. Leszczuk, M., Janowski, L., Romaniak, P., Głowacz, A., Mirek, R.: Quality assessment for a licence plate recognition task based on a video streamed in limited networking conditions. In: Dziech, A., Czyżewski, A. (eds.) MCSS 2011. CCIS, vol. 149, pp. 10–18. Springer, Heidelberg (2011)
16. House of Lords, P.U.: Science and technology - fifth report (February 1998), http://www.publications.parliament.uk/pa/ld199798/ldselect/ldsctech/064v/st0501.htm
17. Mihçak, M.K., Venkatesan, R.: New iterative geometric methods for robust perceptual image hashing. In: Sander, T. (ed.) DRM 2001. LNCS, vol. 2320, pp. 13–21. Springer, Heidelberg (2002)
18. Nikolaidis, A., Pitas, I.: Asymptotically optimal detection for additive watermarking in the dct and dwt domains. IEEE Transactions on Image Processing 12(5), 563–571 (2003)
19. Schaefer, G., Stich, M.: Ucid - an uncompressed colour image database. In: Proceedings of SPIE Storage and Retrieval Methods and Applications for Multimedia 2004, pp. 472–480. SPIE, San Jose (2004)
20. Swaminathan, A., Mao, Y., Wu, M.: Image hashing resilient to geometric and filtering operations, pp. 355–358 (2004)
21. Venkatesan, R., Koon, S.M., Jakubowski, M.H., Moulin, P.: Robust image hashing. In: Proceedings 2000 International Conference on Image Processing (Cat. No.00CH37101), vol. 3, pp. 664–666. IEEE (2000), http://dx.doi.org/10.1109/ICIP.2000.899541
22. Zhang, X., Wang, S., Feng, G.: Fragile watermarking scheme with extensive content restoration capability. In: Proc. of International Workshop on Digital Watermarking (2009)
23. Zhang, X., Qian, Z., Ren, Y., Feng, G.: Watermarking with flexible self-recovery quality based on compressive sensing and compositive reconstruction. IEEE Transactions on Information Forensics and Security 6(4), 1223–1232 (2011)

Author Index